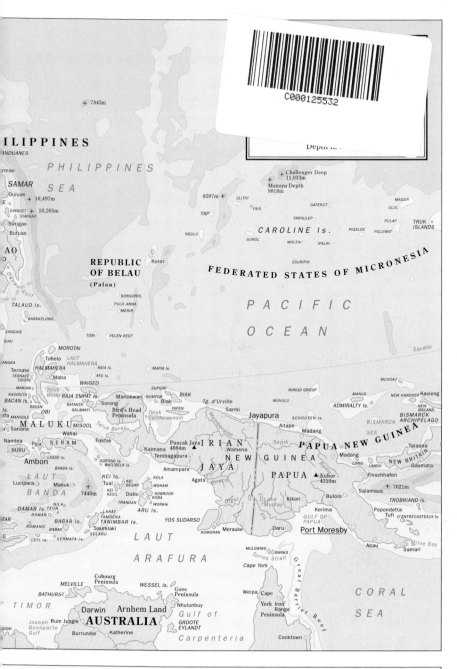

Republic of Indonesia, with 190 million people, is the world's fourth largest ...ry. Originally controlled by several Ḥindu and Islamic kingdoms, these 18,508 islands ...cted the interest of European spice traders beginning in the 16th century. By the 19th ...ry, the East Indies were a colony of Holland. Nationalist sentiment grew in the early 20th ...ury, and after World War II and a difficult Japanese occupation, Sukarno, who was to be ...nesia's first president, declared independence on August 17, 1945. The Dutch were oust-...ve years later. The Indonesian language is a variant of Malay, long the region's lingua ...a. The largest Islamic nation in the world, 88 percent of Indonesians are Muslims. In the ...e remote parts of the archipelago, traditional lifestyles are still practiced.

Diving Indonesia

A GUIDE TO WORLD'S GREATEST DIVING

Kal Muller

Edited by David Pickell

PERIPLUS

Published by Periplus Editions (HK) Ltd.

ISBN 962-593-314-X
Printed in Singapore

Publisher: Eric Oey
Editor: David Pickell
Production: Mary Chia
Cartography: David Pickell, Violet Wong
Design: David Pickell

Distributors

Asia-Pacific   Berkeley Books Pte. Ltd.
                      5 Little Road, #08-01
                      Singapore 536983
                      Tel: (65) 280-3320
                      Fax: (65) 280-6290

Indonesia   PT Wira Mandala Pustaka
                      (Java Books—Indonesia)
                      Jl. Kelapa Gading Kirana
                      Blok A-14 No. 17, Jakarta 14240
                      Tel: (62-21) 451-5351
                      Fax: (62-21) 453-4987

Japan   Tuttle Shokai Ltd.
                      1-21-13, Seki
                      Tama-ku, Kawasaki-shi
                      Kanagawa-ken 214-0022
                      Tel: (044) 833-0225
                      Fax: (044) 822-0413

United States   Tuttle Publishing
                      Distribution Center
                      Airport Industrial Park
                      364 Innovation Drive
                      North Clarendon, VT 05759-9436
                      Tel: (802) 773-8930, (800) 526-2778

Cover: Diver in Irian Jaya, hovering near soft coral and crinoid. Photograph by Mark Strickland.

Pages 4–5: A reef whitetip shark, *Triaenodon obesus,* snatches some food on a reef in the Bunaken group, North Sulawesi. Photograph by Ed Robinson/IKAN.

Frontispiece: The most dramatic animal in this composition is a beautiful gorgonian in the very unusual genus *Semperina*. Selayar Island. Photograph by Mike Severns.

Contents

See page 46

See page 119

See page 141

See page 149

See page 66

Nusa Tenggara

Sulawesi

Maluku

Irian Jaya

Practicalities

See page 51

See page 69
See page 63

Author's Dedication

To my editor, David Pickell

He missed out on the fun part of this effort—the diving—and instead struggled behind his computer to whip the book into shape from the mess of my manuscripts.

Essential to this book were the many dive operators, guides and dive buddies who contributed their time and knowledge, and who made certain I stayed out of trouble underwater (and sometimes above). Very special thanks to **Easy Ed Donohue**, who kept a close watch over me in my PC (Pre-Computer) days. Also to **Cody Shwaiko**, a close friend and my most frequent dive buddy, who traveled across Indonesia from his home in Bali several times to join me during the research for this book. And to **Wally Siagian**, who stands head and shoulders above all dive guides, who took me to all the right sites in Bali, and found me a cold beer whenever I could not live without one. And to **Loky Herlambang**, pioneer dive operator, founder of Nusantara Diving Centre, and conservation prize-winner, who did the same in Manado. And to **Edi Frommenwieler**, operator of the *Pindito* and **Peter**, the dive master, for the best dive series of my life. And to **Graeme** and **Donovan Whitford** for their sense of humor and never ending enthusiasm, along with truly world-class diving on Alor. And to **Larry Smith**, the most professional of instructors/guides, over 11,000 dives under his weight belt, the best of buddies if anything should go wrong. And to my most recent dive buddy, my son **Kalman**, in the hopes that his interest in marine biology may quickly surpass my own.

Editor's Acknowledgements

Any book of this scope represents the sweat and talent of many people, and an awful lot of both have gone into this one.

The fieldwork for this volume—hundreds of dives, thousands of kilometers of airplane and boat travel, sometimes weeks at a time without a cold beer—was conducted by Kal Muller, a Hungarian-born photographer and writer who has spent some 20 years tromping around the archipelago with his cameras and notebook. Kal is an old friend and probably the most tireless and good-humored person I know. Others who have contributed to this volume:

Dr. Charles Anderson, a marine biologist with the Marine Research Section of the Ministry of Fisheries of the Republic of the Maldives, co-authored the marine life section and updated the practical section for Sumatra.

Cody Shwaiko, an experienced diver living in Bali, provided the Kangean Islands section, parts of the Banda dive narrative, and the sections on Sumba and Sangihe–Talaud. Cody has also provided several interesting photographs.

Dive guide **Wally Siagian** not only kept Kal out of trouble while he was researching the Bali section of this book, but also provided detailed sketch maps of the Bali and Banda Islands sites, and to this edition, several photographs. Wally, who has an instinct for finding underwater life that is second to none, also pioneered all the best sites around Komodo Island.

Helmut Debelius, founder of the IKAN agency, provided us with his own photographs, as well as those of agency photographers **Ed Robinson**, **Jan Post** and **Lionel Pozzoli**. Helmut also provided a

nice anecdote about discovering the beautiful reef lobster that now bears his name.

Photographer **Mike Severns**, who runs a dive operation in Maui with his wife, marine biologist **Pauline Fiene-Severns**, provided us with some of his very fine work from North Sulawesi. Mike's most recent book of photographs, *Sulawesi Seas*, co-authored with Pauline, has garnered widespread praise from both journalists and fellow professionals.

Rudie Kuiter is an experienced underwater photographer and the author of one of the best fish identification guides to the region: *Tropical Reef-Fishes of the Western Pacific*. Rudie provided an essay on discovering new species and a series of very interesting photographs.

Mark V. Erdmann, a coral reef ecologist who has conducted research in Indonesia for four years, provided the section on South Sulawesi. Mark's primary concern is marine conservation and development, and he has authored several articles on destructive fishing techniques in the archipelago.

Janet Boileau and **Debe Campbell**, both freelance writers living in Jakarta, wrote the Java section, and Debe helped update the practical section for Bali.

Andy Udayana, a student at the National Tourism University in Bali also helped update the practical section for Bali.

Lastly, I wrote some of the marine life and background sections, and updated the volume for this printing.

— **David Pickell**
San Francisco 1998

Introducing the Indonesian Islands

The islands of Indonesia spread in a wide arc, more than 5,000 kilometers long, from mainland Southeast Asia to Papua New Guinea. Dotted with volcanoes, covered with thick tropical vegetation and bright green rice fields, and surrounded by coral reefs, the Indonesian archipelago is one of the world's most beautiful places.

The most reliable figure offered for the number of islands in Indonesia is 17,508, including rocks and sandbanks exposed by the tides. Some 6,000 of these are important enought to have names, and perhaps 1,000 are inhabited.

Indonesia is the largest archipelagic nation in the world, with at least 80,000 kilometers of coastline. Some estimates run as high as 200,000 kilometers, but even the lower figure makes Indonesia's coastline longer than that of any other nation. The territorial waters of Indonesia include 3.1 million square kilometers of tropical seas.

Indonesia is the world's fourth-largest country, with 204 million inhabitants. Most are Muslims, but there are significant Christian and Hindu minorities. Racially the majority of Indonesians are Malayo-Polynesian, with Chinese and Papuan minorities. The capital and largest city is Jakarta.

The Indonesian language is a variant of Malay, which, in this nation of hundreds of languages, has long served as the lingua franca of trade.

Seafaring Empires

Indonesians refer to their country as *tanah air kita*—"our land and water"—and have always considered the seas as an integral part of their country. The ancestors of the great majority of Indonesians—the Austronesians—arrived in the archipelago by boat. The invention of the outriggered canoe some 5,000 years ago was as essential a development to seafarers as the wheel was to land-locked people.

Spreading first from the Asian mainland to Taiwan, and then—about 3,000 B.C.—through the Philippines and into the larger islands of western Indonesia, the Austronesians brought with them rice and domesticated animals, and thrived on the rich volcanic soil of the Sunda Islands.

But seafaring skills were not forgotten. Starting in the 4th century, Indonesians from south Kalimantan (Borneo) sailed across the Indian Ocean to settle in uninhabited Madagascar, just off the coast of Africa.

The first great Indonesian empire, the Buddhist Srivijaya, was a maritime empire based around the port of Palembang in southeast Sumatra. The Srivijaya controlled the Straits of Malacca, the key to the crucial China–India trade route, from the 7th to the 13th centuries.

Influences from the Asian subcontinent continued to reach the archipelago, which became increasingly Indianized in culture and religion.

From A.D. 1294 to the 15th century, most of western Indonesia was controlled by the powerful East Java kingdom of Majapahit, the most famous of the archipelago's ancient kingdoms. Majapahit is thought to have exacted tribute from islands as far away as New Guinea.

Above: *Many of Indonesia's 17,508 islands are graced with beautiful, palm-lined beaches. This is the south coast of Bali.*

Overleaf: *A porcelain crab,* Neopetrolisthes ohshimai, *in Merten's carpet anemone,* Stichodactyla mertensii. *The porcelain crab is a shy filter-feeder that uses the stinging tentacles of the anemone for protection. Photograph by Mike Severns.*

Opposite: *Two snappers,* Macolor macularis, *and a cloud of peach anthias and lyretail anthias,* Pseudanthias dispar *and P. squammipinnis, at Mike's Point, on the northwest corner of Bunaken Island in Sulawesi. This site was named after the photographer. Photograph by Mike Severns.*

KAL MULLER

Above: *A fisherman tries his luck off the dock at Ampenan, Lombok.*

During World War II, the Japanese quickly swept through the Dutch Indies, evicting the colonialists in 1942. At the end of the war, Indonesian nationalist leaders declared independence —on August 17, 1945—but it took four more years to oust the Dutch. Irian Jaya, the western part of New Guinea, was transferred to Indonesia in the 1960s; the former Portuguese colony of East Timor was annexed in 1976.

Lush Islands

The "Ring of Fire" runs through Sumatra, Java, the Lesser Sundas, and then up through the Moluccas. These islands are marked by jagged volcanoes, and the rich, black soil that produces the great rice crops of Java and Bali. Some of the islands—for example, Timor, Seram and Biak—are formed of uplifted coral limestone. Here the soil is poor, and some areas—particularly parts of Timor—exhibit dry grassland that is more reminiscent of Australia than the tropics.

Two seasons of wind sweep through Indonesia each year. The northwest monsoon, usually starting (depending on the area) between late October and late November and ending between March and April, brings rain and wind. The southeast monsoon, with wind but much less rain, begins around late April to late May, and ends in early September. The *pancaroba*—between monsoons—brings generally calm seas and good weather, and falls just about everywhere in the archipelago in October and April.

The worst of the rainy season in most of Indonesia is in the months of December and January. The weather in the eastern province of Maluku is the most out of step with the rest of the country, and the worst comes in July and August. Some islands—such as Bali—have mountains that block the rains, creating a dry rain shadow in their lee.

Islam and the Europeans

Beginning in the mid–13th century, Indonesian traders and rulers began converting to Islam, for both political and religious reasons. The biggest boost to Islamization of the archipelago came with the conversion of the ruler of Malacca, which sat in a very strategic position on the strait between Sumatra and peninsular Malaysia.

Most of these conversions were peaceful—the Sufi doctrine offering a theologically smooth transition for the Hinduized kingdoms—but Majapahit, past its prime, fell by force to the neighboring Islamic kingdom of Demak in the early 16th century.

This was also about the time the Portuguese, seeking spices, arrived in the archipelago, conquering Malacca in 1511. Soon after, the Spanish and English also sought Indonesia's valuable spices, but it was a century later that Holland, newly independent of the Holy Roman Empire, ruled from Spain, succeeded in controlling the market in cloves, nutmeg and pepper. During much of the 17th and 18th centuries, the Dutch East India Company held a virtual monopoly.

The company went broke in 1799, and in the 19th century, the Dutch concentrated their colonial efforts on Java, leading to a huge increase in the population of this island.

Fantastic Diving, but Kafkaesque Transport

KAL MULLER

Indonesia is the least known of the world's best dive locations. The introduction of scuba gear and the beginning of dive operations here are barely a decade old, and new locations are still being explored and opened, albeit slowly.

It will be many years before diving in Indonesia reaches its full potential, which has both great advantages and serious drawbacks. Experienced divers will be excited by the possibility of diving clear, rich waters without being surrounded by hordes of human beings. It is still very possible to dive areas where no one has yet gone underwater. This will be a refreshing change from sites like the Caribbean, Hawaii, the Great Barrier Reef, the Maldives and the popular spots in the Pacific Islands.

In all of the huge Indonesian archipelago, containing 10–20 percent of the world's coral reefs, there are few locations with dive services, and a handful of year-round live-aboard boats.

The diving is excellent, inexpensive (averaging around $75 a day for two dives) and uncrowded. This does not come without a cost, however: flights can be unceremoniously cancelled, the quality of guides is variable, and the weather is sometimes fickle.

Live-aboards are the obvious solution to diving in Indonesia, with its thousands of islands and huge area. Some of the boats are luxurious and expensive but take you to the top dive locations in Indonesia. A few are more basic.

Indonesia's Dive Sites

The sites listed below are the main ones in Indonesia, with compressors, equipment and other facilities for diving. They appear here in the order they appear in this book, roughly west to east across the archipelago.

West Java. The Pulau-Pulau Seribu—"Thousand Islands"— dive area is quite close to the capital of Indonesia, Jakarta, and many efficient dive clubs provide all the necessary transportation and services to these islands. There is some interesting diving here, but in general coral and fish life is quite limited, and the visibility poor. The clubs will also take you diving off the islands

Above: *Although it makes a heroic effort to connect the archipelago's far-flung islands, Merpati Airlines is often the bane of travelers to Indonesia. Above is one of the airline's rugged Twin Otters in Karubaga, Irian Jaya.*

Below: *A diver in the waters off Bali peers into a large barrel sponge,* Xestospongia testudinaria.

HELMUT DEBELIUS / IKAN

Above: *Beautiful Bali cattle wander the rocky beach at Tulamben, Bali, one of the most popular dive sites in Indonesia. These placid animals are a domesticated form of the wild cow or banteng.*

HELMUT DEBELIUS / IKAN

around the famous Krakatau volcano, and off the Ujung Kulon Nature Reserve on the tip of southwest Java.

If your plans will take you through Jakarta, these dives might be worthwhile, but the diving is much better at points east. If you are coming all the way to Indonesia expressly to dive, your destination should not be Java.

Sumatra. Just an hour's ferry ride from Singapore, north Bintan Island has opened for diving. Visiblity is limited, but there's a wealth of life to see, especially at night. On the opposite side of the island, offshore Padang and the Mentawai Islands promise great diversity—shipwrecks and fringing reefs to wall dives. And much of it is still relatively unexplored.

Bali. Bali has more tourist services than anywhere else in Indonesia. It is a beautiful island, and the diving is excellent. There are many different sites here, from the clear water and steep walls of Menjangan to the famous Tulamben wreck to the 4-knot currents and cold water of Nusa Penida. The visibility is usually very good, and the fish and coral life are excellent. One caveat: almost 1 million tourists a year visited Bali at last count, and here is one of the few places where you might find a crowd.

Live-aboards and chartered boats from Bali can also take divers to the islands south of Sulawesi, the Lesser Sundas, and the dive sites in the Banda Sea.

Lombok. The only diving available on this island, just a cheap ferry ride or short flight from Bali, is on the Gilis, three tiny islands off Lombok's west coast. Gili Trawangan and Gili Air have quite good reefs, but even these are far from Indonesia's best. But the Gili islands have fine white beaches and a get-away-from-it-all kind of appeal, and the diving is just offshore. You can find luxury accommodations in Senggigi beach on the mainland, an hour's ride from the islands. The dive businesses are all based there. With prior arrangements for pickup, it's better to rough it at the small places on the beach in the Gilis, with the young frisbee-tossers and sunbathers.

Komodo Island. The waters between Komodo Island (home of the fabled "dragon," a large monitor lizard) and Labuhanbajo, Flores are speckled with small islands ringed with coral. It is also swept by fierce currents. There are several places in Labuhanbajo which sometimes offer day trips for diving.

For the best locations, try the inexpensive live-aboards the *Komodo Plus I* and *II*. These ships do not offer luxury, but their charts show all the best locations in this world-class area, all pioneered by the outfit.

Maumere, Flores. Early in the decade, Maumere Bay was hit by a triple whammy: earthquake, tsunami, and a cyclone. Many of the reefs were devastated, but there are still good locations. Life is returning to the area, and this process of recovery can be very interesting from a diving perspective. Diving services are now very limited, but the essentials are there.

Sumba. It's no piece of cake to get there, but the south coast of Sumba offers a top location, dubbed Magic Mountain. It's an undesea mound, teeming with large fishes. The resort on land has been bought by the internationally acclaimed Oberoi chain.

Kupang, West Timor, and Roti and Alor. This area provides the closest diving for North Australia–based divers. The marine life is plentiful, and the operators are very good, experienced and enthusiastic. The only drawback to Kupang is the visibility, which is poor to just fair by Indonesian standards: 6–12 meters. Roti is better.

For the best diving, the operators have pioneered Alor Island, where a couple of dozen spots, along with some in the Banda Sea, top our best-of-the-best in Indonesia list. Currents can be strong, but for hard core divers, Alor gets our highest recommendation. Now the live-aboards *Komodo Plus I* and *II* also visit Alor.

Sulawesi. The steep coral walls ringing the islands off Manado are some of the very best in the world. The visibility is very good, and the variety of marine life is superb. Some of the dive operators could use more reliable dive boats, and English-speaking dive masters with international certification. Bangka Island offers excellent spots, without the crowds at Bunaken. A new dive center, quiet and luxurious, offers very good diving from just north of Bitung, on the other side of the peninsula from Manado. The waters of the Lembeh Strait are very rich, and hold interesting wrecks.

The *Serenade* and its daughter ship *Arlena,* both operated by Murex, and the live-aboard operated by Liburan Adventure Diving Tours, all run out of Manado to the Sangihe-Talaud Islands. The Spermonde archipelago off Ujung Pandang, Selayar island just off the southwest peninsula, the Tukang Besi archipelago off the southeast tip, and the Togian islands tucked away in the Gulf of Tomini in central Sulawesi all offer exciting exploratory diving opportunities.

East Kalimantan. Manta rays and a salt-water inland lake are the top drawing cards here. World-famous Borneo Divers, the folks who pioneered Sipandan diving, started operations in

Below: *A school of pennant butterfly-fish,* Heniochus diphreutes. *Swarms of these beautiful butterflyfish are a common sight on Indonesian reefs.*

Sangalaki. After a period of suspended operations, they are planning to reopen their dive business with a new Indonesian partner. Another dive outfit, based on nearby Derawan Island, also offers diving on Sangalaki, and this has evolved into a well-run operation.

Ambon. Dive operations in Ambon and the Lease Islands are smoothing out. Operators now have adequate boats, with all the essentials. The diving here is very good and there will be no crowds at all. But the quality of dive personnel varies greatly. New sites here are still waiting to be discovered.

Our favorite live-aboard, the wooden *Pindito,* operates out of Ambon. Most of the year, it covers the Banda Sea. When the weather gets bad there, it runs dive cruises to Irian Jaya. The *Pindito* has pioneered most of the best dive spots in the Banda Sea and they know the area well. With the deepest seas in Indonesia and islands jutting up from abyssal depths, this is truly spectacular diving, second to none.

Unfortunately, the *Pindito* is quite expensive, and markets chiefly to Europe. Other live-aboards that make Banda Sea runs can be found in Bali.

Banda Islands. The Banda Islands are a tiny group rising incongruously out of the middle of the wide Banda Sea—the Hawaii of Indonesia. Some of the dive sites here are fantastic, and large pelagics are commonly seen. There's not always someone around with formal dive training, although recently a European divemaster has taken up residence in Banda. The real problem is getting to these beautiful islands, however. They are really out of the way, and the bottleneck is the final leg on a small plane from Ambon.

Irian Jaya. Abundant reef life and little-explored ship and aircraft wrecks make diving in the Raja Ampat islands and Cenderawasih Bay on the north coast of Irian Jaya exciting adventures. A new hotel on the tip of Biak Island also offers diving in the Padaido group.

Exploratory dives

In addition to the few locations in Indonesia where compressors, tanks, weights and guides are available, dozens of others have been prospected, and await investment to be opened. To this list, add hundreds of sites—a few "discovered" but most unexplored—accessible only by the live-aboards.

You can also simply charter a large enough boat, and head off to a location of your own choosing. The problem, of course, is finding a compressor. This may be possible in Bali, however, which would open up locations such as the Kangean Islands, Taka Bonerate and the Bonerate group. This is territory for real explorers, and if you have the time, patience, and self-sufficiency, this could provide a once-in-a-lifetime experience.

Scuba Guides: Variable

The quality of dive services and guides in Indonesia is, to be polite, "variable." Most of these guides have spent more time underwater than their customers, accumulating thousands of dives, and are excellent scuba divers. But this does not make them good guides. They usually fall short in emergency training and organization.

It best to dive with the foreknowledge that you probably can not expect any help from your guide. Many guides may even have had some theoretical training in emergency procedures. But we have only rarely seen a first-aid kit on any of the local dive boats, let alone oxygen. Do not expect your guide to rescue you if you get into trouble.

This is not much of a problem

for well-trained, experienced divers, particularly those who are traveling as a group. In fact, if you fall into this category, Indonesia is going to be a paradise for diving—no crowds, virgin reefs, and a lot of underwater time for your buck.

Beginners, on the other hand, are advised to use extreme caution—especially those who take a resort course after arrival here. Instructors' command of English is usually incomplete, and safety procedures are sometimes neglected. Being "certified" in Indonesia does not make you a competent diver. If a resort course here is your only diving experience, stick to the easy locations, and be very particular in choosing an operator and guide.

In all cases be extremely wary of rental gear. This equipment is very expensive to buy with Indonesian rupiah, and operators use it to within an inch of its life. If maintenance were regularly scheduled and carried out properly, this wouldn't be a problem. But spare parts are expensive and very hard to get here, and training in repair and diagnostics of dive equipment is basically non-existent.

In most places, dive guides and assistants will ready your gear for you, but we suggest you do this yourself. If you are in the habit of just looking at the pressure gauge to make sure you have a good fill, you better change your way of thinking in Indonesia. Test *everything*—regulator, gauges, BC valves and straps. You should infer from this advice that we highly recommend you bring your own gear.

Indonesia is not the place to push your limits as a diver. We discourage dives below 30 meters, especially if decompression stops are required. Take your dive tables (better yet, a computer) and follow them scrupulously. Don't even think about a decompression cham-

bers being available—except perhaps in Bali and Manado, they are too far away.

Dive-tour operators, particularly in Europe, are reluctant to send their clients to Indonesia because of the poor training of local guides. This situation will be remedied only when more dive guides receive adequate instruction in dive planning, emergency procedures and language skills.

Transportation: Kafkaesque

Marine tourism in Indonesia is also stalled by the archipelago's transportation infrastructure. Bali, Java and Sulawesi are easy to get to, but particularly at the height of the tourist seasons, July–August and December–January, travel to Maumere, Banda, and other points in eastern Indonesia can be an exercise in

Above: *Since most of the Indonesian dive sites are the steep outer walls of fringing reefs, access is usually just a matter of a short ride by outboard-powered canoe. This is the fringing reef off Bunaken Island in northern Sulawesi.*

Above: *Tulamben in Bali is famous for the World War II* Liberty *shipwreck, lying just 30 meters from the beach. This dive location is also noted for its remarkable diversity of marine life.*

frustration. Delays, overbooked flights, and broken computers will make a mess of your schedule. The guilty airport is Ujung Pandang in South Sulawesi. This is the main hub to eastern Indonesia, but too few planes fly there to and from Bali.

The scene at the ticket counters of the Indonesian government airlines—Garuda and Merpati—often produces a strange mix of Kafkaesque angst and hilarity.

It's not always this bad. Things are better in the off-peak months, and even during the middle of the tourist rush, only perhaps 25 percent of the confirmed passengers have problems. The basic problem is that Merpati—the main internal carrier—has too few airplanes, lacks organization, and owns a computer reservation system that is, in fact, often worse than useless.

Start with the obvious—it can't hurt. Ask the travel agent with whom you made your original booking if the company has a local correspondent. Many have agents in Bali who can re-check confirmations. Even before you arrive, try to obtain something tangible from this agent and/or Merpati airlines, such as a fax or telex showing your confirmed dates. As soon as you get to Bali, re-check your bookings.

As soon as you make it to your destination, confirm your return booking. The dive resorts

and many hotels are quite efficient at doing this—they will usually ask you for your plane details right away—but still make sure that it's been done.

If you do all this, it's likely—but not guaranteed—that things will work out as planned. But, just in case, keep some flexibility in your schedule in case there is a day or two of delay. If you have to sit in Bali for a day or two, there are plenty of good day-trips for diving. Unless you are traveling in a large group, go to the airport and try to get on your desired flight, even if you have been told that it's full. We've been on many of these over-booked flights where half or more of the seats are empty.

If you don't get a seat on the plane, forget about lodging an official complaint, getting mad, or punching somebody. If you throw a fit, you will provide a great deal of entertainment to the people waiting around the counter, but such unsavory behavior will inevitably lead to more delays. Sometimes—but not always—it might help to offer to pay "something extra" to get on your flight. It is not unknown that even someone with a confirmed reservation has been "bumped" due to a shady deal.

Still Worth It, Though

Are all these potential hassles worth it? You bet. Chances are you won't have problems. We just wanted to warn you—not scare you away. Remember: the diving is great out there. If you can schedule your visit from April through June, or September through early November, planes will be less crowded and everything will be much easier.

When planning your visit, don't try to visit too many places. If you have a week, go just to one place. Otherwise, you can spend much of your precious vacation time contending with the difficulties mentioned above.

Coral Growth and the Formation of Reefs

Diving over a tropical coral reef has been compared to stepping into a time machine. You find yourself in a strange place, millions of years out of sync with the land. The reef is a reminder of a time when all the life on earth existed in shallow, tropical seas, the original soup of creation.

The myriad fish and invertebrates that shelter among and encrust the rugged surfaces provided by the clumps, shelves and branches of coral are overwhelming in their numbers, shapes and colors. Nowhere else is there such a diversity of animal forms.

Clear tropical seawater is nutrient poor, an aquatic desert. The strange and varied forms of the members of coral reef communities allow each to fill a niche in a complex nutrient cycle, beginning with the fixing of nutrients by the photosynthesis of algae, and working up to the barracuda that snatches an aging fish from the school. The ammonia and feces secreted by the predator are cycled right back into the reef ecosystem.

Over 240 million years, when scleractinian coral reefs first formed, this community has made a remarkable geological impact. The stony coral skeletons become overgrown and compacted into rock, eventually building up a prodigious thickness of limestone. When forced upward by the buckling of the earth's crust, this old reef rock forms islands.

Distribution of Coral Reefs

Reef-building corals require large amounts of sunlight, and thus are only found in the trop-ics, and even there only in shallow water. The effective limit of coral growth is usually given as 100 meters, although in Indonesia coral usually stops at 60–70 meters. Corals, even stony corals, are found as deep as 6,000 meters, but these grow slowly and do not form the diverse communities of tropical coral reefs.

The Indo-Pacific region, centered around the islands of Indonesia, harbors most of the world's coral reefs. Of the total area covered by coral reefs, 55 percent is in southeastern continental Asia, Indonesia, the Philip-

Below: *The presence of large gorgonians, crinoids and schools of planktivores like these anthias indicates plankton-rich waters, which can provide a spectacular concentration of marine life. Mike's Point, Bunaken Island, Sulawesi.*

MIKE SEVERNS

pines, North Australia and the Pacific islands; 30 percent is in the Indian Ocean and the Red Sea; 14 percent is in the Caribbean; and 1 percent is in the North Atlantic. In variety, central Indonesia is the richest in the world: 80 genera, 450 species.

Reef-building corals grow only in water from 18°C (65°F) to 33°C (91°F). And the extremes of this range can only be tolerated for very short periods.

This explains why reefs are generally found only on the eastern coasts of large continents. The wind patterns caused by the rotation of the earth create currents that bring an upwelling of cold water (14°C [57°F]) from the depths at least part of the year to the western coasts of the Americas, Europe and Africa. Thus the Indian Ocean side of Africa has extensive reefs, and the Atlantic side almost none.

No cold currents flow through Indonesia, but even temporary rises in sea temperatures can devastate reefs. In 1983 sea temperatures around the Pulau Seribu islands off western Java rose to 33°C (91°F), killing much of the shallow reef coral there. Most has now recovered.

Turbid waters, those carrying a great deal of suspended sediment, deter reef formation. This is a very important in South and Southeast Asia, where rivers dump 70 percent of all sediments delivered to the ocean worldwide. (The Ganges is the champion, carrying almost 1.7 billion tons a year to the Bay of Bengal.) In Indonesia, the larger rivers in Kalimantan and Sumatra produce enough sediment to discourage reef formation a significant distance from their mouths, although even here some rich reefs have formed.

The Biology of Corals

True reef-building or hermatypic corals are animals grouped in the phylum Cnidaria, order Sclerac-

tinia. They all have an indispensable symbiotic relationship with dinoflagellate algae called zooxanthellae. (see "Zooxanthellae and Corals," opposite.) These algae are essential for respiration and nutrient uptake, and the vigorous deposition of calcium.

Coral skeletons are made of aragonite, a very soluble form of calcium carbonate. The material is secreted as a way of disposing of excess ionic calcium.

Grazing and predation of fish and invertebrates causes portions of the coral skeletons to die, and these are immediately encrusted with algae, sponges, soft corals, or any of a myriad forms of small invertebrates. Over time, these too are grazed, silted over by coral sand, or outcompeted by other organisms and their remains become part of another compacted layer.

The lithification of coral rock is not well understood, but a fine-grained carbonate cement seems to form in the pores of the old coral, turning it into dense coral rock. This is thought perhaps to result from bacterial action.

The buildup of limestone on the reef is not a simple process of accumulation. It is a cycle just like the nutrient cycle. Scientists studying a 7-hectare reef in the Caribbean measured an annual production of 206 tons of calcium carbonate; they also measured an annual loss of 123 tons. The greatest part of this erosion was produced by boring sponges and the rest by grazing fishes and echinoderms.

Not all the limestone produced is created by corals, either. In some areas, particularly where there is very strong wave action, calcareous algaes are the primary producers of carbonate, forming algal ridges at the outer edge of the reef.

Coral Reef Architecture

Coral reefs are generally defined as falling into three main types

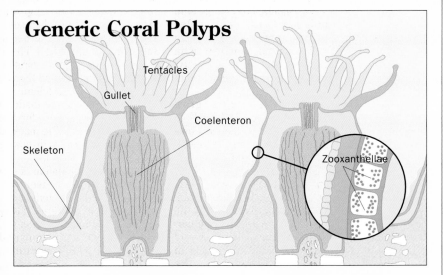

Generic Coral Polyps

Tentacles

Gullet

Coelenteron

Skeleton

Zooxanthellae

Zooxanthellae and Corals

Reef-building corals have evolved an indispensable, symbiotic relationship with a type of yellow-brown algae called zooxanthellae, which is "farmed" in the tissues of the coral polyp. The relationship is mutually beneficial: the coral receives oxygen and nutrients, and the algae receives carbon dioxide and "fertilizer" in the form of animal waste.

The presence of zooxanthellae is so important to the health of the coral that scientists speculate the symbiotic algae must have been present in the polyp tissue almost throughout modern coral's 50–100 million years of evolution.

The zooxanthellae alga has been dubbed *Symbiodinium microadriaticum,* part of a "supergenus" of marine dinoflagellate algas, but recent research suggests there are more than one species. These algas are dinoflagellates, which have whip-like processes giving them some limited ability to move. This is probably how the cells initially enter the corals, although once they are there they divide vegetatively, and take on a simpler structural form.

Corals are not the only reef animals to have zooxanthellae. Sea anemones and other cnidarians host the algae, as do some molluscs, most famously the giant clams (*Tridacna*). Because zooxanthel-

lae is a yellow-brown algae, and the host tissues are generally colorless—to pass the greatest amount of light to the algae—zooxanthellae-containing animals are usually a dull color: beige, brown, olive green. There are exceptions, however, including some of the giant anemones and *Tridacna* clams, which can be richly hued. As a general rule, however, the most brightly colored invertebrates—such as some of the soft corals—do not harbor zooxanthellae.

Coral nutrition

Corals derive their food energy from three sources: plankton captured by their tentacles, organic nutrients absorbed directly from the water, and organic compounds provided by the zooxanthellae. For the reef-building corals, the latter is by far the most important.

In the presence of sunlight, the zooxanthellae produce oxygen and photosynthetically fix nutrients—glycerol, glucose and amino acids—which are "leaked" to the surrounding tissues of the coral polyp. The raw materials for this process are the waste products of the coral animal: carbon dioxide, ammonia, nitrates and phosphates. It is a very efficient, almost self-sustaining partnership.

— *David Pickell*

fringing reefs, barrier reefs and atolls. In a sense, these types also form a historical progression. As a fringing reef grows outward, a boat channel forms behind. As the reef widens, the boat channel becomes a lagoon, and the fringing reef graduates to a barrier reef. If the fringing reef began around an island, and the island subsequently sinks or the sea level rises, the final result is an atoll, a near circular reef surrounding a central lagoon.

These are not the only forms, and scientists studying reef topography offer many more types. For example, bank reefs, reefs that grow up more or less in patches in open water where the depths are relatively shallow, are an important type in the Coral Sea off Australia. These reefs often form at the edge of undersea plates, and appear when geologic activity causes an uplifting of the bottom. If the bottom is pushed up high enough that sunlight can reach it, a bank reef will form.

Fringing reefs. Most of the reefs a diver will be exploring in Indonesia are fringing reefs, coral formations that grow right up to the edge of an island. These reefs can take many forms. The steep coral walls for which Indonesian diving is famous are fringing reefs, with sometimes just a few meters of reef flat, and a reef edge that has an almost vertical slope.

Walls, or drop-offs, fascinate divers because these are where deeper dwelling animals come closest to the surface. Some of the deep-dwelling dwarf angelfish (*Centropyge* spp.), damsels, and anthias (e.g., *Pseudanthias pleurotaenia*) can be found at comfortable depths only along steep drop-offs.

Generally, a fringing reef consists of a reef edge of stout corals, which absorb the brunt of the waves and current; a reef flat, a shallow area exposed at the lowest spring tide; and perhaps a boat channel or back reef, deeper than the reef flat and quite calm.

The reef edge, and the fore-reef area towards the open sea, are the most rewarding areas for the diver. Here the current is strong, bringing plankton and fresh water from the open sea.

Below: *On the steep walls of Indonesian reefs, normally deep-dwelling species can be seen at relatively shallow depths. This is a male square-spot anthias,* Pseudanthias pleurotaenia.

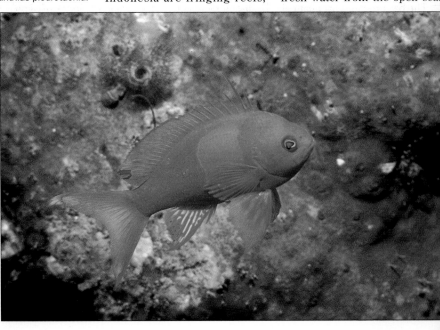

Here also is where divers will see larger reef fish, and occasional pelagic visitors to the reef. Sometimes the reef edge is indistinct, marked by pinnacles or other formations. And sometimes the area just back of the reef edge will not immediately become part of the reef flat, but instead, protected from the full force of the current, will be rich in more delicate corals and animals.

The reef flat is shallow, and usually light brown with sediment. This is an area of coral sand and detritus, with small boulders of hardy massive corals and clusters of branching *Acropora* coral, growing in pools. Usually there are fewer than a handful of very hardy coral species on the reef flat.

Most divers will walk or wade across this area (wearing a pair of dive boots, of course) without even looking down. Here there are echinoderms—particularly brittle stars, which sometimes occur in great numbers—small fish, a variety of molluscs and soft algaes. Sometimes there will be meadows of the calcareous alga *Halimeda*.

The back reef or boat channel is a deeper area, between the reef flat and the shore. Although often deep enough for swimming, the coral growth here is poor because of sediment run-off from the shore. Resistant *Porites, Acropora* or *Goniastrea* grow in the boat channel in patches. Further inland, there may be beds of turtle grass, a rich habitat for juvenile fishes and many crustaceans.

Barrier reefs. The most famous barrier reefs are the Great Barrier Reef off Queensland, Australia, which is 2,000 kilometers long and 150 kilometers wide, and the large barrier reef off the coasts of New Caledonia in Melanesia. A barrier reef is a fringing reef where the back reef or boat channel has become a large lagoon. In the

Trepang drying on a dock in Pagimana, Sulawesi

Trepang Fishing

The lowly sea cucumber, a lumbering, inoffensive detritus feeder, hardly looks like something you would want to touch, much less eat. But this homely animal is the target of small-scale fishermen all over Indonesia, and for many it serves as a major source of cash income.

Plucked from the shallow reefs of Indonesia, the sea cucumbers are dried, cleaned and sold in small lots to local businessmen, who ship them to Ujung Pandang, the center of the trade. There they are graded, and sold to the Asian market where this trepang becomes the key ingredient in a Chinese soup.

Most of the collectors are young boys. Wearing homemade goggles made of circles of glass fitted with pitch into carved sections of bamboo, the trepang collectors scan the shallows for their foot-long quarry.

Although the animals are not dangerous, they have a tendency to eject their Cuvierian tubules—long, sticky white strands—when disturbed. Collectors invariably get this goo, designed to immobilize a predator, all over their hands.

Some 30 species—generally *Holothuria*—are collected. The inferior, small black ones are sold to the Chinese market, where they fetch up to $2.40 a kilo for the wholesalers in Ujung Pandang. The real prize, however, is *H. aculeata,* fat and whitish when dried. These are saved for the more lucrative Hong Kong market, where they sell for up to $17/kilo wholesale.

Trepang, a Malay word, is also called bêche-de-mer, a pseudo-French word derived from an old English word, derived from the Portuguese *bicho do mar,* "sea worm." The original Latin, however, is more evocative: "little sea beast."

— *David Pickell*

Biak Fish Bomb Industry

Fish bombing and dynamite fishing are unfortunately widespread in Indonesia. The practice began in earnest after World War II, as wartime construction brought dynamite to Indonesia, the Philippines, and the Pacific Islands. In Indonesia, a flourishing cottage industry has developed to remove the cordite from surplus Allied shells—dumped in the sea at war's end—and distribute it to markets across the archipelago for fish bombs.

Fish bombing is a simple process. A likely spot is located and staked out by a fisherman. A small bomb, usually powder packed into a beer bottle, is stuffed into a cored papaya and thrown overboard. After the explosion, the stunned

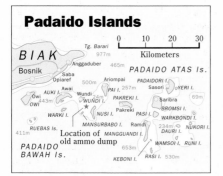

Padaido Islands

and killed fish are scooped up with nets as fast as possible. The papaya helps the bomb sink and muffles the blast; one doesn't want any unsolicited "helpers" when the fish start floating upward.

To a fisherman, who works a long, hard day to bring a few fish to market, the appeal of bombing is obvious. Unfortunately, the impact on the reef is disastrous. Not all the dead fish float, of course, and method is very wasteful. But the most damage is caused by the destruction of the coral by the blast. Fish will essentially reproduce to fill the environment. Coral *is* the environment.

Flourishing Cottage Industry

According to a report by Stephen Nash of the World Wildlife Fund for Nature, an old Allied ammo dump in the Padaido Islands has been the source of a cottage

industry supplying the fish bombs used in Biak and the Cenderawasih Bay, and may supply powder to markets as far away as western Indonesia. The report was written several years ago, and at the time the supply of easily-found shells was running out. But the author feared that scuba gear, brought to Biak to equip collectors of tropical marine fish, would make accessible new supplies of bombs.

The Padaido islanders are masters of the very delicate art of live bomb recovery. The shells are found by dragging the sandy bottom with a piece of iron tied to a rope. When it is felt to hit something hard, a diver puts on goggles and dives to the bottom—18 meters—ties the bomb to the rope, and returns to the surface. Then the bomb is hauled up. Once on land, the bomb is carefully opened, and the priming mixture and cordite are extracted for packaging and sale.

The trickiest part of building the fish bombs is constructing the fuse, which is made of the flat, malleable aluminum from a tube of toothpaste. Priming mixture is "diluted" with crushed matchheads and the aluminum sheet is rolled around it like a cigaret. The aluminum makes the fuse waterproof; heat and combustion gases keep the water from rushing in the open end. Different lengths of this waterproof fuse are used depending on how deep the fisherman wants the bomb to go before exploding.

The fuse is attached to a standard beer bottle—or a large ale bottle, or a small medicine bottle—with coconut husk rope and pitch. The whole package is stuffed into a papaya, and thrown overboard. According to the report, fish bombers off the south coast of Biak near the airport time their bombs with the noisy arrival of the Garuda flight, which effectively masks the explosion.

Today, the supply of cordite and gunpowder has for the most part disappeared. Unfortunately, the clever fishermen have now discovered how to make bombs using ingredients found in widely available chemical fertilizers.

— David Pickell

case of the Great Barrier Reef, this "lagoon" is in places 100 kilometers wide.

A barrier reef that forms around an island is sometimes called an "almost atoll." There can be multiple barrier reefs, extending outward like ripples, and the large lagoon behind a barrier reef can harbor small patch reefs and sandy cay reefs.

Atolls. Some 425 of these characteristic circular reefs, with a large central lagoon, have been recorded throughout the tropics. The vast majority (more than 300) are in the Indo-Pacific. The largest is Kwajalein in the Marshall Islands, which forms an oval 120 by 32 kilometers.

The largest atoll in Indonesia—and the third-largest in the world, just 20 percent smaller than Kwajalein—is Taka Bone Rate, in the Flores Sea south of Sulawesi. Taka Bone Rate (called Tijger in older texts) stretches 72 by 36 kilometers, covers 2,220 square kilometers, and includes 22 sandy islands. "Taka,"probably a Bugis word, is a generic term used throughout Indonesia for atoll or bank reef.

The lagoon of an atoll, because it is so thoroughly cut off from the open ocean, forms a unique environment, and is often much richer in life than the lagoon side of, say, a small barrier reef. The level of organic matter in the water inside the atoll's lagoon is considerably higher than outside, allowing it to support as much as 10 times the biomass as the outer reef edge. And, because it is not adjacent to a large land mass, problems caused by run-off and turbidity are eliminated.

The richness of the lagoon water is thought to be the result of deep ocean water percolating through the walls of the basement structure of the reef, bringing with it nutrients that previously had been locked away in geological storage.

The Formation of Reefs

Darwin's theory. British naturalist Charles Darwin first published his theory of coral reef formation in 1842, and it is still the dominant theory today. Darwin, in *The Structure and Distribution of Coral Reefs,* suggested that a fringing reef around the edges of an island would gradually grow outward, leaving a lagoon in its wake, and evolving into a barrier reef. If the island, over geological time, subsided, then what would be left would be an atoll:

"Now, as the island sinks down, either a few feet at a time or quite insensibly, we may safely infer from what we know of the conditions favourable to the growth of coral, that the living masses bathed by the surf on the margin of the reef, will soon regain the surface…

"Let the island continue sinking, and the coral-reef will continue growing up its own foundation, whilst the water gains inch by inch on the land, until the last and highest pinnacle is covered, and there remains a perfect atoll." (See diagram at right.)

This, like natural selection, was pure speculation on Darwin's part. Atoll-formation was a phenomenon of history, and not something that he could "prove" with 19th century technologies. In fact, it was not until the 1951, when the U.S. Geologic Survey drilled Enewetak Atoll in the

Above: *In the clear waters of Indonesian reefs, ultraviolet radiation can penetrate several meters underwater. Pigments made up of amino acids, called S-320, shield the delicate growing tips of shallow-water corals such as this Acropora sp.*

Step 1. *A fringing reef forms around an island.*

Step 2. *The island sinks, and the fringing reef grows into a barrier reef.*

Step 3. *The island sinks below the surface, and only an atoll remains. (After Darwin, 1842)*

Step 1. Limestone is exposed by geological forces.

Step 2. Rainfall erodes exposed limestone.

Step 3. Water level rises, and eroded limestone is colonized by coral. (After Purdy, 1974)

Below: The emperor angelfish, Pomacanthus imperator.

Marshalls to 1,340 meters, that Darwin's theory was confirmed: deep down, below the layer of coral in the atoll lagoons, the core samples revealed the volcanic rock of a former island.

However, this still did not explain the mechanism for Darwin's subsistence of the island. We now know, for example, that the Ice Ages, by locking up much of the earth's water into ice, brought about large changes in the level of the earth's oceans. At the peak of the last Ice Age, 18,000 years ago, the sea level stood almost 130 meters lower than it does today. In some cases it has probably been the rising of the oceans and not the sinking of the island that has created atolls.

Karstic saucers. Darwin's is not the only theory of reef formation, and there are some areas where geological evidence does not accord well with his speculations. A newer explanation has been offered, called the karstic saucer theory. "Karst" is the name given to the formations caused by the action of rainwater on exposed limestone—caves, sinkholes and underground channels. (The name comes from the type region around the Dinaric Alps, near the Adriatic coast of Yugoslavia.)

This theory proposes that an area of exposed limestone, acted upon by the weak carbonic acid produced by rainfall, would take the shapes Darwin's theory attributes to reef growth. When the water level subsequently rose, corals would colonize the already shaped and eroded limestone. (See illustration at left.)

One of the great appeals of this theory to scientists is that it can be tested in the laboratory. Weak acid applied to a flat-topped block of calcareous rock will tend to erode it into the shape of a saucer, the acid acting to a greater degree in the center than at the edges. It also better explains some of the structures, like blue holes, found in Caribbean reefs.

Products from the Sea

Indonesians have always been sea-farers, and for an archipelagic nation, the ocean is still its greatest resource. Fish provides the main source of protein to

Indonesia's 204 million people. The waters off Indonesia are thought to be able to support a fishing industry of 5 million tons a year, with actual catches just 20 percent of this.

Commercially valuable sea products also provide some cash to people living on sandy islands with little or no resources, save perhaps copra from coconuts. Ujung Pandang, the capital of South Sulawesi, is the Indonesian leader in the export of sea products, shipping several thousand tons a year. These include pearl oysters, mother-of-pearl or *Trochus* shells, other shells and dried sea cucumbers. The sea cucumbers, or *trepang,* are used in Chinese soup. (See "Trepang Fishing," page 27.)

Although collecting these animals provides necessary income to the islanders, over-harvesting by itinerant Bugis and Bajo fishermen has all but wiped out certain species in some areas. Particularly hard-hit are the giant clams (*Tridacna*). The meat is canned and then sold at considerable prices in East Asia. These clams used to grow in huge "fields" in the reefs of eastern Indonesia. You can now dive in the same areas and not see a single one.

Triton shells (*Charonia tritonis*), helmet conchs (*Casis cornuta*) and turban shells (*Turbo marmoratus*), which are sold as trinkets, have also disappeared from some areas.

Future of Coral Reefs

Although Indonesia has some of the most untouched coral reefs in the world, even in the remote parts of the archipelago, where industrialization has not yet reached, the reefs are not free of danger. According to officials of the World Wide Fund for Nature (WWF) in Irian Jaya, the Indonesian half of the island of New Guinea, it is predominantly the reefs, and not the great forests of

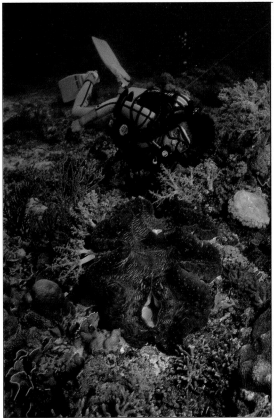

that island, that are most at risk.

Like forests, reefs are subject to succession. A diverse, well-populated reef does not just spring from the sandy bottom. Once a reef is wiped out, unprotected wave action and current may prevent regrowth from taking place.

In the more developed areas of Indonesia, dredging of channels, harvesting of coral for construction materials, and filling of estuarial waters has had a devastating impact on the reefs. The Bay of Ambon, in the central Moluccas, once had a reef that moved naturalist Alfred Russel Wallace to write: "There is perhaps no spot in the world richer in marine productions, corals, shells and fishes, than the harbour of Amboyna." During the post-war building boom, the coral was dragged up for build-

Above: *Giant clams like this* Tridacna gigas *were once common on Indonesian reefs. But a market for the canned meat in Asia, and the use of giant clam shells in making terazzo in Surabaya, Java have decimated the population in many areas.*

KAL MULLER

ing material in Ambon town. Today, the bay is a wasteland.

Also damaging is the continuing practice of fish bombing, in which small charges are thrown overboard to stun fish so they can be easily captured for market. (See "The Biak Fish Bomb Industry," page 28). The bombs don't just kill the fish. They create lifeless craters in the reef, deserts where all the coral and the life it supported have been destroyed. In some places this practice has reduced all the nearshore reef to barren rubble. Fishing for aquarium specimens and groupers for the live seafood trade using sodium cyanide is just as damaging.

In the long run, however, the greatest damage to reefs will probably be a result of bad land use: poor farming practices, including overgrazing, public works projects that expose the thin tropical soil to erosion, and deforestation through timbering.

These practices increase runoff and erosion, loading rivers up with silt, which is then carried out to sea. Silt chokes off coral growth, and leads to eutrophica-tion, a great increase in nutrients in the water. This, in turn, causes an algae bloom, which robs the water of oxygen and can form a lethal mat over the coral.

Divers in Indonesia also have a responsibility to keep the country's reefs, many of which truly are in pristine condition, in a continued state of health. This means taking no souvenirs, developing good diving habits so as not to break off or damage fragile corals, and not harassing animals. In some areas, careless placement of dive boat anchors has already caused damage.

In many areas the guides are not educated in reef conservation. I have been served fresh giant clam after a dive by a guide who took the animal while diving on an Indonesian reef that was a protected marine reserve. He couldn't at first understand why we were upset. As visitors—and customers—divers are in an excellent position to help dive operators develop good conservation habits. I think we owe it to the people and reefs of Indonesia to do at least this much.

— *David Pickell*

Below: *A gorgonian goby (*Bryaninops *sp.) on an antipatharian wire coral. This little animal is no more than 4 centimeters long. Many fishes rely on invetebrates for food, shelter, and protection, but few are as particular as the gorgonian gobies. Some species of* Bryaninops *live and lay their eggs on only a single species of gorgonian or antipatharian.*

The Varied Inhabitants of Indonesia's Reefs

The waters surrounding the islands of Indonesia form the richest marine habitat on earth. Indonesia lies at the epicenter of species diversity for the entire tropical Indo-Pacific region, which stretches from Madagascar and the Comoros islands in the west to the easternmost of the Pacific islands—a vast 12,000-mile sweep through the Indian and Pacific Oceans.

Perhaps 3,000 species of fish, and several hundred species of coral populate the reefs off the larger Indonesian islands. A 19th century Dutch ichthyologist cataloged 780 species of marine fish just in Ambon Bay alone, almost as many as can be found in all the rivers, lakes and seas of Europe. (Alas, this reef has been destroyed, dredged after World War II to provide building materials for booming Ambon town). Even the healthiest Caribbean reef has just 10–20 percent of the species diversity of a comparable Indonesian reef.

The islands that now make up Indonesia are likely to have been the genetic "source" of Indo-Pacific marine life. This region has remained tropical for 100 million years, exposed to the strong sunlight that makes tropical waters so much richer than temperate waters, giving the animals a long time to diversify.

Although ocean currents distribute fish widely, the further across the Pacific one goes from Indonesia, the fewer species will be found. For example, 123 species of damselfish are found in Indonesia.* (see note at right.) In the Philippines, 118. In Papua New Guinea, 100. In Fiji, 60. In the Society Islands, 30. In the Galapagos, just 18. The entire Caribbean holds just 16 species.

One million years ago the Ice Ages began, periodically tying up much of the earth's water in ice. This lowered sea levels by as much as 130 meters, reducing the tropical Atlantic to a small refuge in the south Caribbean, decimating the animal population. The Indo-Pacific never suffered such an extinction.

But volcanism and continental drift caused similar disruptions in Indonesia, and it is probably because the islands provide such a wide variety of habitats—deep sea trenches, rocky shores, sand and mud flats, sea grass beds, mangrove swamps and, of course, coral reefs—that the fauna here is so diverse.

While muddy turtle grass beds, mangrove swamps and estuarial waters are of immense interest to the biologist, divers usually find little in these shallow, turbid waters to hold their attention. When divers talk about tropical water diving, they mean coral reefs.

A Compendium of Reef Life

There are so many species present on the Indonesian reefs that even specialists can not give an exact tally of their numbers here. With this in mind, the aim of this chapter is to provide an introduction to the major groups of animals that will be seen when diving on Indonesian reefs. No attempt at comprehensive coverage is made.

Algae

Although people often mistakenly think of many of the reef animals—corals, gorgonians, sea

Above: *A long-nosed hawkfish,* Oxycirrhites typus, *sitting among the lacy antipatharians encrusting a wreck, just off Molas beach near Manado, Sulawesi.*

*Australia, chiefly because it includes both tropical and colder-water habitats, hosts the most damselfish species, 132.

Above: *Turtle grass,* Thalassia *sp., is one of the very few true marine plants. Although not found on reefs, back-reef areas may have beds of turtle grass, which nourish crustaceans and juvenile fishes as well as the dugong.*

Below: *The marine algas* Udotea *(top) and* Halimeda *can both be occasionally found on the reef.* Udotea *is only lightly calicified, but the calcium carbonate disks of* Halimeda *are in some areas a major component of the reef substrate.*

"anemones"—as plants, what is perhaps most striking about the coral reef is the apparent lack of plant life. Other rich coastal marine environments, for example the kelp forests off California or the sea-grass beds and mangrove swamps off some of the Indonesian islands, are obviously based on the photosynthetic production of oxygen and nutrient-fixing by algae or higher plants.

On the reef, however, despite its teeming life, plants seem absent. In fact, plants are the primary producers on the reef, just like every other environment. Most of the algae found on the reef grows as a short "turf," a fine carpet of hairs that is a mix of dozens or hundreds of species of brown, red and green algaes. While diving, look closely at an area of bare coral rock and you will probably see a fine carpet of "hairs" growing on it.

The algal turf grows at a prodigious rate, but a herd of grazers—tangs, parrotfish, damselfish, sea urchins, snails and many others—keeps it clipped short. If an area of reef were caged off to prevent the entry of herbivores, the turf would quickly sprout into a thicket. The farmerfish damsel (*Stegastes lividus*) does just this, by force of personality keeping out all intruders from his own luxurious green patch of hair algae.

Some reef algaes, the so-called coralline algaes, are calcified, providing them with protection both from grazers and physical damage by surge. These appear as small pink "trees," or flat, encrusting pink or lavender growths on old chunks of coral. Some of the coralline algaes grow in areas of very high wave action, indeed preferring areas that are too turbulent for even corals to survive.

On reefs facing the open ocean, it is a ridge of coralline red algae that receives the full force of the crashing ocean

waves, dissipates their energy, and allows less robust organisms including corals to thrive. Other varieties of coralline algae grow deep on the reef, below the level at which reef-building corals can survive, where they contribute significantly to reef growth and sand production.

One recognizable green macro-alga that can sometimes be seen on shallower reefs is *Halimeda,* a heavily calcified alga made up of chains of green disks, each the size of a small button. These disks are calcium carbonate, like coral, and in some areas *Halimeda* rubble is a major component of the reef substrate.

Sometimes an inshore reef will merge with shallow beds of turtle grass, one of the very few true marine plants. These grassy beds provide an environment for seahorses, pipefish, damselfish, wrasses, and the young of some reef fishes, including butterfly-fish, as well as small crustaceans, mollusks and worms. The sea grass also provides forage for the rare dugong (*Dugong dugon*), or sea cow, which ranges across Indonesian waters.

Plankton

The diver will rarely *see* plankton, and if he or she does, it will usually be apparent as a cloudiness of the water, or an irritating backscatter in photographs. But plankton is an important link in the reef food chain. Reef areas rich in plankton will be characterized by an abundance of filter-feeders, animals that have evolved methods of sifting or snaring plankton from the current—including soft corals, mussels and oysters, anemones, crinoids, gorgonians and sponges.

Plankton consists of both "plants"—phytoplankton—and "animals"—zooplankton, and the larger zooplankters are predatory on the diatoms and algae of the phytoplankton. The plankton also contains some temporary

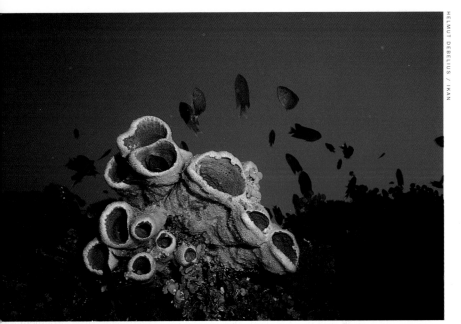

members, the meroplankton, which consists of the larval stages of fish and invertebrates. As these grow, they settle out of the plankton stream to become part of the swimming nekton (fish, jellyfish) or the crawling or fixed benthos, or bottom dwellers (sea urchins, gorgonians).

Sponges

Indonesian reef sponges vary in size from tiny to huge, from the small patches of color provided by encrusting sponges (family Clionidae) to the meter-high barrel sponges (*Xestospongia*). All sponges are members of the phylum Porifera, "the hole-bearers," and their porous, "spongy" nature is crucial to their mode of feeding. Sponges are the archetypal filter-feeders, straining plankters from the water through myriad microscopic pores.

A cross-section of a sponge shows a very sophisticated system for moving water. Small intake pores lead to an internal system of tiny canals and chambers lined with cells bearing whip-like processes. Beating constantly, these cells create a cur-

rent through the sponge that moves its own volume of water every 4–20 seconds. Even a relatively small sponge can circulate as much as 5,000 liters a day. The chimney or barrel shape of many larger sponges helps increase surface area and the water flow through the animal.

Sponges are notoriously difficult to identify. Colors vary and even the shape or size of a sponge does not necessarily mark its species; sometimes shape is just a response to local conditions. Scientists would call this new form an "ecomorph."

Scientists rely on detailed examination of the internal "skeleton" to identify sponges. Sponges are made of a proteinaceous secretion called spongin. This fibrous net forms the useful part of the bath sponges (*Spongia* and *Hippospongia*) harvested in the Mediterranean and Caribbean. Many sponges also contain spicules of silica or calcium carbonate, or both, bound together with spongin.

There are an estimated 830 species of sponges in Indonesia. The giant barrel sponges are

Above: *Sapphire damsels,* Pomacentrus pavo, *take shelter in the sponge* Cribrochalina. *Halmahera, Maluku.*

Below. *Marine dinoflagellate plankters, top to bottom:* Gymnodinium, Gonyaulax, Peridinium, Ceratium.

most impressive to divers, but the smaller tube sponges and vase sponges also create colorful and aesthetically pleasing forms.

Like many invertebrates, sponges can grow to a remarkable age. Experiments with commercial farming of bath sponges in the Caribbean have led researchers to estimate that larger specimens are at least 50 years old, and maybe much older.

Reef sponges create an environment that is exploited by a variety of other creatures. Small crabs and shrimps and even fish hide in the tubes and cavities. Crinoids perch on upright sponges to filter plankton from the current. And sea cucumbers and other detritus feeders graze on the organic material that collects on the sponge's surfaces.

Corals and their relatives

Corals, soft corals, sea anemones, gorgonians, hydroids, jellyfish and the other members of the phylum Cnidaria (formerly Coelenterata) cause a great deal of confusion for the diver trying to identify the teeming mass of branched and tentacled life he sees attached to the reef. Taxonomists identify these animals by their stinging cells, nematocysts, and simple coelenteron, from the Greek *koilos,* "hollow," and *enteron,* "gut." All have the form of a polyp at some stage in their lives. Other than these shared characteristics, the form of these animals varies widely.

Aristotle considered them an intermediate form between plants and animals, and they were first placed by taxonomists in a group called Zoophyta, "animal-plants." Only in 1723 were corals properly identified as animals, and Jean André Peyssonel, the naturalist who proposed this to the French Academy of Sciences, was laughed at and quit science in disgrace.

Phylum Cnidaria is usually divided into four classes: Hydro-

zoa, hydroids and fire corals; Anthozoa, corals and anemones; Cubozoa, box jellies; Scyphozoa, jellyfish. Anthozoa, in turn, is split into three sub-classes: Alcyonaria (Octocorallia), containing the soft corals and gorgonians; and Zoantharia (Hexacorallia), containing the stony corals and anemones; and Ceriantipatharia, including the black corals and cerianthids, or tube anemones.

The Stony Corals

The stony or hard corals are the reef-builders. They are in the order Scleractinia, and are sometimes called scleractinian or "true" corals. The skeletons these animals secrete range in shape from the massive, smooth boulders of *Porites* and stout-branched *Pocillipora* that take a pounding at the reef edge to the finely foliated needle coral *Seriatopora histrix.*

These corals are colonies, comprised of thousands of individual coral animals, or polyps. Each polyp, upon close examination, will be seen to have much the same shape as a sea anemone, with tentacles ringing a central mouth. What makes the stony coral polyp distinctive, and so ecologically important, is that it deposits calcium carbonate around its lower part, forming a

Right: *The presence of whip coral gorgonians often indicates very clean water and plenty of plankton. This is* Ctenocella *(formerly* Ellisella*). Bunaken group, Sulawesi.*

skeletal cup. The skeleton is essentially formed of repeated casts of the tiny polyp.

Most reef-building corals are nocturnal. During the day, the polyps are retracted, drawn down into the skeletal cup. At night, these corals are transformed from dead-looking lumps of rock into miniature forests thick with polyps, which expand to feast on the abundant night plankton. Tiny plankters are snared by the polyp's tentacles, which are armed with stinging nemato-cysts. Although they feed on plankton, the vast majority of the nutrition of reef-building corals is provided by the symbiotic zoox-anthellae in their tissues. (See sidebar, "Zooxanthellae and Corals," page 25.)

Corals, like other reef animals, also spawn at night, releasing pink clouds of sperm and eggs. To increase the chances of fertilization, corals of the same species tend to coordinate the release of their eggs and sperm. Many reef animals spawn around the time of the full moon, when tidal currents are strongest, to ensure wide dispersal of the larvae. On the Great Barrier Reef of Australia the majority of corals spawn 4–5 days after the November full moon. Some corals in Indonesia spawn at this time too, but the full pattern of coral spawning has not yet been determined here.

According to travel brochure clichés, corals are supposed to be "kaleidoscopic" with color. Divers, of course, know that at least for the reef-building corals, this is not at all the case. Most shallow water corals are a dull brown color, a consequence of the pigments in their zooxanthellae. Still, some are blessed with subtle pastel tints. In particular, the growing tips of *Acropora* can be colored with a pinkish or purplish pigment, a group of amino acids called S-320 which serves as an ultraviolet filter to protect

KAL MULLER

the still-young polyps.

The shape of stony corals, rather than their color, is their most salient characteristic. The form the coral will take is strongly influenced by wave action and currents, and even the same species may take different forms under different conditions. A specimen of the distinctive palmate Caribbean elkhorn coral (*Acropora palmata*) placed in a research ecosystem at the Smithsonian Institute in Washington, D.C. sent up new growth in the bushy form of *A. prolifera*. This, it would seem, further complicates the already difficult project of stony coral identification.

Massive forms. In general, massive, boulder-like forms grow in shallow water where light is plentiful, and along the reef edge where the current is strong. These include the common *Monastrea, Pocillopora,* and *Porites.* In the shallow, often turbid water of the back reef, the more robust branching forms (*Acropora*) can out-compete the massive forms, which are more vulnerable to siltation.

Massive corals sometimes form "micro-atolls" in relatively calm backreefs and reef flats. These are flat-topped forms in which the center has been killed by excessive siltation or regular exposure by low tides. The sides continue to grow outward, demonstrating Darwin's theory in miniature.

Above: *A detail of the eponymous vesicles of the bubble, or grape coral,* Plerogyra sinuosa. *These sacs, called acrorhagi, possess stinging nematocysts. During the day they are inflated with water and protect the polyp tentacles. At night they shrivel, and the polyps are extended to snare plankton. The acrorhagi also discourage other corals from overgrowing* Plerogyra, *blocking its sunlight and supply of plankton.*

Goniopora is an unusual massive coral that extends its polyps during the day. These are also usually large, reaching 20–30 centimeters in length. The effect is of a round stone, covered with little brown flowers.

Branching forms. Deeper in the reef, or in protected parts of the shallows, the diver will encounter finely branched and "leafy" forms. These more delicate structures cannot withstand strong wave action, and the added surface area of their shapes serves to better expose their zooxanthellae to the diminished sunlight of deeper waters.

The most common is the fast-growing and ubiquitous *Acropora*. This genus (there are some 100 species) takes a variety of forms, ranging from branching thickets to table-like formations. The tables are considered to be a defense mechanism, as the *Acropora* quickly grows outward, shading any other corals that might try to overgrow it.

Another branching coral often recognized by divers is the needle coral *Seriatopora hystrix,* sending up delicate, pointed branches of cream, blue or pink. *Seriatopora* is usually found in quiet, rather shallow water.

Smaller corals. Some of the smaller coral colonies have distinct, interesting shapes. These corals are not primary reef builders, but colonize already established areas of the reef.

The mushroom corals (family Fungiidae) are common in Indonesia. These form carbonate skeletons that are flat and oval-shaped, perhaps 15–30 centimeters inches long, with fine, radial structures reminiscent of the "gills" of a mushroom. The skeletons are not attached to the reef, and particularly on drop-off reefs, are often knocked upside down by currents. These corals are capable of limited movement, and can usually right themselves eventually. The long-tentacled *Heliofungia actiniformis* is often mistaken for a sea anemone.

The flower corals (*Euphyllia*) are not as common as *Fungia,* but can be quite beautiful. They form a maze of flat plates that stick up vertically 10–20 centimeters and cover an area 50 centimeters or even much more in diameter. These corals have long, colorful tentacles, which they extend during the day. *Euphyllia* tolerates turbid water, and can be found growing on patch reefs in back reef channels.

The very bright orange polyps of the coral *Tubastrea* (or the similar *Dendrophyllia*) can be seen in small clusters, usually in low-light areas such as deep on the reef or under overhangs. These finger-sized polyps can easily be mistaken for anemones. They are true scleractinian corals, however, and secrete a very fragile internal skeleton. *Tubastrea* contains no zooxanthellae and receives all its nutrition by capturing plankton. At night, you can watch the polyps feeding by using your light to attract the plankton within reach of the polyps' tentacles. (If your light is very bright, shade it so the polyps won't retract.)

Anemones

Despite their soft and fleshy appearance, sea anemones (order Actinaria) are more closely related to stony corals than soft corals. The giant anemones commonly encountered in Indonesia contain symbiotic algae and are most abundant in relatively shallow areas. They can be seen growing in sand, or tucked into the coral rock in the shallows or at the lip of drop-off reefs.

Like the corals, color and even shape varies widely in the giant anemones, and they are often very difficult to identify. In Indonesia, one can find the long-tentacled *Heteractis*, the short-tentacled carpet anemone, *Stichodactyla*, and the unusual

Discovering New Species

For the diving scientist, Indonesian waters are the most exciting in the world. Not only can "new" species be found on just about every dive, but so much of the behavior of these animals is still unknown that underwater observations are full of surprises.

Scuba has radically changed the way scientists study marine animals. No longer is it necessary to collect everything to study in an aquarium, an artificial environment that often produces artificial behavior, or to collect species the old way—netting, trapping, or even poison. A diver can collect very selectively, and make observations without interfering with the animals' ways of life.

Innumerable small crustaceans and other benthic creatures living in the cracks and crevices of Indonesian reefs go undescribed by science. Even among the best-known reef animals—the fishes—new discoveries are made regularly.

The Grandfather of Ichthyology

To find new species of fish, a good eye and thorough knowledge of the literature serves one better than an academic degree. The grandfather of Indonesian ichthyology was Pieter Bleeker, a Dutch army doctor with a keen interest in fishes. He arrived in Jakarta in 1842, and over the following 30 years produced some 500 papers that became the foundation of his famous, nine-volume *Atlas Ichthyologique* (1862–78).

Unlike many 19th century scientists, who were for the most part simple taxonomists, Bleeker had a very modern understanding of the inter-relationship of species. His work is highly respected by today's scientists.

Finding New Species

Bleeker's work was so good that species described 100 years ago are still waiting to be "re-discovered." It is amazing how many deep-water fishes were collected in those days and never seen again. But scientists tend to concentrate on these, and the intertidal areas are often overlooked.

Above: *The red-headed wrasse,* Halichoeres rubricephalus, *is sexually dichromic (male at top). This beautiful wrasse was discovered by Kuiter in 1986 in Maumere Bay. Common there, it has not been seen anywhere else.*

A knowledgeable diver, with sharp powers of observation, has a very good chance of finding an unknown animal on just about any dive in Indonesia.

I have been visiting the Flores Sao Resort on a regular basis since 1986, photographing and observing the animal life of Maumere Bay. Despite my many dives in these waters, new species turn up on every trip. Often a "new" species looks very similar to a well-known one, and thus has been overlooked. But in other cases the new species is so spectacular one wonders how it could possibly have ever gone unnoticed.

I started underwater photography 20 years ago, and even among my first dives with a camera, I photographed things that I have never seen since. I always take the picture first, and try to sort out the story later. The underwater world is so diverse you may never see it again.

—*Rudie Kuiter*

Entacmaea quadricolor, with bulbous-tipped tentacles. These anemones are large, sometimes growing to half a meter or more in diameter, although what at first seems to be one anemone is sometimes a group of several.

Giant anemones are easy to spot because they nearly always host a pair, or small group of clownfish *(Amphiprion* and *Premnas)*. (See "Clownfishes and their Sea Anemone Hosts," page 46.) These fish are not the only animals to take advantage of the security of the anemone's stinging tentacles. Porcelain crabs *(Neopetrolisthes)* and shrimps are also anemone commensals.

Corallimorphs. These animals (order Corallimorpharia) have some of the characteristics of anemones, and others of corals. In fact, however, they look like small anemones. They are mostly colonial, and consist of flat disks, 2–4 inches in diameter, with a smooth, napped or tentacled surface. One genus, *Discosoma,* is particularly colorful, overgrowing rocks with its bright blue, purple or red disks.

Soft corals and gorgonians

These animals (subclass Alcyonaria) are among the loveliest of the cnidarians. In the clean, plankton-rich waters of Indonesia, soft corals and gorgonians—sea whips or sea fans—are common. Some contain zooxanthellae, but many frequent the deeper parts of the reef, where they filter plankton from the water. Semi-precious pink "coral" is a gorgonian *(Corallium)*, harvested from deep waters off Japan and in the Mediterranean.

Soft corals. Soft corals, as the name suggests, lack the hard limestone skeletons of their reef-building relatives. Instead, the numerous polyps that make up the colony are supported by a fleshy central "body"; in some cases strengthened by spicules, spines of silica or calcium.

Soft corals (order Alcyonacea) have few obvious defense mechanisms, and might seem to be vulnerable to attack by predators and parasites, or to fouling by overgrowth. The animals avoid these problems by secreting various bioactive substances, a kind of chemical defense. Substantial efforts are being made by biochemists and pharmaceutical companies to identify compounds in soft corals—and also sponges—that may have properties useful in medicine. Since many of these compounds have evolved to prevent alien growths, they are receiving attention as potential anti-cancer drugs.

A very common group of soft corals in Indonesia are the leather corals *(Lobophytum, Sarcophyton* and *Sinularia)* so-named because of their color and texture. These corals grow as wrinkled lobes in well-lit, shallow areas of reef. Because of their symbiotic zooxanthellae, they are a dull brown, sometimes with a slightly green or yellow tinge. When their white polyps are extended for feeding they are easy to identify as soft corals, but when their polyps are retracted they could be mistaken for sponges. The leather corals, however, have a much smoother surface than sponges.

Perhaps the most beautiful of the soft corals is *Dendronephthya,* a soft coral with fuzzy branches of vivid pink, white, orange, red, red-and-white, and a variety of other colors. The main "stem" is normally translucent and contains numerous white spicules, which offer some structural support. Most of the color comes from the polyps, which also contain sharp spicules to deter browsing by fishes. *Dendronephthya* grows deeper on the reef and in areas of low light, and always where currents can provide it with abundant plankton.

Xenia, particularly common in Indonesia, has perhaps the

largest individual polyps of any soft coral, each 6–8 centimeters long. The white (also tan, or light blue) polyps grow in clusters, and the tentacles at the end of each are feathery. These continually open and close, like numerous grasping hands. In *Xenia* one can easily count eight tentacles, which is one feature that distinguishes soft corals (Octocorallia) from hard corals and anemones (Zoantharia) which have six, or multiples of six, tentacles.

Gorgonians. Gorgonians (order Gorgonaceae) have a strong, horny skeleton, which gives strength and support without sacrificing flexibility. They tend to grow on the deeper parts of the reef, away from strong wave action. They live by filter feeding, and to maximize the water flow across their surfaces always grow at right angles to the prevailing current. Where the tidal current flows along the reef, gorgonians grow with their long axis vertical. Sometimes, however, particularly on some of the big walls in Indonesia, large sea fans can be seen growing horizontally out from the reef wall, to take advantage of the current upwelling.

There are many species of these animals. Some have a twig-like structure, like a branch from a delicate tree. Many are brightly colored. The sea fans (Melithaeidae and Plexauridae) are flat nets, growing in some cases to three meters across. The skeleton of a sea fan is coated with a kind of "rind," which is sometimes a delicate shade. When you see a big gorgonian it is worth spending a few moments looking closely at its surface because they often host an assortment of small symbiotic animals.

Sea pens. These animals (order Pennatulacea) are filter-feeders related to the gorgonians. Their common name comes from their resemblance to the old-fashioned quill pen. Although common in Indonesia, they are not really reef dwellers, and will usually only be seen by night divers who venture out over mud or sand bottoms. Sea pens, sometimes growing in large fields, rotate gently back and forth with the current, their "feathers" sifting plankton from the current.

Below: *Closeup of the lovely soft coral* Dendronephthya. *In this photograph the strengthening spicules are clearly visible in the animals' transparent tissue.*

KAL MULLER

Above: *The poisonous sea wasp,* Chironex. *This animal has been responsible for human fatalities in Australian waters.*

Black corals. Black coral (subclass Ceriantipatharia, order Antipatharia) looks to the diver like a gorgonian, although it is more closely related to the stony corals and anemones. On deeper dives in Indonesia, one can see wire corals (*Cirrhipathes*) and black coral bushes (*Antipathes*).

The polished skeleton of the latter, particularly the thicker branches, is the precious black coral. Black coral is scarce, and its export from Indonesia and import into many other countries is prohibited by laws.

Cerianthids. In some areas, particularly with sandy bottoms, one can find cerianthids (subclass Ceriantipatharia, order Ceriantharia) or tube anemones. These are quite different from true anemones. Cerianthids have fine tentacles arranged in two concentric bands, and a tube—made of fibers created by special nematocysts—into which they can retract if disturbed.

ED ROBINSON / IKAN

Above: *A pair of* Chromodoris willani, *perhaps mating. All nudibranchs are hermaphrodites, although they require a partner to produce viable offspring. Bunaken group, Sulawesi.*

Fire coral and hydroids

All cnidarians have stinging cells on their tentacles with which they can defend themselves and immobilize their prey. In most cases, however, these are rather weak and are usually not capable of penetrating human skin. One group, class Hydrozoa, which includes the fire corals and their relatives, has members capable of inflicting very painful stings.

The notorious Portuguese-man-of-war (*Physalia physalis*) is a hydrozoan, and not, despite its appearance, a jellyfish. Fortunately for divers this animal is more of an open ocean dweller.

Stinging hydroids. A far greater nuisance to divers in Indonesia are the hydroids *Aglaophenia* and *Lytocarpus*. Despite their delicate, fern-like appearance, these colonial animals can deliver a burning sting that raises a welt on bare skin. They are fairly common on many Indonesian reefs, and their presence prompts divers to wear Lycra or thin neoprene suits even in the warmest of conditions. The stinging hydroids are sometimes called sea ferns, or sea nettles.

Fire corals. Somewhat less virulent are the fire corals of the genus *Millepora*, but as their name suggests they too should be treated with respect. These hydrozoans are members of a group called hydrocorals for their superficial resemblance to the true corals. Hydrocorals secrete a limestone skeleton, and form colonies that are usually a dull-yellow brown in color (*Millepora*) although some species (*Distichopora, Stylaster*) can be brightly colored.

The unusual blue coral (*Heliopora coerulea*), is a fire coral which has a skeleton that when dried displays a light blue tint. It is taxonomically distinct, however and has been placed in class Anthozoa with the octocorals.

Some hydrocorals are important reef-builders, particularly *M. platyphylla,* which can be found growing with massive scleractinian corals at the pounding edge of the reef.

Jellyfish

These familiar animals (class Scyphozoa) are characterized by a dominant medusa stage. Like all cnidarians they form a polyp for part of their lives, but for the jellyfish, this is just temporary. Occasionally, large jellyfish can be seen while diving in Indonesia, particularly in areas of rich plankton. These can be quite beautiful to observe. More bothersome are the cubomedusae, or sea-wasps, tiny jellyfish that can have an irritating sting. Members of the genus *Chironex* have even been responsible for human fatalities in Australia. Because they tend to inhabit the surface layer during the day, they are more of a bother for snorkelers. The lights of night divers, however, can often attract an unwelcome swarm of these creatures.

Worms

Although the word conjures up a dull, and faintly repulsive animal to many people, the worms found on the reefs of Indonesia show a diversity of form and color that often astounds the observer.

There are many different sorts of worms, but most likely to be seen by divers on Indonesian reefs are those in the following phyla: the flatworms (phylum Platyhelminthes); the ribbonworms (phylum Nemertina); the tongueworms (phylum Echiura); and the segmented worms (phylum Annelida).

Flatworms. Flatworms often have the strikingly beautiful colors divers associate with nudibranchs (which are molluscs). The species seen on Indonesian reefs rarely grow longer than 10 centimeters, and feed on sessile animals such as tunicates and sponges. Flatworms move by gliding over the bottom, or by muscular undulations. This latter waving action is characteristic, and mimicked by the juveniles of several species of fish. This mimicry and the bright colors suggest the presence of a noxious chemical to deter predators.

Ribbonworms. These animals are longer than flatworms, and not as showy. Many are white, with dark stripes or bands.

They tend to live under rocks and corals or in the sand, and are most likely to be seen by divers at night. Some can grow to astonishing sizes, as much as several meters. They feed on molluscs and other worms.

Tongueworms. The tongueworm *Bonellia* can be seen on reef slopes. However, it hides its sac-like body in a crevice, with only a forked proboscis protruding, is easily overlooked. These

animals have an unusual sex life. All the fully formed *Bonellia* are females; if a larva settles into an area where there are no worms, it becomes a female. If there are already *Bonellia* established in the area, the larva passes into the body of an adult, becoming a dwarf male, which lives like a parasite on the female "host."

Segmented worms. The segmented worms are the most abundant and diverse of all the

Above: *Two dorid nudibranchs,* Notodoris citrina *(top) and* Nembrotha sp. *Nudibranchs tend to be very prey-specific.* Nembrotha, *as is shown here, feeds only on hydroids.* Notodoris *was photographed in Halmahera, Maluku;* Nembrotha *in Flores.*

groups of reef worms. Divers are familiar with the feathery feeding parts of the tiny Christmas tree worms (*Spirobranchus*) which extend from lumps of living coral. The body of the worm is hidden in a tube within a *Porites* coral head. The similar, but larger fanworm, or feather duster worm (*Protula, Sabellastarte*), secretes a tube of flexible parchment to protect its soft body. From its tube, it periodically extends a crown of colorful "feathers" to collect plankton. These worms make good subjects for macrophotography, but any sudden movement will cause them to withdraw their crowns.

Some of the segmented worms have evolved unusual reproductive strategies, perhaps the most famous being that of the palola worms, (*Palola siciliensis*). Called *nyale* in parts of Indonesia, these worms spend their lives in coral crevices, but one night a year, their tail parts metamorphose into a sexual form, containing either eggs or sperm.

These sexual forms, called epitokes, break off and swarm to the surface. The timing of the event is set by the moon, and in parts of Indonesia, most notably western Sumba and southern Lombok, the appearance of the epitokes is an important event in the ritual or cultural calender. It is also a great culinary event, as the rich-tasting epitokes are highly prized for eating.

Molluscs

Molluscs are one of the largest and most familiar groups of invertebrate animals, and thousands of species live in Indonesian waters. The phylum is organized into either five or eight classes, the main ones found on Indonesian reefs being: Gastropoda (univalves—single shells), including snails, cowries and conches, as well as the shell-less sea slugs; Pelecypoda (bivalves—two-part shell),

including clams, oysters and mussels; and the Cephalopoda, including octopi, squid and cuttlefish. Despite their differences, animals in these three groups all possess a soft, fleshy body (mollusc means "soft") and most—octopi and nudibranchs are exceptions—have the ability to produce a calcareous shell.

Nudibranchs and snails

Gastropods are abundant on Indonesian reefs, but they are easily overlooked because most are small, many are nocturnal, and some are very well camouflaged. Nevertheless the diver who develops the habit of carefully scrutinizing the reef surface will soon find many of these delightful creatures.

Nudibranchs. Nudibranchs, the "naked gilled" sea slugs, are the most interesting to the diver. Like common garden slugs, they are snail-like animals that have lost their shells. Nudibranchs are often strikingly colored.

In some species the coloration is clearly cryptic, allowing them to blend in with their chosen prey. Nudibranchs are carnivorous, and most are very prey specific, feeding for example only on particular types of soft coral or sponges. Since these prey animals are often very colorful, so are the nudibranchs.

In other species, it seems certain that coloration serves as a warning to would-be predators that the animals are foul-tasting or poisonous. Nudibranchs are known to produce some very concentrated toxins. Some even have nematocysts, which they obtain from their cnidarian prey and concentrate in the outer layers of their own skin.

Most nudibranchs are small, although a few mainly nocturnal forms grow to 20 centimeters or more in length. One of the largest and certainly the most spectacular nudibranch found in Indonesia is the Spanish dancer,

Above: *The triton shell,* Charonia tritonis. *This gastropod preys on crown-of-thorns starfish.*

Above: *The helmet conch,* Casis cornuta. *Indonesians call this* kima kepala kambing, *the "goat's head shell."*

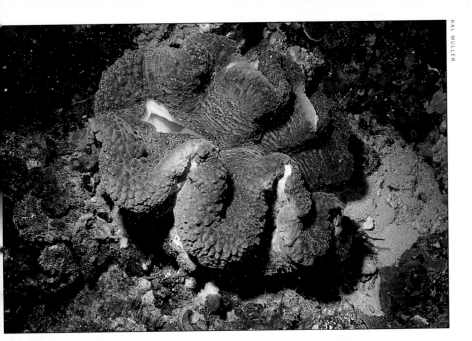

Hexabranchus sanguineus, a beautiful, crimson-colored animal. This nudibranch only wanders out at night, and if it is found and gently picked up, it will begin its "dance." The wild undulations of its body and surrounding skirt are thought to serve as part of a warning display. Like many nudibranchs, Spanish dancers lay their eggs in huge numbers, in spiral ribbons that can look like flowers.

Rock shells. The rock shells or murex (*Murex* spp.) feed heavily on small bivalve molluscs such as oysters. This is not an easy task, because the bivalves clamp their shells shut when attacked. A murex shell overcomes this resistance by chipping away at the edge of the oyster with its sharp radula or mouthpart, and then pokes its proboscis into this opening to feed on the fleshy tissues within. Another species, with similar tastes in prey, is the drill (*Thais*). This small gastropod literally drills a hole through the oyster's shell. The large number of bivalve shells with neat holes drilled in them that are washed

up on Indonesian beaches testifies to the efficiency of this feeding method.

Tritons. The triton shell (*Charonia tritonis*) is famous as a predator of the troublesome crown-of-thorns starfish, which has devastated Australian reefs. This large shell (to more than 30 cm.) is a popular souvenir, and over-harvesting has been blamed for population explosions of the crown-of-thorns. The helmet conch (*Casis cornuta*) is another large, predatory gastropod found in Indonesia. Because of collectors, both the triton and helmet conch are endangered in parts of Indonesia.

Cone shells. Cone shells (*Conus* spp.) are even more rapacious predators. Their radulas are modified as barbs, with which they stab their victims. They then immobilize their prey by injecting a neurotoxic poison. Most cone shells eat worms, although a few are piscivorous. The poison of some of the fish-eating *Conus* species is powerful enough to kill a human, so treat them with respect.

Cowries. Cowries (*Cypraea*

Above: Tridacna gigas *is the largest of the seven species of giant clams. It can be distinguished by its size and the pebbly texture of its mantle. Scientists believe these to be among the longest-lived animals, some surviving as long as 200 years. A specimen as large as the one pictured here is probably well over 50 years old.*

Above: *A predatory gastropod prying open a bivalve.*

HETERACTIS MAGNIFICA

Above: *The colorful magnificent anemone, one of the largest clownfish anemones.*

Below: *Juvenile Clark's anemonefish, in the distinctive bulb-tentacled anemone. 15 meters, Bunaken Island, Sulawesi.*

Clownfish and their Sea Anemone Hosts

There is perhaps no sight more charming than a pair of bright clownfishes nestled in one of the colorful giant reef anemones. Although known to possess powerful stinging cells, the anemones clearly don't harm the clownfishes, which look downright snug tucked into the soft tentacles of their host.

The relationship between the fish and the actinian is commensal; the anemonefishes clearly benefit, receiving protection for themselves and their offspring. They even pluck at the tentacles and oral disk of the anemone, eating the organic material that has collected there.

The benefit to the anemone is less clear. The constant prodding, cleaning and stimulation provided by the fishes certainly *seems* enjoyable, but this maybe just to us. Anemonefishes are never found without anemones;

anemones, however, are sometimes found without the fish.

A Delicate Operation

It had been thought that clownfishes were somehow immune to the anemone's stinging nematocysts. Close observations, however, have shown this not to be the case. The fish, through a series of brief—and careful—encounters with the actinian, picks up a substance in its mucous that the anemone recognizes as its own. The nematocysts don't fire when touched by the fish for the same reason one tentacle doesn't sting another.

Some cold-hearted experimenters tested this theory by scraping the mucous off a clownfish and placing it back with its anemone. The hapless fish was immediately and unceremoniously stung.

Clownfishes are protandrous

AMPHIPRION CLARKII   ENTACMAEA QUADRICOLOR

hermaphrodites; that is, all mature as males, and then a few sex-reverse to females. A typical anemone will contain a pair of clownfish, and perhaps a few young ones.

The largest fish in the group is the female. If she should die, the reigning male sex-reverses, and the dominant juvenile becomes the functional male. Juveniles sharing an anemone with an adult pair are hormonally stunted, and remain small.

Although clownfish are the only fishes to require an anemone host, other small damsels will opportunistically occupy anemones as juveniles, especially various species of *Dascyllus*.

Sea Anemones

Some of the giant reef anemones can reach a meter in diameter. All have zooxanthellae, and are thus found in relatively shallow water. They derive most of their nutrition from the algae, but also consume plankton and any other small animal unlucky enough to blunder into their tentacles.

Anemones can live to a ripe old age. In the 19th century, British naturalist John Dalyell kept a coldwater *Actinia* sp. anemone for 66 years. Over this period, it produced 750 young (by budding), 150 of these after the age of 50. The anemone eventually outlived the scientist.

Some 10 species of Indonesian anemones, in three families, host clownfish. The systematics of this group was in some confusion until Dr. Daphne Fautin reorganized it in 1981.

Cryptodendrum adhaesivum. Lies flat; very short tentacles. Hosts only Clark's anemonefish.
Entacmaea quadricolor. The bubble anemone. (See photo at left.) Hosts 11 species.
Macrodactyla doreensis. Very long, widely spaced tentacles.

AMPHIPRION CLARKII   HETERACTIS AURORA

KAL MULLER

PREMNAS BIACULEATUS   ENTACMAEA QUADRICOLOR

MIKE SEVERNS

AMPHIPRION OCELLARIS   STICHODACTYLA HADDONI

HELMUT DEBELIUS / IKAN

Usually dull color, buries column in sand. Hosts 2 species.
Heteractis aurora. Dull color, buries column in sand. Distinctive tentacle shape (see top photo above.) Hosts 7 species.
H. crispa. Long, thin, almost pointed tentacles that often seem tangled. Hosts 11 species.
H. magnifica. Brightly colored column, blunt tentacles. Often photographed. (See small photo opposite.) Hosts 10 species.
H. malu. Buries column in sand, fairly short tentacles, limited range. Hosts only Clark's.
Stichodactyla haddoni. Haddon's carpet anemone. Short-tentacles. Grey, with white radial stripes. Hosts 6 species.
S. gigantea. Bludru anemone. Longer tentacles, larger than Haddon's. Hosts 6 species.
S. mertensii. Merten's anemone. Colorful; largest carpet anemone, to 1m across. (See bottom photo above.) Hosts 10 species.
— *David Pickell*

Above: *One of the piscivorous cone shells* (Conus sp.) *devouring a small goby. Most cone shells eat worms, but the relatively few fish-eating species are very dangerous.*

Below: *The octopus has highly developed eyes and a very sophisticated nervous system. It is thus considered "intelligent," and people find it hard to believe that it is a mollusc. The white color of this specimen suggests exhaustion, and perhaps the photographer was a bit overzealous in getting this shot.*

spp.) are common, small (most just a few cm.) gastropods with a smooth shell that is completely covered by the animal's fleshy mantle. Both the shells and mantles can be beautifully marked, often with very different patterns. The cowries are omnivorous, feeding on algae as well as a variety of sedentary animals such as soft corals.

Trochus. Top shells (*Trochus* spp.) are relatively large (6–8 cm.), and conical. Before the advent of plastics they were widely collected for the manufacture of buttons. Removing the grubby outer layer of shell reveals the lustrous nacre, or mother-of-pearl beneath. Until the invention of Bakelite, and the many plastics that followed, shell nacre for buttons was an important business in Indonesia. Today they are still collected, most to be used in souvenirs and to supply the small market for "real" buttons.

Clams and Oysters

The bivalves include such familiar forms as clams, oysters, mussels and scallops. All have two articulated shell halves that can be closed with a large muscle. It is this muscle that makes bivalves so prized as seafood. With a very few exceptions, bivalves cannot move, like gastropods, and thus most have adapted to filter-feeding. They draw water in through one tube or "siphon" and pass it out through another. This stream of water passes through the animal's gills, which serve the dual purpose of respiration and filtering out food particles.

All bivalves must hold their shell halves at least slightly ajar to maintain water circulation through their bodies. But when danger threatens they are clamped shut. Some Indonesian bivalves gain further protection by boring into corals and reef rock, so that predators cannot reach them. The boring is achieved by a combination of chemical action and rasping with the two shell haves. Eventually, reef bivalves become so encrusted with sponges, coralline algae, bryozoans and cnidarians that they are barely visible.

Giant clams. The giant reef clams, *Tridacna* spp., have a different means of feeding. Like reef-building corals, *Tridacna* clams harbor zooxanthellae in their fleshy mantles, and can thus "manufacture" most—or perhaps all—of their own food. Like corals, they require lots of light, and tend to be found in the shallows. They grow with the hinge of their shells down, and their rippled gape facing the sun.

There are seven species of *Tridacna*, of which the giant clam, *T. gigas*, is the most dramatic. These animals can reach a meter and a half in diameter. An animal that big could be a century old. Although smaller than *T. gigas*, *T. squamosa* has a beautiful ruffled shell. The fleshy mantles of *Tridacna* clams are beautiful, varying in color from brown to yellow to green to blue, with contrasting spots or mottling.

Tridacna clams are a great delicacy in Asia, particularly in Taiwan, and their shells are made into terrazzo in factories in Surabaya. Over-harvesting has greatly reduced their numbers throughout Indonesia. Shallow reefs in Eastern Indonesia that used to support literally fields of giant clams have been stripped in just the past few years. There is fear that the population in many areas is no longer at a self-sustaining level.

Recently, however, researchers at the Micronesian Mariculture Demonstration Center in Palau, headed by Gerald Heslinga, have discovered a method of "farming" giant clams by inoculating the veliger larvae with zooxanthellae. Once the symbiotic algae is in place, the clams need only a good supply of seawater and plenty of light to thrive. The farming operation requires little room, and the clams reach 10 centimeters across in just two years. Because of the commercial potential for these clams, a number of pilot farms have recently been established in the Pacific region.

Oysters. A number of oysters can be found on the reef, in many cases so well camouflaged with encrusting growths that they are at first invisible. The cock's comb oyster (*Lopha cristagalli*) has a distinctive sharp, zig-zag opening, and is often covered by encrusting sponges.

The colorful mantle of the thorny oyster (*Spondylus* spp.) stands out, although its rough shell is usually overgrown with algae, sponges, and small cnidarians.

In many parts of Indonesia, Japanese operators seed pearl oysters (*Pinctata*) and hang them in the shallows to grow pearls. The oysters are purchased from local collecters, and the "seed" comes from a freshwater mussel found in the Mississippi basin. Security on these "farms" is high, and divers are unwelcome.

Cephalopods

These animals, despite their close relationship to the snails and clams, are active, "intelligent" predators with highly developed eyes and sophisticated behaviors. The octopus has eight suckered arms, while squid and cuttlefish have an additional two grasping tentacles. Both octopi and squids have a hard, chitinous beak. The nautilus—of which only one genus is extant—differs markedly from the other cephalopods. It has 90 arms,

Above: *The thorny oyster (*Spondylus sp.*) is often so encrusted with sponges, algae, tunicates and other organisms that only when it is agape with its bright mantle showing (as here) can it be seen. Halmahera, Maluku.*

without suckers, and a well-developed shell. Unlike other cephalopods, the nautilus has very primitive eyes, lacking a lens and open to the water.

Octopi. These familiar animals can be found on the reef, although they normally hide in small caves or crevices. They have no internal skeleton so are able to squeeze into surprisingly small spaces.

Chromatophores on their skin give octopi remarkable abilities to change color, which they do either to blend in with their surroundings or to display emotion. Some species can also change their surface texture, from smooth to lumpy and back, producing very believable imitations of shells, and even lionfish.

Octopuses are particularly fond of eating crabs and other crustaceans, and a pile of shells often marks a hole where one is resident. Normally an octopus crawls rather slowly across the reef, but it can also swim by contractions of its legs, much like an umbrella opening and closing. If disturbed, it can produce a short burst of speed by squirting water out of its large gill cavity through a muscular siphon.

Beware of the common, small blue-ringed octopi (*Hapalochlaena*) which can be found under rocks on the reef flats in Indonesia. Do not pick one up. They possess a very virulent poison.

Squid. Squid are free-swimming animals, usually seen in groups in shallow lagoon areas or along the reef edge. They have perfected the mode of jet-propelled movement. While stationary they maintain position with gentle undulations of their lateral fins. Movement, either forward or backward, is achieved by the highly maneuverable water jet. Like the octopus, squids can change their coloration, adopting a sparkling array of brilliant colors and patterns.

Squid have a rudimentary internal "shell," actually a non-calcareous strengthening device called a pen. It is of a clear, flexible substance that looks and feels like a piece of plastic.

Although you will never see one on the reef, the largest cephalopods by far are the giant squids (*Architecteuthis*), which can reach a length of 18 meters. These animals frequent very deep water, and little is known of their habits. They are the preferred prey of the sperm whale.

Cuttlefish. Cuttlefish (*Sepia*) superficially resemble squid, but can be distinguished by their generally larger size and more robust shape. Unlike squid, which often travel in large groups, lone cuttlefish can often be seen foraging on the reef slope, and are the most frequently encountered cephalopods.

Like the other cephalopods, cuttlefish can squirt out a blob of ink if threatened. The shape of this blob, roughly the size of the animal that ejected it, and its strong smell, distracts the would-be predator while the cuttlefish jets away. In earlier times, this ink was used for writing, as is suggested by the cuttlefish's genus name, *Sepia*.

Instead of the squid's flexible pen, cuttlefish have a "cuttlebone," a calcareous structure perhaps most familiar for its use as a dietary supplement for cage birds. Although it provides some stiffness, the most important use of the porous "bone" is for buoyancy control, balancing the animal's vertical movements across the reef face.

Nautilus. These animals, with their distinctive spiralled shell, are the most unusual of the living cephalopods. The chambered shell serves as a form of buoyancy control, like the cuttlefish bone, but much more sophisticated. This control is necessary as the animals undergo a considerable daily vertical migration. During the daylight hours, the

Opposite: A mantis shrimp, Odontodactylus scyllaris. *These animals are fierce predators, using their modified front claws to seize or bludgeon prey in the manner of their namesake, the praying mantis.* Odontodactylus *is the most colorful and one of the larger mantis shrimps—it is said to be able to smash a four-inch crab with one strike. Some divers call these animals "thumb-splitters" and with good reason. Do not try to touch one! Tulamben, Bali.*

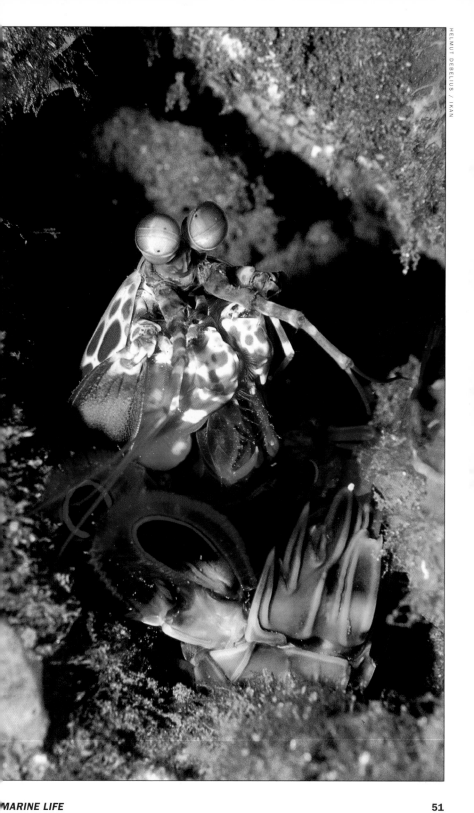

nautilus stay at 1,000–1,500 meters, and only rise into relatively shallow water at night. Only very rarely are they found in depths a sport diver could reach. In this way they avoid predators, and perhaps also are able to more easily find their food—carrion and, particularly, the molts of crustaceans.

There are several species, but the most common on Indonesian reefs is the pearly nautilus (*Nautilus pompilius*).

Crustaceans

The jointed-foot animals—Arthropoda—is the single most successful phylum of animals. On land, the insects and spiders dominate; in the water, the subphylum Crustacea is king, with almost 40,000 species. Crustaceans—crabs, shrimp and lobsters—are very abundant on Indonesian coral reefs, but many keep themselves well-hidden, particularly during the day. They are most likely to be seen by night divers.

The largest commonly seen crustaceans are the spiny lobsters, *Panulirus*. By day spiny lobsters hide in caves and crevices, often in small groups, with only their long antennae protruding. But at night they venture out of their retreats in search of food. If surprised out in the open, spiny lobsters can swim backwards with great speed using powerful flicks of their tail.

These lobsters, of course, make very fine eating, but visiting divers should resist the temptation of trying to catch a lobster for the table. Removal of animals from a dive site is short-sighted, and lobster catching is quite a skilled operation. An unpracticed diver who attempts it is likely to be left only with painful cuts and a handful of antennae.

Shrimps

On night dives large shrimps can sometimes be spotted out in the open where their reflective eyes catch the light and stand out as two bright red spots. But even by day the careful observer should be able to spot several species of small shrimp.

Commensals. A variety of sometimes colorful shrimp associate with anemones, coral and echinoderms for protection, making them easy to spot. The tiny bumble-bee shrimps (*Gnathophyllum*) associate with sea urchins. Various species of *Periclimenes,* some quite colorful, associate with anemones, gorgonians, and echinoderms. One, *P. imperator,* lives in the folds of the Spanish dancer nudibranch.

Cleaner shrimps. Also easy to see are the cleaner shrimps, protected from predation by the services they offer. These cleaners pick parasites and bits of dead tissue from fish, and can al-

Below: *A dispute developed between these two prawn gobies,* Mahidolia mystacina, *when the yellow goby and its shrimp wandered into the grey goby's territory. When the grey fish came out of its burrow, the sand started to fly. Both of these gobies are females. Tulamben, Bali.*

RUDIE KUITER

be recognized by long, white antennae.

The candy shrimps (*Lysmata*) are beautiful red striped or spotted cleaners. The coral shrimps (*Stenopus*) live in pairs in small caves or holes extending their large white antennae to attract the attention of passing fish.

The common banded coral shrimp, *Stenopus hispidus,* has well-developed front claws, and is sometimes called the boxer shrimp. Various species of *Periclimenes* also serve as cleaners.

Cleaner shrimp often set up a "station," that fish visit repeatedly. It is quite a sight to watch a tiny shrimp crawl into the mouth and gills of a grouper or large angelfish. If approached slowly enough cleaner shrimps will climb onto a diver's outstretched hand, to see if it too needs cleaning, or even into his mouth.

Pistol shrimp. These animals (*Alpheus* and *Synalpheus*) have well-developed pincers, one much larger than the other. By some means that is not well understood, the pistol or snapping shrimp is able to create an audible clicking sound with its large claw.

Some of the blind or near-blind pistol shrimp have developed interesting relationships with small gobies. In lagoons and on sandy patches around the reef you can see these small fish sitting up on their fins outside a small burrow. Next to the fish will be one or more pistol shrimps. The shrimps rely on the gobies, with which they keep in contact by their long antennae, to warn them of the approach of any danger. The gobies benefit from this relationship by having a safe burrow dug for them.

Crabs

Many species of crabs live on Indonesian reefs, but they are not always easy to find. Crabs would soon be eaten by strong-jawed fish such as wrasses if they ventured out boldly by day. Many species are therefore only seen at night when they come out under the cover of darkness to feed. If you look closely at a well-protected coral thicket, however, you will likely see a few small crabs safely wedged in.

Hermit crabs. These familiar, and comical creatures use the discarded shells of gastropods as portable refuges. Some of these small animals are very colorful, particularly *Aniculus* and the demon hermit crabs, *Trizopagurus*. A few species of hermit crabs go one stage further, carrying small sea anemones on their shells as additional discouragement to potential predators.

The large terrestrial coconut or robber crab (*Birgus latro*), a delicacy in the Moluccas and other parts of Indonesia, is actually a hermit crab that abandons its shell when it reaches adulthood. Small land hermit crabs (*Coenobita*) are common along the high tide line on some Indonesian beaches.

Decorator crabs. These are types of spider crabs that protect themselves by sticking live sponges, gorgonians or other material onto their fuzzy or spiny backs as camouflage. Small decorator crabs may be spotted at any time on sea fans or black coral trees. But look out for the large nocturnal species that carry massive chunks of soft coral or sponge on their backs, held on with their last pair of legs.

The small and colorful boxer crab, *Lybia tesselata,* grasps a pair of tiny sea anemones in its claws which it then uses for both defense, and to collect food.

Porcelain crabs. The porcelain crabs (*Neopetrolisthes*), so-named for their smooth, colorful shells, are sometimes called "half-crabs," for they are structurally similar to prawns and lobsters. They are commensals on the giant anemones where, protected from predators, they strain plankton from the water with mouthparts that have been modified for filter-feeding.

Echinoderms

Everyone is familiar with the common starfish or sea star. But starfishes are only one of five groups that together form the Echinodermata, "hedgehog-skinned" animals. The others are the sea urchins, the brittle stars, the feather stars and the sea cucumbers. Most echinoderms have a skeleton of spiny plates—most developed in the sea urchins, and least developed in the sea cucumbers—and five-sided symmetry.

Starfish. The five-sided symmetry of the echinoderms is clearly displayed in the starfishes. Most Indonesian species have five arms, although some individuals may have one arm more or less. The common cobalt-blue starfish *Linckia laevigata* is particularly variable in this regard. Some of the larger starfishes may have a great number of arms.

Starfishes are predators, feeding on a wide variety of bottom-dwelling animals, or detritivores. A feeding starfish envelops its prey with its arms, then actually pushes part of its stomach out through its mouth over the victim, digesting it externally. Starfishes are able to hang on to even actively struggling prey with their myriad tube feet, tiny suckers that cover the undersides of their arms. The gripping power of these animals is considerable, and over time they can even overpower the strong muscle of a bivalve. The tube feet are also used for locomotion.

Some starfish have very thick arms, particularly the pincushion starfish (*Culcita* spp.) common on Indonesian reefs. These animals can inflate their bodies to the point where they become almost spherical. *Culcita* normal-

ly have tiny symbiotic shrimps living on their lower surfaces.

The most notorious starfish in Indonesian waters is the crown of-thorns, *Acanthaster plancii*, which is found throughout the tropical Indian and Pacific Oceans. This animal feeds exclusively on coral polyps.

Normally the crown-of-thorns large, multi-armed and bristly occurs in very low numbers on coral reefs—divers usually see perhaps one per dive. But population densities have occasionally reached plague proportions, and at these times whole reefs can be destroyed. Some of the greatest damage has been on the Great Barrier Reef of Australia and on the reefs of southern Japan, but *Acanthaster* outbreaks have occurred throughout its range including Indonesia.

These plagues have been the subject of a long and heated debate by reef scientists. Some argue that over-fishing, over-harvesting of predators like the triton conch, and agricultural runoff have contributed to the disastrous outbreaks. Huge coral heads, hundreds of years old have been destroyed by the ravages of the starfish. These scientists argue that control measures are necessary, and advocate the removal of *Acanthaster* whenever seen by divers. (Note: The crown-of-thorns is spiny, and some people have a toxic reaction to its thorns. Do not touch one unprotected.)

Another opinion suggests that the outbreaks are a natural phenomenon, and point to core samples taken on the Great Barrier reef that show periodic accumulations of *Acanthaster* spines. These scientists say the outbreaks remove dominant coral species, and may be necessary to increase the species diversity of tropical reefs. They note that the reefs have recovered relatively rapidly from the outbreaks, and suggest removal of crown-of-horns would in the long run be counter-productive.

Brittle stars. Brittle stars are quite similar in appearance to starfish, but have thin, flexible arms. These arms are easily broken off, hence the name. While starfish move mainly by the action of the tiny tube feet on the underside of their arms, brittle stars move by movements of the whole arm.

Many brittle stars have spines on their arms which are very sharp and can give the unwary diver a nasty sting. Despite these spiny defences and their unappetizing appearance, brittle stars are preyed upon by several species of fish, and thus tend to remain well-hidden.

On the shallow reef flats one can sometimes find literal "fields" of brittle stars, their bodies flat on the bottom and their arms wriggling in the water, filtering plankton and debris. On deeper areas of the reef, these animals are less bold, and extend just an arm or two from the safety of their crevices.

Serpent stars are brittle stars with smooth arms, and often very striking colors. These animals can sometimes be seen with their arms coiled in tight loops around gorgonians.

Basket stars are the most highly developed filter-feeding brittle stars. They only come out to feed at night, when they extend their branched arms to capture planktonic animals drifting past. Basket stars are beautiful creatures to watch, and they are particularly common on Indonesian reefs, where they can grow to over a meter across.

Crinoids. The crinoids or feather stars are survivors of the sea lilies, animals that once were among the most common in the seas. Although there are still some stalked crinoids extant, those seen on Indonesian reefs are unstalked. They perch on the edge of sponges or gorgonians with a set of small clasping legs, and deploy their delicate arms— of which they have 30 or more— to strain plankton from the water. Feather stars can also walk on these long arms, and if dislodged may swim with them in a beautiful but rather inefficient manner.

Food filtered from the current

Below: *Many species of shrimps act as cleaners. This is a* Leandrites *sp. at work on the mouth of a coral grouper,* Cephalopholis miniata.

by the fine hairs on the crinoid's arms are passed down a channel to the central mouth. Crinoids sit "upside-down" compared to the starfish, and the mouth is on top the animal.

Some feather stars are nocturnal and hide by day in reef crevices. As night falls they come out of hiding and climb up onto prominent blocks of coral or other high points where they are exposed to the strongest current flow. Crinoids are particularly abundant in plankton-rich areas.

Sea urchins. Sea urchins are important and abundant grazers on Indonesian coral reefs. Even the spiniest of urchins may be attacked if they venture out into the open by day, so they tend to confine their activities to the night. By day they wedge themselves into crevices or hollows to avoid the attentions of predatory fish. Sea urchins have a very sophisticated feeding apparatus which they use to scrape at the reef, removing not only algae but

also quantities of coral rock. In fact, some small species actually excavate their own daytime hiding places out of the soft coral rock by the constant scraping of their jaws and spines.

On shallow, quiet reefs in Indonesia one can often see the black, long-spined urchin *Diadema,* so-named for the cluster of glistening "jewels" set into its upper body. This urchin has very

long and brittle spines, and stepping on one would be a real disaster. In harbors and other disturbed areas of reef, very large numbers of these animals can be found. Shrimpfish and urchin clingfish hide among their spines.

The rarely seen slate pencil urchin (*Heterocentrotus mamillatus*) is a distinctive species, with thick, pink spines. No longer used as chalk, the unfortunate animals' attractive spines are in some areas now being made into wind chimes.

The bodies of most sea urchins seem roughly spherical but in fact they are made up of five radial segments, in typical echinoderm fashion. Sea urchins develop a calcareous skeleton or test, which contains the feeding apparatus, the intestines, and the gonads. Prior to reproduction the gonads expand to fill the whole shell, and it is this rich substance that make sea urchins so attractive to hungry fish despite their spiny defenses.

The ripe gonads of the sea urchin *Hemicentrotus pulcherrimus* are prized in Japan for sushi; the taste of this *uni* is strong, but delicious.

Sea cucumbers. Though at first they look just like loose sacks, or large worms, sea cucumbers (class Holothuria) are constructed with the same five-sided symmetry typical of the echinoderms. Because they are so elongate, they have a "head" and a "tail," unlike the starfish or urchins. The head of a sea cucumber is not, however particularly well developed, consisting of little more than a ring of tentacles around the mouth. Sea cucumbers are an important trade item in Indonesia. (See "Trepang Fishing," page 27.)

Most species are detritus feeders, the tentacles being used to pick up sand and pass it into the mouth. Organic matter is digested and the undigested remains are passed out through he anus. Sea cucumbers have to eat a lot of sand in order to obtain enough food, so they often leave a continuous trail of sandy feces behind them. A few species are filter feeders. They hide their bodies in reef crevices and hold their tentacles up in to the water current to feed. The tentacles are rapidly withdrawn if disturbed.

Sea cucumbers appear as elongated and somewhat flaccid forms lying among coral rubble or sea grass, moving slowly in a worm-like way by contractions of their bodies. These are usually black or dull-colored. A few species, such as the sea apple (*Pseudocolochirus*), are very colorful, however.

Many sea cucumbers are active by day. Since they are not attacked by predatory fish it would seem that they must have some efficient means of defense. Some species can discharge sticky white threads if molested, and most tropical sea cucumbers contain toxins.

Tunicates

The tunicates or sea squirts are an entirely marine group of animals, and are unfamiliar to many people. Despite their unimpressive appearance, they are chordates, and—technically—are more closely related to human beings than to any of the invertebrates listed above. They have a notochord, a primitive backbone, only in their larval form. Once they settle out of the plankton and become sessile filter-feeders, the backbone is unceremoniously shed. (So much for the vaunted evolutionary superiority of "higher order" forms.)

The tunicates seen on Indonesian reefs are all in the class Ascidiacea, a name derived from the ancient Greek word for leather bottle. They are rather like little bottles, with (usually) two openings rather than just one. Water is drawn in through the uppermost of these siphons,

filtered through a basket-like arrangement internally, and then passed out through the lower siphon. Peer into the opening of a large tunicate and you may be able to make out the fine sieving apparatus within. Many tunicates have stout spikes projecting from the inner wall of their siphons, to thwart small fish or other unwanted intruders.

One of the most common and

KAL MULLER

conspicuous tunicates on Indonesian reefs is the beautiful white, purple and yellow *Polycarpa aurata*. These creatures are about the size of a man's thumb, and have a tough leathery outer coating, or tunic. *Polycarpa* is a solitary and very distinctive animal and easy to identify underwater. But many tunicates are colonial, and can easily be mistaken for sponges. If the siphons

Above: *A cluster of tunicates,* Rhopalaea crassa. *Water enters through the uppermost opening, is filtered of plankton and nutrients, and then passed out the lower opening. Bunaken group, Sulawesi.*

Above: *The blue ribbon eel,* Rhinomuraena quaesita, *is one of the most attractive moray eels. Young eels are black, and don't turn electric blue until they reach a bit over a half-meter in length. Bunaken group, Sulawesi.*

of a sea-squirt are touched (gently so as not to harm the animal) they will squeeze shut. Sponges do not react to touch. If a tunicate is lifted out of the sea this same contraction will cause water to be squirted out of its siphon—hence the common name sea squirt.

Most colonial tunicates are overlooked because they tend to be tucked away in dark corners. An exception are the marble-sized, white-and-green grape ascidians, *Diademnum molle,* a common compound tunicate on shallow reefs in Indonesia. Diademnid tunicates have a single large inhalent opening, and many small exhalent openings around their globular tunics.

Their green color comes from a symbiotic algae living within its tissues, much like the zooxanthellae of stony corals. The relationship between this tunicate and its algae is one of mutual dependency, neither party being able to survive alone. *Diademnum* larvae even carry samples of the algae with them to ensure that the relationship is continued in the next generation.

The Fishes

Corals and other invertebrate animals can provide a lifetime of interest for a diver in Indonesia, but the fish are what really grabs one's attention. On most reefs, brightly colored and beautifully patterned fish are everywhere,

darting among the corals or lying sedately in mid-water. It would be impossible in the space available here to offer a complete description of the thousands of fish species found on Indonesian reefs, so all that will be attempted is a brief survey. Consult "Further Readings" page 321 for more complete resources.

Elasmobranchs

Sharks and rays are elasmobranchs, and differ from true bony fishes by having a cartilaginous skeleton, only parts of which are calcified (e.g., the jaws of a shark). Gill structure—elasmobranch means "plate-gilled"—and other physical features differ between bony fish and sharks and rays, which are considered a more primitive form.

Sharks. There are many species of sharks in Indonesian waters, but those most commonly seen by divers are the reef white-tip shark (*Triaenodon obesus*), the gray reef shark (*Carcharhinus amblyrhynchos*), and the reef black-tip shark (*C. melanopterus*).

The reef white-tip shark grows to 1.7 meters, and is a thin, gray fish with white tips to its dorsal and tail fins. This is the most commonly seen shark on the Indonesian reefs. This small shark can be often be found hiding under overhangs.

The gray reef shark grows up to 2.3 meters, and has a very dark trailing edge to its tail. Although this animal is known to be aggressive in some areas, it is not considered dangerous in Indonesia.

The reef black-tip shark grows to 1.8 meters, and is pale gray or brown with distinct black tips on all its fins. This shark sometimes comes up into very shallow water on reef flats and in lagoons to look for food.

The largest fish extant is the whale shark (*Rhincodon typus*), a harmless animal that strains kril nd small fish from the water. Growing to more than 12 meters in length (although specimens of 4-7 meters are more common), the whale shark is not a reef fish, although it can be found seasonally off some reefs in Indonesia.

The only really dangerous sharks a diver might encounter on an Indonesian reef are the tiger shark (*Galeocerdo cuvieri*), a large—up to 5.5 meters—scavenger that sometimes comes up onto the reefs at night or in the late afternoon. These sharks, however, are very rarely seen.

Rays. Structurally, rays are essentially flattened sharks. The stingrays have one or two stout spines at the base of their tail, which are their main means of defence. They will not normally be used against divers, although you should always take care to avoid stingrays while walking in shallow water.

Stingrays are bottomfish, and have strong teeth which they use to crush shellfish. In areas where stingrays are common you may see large craters in the bottom, caused by their feeding activities. Perhaps the most common stingrays in Indonesia are two species of blue-spotted stingray: *Taeniura lymma*, which frequents coral rich areas, and *Dasyatis kuhlii,* which lives in sandy areas of disturbed reef, or between patch reefs. A much larger animal is the grey reef ray (*Taeniura melanospilos*).

Not all rays are bottom-dwellers. The spotted eagle ray (*Aetobatis narinari*) cruises the reef edge looking for crustaceans. Eagle rays can reach 2.3 meters across.

The largest ray, however, is the manta (*Manta birostris*). Like the whale shark, mantas are essentially open water fish, but they are regularly seen by divers in Indonesia. The manta ray, growing up to 6.7 meters across and weighing 1,400 kilos, is a planktivore. Both whale sharks and mantas occur only seasonally in different parts of the country, as they migrate to the areas where the plankton is thickest.

Because they are found in areas dense with plankton, mantas tend to be seen at times when visibility is relatively low. This, however, is a small inconvenience when weighed against the pleasure of swimming with such magnificent creatures.

Sometimes seen in the same places that attract mantas are the smaller, but very similar devil rays (*Mobula*). These animals travel in groups and sometimes large schools.

Bony Fishes

Eels. The moray eels (family Muraenidae) are common both in folklore and on the Indonesian reef. Although not as dangerous as Hollywood would have us

Below: *The ornate ghost pipefish,* Solenostomus para-doxus. *This strange animal is a relative of the seahorses and pipefishes, however in* Solenosto-mus *the female broods the eggs. The coloration and growths are cryptic. This juvenile stands out here against the brilliant red crinoids, only because it has moved from a neigh-boring white crinoid or antipatharian. Tulamben, Bali.*

RUDIE KUITER

believe, they have sharp teeth and should not be provoked. The largest species, the giant moray (*Gymnothorax javanicus*), can reach more than two meters in length, and weigh 35 kilos. Many morays are nocturnal hunters, resting in holes by day and prowling the reef by night. They feed on dozing fish which they detect by smell.

A very beautiful eel, related to the morays but more delicately built, is the blue ribbon eel (*Rhinomuraena quaesita*). The adult coloration of this animal is electric blue and yellow, and adult females turn bright yellow. Juveniles are black.

Several species of the unusual garden eels (a subfamily of the conger eels) can be found on sandy bottoms in Indonesia. They live in burrows in often large groups, and the sight of all their thin bodies waving in the current gives them their common name. They have small mouths, and pluck plankton from the current. If you swim over the "garden" the eels will slip back down into their burrows, disappearing in a wave before you.

Although garden eels are usually found in deeper water, particularly the sandy channels between reefs, they can sometimes be seen in very shallow sand patches on the reef. There is a colony of garden eels in shallow water on the approach to the popular wreck at Tulamben, Bali

Seahorses and pipefish
These fishes (family Syngnathidae) are generally slow-moving and secretive, and are not often easy to find. They are planktivores, and can be found in seagrass beds and estuaries as well as in coral reefs. In fact, their fins are poorly developed, and they shun areas of high current or surge. Seahorses (*Hippocampus*) can be highly camouflaged, some exactly matching a single species of gorgonian.

The master of camouflage however, is the ghost pipefish (*Solenostomus cyanopterus*), an animal whose shape and color precisely duplicate a blade of turtlegrass. A strikingly colored relative is the ornate ghost pipefish, *S. paradoxus*.

Pipefish are long and thin and superficially appear quite dif

Below: *A school of shrimpfishes,* Centriscus scutatus. *The shrimpfishes always swim with their noses pointed downward. In the process of evolution their dorsal, tail and anal fins have migrated to a position on the side fo the body, where they can produce lateral motion while the animal is oriented vertically.*

erent from seahorses. In fact, structurally they are quite similar, the pipefish just being a stretched-out version. The male incubates the eggs in a pouch on its stomach, and the young are born "live."

The large trumpetfish (*Aulostomus chinensis*) looks like a pipefish on steroids (these can be a half-meter or longer) and feeds on small fish. It has the curious habit of hiding behind larger fishes until it comes within range of its prey. One color morph is bright yellow.

Scorpionfish. The most commonly seen of this family (Scorpaenidae) are the lionfishes (*Pterois* and *Dendrochirus*). During the day these lavishly colored fish can be seen perching on coral heads. Perhaps because of their poisonous fin rays, they are relatively unperturbed by the presence of divers.

Lionfishes feed mainly at night on shrimps and small fishes. They use their elaborate fins to shepherd their prey into a suitable position, whereupon they shoot forward and inhale it whole into their large mouths.

Scorpionfish are less commonly seen, chiefly because they are so well camouflaged. Covered with folds and flaps of skin, they blend right in with the algae and other growths.

The scorpionfishes and lionfishes have a row of poisonous spines along their backs. So, despite their usually benign behavior these fish should be treated with some respect. More than one underwater photographer has been stuck by a lionfish while trying to encourage it into position for that perfect photograph. Lionfish poison is not strong enough to kill an adult, but it will certainly give you many hours of acute pain.

Some victims have required hospitalization. The best treatment is to immerse the affected part in very hot water, as heat breaks down the venom.

Much more dangerous is the stonefish (*Synanceia verrucosa*), which carries a toxin responsible for several well-publicized deaths. These animals are masters of disguise, and encrusting algae and bryozoans actually grow onto their skin. When a small fish or crustacean absently wanders within range, it is engulfed by the animal's formidable mouth.

Groupers. The groupers (family Serranidae), are a common family on Indonesian reefs, ranging in size from more than a meter to the tiny dottybacks or pseudochromids, colorful planktivores no larger than a man's little finger.

Most of the larger groupers are plainly marked, but some, most notably the bright red and blue-spotted coral grouper (*Cephalopholis miniata*) and the flagtail grouper (*C. urodeta*) are exceptions. One of the largest fish on the reef is the giant grouper (*Ephinephelus lanceolatus*), which can reach 2 meters and weigh 400 kilos.

The fairy basselets or anthias (subfamily Anthiinae) are also groupers. Anthias, which hover in large schools around coral heads and soft coral colonies, picking plankton from the water, are very beautiful, and staples of underwater photography. Their names—the peach fairy basslet (*Pseudanthias diaspar*), the purple queen (*P. pascalus* and *P. tuka*) and the square spot anthias (*P. pleurotaenia*)—hint at their lovely colors.

Anthias are protogynous hermaphrodites, meaning that the fish all mature as females, and then a few undergo a terminal sex-change to male. These terminal males exhibit distinct, and very striking colors.

The dottybacks (Pseudochromidae), also among the real jewels of the reef, are small, secretive fishes that hide in caves and under ledges.

Another unique member of the grouper family is the comet (*Calloplesiops altivelis*). This small fish has long, black fins covered with a multitude of white spots. Because of the ocelli on the fins, and the fish's movements, it is thought to be a Batesian mimic of the juvenile spotted moray eel (*Gymnothorax meleagris*). A Batesian mimic uses its

Ciguatera Poisoning

Ciguatera is a toxin produced by a tiny dinoflagellate alga, *Gambierdiscus toxicus*. The alga itself is harmless enough, living around rocks, seagrass and filamentatious algae. The quantities of poison in each organism are minute.

But the dinoflagellates are eaten along with the algae in which they live by herbivorous fish and invertebrates. These herbivores are then eaten by larger, carnivorous fishes, and these are in turn are eaten by even larger, and more voracious predators. Since the ciguatera is not broken down, it concentrates in the tissues of these higher order predators.

A human being who eats a ciguatoxic fish will experience numbness in hands and feet, disorientation, weakness, vomiting, diarrhea, shortness of breath and even cardiac arrest. The poison is very serious. People have died from ciguatera and there is no available cure.

The greatest danger comes from fish at the highest levels of the food chain: snappers, groupers, large jacks, barracuda, some triggerfish and moray eels. For reasons not well understood, certain species are more frequently ciguatoxic than others: particularly the red snapper (*Lutjanus bohar*), and also the giant moray (*Gymnothorax javanicus*), the saddleback grouper (*Plectropomus laevis*) and the giant grouper (*Epinephelus lanceolatus*).

Open-water fish (tuna, mackerel, etc.) are not part of the same food chain and are not affected, but any large, predatory reef fish is a candidate.

— *David Pickell*

from their predatory habits These small fish (6–10 cm.) perch on coral heads or sponges—anything that gives them a good lookout—and when a small crustacean or fish comes within range, they swoop down on it like a hawk. Because they are so sedentary, they make very easy photo subjects. Some species are also quite colorful—particularly the large Forster's hawkfish (*Paracirrhites forsteri*)—and the long-nosed hawkfish (*Oxycirrhitus typus*) has an interesting, pointed "beak."

Jacks. The jacks or trevallies (family Carangidae) are often seen patrolling the upper reef slope in small groups. They are among the most active predators on the reef. Jacks are always on the lookout for a meal, and groups regularly interrupt their steady cruising with powerful bursts of speed as they chase unwary smaller reef fish. Sometimes a few jacks will make a sortie into a lagoon in search of prey. If they find and attack a school of fish the sea surface erupts as the hunted fish desperately try to escape, sometimes throwing themselves onto the beach in the attempt.

Snappers and sweetlips. Snappers (*Lutjanus*) are common predatory fish around deeper reefs, and are an important food fish. The red snapper (*Lutjanus bohar*), although delicious, is in some areas one of the most frequently ciguatoxic fishes (see "Ciguatera Poisoning," at left).

Perhaps the most commonly seen reef fish in Indonesia is the yellow-backed fusilier (*Caesio teres*), a streamlined, 20–30 centimeter fish marked with bright blue and yellow. These planktivores, related to snappers, travel in large aggregations that provide a measure of protection against predators such as jacks.

Sweetlips (*Plectorhinchus*) are medium-sized, strikingly marked fish related to the snappers. They

resemblence to a known dangerous animal to discourage predation.

Hawkfish. Hawkfishes (family Cirrhitidae) get their name re common in Indonesia, where they can often be seen in mixed schools. The juveniles are especially attractive, with bold stripes and dots of white against a brown or black background.

Batfishes. The batfishes (*Platax*) are common inhabitants of Indonesian reefs. As adults, these animals take the shape of a large, silvery platter, as much as half a meter in length, with two or three broad black vertical bands. Traveling about the reef in small groups, they have a reputation for being very "intelligent," and seem to regard divers with curiosity.

There are three species commonly seen in Indonesia, the orbiculate (*Platax orbicularis*), the round-faced (*P. tiera*) and the pinnate (*P. pinnatus*). As adults, orbiculate and round-faced batfish are almost impossible to distinguish. The pinnate batfish can be recognized by its long snout.

As juveniles, the fish are very different in shape, with greatly elongated dorsal and ventral fins. Juvenile orbiculate batfish are mottled brown and have a transparent tail, which—together with their habit of floating on their sides in the shallows—allows them to match a dead leaf. Juvenile round-faced batfish are black and white and have long fins.

The most beautiful as a juvenile is *P. pinnatus*, which has a band of electric orange all around its body and fins. This juvenile, sometimes called the orange-rimmed batfish, is thought to mimic a toxic flatworm.

Butterflyfishes. The butterflyfishes (family Chaetodontidae) are beautiful, delicate looking fish that feed on small benthic animals. Some species feed heavily on coral polyps. They have laterally compressed bodies, and snouts and teeth adapted to their particular feeding habits, enabling them to pick up their preferred prey deftly. In particularly, the long-nosed butterflyfishes (*For-*

cipiger) have long, thin mouths perfect for snatching small animals from cracks and crevices in the reef. These bright yellow fish will be seen hovering under overhangs in the reef, sometimes even upside down.

Some species, occur singly or in pairs, e.g. *Forcipiger*. Others are schooling fish. The black, white, and yellow pyramid butterflyfish (*Hemitaurichthys*

polylepsis), for example, occurs in massive aggregations along the walls in Manado and other parts of eastern Indonesia. Common schooling butterflyfish include the bannerfish (*Heniochus*), the most distinctive of which is the pennant bannerfish (*Heniochus diphreutes*), which has a very elongated dorsal fin and bright yellow, white and black markings.

Angelfish. The angelfishes

Above: *The twinspot lionfish,* Dendrochirus biocellatus, *is one of the most attractive of the dwarf lionfishes. It is much smaller than* Pterois sp., *growing to just 8 centimeters. Halmahera, Maluku.*

(family Pomacanthidae) probably make it onto more postcards than any fish other than the Moorish idol. They browse the reef for sponges, algae and occasional small crustaceans. Adult angelfish, some of which can reach 30 centimeters, are truly magnificent animals.

In Indonesia, one can often see emperor angelfish (*Pomacanthus imperator*), with thin, horizontal stripes of blue and yellow; blue-girdled angelfish (*P. [Euxiphipops] navarchus*), with a deep blue "girdle" against bright orange; and regal angelfish (*Pygoplites diacanthus*), the most shy of the bunch, with vertical stripes of yellow, white and blue.

All *Pomacanthus* species have very similar juvenile coloring, a series of thin white or light blue stripes against a dark blue background. Two fish with dramatically different adult coloration, for example the blue-girdled and emperor angelfish, look so similar as juveniles that only an expert could tell them apart.

Damselfish. These small, ubiquitous fish (family Pomacentridae) are members of one of the largest groups of tropical reef fish. In addition to the reef itself, they occur along rocky shores, algal flats, and even in silt-choked harbors. The damselfish feed on plankton and algae, some even setting up small territories from which they aggressively keep all herbivores away, "farming" the algal turf that then grows on the coral rock.

The black and white three-striped damselfish (*Dascyllus aruanus*), the blue devil (*Chrysiptera cyanea*), and the blue damsels (*Pomacentrus*) are common among the coral heads and rubble of the shallow reef. The pugnacious black farmer fish (*Stegastes lividus*) also defends its patch of algae in the shallows.

Deeper on the reef, the planktivorous blue-green chromis (*Chromis viridis*) is common,

occurring in large schools lik anthias, which it superficiall resembles. Along rich drop-offs the pugnacious yellow Golde sergeant (*Amblygliphidodo aureus*) is often seen. A singl good Indonesian reef can hos more than 100 species.

Favorites among divers ar the anemonefish (*Amphiprio and Premnas biaculaeatus* These beautiful and plucky littl fish will even nip a diver t defend their anemone home (See "Clownfish and their Se Anemone Hosts," page 46.)

Wrasses. The wrasses (fam ly Labridae) are a large and suc cessful family on the coral reefs Most are small, elongated fishes with a distinct swimming styl that depends more on the pec toral fins than the tail. Many ar colorful, and inhabit the shallo parts of the reef and reef flats although some (such as the hog fishes) are characteristic of th deep reef.

Wrasses undergo sometime dramatic color changes as the pass from juveniles to adults Many of these predators o worms and small crustacean bury in the sand at night to sleep or dive into the sand to escap predators.

Most familiar to divers is th blue-streak cleaner wrass (*Labroides dimidiatus*), which se up stations to clean small para sites and pockets of decay from the skin, mouth and gills of larg er reef fish. Some wrasse act a cleaners only when young (fo example, the colorful lyretai hogfish, *Bodianus anthoides*).

The largest of the family i the Napoleon wrasse (*Cheilinu undulatus*), which can reach 1.8 meters. This is one of the larges fish a diver will see on man dives. These stately animals, als called the humphead wrasse have a prominent forehead an formidable-looking snout an cruise the outer edge of the ree in loose groups, with one larg

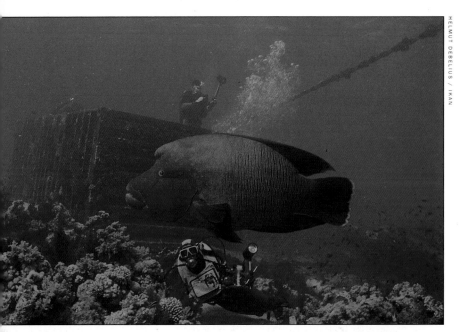

nale and a few smaller females.

Parrotfish. The parrotfishes (family Scaridae) are among the most important herbivores on the reef. They get their name from their bright colors, curious flapping "flight" (much like wrasses), and their strong, bird-like beaks, which they use to scrape algae and other living matter from rocky surfaces. In so doing they inevitably take in great quantities of coral rock. This is ground down by powerful sets of teeth in the throat so that the organic material can be more easily digested. The waste product of the feeding activities of parrotfish is coral sand—a major component of Indonesian beaches especially on the offshore islands.

Parrotfishes are protogynous hermaphrodites that undergo a series of color changes with age and sexual status. Primary phase parrotfish—whether males or females—are exceedingly difficult to identify, all being relatively drab grey or rust-colored. The terminal males are striking, however, usually green with bright markings, particularly around the cheeks and eyes. In most species the primary phase is made up of mixed males and females (diandric); in others the primary phase is all females (monandric).

One notable exception to this pattern is the bumphead parrotfish (*Bolbometopon muricatum*). All bumphead parrotfish (males, females and juveniles) are a dull green in color. Although parrotfish have popularly been considered coral-eaters, they are chiefly herbivores, scraping the reef surface to extract the algal turf, not to eat coral polyps. The bumphead parrotfish is an exception, and feeds for the most part on living coral. They are massive beasts which grow to over a meter in length and travel along the reef in groups looking for all the world like squadrons of army tanks, leaving clouds of coral sand in their wakes. Sometimes their crunching can be heard underwater.

They should not to be confused with the Napoleon wrasse (see above), a superficially similar fish. The bumphead parrotfish has a more rounded head.

Above: *The Napoleon wrasse, or humphead wrasse, Cheilinus undulatus, is the largest wrasse and—at up to two meters— often the largest fish of any kind one will see on a given dive. This predator on crustaceans, gastropods, fishes and echinoderms is usually a solitary rover, but sometimes a pair or a small "squad" will be seen. Australians call this fish the Maori wrasse.*

At night, parrotfish secrete a transparent cocoon of mucus in which to sleep. At first glance such a fragile structure would seem to offer little protection against predators, but at night, most predators hunt with their sense of smell, not their eyes, and the cocoon is an effective defense against them.

Barracudas. These familiar fish (family Sphyraenidae) are

ED ROBINSON / IKAN

Above: *The bump-head parrotfish,* Bolbometopon muri-aticum. *This, the largest parrotfish, is also one of the few true coral feeders. With its impressive fused "beak" it can crunch on corals like they were pret-zels. It is some-times confused with the Napoleon wrasse, but a com-parison of this photo with the one on the previous page should make clear the physical differences between them.*

one of the most important preda-tors on the reef, but their reputa-tion for ferociousness is exagger-ated. Despite their formidable teeth, in Indonesia they are not known to attack divers. Smaller species of barracuda often gather in schools during the day, some-times numbering many hun-dreds of individuals. In contrast, large barracudas (which may grow up to 1.7 meters) tend to be solitary. Such giants may be quite old, so are less likely to be seen near heavily populated areas where there is a lot of fish-ing pressure.

Blennies. These little fishes (family Blenniidae) often go unnoticed by divers. They are most abundant in the shallows, and can also be found on back-reefs and in murky estuarial waters. Most are not very color-ful. Some have interesting "faces," although these are only really visible to the macro lens.

The mimic blenny (*Aspidon-tus taeniatus*) mimics the color

and even the movements of the blue-streak cleaner wrasse *Labroides dimidiatus.* However instead of cleaning parasite from the larger fish, the mimic blenny bites off a tender chunk of scales and flesh, and then beats a hasty retreat.

Dartfishes. One group the diver will notice, because of their striking colors and their habit of hovering in small groups above the coral sand, are the firefishes (*Nemateleotris* spp.), particularly *N. magnifica,* a beautiful fish with a greatly elongated dorsal fin which it flicks in nervous little movements.

Gobies. These fish (family Gobiidae) are small, usually dull colored, and often remain hidden in crevices and the branches of coral. There are many hundred of species and perhaps 100 gen-era in the Indo-Pacific, making them the single most successful family on the coral reefs. Identi-fying these fishes is very difficult and there are probably hundreds still undescribed.

Although not reef-dwellers the curious mudskippers (*Perio-phthalmus*), which can be found in Indonesia on the brackish mudflats around mangrove swamps, are also gobies. As long as their gills and skin remain wet, these small brown fish can hop about on land.

Related to the gobies are the little dragonets. These are found in weedy areas and sea grass beds as well as the reef itself. Perhaps the most spectacular is the mandarinfish (*Synchiropus splendens*), with a pattern that could have come off a bright pais-ley silk tie.

Surgeonfish. The surgeon fishes and tangs (family Acan-thuridae) are a particularly important group of herbivores. They are sometimes seen singly in shallow water over coral flats. Since single grazers are often chased by damselfishes protect-ing their territories, surgeonfish s sometimes form large feeding aggregations.

Despite their apparently destructive feeding habits, herbivorous fish are of immense value to the coral reef community. By breaking down hard-to-digest plant material they make the nutrients in it available to other animals. Furthermore, by limiting the growth of plants they may actually enhance that of corals. Without grazing, the plants would grow to such an extent that they would soon cover the reef, making new coral settlement virtually impossible.

The surgeonfish family includes some of the most exquisitely patterned and colored of all reef fishes. But one feature that is common to all is that they all have one or two pairs of scalpel-like blades on the sides of their tails. These give the family its name and can inflict serious cuts if the fish are handled carelessly.

The orangespine unicornfish (*Naso lituratus*) with its bright orange spots warning of its spines; the hepatus tang (*Paracanthurus hepatus*) with its electric blue and black body, and the clown surgeonfish (*Acanthurus lineatus*), orange-and-blue striped, are just a few examples.

Moorish idol and Rabbitfishes. The Moorish idol (*Zanclus cornutus*) and the rabbitfishes (*Siganus*) are close relatives of the surgeonfishes. The Moorish idol is for many people the quintessential reef fish; with its bright, contrasting yellow, white and black color, prominent snout, and long, thin dorsal fin, it is indeed an elegant-looking animal. They are fairly common grazers, and can be found all the way from the east coast of Africa to the west coast of Central America.

The rabbitfishes look much like surgeonfish or Moorish idols, although with the exception of the foxface (*Siganus volpinus*) and the coral rabbitfish (*S. corallinus*), not as brightly colored. They have no "scalpels," but they do have a strong venom in the short spines of their fins, and should not be handled.

Tuna and Mackerels. Although one or two members of the family Scombridae patrol reefs—particularly the dogtooth tuna (*Gymnosarda unicolor*)—most are true pelagics, living in

the open sea, and will only occasionally be seen on the outer reef edge. When traveling by boat between islands or to offshore dive sites it is not unusual to see big schools of tuna splashing at the surface, often with attendant flocks of seabirds overhead. These schools are usually composed of skipjack tuna, although there are several other species found in Indonesia.

Above: *A school of pyramid butterflyfishes,* Hemitaurichthys polylepsis. *These plankton feeders gather in large groups around the lip of drop-off reefs in eastern Indonesia. The Bunaken group, Sulawesi.*

Above: *Indonesian flashlight fishes.* Anomalops katoptron, *top, is the more common of the two.* Photoblepheron palpebratus *tends to be found in smaller groups in rather deep caves. Both species are easy to see in Tulamben Bali:* Anomalops *on the wreck, and* Photoblepheran *on the wall. Both grow to about 10 centimeters long.*

Skipjack (*Katsuwonis pelamis*) grow to just under a meter in length, and are plump and streamlined, with a characteristic series of about five black lines on their bellies. They will not be seen on the reef itself, however, although there will be plenty in the fish market.

Triggerfish. Triggers (family Balistidae) are common fish at moderate depths on the reefs, where they hunt spiny crustaceans and echinoderms. Shaped like a compressed football and often exquisitely marked, they use powerful jaws to dispatch their hard-shelled prey. Large schools of the black triggerfish (*Odonus niger*), which is actually more blue in color, can be seen hovering off the reef walls, swimming with characteristic undulations of their fins. This fish is sometimes called the red-toothed trigger, although you have to look very closely to see that its teeth are, indeed, red.

Some distinctively marked triggers include the Picasso trigger (*Rhinecanthus aculeatus*), so-named for its cubist markings, and the undulate trigger (*Pseudobalistes fuscus*), covered with wavy markings. The largest trigger you will see on the Indonesian reefs is the Titan triggerfish (*Balistoides viridescens*), a loopy-eyed and sometimes aggressive animal that grows to more than 60 centimeters.

The most dramatic of the family is the clown triggerfish (*Balistoides conspicullum*), with its bright orange snout, blue body, and white-spotted belly. The clown trigger is very territorial, and will patrol the same area of reef. When threatened, a clown trigger will wedge its body head-first into a crack in the coral wall, and extend its dorsal spine. The first spine, once raised, is locked in place by the second, making it impossible to pull the fish out of his hole. A diver who knows what he is doing can reach in and gently push back the second spine, unlocking the fin. He can then extract the irritated fish.

Puffers. The curious pufferfishes (family Tetraodontidae) are solitary omnivores, often seen wandering about the reef in their slow, almost clumsy way and plucking at algae, crustaceans, molluscs, worms and sponges. When threatened they inflate themselves with large quantities of water, which either locks them into a coral crevice, or makes it impossible for a predator to swallow them. In addition to this protection, the skin and most of the internal organs of puffers contain a deadly poison. This poison is absent from the flesh, which in Japan is the highly prized *fugu*.

A common puffer on Indonesian reefs is the dog-faced or black-spotted puffer (*Arothron nigropunctatus*), which exhibits a great deal of color variability, from the usual dull brown to bright yellow, always with many small black spots.

The related porcupinefishes (family Diodontidae) possess the same defenses as the puffers, with the addition of numerous spines, which become erect when the animal is inflated. The common porcupinefish (*Diodon hystrix*) is often seen. Boxfishes (family Ostraciontidae) are similar to puffers, except their protection comes in the form of a hard, roughly cubical external covering.

Nocturnal fish. At night the schools of day active species break up and the fish take refuge in holes in the reef. They are replaced by nocturnal species such as the cardinalfishes (family Apogonidae), bigeyes (family Priacanthidae), and squirrelfishes or soldierfishes (family Holocentridae), which feast on the abundant night plankton.

One of the most interesting families of fish to come out at night are the flashlight fishes family Anomalopidae). These delightful little black fish have special organs under their eyes which contain millions of light-producing bacteria. The fish are able to cover and uncover these organs to produce characteristic flashes of blue-green light. The function of these lights is not fully understood, but they are probably used to communicate, to see by, and perhaps to confuse predators.

Two species of flashlight fish are found in Indonesia. The most often seen is *Anomalops kataptron*, a 6–8 centimeter fish that forages for plankton in shallow reef waters, often in large schools. (*Anomalops* also occurs in a much larger—27 centimeters—deepwater form that lives in up to 400 meters of water.) *Photoblepharon palpebratus* is rare and tends to occur in relatively small groups in deep caves.

Marine Reptiles

Sea turtles. One of the most delightful experiences a diver can have is swimming with turtles, and in Indonesia such encounters are quite common.

Six species of marine turtles are found in Indonesian waters, but the two most likely to be seen by divers are the hawksbill turtle (*Eretmochelys imbricata*) and the green turtle (*Chelonia mydas*).

They are not always easy to distinguish underwater, although the hawksbill has a distinct beak, and the trailing edge of its shell is jagged. The hawksbill is also generally smaller, and is tortoiseshell brown (instead of olive green) although such relatively minor color differences are very hard to determine underwater. A third species that may be seen by divers is the loggerhead (*Caretta caretta*), which is much like the green turtle, except it has a massive head.

The green turtle feeds almost entirely on sea grass, while the hawksbill and loggerhead are both largely carnivorous. The shell of the hawksbill is covered with large horn-like scales, the source of "tortoiseshell." Tortoiseshell products—and even stuffed and varnished hawksbill turtles—are offered in Indonesian markets, although import into most Western countries is

Below: *A bluestreak cleaner wrasse,* Labroides dimidiatus *picks at the eye of a bright, terminal male purple queen,* Pseudanthias tuka. *The little cleaners provide an essential service and are never molested by their "customers."* Manado, Sulawesi.

Above: *Traditional whaling still takes place in two villages east of Flores. These men, from Lamalera, Lembata, are flensing a sperm whale they caught with a hand-hurled spear from their small wooden boat. The men catch no more than 15–20 small whales a year, although they will also harpoon whale sharks, marlin or any other large fish they come across.*

strictly prohibited.

Marine turtles spend nearly all their lives at sea, but their eggs have to be laid on land. At certain secluded beaches females regularly emerge at night to deposit their eggs above the high water mark.

Sea snakes. Most sea snakes (family Hydrophiidae) never come onto land at all, even giving birth at sea. There are some 60 species of sea snakes in the world, over half of which are found in Indonesia. They tend to be patchily distributed, very common in some areas and absent from others. As reptiles, they must come up for air, although they have a very large lung and can stay under for many hours.

Sea snakes can be seen underwater poking their small heads into cracks and crevices, searching for small fish and crustaceans. The head of a sea snake is often difficult to distinguish from the tail, as both are blunt, although the head is always smaller, and the tail is laterally flattened, to aid in swimming.

Sea snakes are equipped with extremely toxic venom which can be delivered through two short fangs on the upper jaw. The venom is used to subdue prey such as spiny fish or moray eels, which could cause the snake considerable damage if not killed very quickly. Since fish are quite resistant to most toxins, it is not surprising that sea snake venom is so strong.

Sea snakes are rarely aggressive towards divers, however, and unprovoked attacks are virtually unknown. They are sometimes inquisitive, however, and may inspect a diver.

The grey-and-black banded colubrine or amphibious sea snake (*Laticauda colubrina*) is common in Indonesia. This animal—collected in huge numbers in the Philippines for its skin—It is an inoffensive creature, and slow to anger. Guides often catch the animals for their clients to pose with. We don't suggest you try this, however.

The yellow-bellied sea snake (*Pelamis platurus*) is the most numerous reptile on earth. This colorful animal is so completely adapted to an aquatic life that, if washed ashore, it will die. It can-ot even crawl back to the water.

Crocodiles. One marine reptile that is truly dangerous is the salt water crocodile (*Crocodylus porosus*). These monsters can grow to many meters in length, although real giants are very rare these days. Fortunately for divers they usually live in murky estuarine areas, not on coral reefs. Saltwater crocodiles are found in Irian Jaya, and in scattered locations in Maluku.

Marine Mammals

While common enough in Indonesian waters, sea mammals are rarely seen while diving, and swimming with whales or dolphins is a rare occasion indeed for a diver.

Dolphins. Schools of dolphins are a frequent sight while traveling out to dive sites by boat. Sometimes their "whistling" can be heard during a dive (a sound that is sometimes uncannily like a leaking air cylinder) but they will normally stay well beyond the range of visibility. The best way to see them underwater is to snorkel from the dive boat when a school is encountered in deep water. Usually they will move away, but you could get lucky.

There are several dolphin species in Indonesia and identifying them at sea is a far from easy task. Common species here include the spinner dolphin (*Stenella longirostris*), so-called because of its characteristic high, spinning jumps; the common dolphin (*Delphinus delphis*), which has a black-tipped snout, and a crisscross pattern on its flanks; and the spotted dolphin, with a pattern of fine spots on its sides.

Whales. Several species of large whales also occur in Indonesia, some arriving seasonally from polar regions, others being year-round residents. Like dolphins they are best watched from a boat rather than the water. Some whales breed in Indonesian waters, so it is very important not to harass them by chasing them in boats.

Most of the species seen are plankton-eating baleen whales which have vertical spouts and a small, but distinct, dorsal fin. They might be distinguished on the basis of size, but this requires some experience. The blue whale (*Balaenoptera musculus*) is known in Indonesian waters, as are several smaller but very similar species, including the fin whale (*B. physalus*) and minke whale (*B. acutorostrata*). The humpback, (*Megaptera novaeangliae*), is easier to identify.

The sperm whale (*Physeter catodon*), of *Moby Dick* fame, is a very different animal. These are toothed whales, which feed on giant squid and fish snatched from great depths. The sperm whale has a characteristic forward pointing spume and hump-like ridges rather than a dorsal fin on its back. Pygmy and dwarf sperm whales (*Kogis*) also inhabit Indonesian waters.

Dugong. It is very unlikely that a diver will see this rare animal. The dugong or sea cow (*Dugong dugon*) is a slow-moving animal, up to 2.5 meters long, that looks like a walrus without the tusks. There are only three other members of order Sirenia, manatees from Florida, the Amazon basin and West Africa.

The dugong is the only herbivorous marine mammal, and is strictly aquatic. The animals can eat 10 percent of their body weight a day in sea grasses, and are found mainly in sheltered bays where these plants grow.

Dugongs are threatened throughout their range, because they are slow-moving, easy targets for hunters—their tusks are used for cigaret holders—and because they take so long to reproduce. Calving takes place only once every 3–7 years, and dugongs take 15 years to mature.

—*Charles Anderson and David Pickell*

Introducing the Island of Java

Lush and populous Java—together with Bali the most familiar of Indonesia's many islands—is the political, cultural and industrial heart of the island nation. Some 115 million people live on Java, almost two-thirds of Indonesia's total population on just 7 percent of the nation's land area.

The island is rugged and volcanic, and its rich soil makes it one of the world's most productive agricultural regions. In Dutch colonial times, Java was called "The Garden of the East."

Jakarta

The Ibu Kota—literally "Mother City"—of Indonesia is Jakarta, on the northwest coast of Java. With more than 10 million inhabitants, it is one of the world's biggest cities. Jakarta is the fourth most densely populated city in the world, more dense, even, than Bombay. This richness of humanity—or crush, depending on your outlook—is essential to Jakarta's bustling (and hustling) charm.

History of Java

Java, which until 10,000 years ago was connected together with Sumatra and Borneo to the southeast Asian mainland, is one of the world's earliest populated spots. In 1894, Dutch naturalist Eugène Dubois announced that he had discovered a "Java ape-man," the first known fossil remains of what scientists now call *Homo erectus*.

Between "Java Man," who lived more than 1 million years ago, and the first Bronze Age Javanese, who lived 2,000 years ago, there is little surviving archaeological record on Java.

The ancestors of modern-day Melanesians and the Australian aboriginals are thought to have passed through Java some 50,000 years ago. But the ancestors of today's Javanese were the Austronesians, the region's great seafarers and most successful settlers, who moved into Java about 5,000 years ago.

Java is most famous for her great Indianized kingdoms, which developed out of trading contacts with India, beginning in the first millennium A.D. The Hindu and Buddhist kingdoms of central Java produced the largest Buddhist stupa extant, Borobudur on the Kedu plain, and the many Hindu monuments of Prambanan, including the 47-meter high Loro Jonggrang.

East Java's Majapahit, which lasted through the 14th and 15th centuries, was the most successful of the early Javanese kingdoms. According to an old manuscript, Majapahit claimed an area under its control greater than that of present day Indonesia.

By the 16th century, Islam had displaced the old Indianized kingdoms and at the same time, European traders seeking spices began arriving. The Portuguese were first, but it was the Dutch East India Company, the Vereenigde Oostindische Compagnie, that established a chokehold on the spice trade. After the V.O.C. went bankrupt in 1799 the Dutch government ran Indonesia as a colony.

With the imposition of the "Cultivation System" in Java, Dutch planters grew wealthy, and the Javanese worked as near slaves growing export crops like coffee and sugar. Resentment

Overleaf: *A school of sleek unicornfish,* Naso hexacanthus. *Photograph by Ed Robinson of IKAN. Manado, Sulawesi.*

Opposite: *A pair of spine-cheeked anemonefish,* Premnas biaculeatus, *in their host anemone,* Entacmaea quadricolor. *Photograph by Helmut Debelius of IKAN. Flores.*

grew and nationalism boiled at the turn of the 20th century.

After World War II and a cruel Japanese occupation, the nationalists declared independence on August 17, 1945. The Dutch were unwilling to relinquish their colony, however, and it took five years of fighting and mounting international opposition to the Dutch to drive them out. The Dutch signed sovereignty to the Republic of Indonesia in December 1949.

People and Culture

The great majority of the Javanese—88 percent—are Muslims, and in fact Indonesia is the largest Muslim country in the world. Still, older threads of Hinduism, Buddhism and many regional ethnic cultures are deeply woven into Javanese culture. Hindu epics, the *Mahabharata* and *Ramayana,* are still the chief source of material for the very popular shadow puppet theater, *wayang kulit*, and drama, *wayang orang.*

Javanese music, played on the famous gamelan orchestra of metallophones, drums, gongs and other mostly percussion instruments, is a holdover from the days of the Hindu courts.

Batik, fabric that has been patterned through repeated dyeings over a wax resist, is sometimes considered a Javanese invention, although it is perhaps more likely that the techniques came from India. Whatever the source, Javanese batik is today very popular.

Geography

Several of Java's volcanoes are still active, and Merapi erupted in November 1994, killing more than 60 people. Java's most famous eruption occurred in 1883, when Krakatau exploded.

The Java Sea to the north of the island is quite shallow, less than 200 meters. But to the island's south is the Java trench, where the Indian Ocean reaches its deepest point, 7,450 meters.

Much of the island's forest has been given up to cultivated land. The last wilderness area is Ujung Kulon National Park on Java's westernmost peninsula.

— Janet Boileau and Debe Campbell

Diving Krakatau and Ujung Kulon Park

Diving in the waters off Krakatau, the rocky islands forming the crater of an underwater volcano in the Sunda Strait off West Java, or in the waters around the Ujung Kulon peninsula in southwest Java, is not the best to be found in Indonesia. But the seascape of cracked volcanic rock around Krakatau, and the caves and tunnels around Ujung Kulon provide an interesting underwater experience.

Reaching either of these sites requires some patience and initiative. There is little chance of making a day of it from Jakarta. One must overland to Anyer or Labuhan, and then take a boat to the dive sites.

Recent road repairs make the trip from Jakarta to Anyer quite pleasant. From there, a boat will take you the 50 kilometers to the Krakatau group, a 4-hour crossing (see map page 78). To reach Ujung Kulon, one can go either by train or car to Labuhan, and then by boat to Ujung Kulon.

We strongly suggest that you organize your jaunt with a Jakarta dive outfit. (See "Java Practicalities" page 273). You can either go with your own group, or hook up with one of the many weekend dive excursions. It can be a challenge to find a seaworthy boat, and strong and unpredictable winds in the strait could prove quite troublesome to an inexperienced captain.

If our warning does not deter you, you can charter a boat through the ranger stations at Labuhan, Carita, or Ujung Kulon Park, or through one of the many small hotels scattered along the way. Alternately, a tour agent in Jakarta could arrange a boat charter for you. In any case, do not expect a purpose-built dive boat with an attached Zodiac. What you will likely find is an older wooden *pinisi,* a traditional sailing craft that has been converted to diesel power.

Krakatau

The famous eruption of Krakatau on August 26, 1883 sent up a plume of ash and pumice 26 kilometers high and 6,000 kilometers wide, and the explosion could be heard from Myanmar to Australia. The huge tsunamis created by the blast destroyed some 165 villages in Sumatra and Java, and killed more than 36,000 people.

The original caldera collapsed in on itself, leaving three islands remaining of its rim: Sertung, Panjang and Rakata. In 1928, Anak Krakatau—"Child of Krakatau"—appeared. This still active daughter cone continues to eject tephra and lava, growing

---

AT A GLANCE
Krakatau and Ujung Kulon

Reef type: Volcanic rock slabs and formations, some reef

Access: 4 hrs from Anyer by boat for Krakatau; Ujung Kulon sites 15–30 min from ranger station

Visibility: Fair to good, 10–20 meters

Current: Gentle, to 1 knot; swells and 1.5 knot current at Ujung Kulon sites

Fish: Fair to good variety

Highlights: Underwater landscape at Krakatau; rock tunnels at Karang Copong; good coral at Tg. Jajar

---

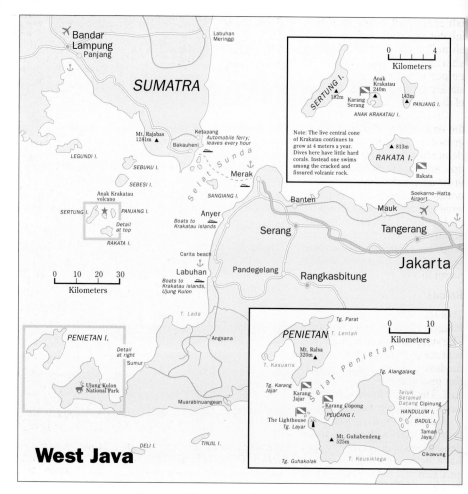

SUMATRA

Bandar Lampung
Panjang
Labuhan Meringgi

Mt. Rajabas 1281m
Ketapang
Bakauheni
Automobile ferry; leaves every hour

LEGUNDI I.
SEBUKU I.
SEBESI I.

Selat Sunda

Merak

Anak Krakatau volcano
SERTUNG I.
PANJANG I.
Detail at top
RAKATA I.

SANGIANG I.

Anyer
Boats to Krakatau islands

Banten

Serang

Mauk

Tangerang

Soekarno–Hatta Airport

Carita beach

Labuhan
Boats to Krakatau islands, Ujung Kulon

Pandegelang

Rangkasbitung

Jakarta

0   10   20   30
Kilometers

PENIETAN I.
Detail at right
Sumur

Angsana

Ujung Kulon National Park

Muarabinuangean

DELI I.
TINJIL I.

West Java

0   4
Kilometers

SERTUNG I.   182m
Anak Krakatau 240m
Karang Serang
143m   PANJANG I.
ANAK KRAKATAU I.

Note: The live central cone of Krakatau continues to grow at 4 meters a year. Dives here have little hard corals. Instead one swims among the cracked and fissured volcanic rock.

813m
RAKATA I.
Rakata

PENIETAN
Tg. Parat
T. Lentah
Mt. Ralsa 320m
T. Kasuaris

Selat Penietan

Tg. Alangalang

0   10
Kilometers

Tg. Karang Jajar
Karang Jajar
Karang Copong
PEUCANG I.
The Lighthouse
Tg. Layar
Mt. Guhabendeng 525m

Teluk Selamat Datang   Cipinung
HANDULUM I.
BADUL I.
Taman Jaya

Tg. Guhakolak
T. Keusiklega
Cikawung

at the rate of 4 meters each year, now having reached 240 meters.

A rocky, wide skirt of black sand rings the island. Being so new, Anak Krakatau has provided a perfect laboratory for scientists studying early colonization of islands by plant and animal life. So far, 120 species of plants have found their way to the little island. The shoreline is dominated by feathery casuarinas, and a few tough succulents have found a niche further up the slope.

It takes just 20 minutes to climb the 150 or so meters to the rim of the new crater. Inside, the steaming cone is surrounded by a lunar landscape of fumaroles. Looking outward, one can see the surrounding island remains of the once-massive original Krakatau. The descent is easy, and is best finished with a refreshing swim along the black sand beach.

Karang Serang Rocks

These rocks, painted white by the sea birds, mark the site of a dive off Anak Krakatau. The underwater scenery consists of large blocks of volcanic rock, seemingly sheered off by the blast. The cracked and sharp-edged rocks make a west-facing submarine cliff look like the ruin of an ancient Greek temple. In the crevices of the rock, coral growth is beginning.

The visibility is fair to good, 10 to 20 meters. Schools of Moorish idols and other reef fish inhabit the area, and one occasionally sees reef whitetip sharks. The bright colors of emperor angelfish stand out starkly against the background of dark rock.

On the south end of the site, the slab scenery is interrupted by growths of staghorn and table *Acropora,* some with blue-tinted tips. Around the rocks to the east grow an astonishing number of orange fan coral gorgonians. The smallest covered three square meters, and the largest, five square meters. The visibility drops here, because of the sandy bottom. Reef blacktip sharks patrol this area.

Rakata

This site, off the southeast end of Rakata, offers a nice drift dive. The steep sides of the island prevent access. The depths here are modest, to just 25 meters, and the gentle current carries you east. The underwater scenery is, again, slabs of volcanic rock.

A decent variety of small reef fish populates the shallower depths, and some of the crevices have been claimed by moray eels. Green turtles are numerous at this site. In the 19th century, before it exploded, Krakatau island was a common stop for sailors, who loaded up on turtles.

An unusual feature of this dive are the many underwater trees, which have been cast from the island cliffs by landslides. These attract large schools of fusiliers and jacks.

Ujung Kulon

This park, covering the peninsula at the southwest tip of Java and Penietan Island (the Krakatau group is also part of the park), is a rich area of lowland tropical rainforest. On these 420 square kilometers are hornbills and mynahs, wild boar and rusa deer, macaques and monitor lizards. The most famous inhabitants,

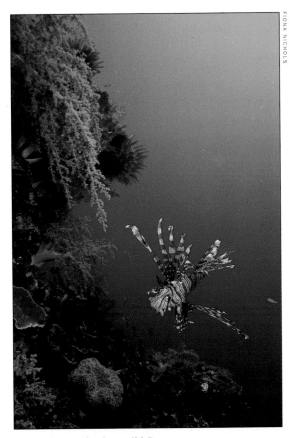

however, are the last wild Javan rhinos. These animals, of which only 57 are still believed to exist, are so elusive that even some park rangers have not seen one.

Accommodations at the Pulau Peucang ranger station, Taman Jaya, and Pulau Handeuleum run $10–$80 a night. There is even a new restaurant at the ranger station on Peucang. The station's 16 units attract surfers, who frequent the peninsula's south side, known for its great waves. Peucang Island also has some beautiful beaches, but beware of the nosey macaques. They will rummage through unattended bags and take to the trees with whatever strikes their fancy.

The Lighthouse

Tanjung Layar lighthouse on the tip of Ujung Kulon is the landmark for triangulating a rocky

Above: *The common lionfish,* Pterois volitans. *Although the dorsal and pectoral spines of this fish carry a potent venom, it is not an aggressive creature. The lionfish's lavish finnage and lazy disposition make it a favorite with photographers. Maumere Bay, Flores.*

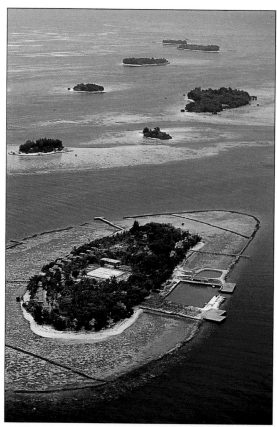

Above: *The Thousand Islands archipelago is very close to Jakarta, Indonesia's largest city, and many of the islands, such as this one, have been developed into fancy resorts providing weekend getaways for rich city dwellers.*

dive location off the west point of the peninsula. Expect swells to rock your dive boat, heavy surface current, and unusually cool water temperatures.

Beneath the surface, however, the sea is surprisingly calm. The visibility is quite good, around 20 meters. The rocks that jut just above the water plunge underneath the surface to 30 meters, looking just like submerged mountains. Coral is scarce, but in the underwater valleys there were large barracuda, schools of fusiliers and other medium-sized fish, and platoons of bumphead parrotfish. We also saw turtles circling the submerged rocks and a fat, nosey reef whitetip shark.

Karang Copong

This is a small island within sight of the northwest tip of Peucang

island. The highlight of this shallow (to 12 meters) dive are tunnels in the rock that lead to caves in the island. Seeing schools of fish swimming in and out of these tunnels is a surprisingly breathtaking experience. Visibility is 20 meters.

The surge here is quite strong, and you are rocked back and forth as the prevailing current carries you from the tunnels across some sandy mounds, where the sea life is abundant—including some nice soft corals—but visibility is quite reduced, to less than 10 meters. This site makes a fine night dive.

Karang Jajar

This site is on the rocks off large Penietan Island's Karang Jajar cape. It is an hour by boat from the ranger station at Peucang. If conditions are right, a drift dive off the south stretch offers a good, and very colorful growth of coral. You drop to 15 meters, and then drift east with a gentle current to a maximum of 20 meters. Below you, the wall plunges to past 40 meters. Turtles frequent the area, and we saw too many stingrays to count.

Badul Island

Tunggal Jaya is a sleepy community on the northern side of the isthmus of the Ujung Kulon peninsula. Just offshore here is a tiny, sandy island, Badul, which is surrounded by a good reef. You enter the water from about 15 meters off Badul's west shore, and an easy drift dive takes you about 3/4 of a kilometer before your air runs out.

Coral growth around the island is not spectacular, but the variety of both hard and soft corals was good. Visibility during our dive was less than 8 meters. Schools of bannerfish and fusiliers inhabit the reef, and we saw some bright nudibranchs.

—*Janet Boileau and Debe Campbell*

Diving on Java's 'Thousand Islands'

Pulau-Pulau Seribu

While not noted for Indonesia's best diving, Pulau-Pulau Seribu —the "Thousand Islands"—can be a good choice because of its proximity to Jakarta, and because of the great number of available sites. The islands, which actually number about 110, are scattered in a vertical group north from Jakarta in the shallow Java Sea.

Some 12,000 people live on Pulau-Pulau Seribu, more than half of them on the island of Pulau Kelapa.

With some advance planning, it is quite easy to get to the islands from Jakarta. Boats, ranging from inter-island shuttles to large cabin cruisers, ferry passengers to and from the various islands for $3.50 to $50, depending on the comfort of the craft and the distance to the island. The nearest islands are just 10 minutes from shore; the furthest can take nearly two hours by speedboat.

Accommodations on the islands also vary dramatically. International standards accommodations that cater to divers can be found on the islands of Putri, Pelangi, Sepa, Kotok, Pantara (Barat and Timur) and Matahari. Each of these also has a shop offering dive equipment rentals and compressors.

Transportation, and bookings for accommodations and dive trips, may be made at the departure pier in Ancol Marina, or through Jakarta travel agents or certified dive centers, such as the Jakarta Hilton's Dive Masters. Also check the English language daily newspaper, the *Jakarta Post,* for trips and special offers. Mid-week diving and accommo-

dations are usually easy to arrange, but be aware that Pulau Seribu is very popular among Jakartans for weekend jaunts.

Popular Resorts

Some of the islands have resort type accommodations, and they may provide some music or a bar at night. On the less "civilized" islands, nighttime entertainment might be limited to the buzzing of mosquitoes.

Upmarket resorts, built in cooperation with Japan Airlines, have gone up on Pantara Timur and Pantara Barat islands. These are very posh, with all the comforts one might expect from a fine hotel in Singapore or Hawaii.

Pelangi and Putri islands offer somewhat less toney accommodations. Putri has small bungalows, a restaurant and bar, and sailboats and sailboards can be rented. Pelangi is a larger resort, and boasts fancy cottages, tennis courts, and a popular restaurant out over the water. Shops here

---

AT A GLANCE
Pulau-Pulau Seribu

Reef type: Coral slopes

Access: 45 min to 2 hrs by boat, depending on location and type of vessel

Visibility: Poor to fair, 8–15 meters

Current: Quite gentle

Coral: In places, good

Fish: Good varieties and numbers

Highlights: Wooden shipwreck at Pulau Piniki; excellent coral at Pulau Kotok and Pulau Gosonglaga

---

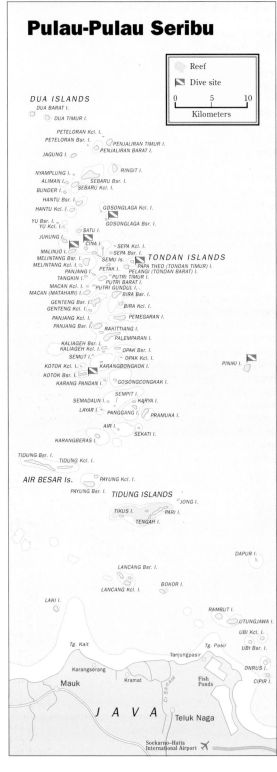

Pulau-Pulau Seribu

Reef
Dive site

0   5   10
Kilometers

DUA ISLANDS
DUA BARAT I.
DUA TIMUR I.

PETELORAN Kcl. I.
PETELORAN Bsr. I.
JAGUNG I.
PENJALIRAN TIMUR I.
PENJALIRAN BARAT I.

NYAMPLUNG I.
ALIMAN I.
BUNDER I.
RINGIT I.
SEBARU Bsr. I.
SEBARU Kcl. I.

HANTU Bsr. I.
HANTU Kcl. I.
GOSONGLAGA Kcl. I.

YU Bsr. I.
YU Kcl. I.
GOSONGLAGA Bsr. I.
JUKUNG I.
SATU I.
CINA I.
MALINJO I.
MELINTANG Bsr. I.
MELINTANG Kcl. I.
SEPA Kcl. I.
SEPA Bsr. I.
SEMU Is.   TONDAN ISLANDS
PANJANG I.
TANGKIN I.
PETAK I.
PAPA THEO (TONDAN TIMUR) I.
PELANGI (TONDAN BARAT) I.
PUTRI TIMUR I.
PUTRI BARAT I.
MACAN Kcl. I.
MACAN (MATAHARI) I.
PUTRI GUNDUL I.
BIRA Bsr. I.
GENTENG Bsr. I.
GENTENG Kcl. I.
BIRA Kcl. I.
PANJANG Kcl. I.
PANJANG Bsr. I.
PEMEGARAN I.
RAKITTIANG I.
PALEMPARAN I.
KALIAGEH Bsr. I.
KALIAGEH Kcl. I.
SEMUT I.
OPAK Bsr. I.
OPAK Kcl. I.
KOTOK Kcl. I.
KOTOK Bsr. I.
KARANGBONGKOK I.
PINIKI I.
KARANG PANDAN I.
GOSONGCONGKAK I.
SEMPIT I.
SEMADAUN I.
KARYA I.
LAYAR I.
PANGGANG I.
PRAMUKA I.
AIR I.
SEKATI I.
KARANGBERAS I.

TIDUNG Bsr. I.
TIDUNG Kcl. I.
AIR BESAR Is.
PAYUNG Kcl. I.
PAYUNG Bsr. I.
TIDUNG ISLANDS
JONG I.
TIKUS I.
PARI I.
TENGAH I.

DAPUR I.

LANCANG Bsr. I.

LANCANG Kcl. I.
BOKOR I.

LAKI I.
RAMBUT I.
UTUNGJAWA I.
UBI Kcl. I.
Tg. Kait
Tg. Pasir
UBI Bsr. I.
Tanjungpasir
ONRUS I.
Karangserang
Kramat
Fish
Ponds
CIPIR I.
Mauk

Ci Sadam

J A V A   Teluk Naga

Soekarno–Hatta
International Airport

and at the other resorts offer basic items like toothpaste and suntan lotion.

Resorts on some of the nearest islands have been in use since Dutch colonial times, and some of the islands have historical interest. Pulau Onrust, just off Tanjung Pasir and 1/2 hour from Ancol by ferry, is where Jan Pieterszoon Coen, the head of the Dutch East India company, planned his final, successful attack on the town of Jayakarta in 1619. Afterward, he named the town Batavia, which it was to be called until 1942, when the invading Japanese renamed it "Jakarta," a name the Indonesians kept.

Diving Pulau Seribu

The dive possibilities are almost countless here. The reefs around many of the 110 islands are excellent in terms of coral growth and fish life. What makes the diving here just fair by Indonesian standards is the visibility, which usually hovers around 10–15 meters. It sometimes improves, but even then only reaches 20 meters.

Daily rainfall here determines how good the visibility will be, but it is generally best in the middle of the dry season, typically May through September.

With few exceptions, the marine life at most Pulau Seribu locations will include an abundant variety of hard and soft corals, a good variety of reef fish and some pelagics, turtles and an occasional shark.

Unfortunately, at some sites the deterioration of marine life is increasingly noticeable. Like the dwindling reef in the Florida Keys, Pulau-Pulau Seribu has suffered for its proximity to a large population center. Pollution, and in some cases, mismanagement, is killing off the coral.

Pulau Piniki

This is an oblong island (see map opposite), oriented along a north–south axis. A few people live here, and the island is marked by a transmission antenna. There is an interesting reef off the western side of Piniki. The reef starts at 5 meters, but has its best coral growth and fish life at around 20 meters.

At the southwest point is the wreck of a 20-meter wooden cargo ship. The ship's cargo of cement has solidified, but the weakened wooden structure is not safe to enter.

Schools of barracuda, batfish, large parrotfish and moray eels have made the wreck their home. There is also a particularly large number of anemones and anemonefish here.

Pulau Papa Theo

This island, formerly called Pulau Tondan Timur, was renamed when the *Papa Theo*, a cargo vessel, sank on the reef here in 1982. The vessel, about 20 meters long, rests now with its port side facing the reef. The bow is at 20 meters, and the stern at 30 meters.

Until April 1991, the ship stood almost upright, but then its stern collapsed, spilling its until then intact cargo of paper products and pharmaceuticals, including condoms.

Until the cargo spilled, the beautiful reef was a favorite dive spot with Jakarta residents. Once the debris has been washed away, the reef may again become a popular spot. All the fittings and other items of value have been removed from the *Papa Theo*.

It is a simple wreck dive, with lots of marine life and an occasional shark in the deeper waters at the stern end. There are parrotfish, some resident groupers, many morays and a particular abundance of stingrays. The north reef is often chosen for night dives.

Papa Theo island is a very pleasant island hideaway, even for non-divers. The simple huts are clean and comfortable, and a basic Indonesian *mandi* or splash bath is provided. The generator shuts down at dark, and then one hears only the sound of the waves through the thatch walls. A candle-lit restaurant serves very fresh fish and standard Indonesian dishes.

Below: *A juvenile pinnate batfish, Platax pinnatus, examines a diver in an underwater grotto off Maumere, Flores. At right is a regal angelfish, Pygoplites diacanthus.*

KAL MULLER

Above: *A hawksbill turtle,* Eretmochelys imbricata. *Hawksbills, the smallest of the sea turtles, are also the most commonly seen on Indonesian reefs. Their shells provide the raw material for tortoiseshell, although the importation of such products is banned in many countries, including the United States. In Indonesian markets, one can see small hawksbill turtles, stuffed and varnished, offered as souvenirs, and even live ones, which are destined for the stew pot.*

Kuburan Cina

This very small island is among the best diving sites in Pulau-Pulau Seribu. The good reef begins due west of the island, continues around the south, then east. There is a small bit of reef at the north tip. Excellent coral growth provides the backdrop for a good drift dive in 8–20 meter depths. In areas, the coral is good to almost 30 meters.

Low tide exposes a wide expanse of reef flat. At high tide, the island shrinks dramatically, with only a sand bank showing.

Pulau Malinjo

A very good reef extends from the west around to the north, and along the south–southwest edge of the island. The best diving is at 8–12 meters. You can find lobsters here up to 30 centimeters long. The reef is also home to a great number of moray eels.

Pulau Kotok

This island sits on the western edge of the Pulau-Pulau Seribu group, and thus offers some of the best coral growth. The

undamaged reef here is good for snorkeling as well as diving. Pulau Kotok is the best in the islands for snorkeling and off-the-beach diving. The west, north and east reefs are good to 20 meters.

Because it faces the open sea, Kotok is the place to see schools of sweetlips, turtles and sharks. Small manta rays have been seen here. The area is abundant in gorgonians and soft corals.

Pulau Gosonglaga

This island is basically a small sandbank surrounded by an immense reef. The entire circumference of the reef is good, and in areas good coral growth extends down to more than 20 meters. Since the island is on the fringe of the Pulau-Pulau Seribu group, it is one of the best places to see larger reef fish and occasional pelagics.

— Janet Boileau and Debe Campbell

Note: The authors would like to thank PADI Dive instructor Vimal Lekhraj of Dive Masters, Jakarta for his invaluable help in preparing this section.

Good, Shallow Diving Close to Singapore

Who says that there's no decent diving near Singapore? How about this, folks: four nurse sharks taking an afternoon siesta, indecently close together, under boulders with several peek-holes; seahorses on two successive dives, tails tightly wrapped around staghorn coral branches; a crocodile fish lying without the slightest twitch, waiting for lunch to come within leaping-range; an absolutely huge banded sea snake, slithering around rocks and sand; a most unusual fish, the comet, showing us its rear end, impersonating an aggressive white-spotted moray; a fat, meter-plus mottled grouper, resting under a ledge.

This was in north Bintan island, forty-five minutes' ferry ride from Singapore's Tanah Merah Ferry Terminal. Visability and the underwater structure here is nothing to brag about, but there's certainly plenty to see.

Our general assessment of diving off Bintan is quite positive in spite of the restricted visibility which ranged from a close to awful 3 meters (but still a lot better than Singapore) to a passable 7 meters. The water clarity was disturbed by fine sediment, and we are not sure if it is just a seasonal aberration. Currents are just about non-existent and the bottom is shallow, a perfect area for beginners.

There is plenty to keep the attention of more advanced divers. Nudibranchs and flatworms—unusual and colorful—are abundant, and we counted at least three dozen species, all competing for the prize in the "small-is beautiful" category.

We saw Tridacna clams—with their hallucinogenic patterns and colors—in the 25–60 centimeter range. Anemones and their spunky clownfish guests (at least three species) enliven most locations. We encountered two species of jellyfish—a large pinkish one, and a smaller-belled, cream-colored one with long, graceful tentacles. Both pulsated beautifully. A fine group of fishes—big, medium and small—also riveted our attention. Hard corals are abundant, in many areas in surprisingly good shape.

Night dives are particularly rewarding here, in fact the vari-

---

AT A GLANCE
Bintan

Reef type: Shallow fringing reefs

Access: 15 min–1 hr by boat, depending on location

Visibility: Poor, 3–7 meters

Current: Almost none

Coral: In places, quite good

Fish: Good varieties and numbers

Highlights: Nudibranchs by day; crustaceans by night

---

ety of life is excellent. Sea urchins of several species, including a couple of exuberantly colorful ones, teach careful underwater movements. Gaudy shrimp and crabs come out of their lairs to scavenge; some bright red, and others imaginatively camouflaged.

Exploring Bintan

An old Mexican saying goes: "So far from God, but so close to the United States" and divers think-

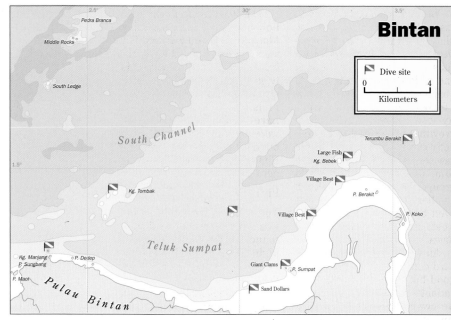

Bintan

Pedra Branca

Middle Rocks

South Ledge

South Channel

Terumbu Berakit

Large Fish
Kg. Bebek

Village Best

P. Berakit

Kg. Tombak

Village Best

P. Koko

Teluk Sumpat

Kg. Manjang
P. Sungbang
P. Dedep
P. Maoi

Giant Clams
P. Sumpat

Pulau Bintan

Sand Dollars

Dive site

0 ⊢——————⊣ 4
Kilometers

ing about Bintan could well be forgiven for giving this their own spin: "So far from eastern Indonesia (scuba heaven), but so close to Singapore (lousy diving)." But being close to Singapore gives distinct advantages to Bintan (we're not sure about Mexico): funds for infrastructure, including resort development, and developing professionally run diving programs.

One of these resorts, the Mana-Mana Beach Club, a water sports complex, offers—among many other aquatic activities—scuba diving under the professional supervision of a well-qualified, personable instructor, Jonathan Ho.

Just before the October 1994 opening of the Mana-Mana resort, Jon conducted a last-minute survey of dive sites around north Bintan. We dove off the Singapore-based power cruiser and dive live-aboard, the *Seri Delima,* owned and operated by Capt. Tan.

We covered a dozen sites, day and night. The Banda Sea it ain't. But to those divers used to Singapore waters and popular and

crowded Tioman, diving on Bintan will be a pleasant surprise: we had a fine dive series, in spite of restricted visibility (3–4 meters) at some sites. Our visibility never exceeded 7 meters, but during our week-long trip (in May), several storms whipped up the sediments. Calmer seas should increase the clarity of the shallow waters.

There are no deep dives here: our computers barely touched the 10 meter mark a couple of times. So there's plenty of time for checking out the underwater scene. It was a real treat to dive 60–70 minutes and still have half a tank remaining. And no decompression stops. In addition, there are plenty of dive locations along the 30-odd kilometer stretch of north Bintan.

Our team included Biologist Carsten Huettche, a young German tropical ecologist, who was then working for Bintan Resort Management as its Conservation Management Executive, a position from which he hoped to do something to help preserve the natural ecosystem of north Bintan Island.

We dove at several places to assess the diving potential. Visibility generally increased from west to east. But two of the better sites were towards the western end of Bintan's north shore. At Tanjung Tondang we were hit by a fairly strong current and visibility was lousy, but the coral growth was surprisingly good, both in variety and health. We saw several fish traps on the bottom, one with a good sized grouper, along with a half dozen smaller species. Coral life was even better a short way to the west, off a small island called Rawa.

As we proceeded west, the hard coral cover remained quite good but the fish life was very variable. Around Pulau Sumpat we saw large spreads of sea dollars, unusual for Indonesia. Invertebrate and fish life were also excellent at Sumapt. But both hard and soft corals, as well as the variety and numbers of fishes improved as we dove towards a place called "Black Rock" on our charts. We saw the most schooling fishes here and consider it the best site on Bintan Island.

The best diving in the area, however, is off an island called Mapor, northeast of Bintan. This marked the top of our dive series from every point of view: visibility, invertebrates and fishes, variety and absolute numbers of animals. Only the night dives here—which are excellent— were not noticeably better than our dives near the north shore of Bintan. The variety of life is staggering.

Fish life

The single largest fish we saw was a huge grouper, which we found sleeping in a crevice at night. Sensing us, it woke up, swam like mad, then settled down between two vertical rocks. Other biggies included normal-sized groupers in the 20 to 40 centimeter range, a school of jacks, several individual queenfish (*Scomberoides*) and blue-spotted stingrays.

During another night dive, an incredibly long banded sea snake slithered into view. It fled in panic as we tried to approach it, but then returned a few minutes later to check up on our activi-

Below: *A large Semaeostome jellyfish (perhaps Cyanea) off Bintan. The waters off north Bintan, though not particularly clear, are rich in life.*

ties. After we swam back to our boat and clambered on, the snake came by again, brightly lit by the ship's lights. It was followed by two smaller relatives. Other night camp followers, basking in our ship's lights, included a flock of gracefully undulating flatworms, mini magic carpets. We were also treated to visiting wide-eyed squid.

During an afternoon dive, We spotted a couple of sleeping sharks. A closer look revealed two more, the biggest one with a sharksucker tightly fastened to its back. The sharks, packed like sardines in a can, did not seem to mind our peeking through several openings between rock slabs. Only one, whose head was fairly close to a peek-hole, kept a wary eye on the struggling photographer trying to squeeze one of his giant flash units into a tight hole to throw light on the resting beasts.

Keen-eyed Jonathan spotted the unusual comet, a rarely encountered fish. When alarmed, this fish, a relative of the groupers, sticks its head in a crack, displaying the rear of its body and its flowing fins. In this way its head is protected and, because of its spotted pattern and a prominent false eye, the back end of the comet looks convincingly like the head of a lurking white-spotted moray eel. Few carnivorous fish are nervy enought to mess around with this fearsome customer.

Jonathan also came up with a prize reserved for only the best-behaved divers: a pair of sea horses. In just over 1,000 dives in Indonesia, these interesting animals have always kept well out of my sights. The pair of yellow seahorses that Jonathan found hid inside a protective tangle of branching corals, stubbornly refusing to come out for a portrait. The next day, however, one of the two obliged, swimming out from the coral far enough to pose for my camera.

Unusual species

Also common in this area are beaked coralfish, long-snouted butterflyfish with bright coppery orange bands. This fish uses its long "beak" to pluck invertebrate

Below: A beautiful octocoral in the genus Carijoa (formerly Telesto). This animal usually has white, or sometimes orange, polyps. The photographer, who has dived extensively in Indonesia, has seen this only once, in Bangka island off North Sulawesi.

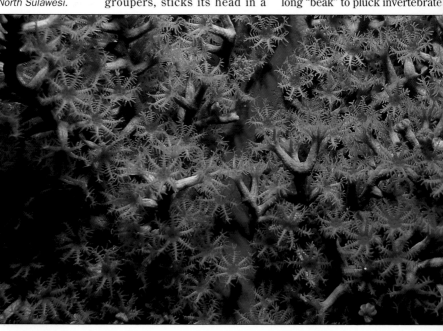

snacks from tiny hard coral cracks. An false eye spot near the back of its body helps to confuse predators. The little juveniles, always in pairs, are curious, checking out buoyancy-controlled divers who make no brusque, threatening gestures. Members of this genus (*Chelnon*) frequent reefs adjacent to large land masses with mangrove—for example, Sumatra—and are never seen on the smaller, more isolated Indonesian islands.

Another colorful species, the majestic blue-ring angelfish, also enlivens the reef with its crazy blue stripes on a yellow body. This is another fish that is common here, but not often seen at some of the more dramatic sites in eastern Indonesia. At one dive site, several adults and their camp followers hung around us, perhaps wanting to play tag, but almost always staying just outside of decent camera range.

Schooling fishes included the ever-present yellow-and-blue fusiliers, sea chubs, rabbitfish, and snappers. Parrotfish and damsels were common. We encountered several large groups of shrimpfish, swimming in their characteristic head down position.

Several other noteworthy denizens of the fish world were spotted. A crocodile fish, confident of his camouflage, allowed us to approach to within a few centimeters. We saw at least one species of shrimp goby, and the banded combtooth blenny, complete with square head and bulging eyes. An occasional harlequin sweetlips, black spots all over its yellow body, finned by quickly to check us out.

We also found a tiny fan-bellied leatherjacket, a filefish that could change its pattern and coloration in a wink, chameleonlike. Fascinating.

We also saw numerous eight-banded butterflyfish, a species that lives strictly on coral polyps, and thus whose presence on a reef has been taken by scientists as a general indicator of stony coral growth and condition. When these "canaries" become scarce, enviornmental biologists become worried about the health of the reefs.

Below: *The puffer* Arothron nigropunctatus *shelters in the barrel sponge* Xestospongia testudinaria.

Introducing
The Island of Bali

KAL MULLER

The tiny volcanic island of Bali is one of the most physically beautiful and culturally rich places in the world. The balmy climate, lush, green ricefields and lavish productions of the Hindu-Balinese cultural calendar never fail to charm visitors. Although writers continue to flatter Bali with adjectives, none has surpassed Indian prime minister Pandit Nehru, who called the island "the morning of the world."

Much of the mythology erected around this "paradise" is more revealing of its western authors than of the island itself—*South Pacific*'s silly "Bali-Hai" comes most immediately to mind—but visitors persistently find themselves drawn here. Today, over 1 million tourists a year visit Bali.

Balinese Culture

Indonesia is the largest Islamic country in the world, but the 2.5 million Balinese are overwhelmingly Hindu. *Agama Hindu Dharma* as practiced in Bali is a philosophy, religion and cultural organizing principal that has resulted from Buddhist and Hindu doctrines and practices arriving from India—partly through Java—between the 8th and 15th centuries. It is a uniquely Balinese meld.

Balinese cultural life cycles according to the Pawukon, a complex 210-day ritual calendar. Holiday celebrations—New Year, temple anniversaries, Galungan—and rites of passage—tooth filings, weddings, cremations—are scheduled according to the Pawukon. These ceremonial events, marked by bright costumes, lavish offerings of food, and dance performances,

leave visitors with some of their fondest memories of Bali.

Bali has been famous for her art since the arrival of the first European tourists in the early 20th century. Balinese masks are now almost *de rigueur* on the walls of fashionable apartments in uptown Manhattan. The island's artists turn out painted Hindu icons like Garuda, whimsical animals, and unfinished abstract and surrealistic figures. Most of Bali's painters work in watercolor, producing intricate and detailed group scenes.

Balinese dance ranges from stately processionals to wild leaping and posturing. In general it is more lively than the very refined Javanese court dances, which are considered ancestors to Balinese dance. Some of the most popular forms—such as the monkey dance or *kecak*—are purely secular events, hybrids of old court dances and modern, western-influenced sensibilities.

Dance is accompanied by the *gamelan,* an all-percussion orchestra of metallophones, gongs and cymbal-like instruments. Rhythm is everything in gamelan music, and the musicians' overlapping runs on their bright-sounding instruments create an unforgettable sound.

History of Bali

Before about the 9th century, when writing and other Indian influences made their way to Bali, little is known of the island's history. Stone altars and sarcophagi, dating back to several centuries B.C. have been found on the island, and these suggest a Bronze Age culture of herders and farmers who practiced a

Above: *Rangda, the antagonist in Bali's famous Barong drama. Rangda is a powerful sorceress.*

Overleaf: *An orange skunk anemonefish (Amphiprion sandaracinos) in Merten's anemone (Stichodactyla mertensii). Photo by Cody Shwaiko.*

Opposite: *Divers on the wreck at Tulamben, perhaps Bali's single most popular dive site. Photo by Kal Muller.*

form of ancestor worship.

From the 9th century onward, Bali had regular contact with Java, at the time being influenced by Indian cultural practices. During the 14th and 15th centuries, East Java was dominated by the Majapahit empire, of which Bali became a colony in 1365.

This event and date—though by no means certain, as its source, the *Negarakertagama,* is something of a panegyric— marks the point when the Hindu caste system, court culture, performing arts, and other Javanese influences came to Bali.

For the next several centuries Bali was ruled by a single court, but factions developed, and by the time the Dutch arrived in the 19th century, Bali was made up of nine realms: Badung, Gianyar, Bangli, Klungkung, Karangasem, Buleleng, Mengwi, Tabanan and Jembrana.

Although they had been in the archipelago since the turn of the 17th century, the Dutch avoided Bali at first. The Balinese had a reputation of being quite fierce, and the fractious internal politics of the little island were considered too great an obstacle to Dutch rule there. Besides, the only important trade item the Balinese offered were slaves.

The Dutch finally subjugated Buleleng (now Singaraja) on the north coast and established a colonial center there in 1849. Then, some 50 years later, a Dutch ship ran aground on the reef off Sanur. The disappearance of the cargo to freelance salvage operators served as a pretext for an armed invasion of the south. The Badung court expired in 1906 in a *puputan,* a ritual mass suicide.

Geography and Climate

The island of Bali was shaped by the action of volcanoes, which produced the rich, black soils that nourish Bali's beautiful and productive rice paddies.

Just 8°–9° south of the equator, Bali is always warm—a mean 27.2°C, although the highlands are about 6° cooler. Humidity is an almost constant 75 percent. Most of Bali's annual 2,500–3,000 millimeters of rain falls from November through March.

—*David Picke*

Splendid Wreck, Fine Walls and Varied Sites

Bali is one of Indonesia's most beautiful islands, and always a favorite with tourists. Although it looks small on the map, Bali's winding and narrow roads can eat up a lot of your underwater time. So, before arriving, think a bit about how much time you want to spend diving, and how much sight-seeing.

Most tourist accommodations are in the south, in the Kuta—Nusa Dua—Sanur triangle. (See map opposite.) If you stay here, there is one interesting, undemanding dive nearby, on the reef off Tanjung (Cape) Benoa, that can give you an introduction—but no more—to Bali's underwater world. The best dive sites require several hours driving from the southern tourist center.

Serious divers should find accommodations close to the best dive spots: at Candi Dasa, Tulamben, or Pemuteran. None of these has the range of *losmen,* restaurants, tourist services and shops as does Kuta Beach or the other resort areas of the south, but they are much closer to the good diving.

Where to Stay

Candi Dasa, in the old Karangasem Regency on the island's east coast, is the best compromise between comfort and proximity to good diving: Cemeluk and Tulamben are within an hour's drive, the little islands of Tepekong and Mimpang are just offshore, Padang Bai is just across the bay, and Nusa Penida is a fairly short boat trip away. Only Menjangan Island, off the far western tip of Bali, is distant.

And Candi Dasa, particularly in recent years, has become quite a bustling little town. There are plenty of accommodations and good restaurants. People have compared it to Kuta beach before the big boom in tourism.

For diving on the *Liberty* wreck off Tulamben, we suggest staying in Tulamben itself—if you can get a room. There are few accommodations, and these are often booked up, especially during the two high seasons, July–August and around Christmas and New Year.

For the dives off Menjangan Island, stay at Pemuteran, a short drive away. There is a very comfortable bungalow style resort there, and an affiliated dive operation offers diving just offshore as well as at Menjangan.

Dive Operators

Unless you are planning just a few, casual dives in Bali, contact one of the dive operators before you arrive and plan a series of dives with them. They can book a hotel for you in your price range, and plan a diving program that matches your interest and experience. (See Dive Operators in "Bali Practicalities," page 277.)

At this same time—well before your arrival—request a good, English-speaking dive guide. Don't wait until you arrive to do this, or you may end up with someone you will be giving English lessons to. Our favorite guide is Wally Siagian of Wally's Special Tours. There are other competent guides and operators as well, but if you wait until the last minute, the best will be booked up.

If you have made plans with an operator, an itinerary will be worked out for you ahead of

Wally's Rankings

Beginning in this section, will be offering dive guide Wally Siagian's rankings of the various sites in Bali and elsewhere. They will be presented as a gloss in the margins.

Basically, Wally's system evaluates sites based on 1) How interesting the bottom is; 2) How good the visibility is; 3) How rich the fish life is; 4) How rich the coral cover is; and 5) Whether there is anything special about the site.

According to this system, the hypothetical best dive in the world would get a 10 as follows:

Best Site

Bottom formation	3
Visibility	2
Coral variety	2
Fish variety	2
Special	1
Total:	**10**

Note that not all categories are weighted the same, e.g. bottom formation, which is unchanging, is considered more important than fish life, which can change with seasons and local conditions time. If not, contact the operators when you arrive—at hotel counters, or at their office. You will be diving with whomever else signs up. Pickups at your hotel are fairly early in the morning, and drop-offs late in the afternoon.

The tours are usually all-inclusive, including tanks and weights, guides and lunch. If you need other equipment, such as a BC and regulator, check to make sure that they are available. It is also a very good idea to take a close look at the equipment the day before the dive.

Bali's Dive Sites

There are five main areas for diving in Bali, working counter-clockwise around the island from the airport in the south: Nusa Dua and Sanur; Nusa Penida; Padang Bai and Candi Dasa; Cemeluk and Tulamben; and Pemuteran and Menjangan.

Each area offers dive locations for novice, intermediate and advanced divers—except for Nusa Dua and Sanur, where no location requires more than a little experience. (Diving is also available at Lovina. It is not really worth a special trip, but if you are passing through you might want to take a look. See "Bali Practicalities," page 277.)

At most sites, you can plan a dive to match your degree of experience—just try to be with divers whose level is similar to yours. It is no fun for either beginners or experts to be lumped together just to convenience the tour operator. Currents of 2–2.5 knots are not going to disturb an experienced diver, but for your first drift dive a half a knot is quite sufficient.

We found very little of interest on Bali's reefs beyond the safe sport diving limit. The best diving in Bali lies between 5 and 40 meters.

Nusa Dua and **Sanur.** The dives here are along the outer edge of a reef that runs from below Nusa Dua to Sanur. Operators ferry their clients over wide, shallow reef flat to the dive site. The passage is difficult or impossible at low tide. The dives are drop-offs, but to only about 15 meters. Coral cover is poor but fish life is fair to good.

Nusa Penida. The dive sites off Nusa Penida, and nearby Ceningan and Lembongan islands, require the longest boat rides and strong currents and surge make conditions tricky although a good guide can usually find an alternate site. These are drop-off dives, and the fish life and coral variety is excellent. The water can be quite cold because of upwelling.

Candi Dasa and **Padang Bai.** The coastal sites in Amuk Bay are shallow and undemanding, with only occasional, mild currents. Visibility can be quite poor. The islands in front of Candi Dasa—Tepekong, Gili Mimpang, and Gili Likuan—offer excellent diving with a great variety of fish life, including many larger species. Temperatures are usually low, and a 3mm wet suit is almost essential. Currents can be strong and unpredictable, including downdrafts and surge.

Cemeluk and **Tulamben.** These areas have excellent coral walls with many species of fish. Some sites also have a great diversity of corals. The Tulamben shipwreck is the area highlight, offering unlimited photo opportunities at shallow depths. There is very little current here. The beach entry over rocks at the wreck dive site can be difficult if the surf is high.

Pemuteran and **Menjangan Island.** Pemuteran offers a variety of rich bank reefs, just offshore or a short boat ride away. Menjangan is an undemanding dive with excellent walls and very clear water—up to 50 meters visibility. There is also an old wreck at 40 meters, and superb coral gardens in just 5–7 meters.

Convenient and Undemanding Dives

The dives just beyond the reef line east of the northern part of Tanjung Benoa peninsula, or in front of Sanur, are not the best in Bali. But the sites are easy to get to, and there is quite a good variety of reef fish to see. These dives serve perfectly as a quick refresher if you haven't dived in a while, or as your first dive if you have just completed a dive course. (See map page 98.)

An outboard-powered outrigger canoe takes you the few hundred meters from the beach to the dive location, just beyond where the waves break. The only way out is over very shallow reef flat, so the tide must be in to make the trip. Be prepared for a bit of spray during the ride out or back and when crossing the (usually low) breaking waves.

On the reef face off Tanjung Benoa, we dropped down to 8–9 meters on a slightly sloping bottom with scattered coral formations. Visibility (late September) was just 6–8 meters, but we were told that it is usually twice this. The majority of the fish were at

AT A GLANCE
Nusa Dua and Sanur

Reef type: Drop-off to moderate depth

Access: 5 minutes by small boat

Visibility: Low, 6–8 meters (can reach 15 meters on occasion)

Current: Very gentle

Coral: Limited coverage, few species

Fish: Surprisingly good variety

Highlights: Feeding frenzy on a fresh spawn

Other: Nusa Dua has slightly better coral cover than Sanur

Below: *A swarm of anthias, mostly red-cheeked fairy basslets,* Pseudanthias hutchii. *Nusa Penida, Bali.*

HELMUT DEBELIUS / IKAN

Nusa Dua and Sanur

Legian

Kuta

Sand and Seagrass

Mud

Mangrove Swamp

SERANGAN (TURTLE) I.

Benoa Port

Ngurah Rai International Airport

Mud

Tg. Benoa

Teluk Jimbaran

Mud

Teluk Benoa

Benoa

Mud

Jimbaran

Mangrove

Sand and Seagrass

BUKIT BADUNG

NUSA DUA

Nusa Dua

★ Whale shark sightings

Seagrass beds

Tg. Lebang

Tg. Gagar

Uluwatu, best fishing grounds

Reef	
Dive site	
0 1 2	
Kilometers	

50m

100m

Sanur

Nusa Dua/Sanur

Bottom formation   1
Visibility   .5
Coral variety   1
Fish variety   1
Special   0

Total: 3.5

Some sites do better, earning perhaps a 6, but recent dredging of the Benoa harbor has ruined visibility and the Nusa Dua and Sanur sites are average at best.

—Wally Siagian

8–10 meters. We made a couple of quick dips to 14 meters, and saw nothing.

Good Variety of Fish

The coral cover here is not fantastic, but the few mini-pinnacles drew plentiful fish life with a good variety of species. We saw several 50–75 centimeter fish glide by, but visibility was too restricted to make an identification. Our guide found a giant moray and pointed him out to us. This big fellow lives in a coral cave with several openings, and for a while he played hide and seek, popping his head out of three different holes.

We saw a fairly large group of yellowtail fusiliers, a nicely compacted hovering mass of blue-lined snappers, a few red bigeyes and several small aggregations of bigeye soldierfish.

Fairy basslets hovered over almost every coral outcrop. Damsels were present in a variety of species. The butterfly fish were well-represented, but the only schooling species we saw was a small group of masked bannerfish (*Heniochus monoceros*). Groupers were common, especially the white-lined grouper (*Anyperodon leucogrammicus*) which we saw in both color morphs: white, and brown-green.

Parrotfish were present in good variety, but the only species we noticed more than once was the blue-barred parrot (*Scarus ghobban*). The only angelfish we saw were the dwarf bicolor angel (*Centropyge bicolor*) and several big emperor angels. Surgeonfish were common, particularly the spotted unicorn fish (*Naso brevirostris*). We saw pairs of rabbit-fish of at least three species, and a single pair of Titan triggerfish.

A Feeding Frenzy

The highlight of the dive came when we saw a furious cloud of several dozen fish of various species whirling around what looked like a bare patch of dark, reddish coral. Caught up in a feeding frenzy, the small fish allowed us to approach as close as we wished. We could even touch them, they were so intent on their meal. We never did identify what it was they were eating, although it is likely it was a fresh spawn of some kind.

Dives off Nusa Dua will probably not offer such a show very often, but are still worth making for the variety of fish here. The reef to the north, off the Sanur coast, is similar—wide tidal flats behind the reef front—and access is also impossible at the lowest tide. The variety of fishes is quite good in Sanur, but there is even less coral cover than at Nusa Dua. If you are a serious diver, either of these dives will just whet your appetite for more challenging locations.

Abundant Pelagics, Some Fierce Currents

Nusa Penida, across the Badung Strait from Bali's southern tip, offers some of the best diving to be found anywhere. But conditions around Penida and its two small sister islands—Nusa Lembongan and Nusa Ceningan—can sometimes be difficult, with unpredictable currents reaching four or more knots. This is not a place for beginning divers, inexperienced boatmen, or engines in less than perfect condition. Also, upwellings from the deep water south of Bali, which keep visibility here clear, can also make the water uncomfortably cold.

Even if you are an expert diver, contract with one of Bali's well-organized diving services to dive Nusa Penida, and make sure that you get a reliable boat and a guide with plenty of experience. The currents in this area can usually be predicted from the tide tables, but they can increase, decrease or shift direction with no advance notice, and vary dramatically with depth. We recommend that your guide bring a buoy, and that you do not wander off by yourself. The dive locations are all close together, and an experienced guide can easily shift you to an alternate site if the conditions at your planned location are unsatisfactory.

Dive boats to Nusa Penida leave from Nusa Dua or Sanur, or from Padang Bai. (See map page 101.) From either of the resorts the 34-kilometer (18-nautical-mile) trip takes 1.5 hours; from Padang Bai, just 17 kilometers (9 nautical miles) from Penida, it takes 45 minutes to 1 hour, depending on the boat. You can also rent a speedboat at Padang

Bai (about $110 round-trip) to shave trip time to the minimum, but if you do, make sure your dive guide knows the boatman. The chap could fall asleep while you're under and be out of whistle range when you come up with the current. It has happened.

Coral Walls and Pelagics

Most of the dive spots are around the channel between Nusa Penida and Nusa Ceningan. The standard reef profile here has a terrace at 8–12 meters, then a wall or steep slope to 25–30 meters, then a fairly gentle slope to the seabed at 600 meters. Pinnacles and small caves are often encountered. At 35–40 meters, long antipatharian wire corals are common, spiraling outward more than 8 meters.

Pelagics are the main attraction here, and you have a good chance to see jacks, mackerel and tuna. Reef sharks are so

Getting to Nusa Penida

The quickest transfer to Nusa Penida is from Padang Bai, using the "Express" ferry, which has twin 85hp engines. This takes 26 minutes to Toyapakeh.

—Wally Siagian

Caution!

Tidal currents between Nusa Penida and Ceningan will get *very* strong to the south.

—Wally Siagian

AT A GLANCE
Nusa Penida

Reef type:	Drop-offs, steep slopes
Access:	45 min to 1.5 hrs by boat
Visibility:	Good, 15 meters
Current:	Moderate to very strong (4+ knots)
Coral:	Very good variety of hard corals; excellent stand of soft corals
Fish:	Excellent variety; many pelagics
Highlights:	Large school of sweetlips, very large hawksbill turtle. Site also hosts sharks, mantas, and even *Mola mola*
Other:	Can be *very* cold; currents are unpredictable and often fierce

Above: *Two clown anemonefish,* Amphiprion ocellaris, *in the host anemone* Heteractis magnifica. *Bali.*

S.D.

Bottom formation	1
Visibility	1.5
Coral variety	1.5
Fish variety	1.5
Special	0
Total:	**5.5**

Malibu Point

Bottom formation	2.5
Visibility	1.5
Coral variety	2
Fish variety	1.5
Special	1
(Sharks, big pelagics, Mola mola)	
Total:	**8.5**

—Wally Siagian

and southwest coasts of Penida, but these areas, swept by tricky currents, require an experienced guide and more time than is available in a daytrip to reach.

A Dive off Penida

We were staying at Baruna's Pur Bagus Beach Hotel in Candi Dasa when the opportunity came to dive Nusa Penida. One of the hotel's minibuses picked us up early, and after a 15-minute ride dropped us off at Padang Bai, where the large diesel-powered *Baruna 05* dive boat was already waiting for us. We waded through waist-high water to load our gear, and were soon on our way for the hour-and-a-half trip.

The boat anchored off the Ped/S.D. area, and we dropped into a practically currentless sea. From an initial 7 meter depth, we followed the slope of 45 degrees down to 37 meters. There was good hard coral cover, and an occasional pinnacle reared up 5–6 meters from the slope. We crossed a big school of black triggerfish mixed with a few sleek unicornfish.

A small cave in one of the coral knolls held a densely packed school of pygmy sweeps (*Parapriacanthus ransonetti*). These greenish, semi-transparent fish feed at night on small plankton attracted by the bioluminous organs located just in back of their pectoral fins.

Early in the dive we crossed paths with a large black-spotted stingray. He allowed us to approach to within just over a meter, but after just one photo flew off to his next appointment. Shortly after we met the ray, we saw a hawksbill turtle, one of the largest we have ever seen. This 1.3–1.5 meter animal flippered off before I could approach within decent camera range.

The rest of our dive passed through busy schools of yellow-tailed and lunar fusiliers, and occasional schools of longfin ban-

common that after a while you stop noticing them. Mantas are frequently sighted. Perhaps the most unusual pelagic visitor to Nusa Penida is the weird mola-mola or oceanic sunfish (*Mola mola*), a mysterious large, flattened fish with elongate dorsal and ventral fins, and a lumpy growth instead of a tail fin.

Dive guide Wally Siagian says he has seen a mola-mola here about once every 15 dives. On two occasions he has been able to swim up and touch the bizarre, up to 2-meter-long animals.

The most common dive spots are just south of the dock at Toyapakeh, or a bit further east, at Ped, the site of an important temple of the same name, Sampalan Point, and "S.D.," named for the *sekolah dasar* or primary school there. There are other dive spots down the northeast erfish. We saw several groupers and even more sweetlips, and an occasional clown or Titan triggerfish. A good-sized barracuda observed us from above. Visibility was good, in the 15-meter range.

When we ascended we noticed the surface current had increased markedly since we began our dive. Wally complained that we had not spotted any big sharks, which are common in this area.

Toyapakeh

We motored a bit further west along the coast of Nusa Penida, and dropped anchor a few hundred meters from the dock at Toyapakeh. We descended through a slight current (less than 1 knot) into veritable clouds of peach fairy basslets (*Pseudanthias dispar*), each the exact color of a blue-eyed Nordic tourist who had done too much time in the sun. The anthias were mixed with large aggregations of firefish, which are more often seen in pairs or small groups.

A long stretch of our dive route—this at 25–30 meters—consisted of an almost unbroken thicket of pastel-tinted *Dendronephthya* soft corals. A school of two dozen or more greater amberjacks swam several lazy circles around our group, mixing sometimes with a larger school of bigeye jacks. As we started upwards, we saw a huge black-

Toya Pakeh

Bottom formation	1.5
Visibility	2
Coral variety	1.5
Fish variety	1.5
Special	1
(Mantas, Mola mola)	
Total:	**7.5**

Gamat

Bottom formation	2
Visibility	2
Coral variety	1.5
Fish variety	1
Special	1
(Turtles, marlin, mantas, Mola mola)	
Total:	**7.5**

—Wally Siagian

Nusa Penida

Reef
Dive site

0 1 2 3 4 5
Kilometers

Gamat Bay

Mouth of bay has coral outcrops, crevices and grottos

Inside of bay is shallow and full of coral; good for snorkeling

Malibu Point. This is guide Wally Siagian's favorite spot in Bali. Visibility is 20m, and there is always strong current, up to 4 knots. The area is small, and the conditions are tricky, but one can see big pelagics, tuna, mantas, turtles, and a wide variety of sharks.

WALLY SIAGIAN
The Best Dive Guide in Bali

Take a group of the most experienced divers in Indonesia and ask them who they think is the best dive guide in the islands. Wilhelm Siagian— "Wally," to one and all—will be at the top of the list, every time.

Wally has shown off his Balinese reefs to top underwater pros, including Gerald R. Allen, Rudie Kuiter, John E. Randall, and Roger Steene—the leading authorities on the archipelago's marine life and some of the world's top underwater photographic professionals. As a result, Wally has become an informal student of Allen, Kuiter and Steene, learning the Latin names of the fish with which he is so familiar.

Wally was born in Bandung, Java in 1960 of Sundanese, Batak and German blood-lines. He was 16 when he first started diving, with a CMAS certificate from Jakarta's Ganesha Diving Club. After some 200 dives around Pulau Seribu and about 30 off Ujung Kulon, he left for a bit of travel. Stints of working and diving around Sorong, Irian Jaya and Balikpapan, East Kalimantan led Wally to decide that diving was all that really mattered in life. (It was while diving near an oil rig off Balikpapan that Wally saw the biggest barracuda of his career—more than 2 meters and fa-a-a-t.)

After Kalimantan, Wally decided to settle with his Swiss wife in Bali. Times were difficult for a while, until he landed a miserably paying job with Baruna Watersports in 1985. Since then, he has made thousands of dives around Bali, pioneering new sites and working his way up the diving ranks: Dive Master rating in 1988 from CMAS, Open Water Instructor from SSI in 1990, and SSI Advanced Open Water Instructor with Dive Control speciality, awarded in Australia, in 1991.

Though training is important, it is his experience and motivation that makes Wally a superior guide. He knows the Latin and English common names of hundreds of fish in the reefs around Bali. He really knows the dive locations, and can set up a sequence of dives to suit the interest and level of competence of any divers in his charge. If necessary, he can cure wounds with traditional medicine and even deliver an excellent massage. A true Renaissance Man.

He has an open personality, a sense of humor and an infectious enthusiasm for diving—and he'll find a cold beer in the most unlikely places. He is my friend, drinking buddy and, of course, my favorite dive guide.   — *Kal Muller*

spotted moray, with about 1 meter of its snaky body sticking out of its lair.

We surfaced just at funnel mouth of the channel between Nusa Penida and Nusa Ceningan. The local fishermen were unfurling the sails of their *jukung*s, and we climbed back on board just as the current began to pick up speed.

The *Baruna 05* tied up to the dock at Toyapakeh, and Wally borrowed a bystander's bicycle to go fetch us some food. While he was gone, a fisherman pulled up in his outrigger, and we bought a just-caught 20-kilo yellowfin tuna for dinner.

Sunset Show

Just before sunset, the current picked up to 5–6 knots. We watched the *jukung*s literally shoot through the channel on their way out for a night's fishing. Others, taking advantage of the wind and a back current, headed for "mainland" Bali in the direction of towering Gunung Agung. This was one of the finest sunset shows I had ever admired in Indonesia.

The tuna we bought ended up as sashimi and charcoal-grilled tuna steaks, and combined with a lobster Wally had snatched from a grotto on our first dive, we had a splendid supper. We then spread our mattresses on the top deck, and settled down to drinking beer. A few little boats fished around us with bright pressure lamps, and we drifted off to sleep.

The night was surprisingly cool, and I woke up at midnight to a sky full of stars. I quickly discarded all thoughts of a night dive as I heard the current rushing by the boat. The beer had taken its usual route, and I relieved myself overboard, creating swirling bioluminescence on the water's surface.

Another Dive at S.D.

The next morning, after the sun

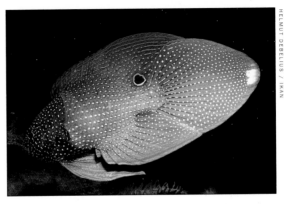

had warmed us thoroughly, we headed back east along Nusa Penida's coast to begin our next and last dive where we had ended the previous morning: in front of the long, red-roofed elementary school.

This was a drift dive, in a 1.5 to 2 knot current that occasionally "gusted" to 3 knots. The fish hovered effortlessly in the current as we sped by. Swimming diagonally, we approached two large map puffers, and several smaller, but exquisitely patterned cube trunkfish. We also took a closer look at a hallucinogenic scribbled filefish.

Between two coral knolls we came on an aggregation of some 40 sweetlips. The fish were split into four groups, all facing the current. The sight of these attractively patterned fish was too much to just pass by, so we carefully grabbed onto some hard corals and crawled along the bottom for a closer look at the sweetlips show.

Perhaps feeling there was safety in numbers, these magnificent animals allowed us to approach to within 2 meters before they drifted off to find a new spot just a bit further away. While we watched our sweetlips, a turtle rose up just ahead and, with no effort at all, swam off straight into the current.

Then, a huge grouper, well over a meter long, appeared out of nowhere, buzzing one of our group before disappearing just as suddenly. Consulting the fish books later, we came to a consensus that our visitor was likely to have been a blotchy grouper (*Epinephelus fuscogattus*).

We later saw triggerfish, a barracuda and a reef white-tip shark; still, it was anticlimactic.

Above: *The comet,* Calloplesiops altivelis. *When alarmed this fish ducks its head into a crevice and displays its long fins and tail, mimicking a moray eel. These unusual fish can be found at the Tulamben drop-off, S.D. on Nusa Penida, and Tepekong.*

Below: *Guide Wally Siagian gets his teeth cleaned by the shrimp* Lysmata amboinensis.

Fair Diving Along the Coast of Amuk Bay

Blue Lagoon

Bottom formation	1
Visibility	.5
Coral variety	1
Fish variety	1
Special	.5

(Some rare species can be found here)

Total:	**4**

Note: This is soon to be a site for a Pertamina oil storage facility

Pura Jepun

Bottom formation	1
Visibility	.5
Coral variety	.5
Fish variety	.5
Special	.5

(Flying gurnards here, also jewel anemones)

Total:	**3**

—Wally Siagian

There are two main dive spots at Padang Bai: Pura Jepun and Tanjung Bungsil. We rate these sites as slightly better than those off Nusa Dua or Sanur, but a damn sight colder. Bring a wet suit if you're going to dive this area. A good, deep chill can take the pleasure out of any dive.

The ride to Padang Bai from the Kuta–Nusa Dua–Sanur triangle is a long, traffic-clogged 60 kilometers. Padang Bai is the port for the five-times-a-day Lombok ferry run, and things can always get a bit congested near the dock area. It's far more convenient to dive this spot from Candi Dasa, just 15 minutes away.

Before diving, you will suit up on the beach, at the restaurant favored by your dive operator. Most small dive groups are taken to the site in little local outriggered fishing canoes powered by small outboard motors. It's usually just two divers per craft, so if you have a large group, the little armada plays follow-the-leader to the site. There will probably be

some spray just as you leave the harbor, and it may follow you further on if the wind is up. Both dive sites are a short 10–15 minutes away. (See map page 106.)

Pura Jepun

We started our first dive about 50 meters from shore, just opposite a small temple shrine (*pura*) called Pura Jepun, after the Balinese word for frangipani, although no flowers were in evidence along the stretch of coast leading to our entry point. (The shrine sits on a little cape, also called Jepun, so the site is sometimes called Tanjung Jepun.)

After leaving the harbor, we headed northeast along the coast, passing Blue Lagoon Bay with an idyllic white sand beach at its back. A rocky point, against which some pretty large waves crashed, marked the end of Blue Lagoon, and from there to the Pura Jepun site the steep hills ended in small cliffs. These look like they drop straight down to the depths, but unfortunately continue only 2–3 meters underwater. At this point the bottom levels off quickly to a wide terrace at 6–10 meters.

We jumped overboard and began our drift dive, pushed back the way we came by a slight, less than one-knot current. Further out from the initial, 6–10 meter terrace, a slight slope eases down to 15–20 meters, followed by flat sand at 40 meters.

After a very quick look in the deeper areas, we restricted ourselves to 6–12 meters, where we had determined most of the animal life was to be found. Coral formations were scattered, although there were quite a num-

---

AT A GLANCE

Padang Bai

Reef type:	Flat-bottomed mixed reef and sandy bottom, some wall
Access:	10–15 min by small canoe
Visibility:	Variable; poor to good, 6–15 m
Current:	Usually gentle, but up to 3 knots
Coral:	Scattered outcrops, fair variety
Fish:	Good variety and numbers
Highlights:	Large feeding Titan triggerfish, blue-spotted stingrays

ber of giant anemones, crinoids of varying colors, odd clumps of tunicates and a few sponges. The bottom remained quite flat across our "flight path" until we reached the rocky point that marks the entrance to Blue Lagoon Bay, where a sheer wall drops close to 40 meters. Visibility throughout the dive was a decent enough 10–12 meters.

Since we remained in quite shallow water during most of the dive, we were treated to several schools of elongated surface feeders: silvery, pencil-thin keeled needlefish (*Platybelone platyura*) and halfbeaks (*Hemiramphus* sp.), and only slightly more substantial arrow barracuda (*Sphyraena novaehollandiae*).

I disturbed a peacock flounder (*Bothus manchus*), delicately patterned to blend in with the sand, quite unlike its namesake. It is only when the fish swims slowly that one can appreciate its colorful back pattern and strangely positioned eyes. The dive's other highlights included a playful few minutes with a cuttlefish, and two small lionfish cowering in a vase sponge. Two blue-spot-

ted stingrays also made a brief appearance but disappeared quickly.

Otherwise, the dive was basically average for Indonesia, which is to say not bad at all. We saw lizardfish, hawkfish, a bright yellow trumpetfish, the odd small grouper, a few oriental sweetlips, goatfish, parrotfish, wrasses, butterflies, emperor and blue-faced angelfish, damselfish—especially plucky sargeant-majors—foxface and lined rabbitfish, a cubefish, a dog-faced puffer, Moorish idols, surgeonfish—including clown surgeonfish and a single electric-blue hepatus tang—and several species of triggerfish. Although the hard coral was not plentiful, we saw a fair number of anemones, crinoids and sponges. Even though I was not carrying a macro set-up, and was looking for overview shots, I noticed a very beautiful nudibranch.

Blue Lagoon

When we arrived off the wall below the rocky point at the end of Blue Lagoon, we dipped down just far enough (25 meters) to see a few larger predatory jacks:

Above: *Photographer Rudie Kuiter caught this moray eel at night in the act of snatching a cardinalfish. The eel is the undulate moray,* Gymnothorax undulatus; *the cardinalfish is an unidentified* Apogon *sp. Tulamben, Bali.*

rainbow runners, a couple of black jacks, and blue-lined sea breams. There are said to be occasional strong down-currents towards the base of this wall, but we felt no pull whatever.

When we were almost out of air, we surfaced and, not seeing our boat around, snorkeled to the beach at Blue Lagoon, stopping along the way to check out a few coral outcrops in the sandy bottom. When we clambered out of the surf in our gear, we were the sunbathers' center of attention. These included four very pretty Italian girls, but unfortunately our boatman showed up immediately, apologizing profusely for the delay. Arivaderci.

Tanjung Bungsil

After a quick lunch, we headed for Tanjung Bungsil, on the south side of Padang Bai harbor. This dive was to be even shallower than the morning's—at the end my computer showed a maximum depth of 10.2 meters. The very slightly sloping bottom was a bit rockier here than at Tanjung Jepun, with corals growing to within a few meters of the sur-

face. Some large carpet anemones grew here in the shallows. In places the visibility dropped to a very poor 5–6 meters.

The good variety of fish life here was similar to the morning's dive. We also saw several six-banded angelfish, and a little group of the curious, headstanding shrimpfish. As I tried (unsuccessfully) to sneak up on a clown triggerfish, a very attractively marked ringtail wrasse (*Cheilinius unifasciatus*) swam up and insisted on posing for a portrait.

The dive's highlight was a Titan triggerfish, doing a headstand while furiously snapping away with its strong teeth at a patch of coral rubble, apparently trying to dislodge an irresistible hors d'oeuvre.

This big boy's energetic activities attracted a host of camp followers looking for a free snack: angelfish, butterflyfish, wrasses, goatfish and even a pair of Moorish idols.

Unfortunately, the triggerfish did not allow human beings into his circle of friends, and abandoned his activities as soon as we approached to within 3 meters.

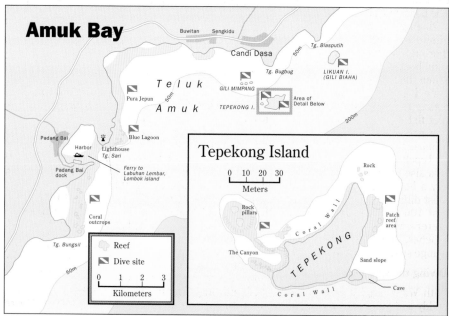

Swirling with the Fish in Tepekong's Canyon

Candi Dasa

Just offshore from Candi Dasa is tiny Tepekong, a little outcrop that offers some spectacular diving. The coral walls are steep, the water is cold, and the current can be strong. But for an experienced diver, drifting with a 3-knot current through The Canyon offers an unforgettable underwater experience.

You can reach Tepekong from anywhere along the southeast coast, but access is easiest from Candi Dasa. There are actually three dive sites here: Tepekong (sometimes called Kambing—"Goat"—Island); Gili Mimpang (three mini-islands sometimes called Batu Tiga, "Three Rocks"); and Biaha Island, sometimes called Likuan Island. (See map opposite.)

Your ride to the dive site is a fishing boat or *jukung,* fitted with a tiny outboard. Two or three divers at most will fit in a *jukung.* The boats must cross the edge of a fringing reef about 75 meters offshore. This will give you a thorough soaking, the skills of your boatmen notwithstanding. When the tide is low, you might even have to get out of the *jukung* to help push it over the reef flat. Once across the reef, you are 10–15 minutes from Mimpang or Tepekong.

Tepekong has the best diving. It is also the coldest—occasionally a bone-chilling 19°C—and most difficult. Tiny Tepekong is just 100 meters long and 50 meters wide. There are no beaches. The sides of the island plunge straight into the sea.

Diving the Canyon

With Wally Siagian as my dive buddy and guide, we twice tried to dive his favorite spot, the southside Canyon, but the combination of over 4 knot current and undertow from swell and waves crashing into Tepekong's western side defeated our attempts. On the third try, however, it worked.

We dropped in about halfway along the western side of Tepekong, descending in a slight current to a sloping bottom at 9 meters, near the vertical underwater continuation of Tepekong's above-water cliff. We were just nearing the bottom when a large Napoleon wrasse appeared at the edge of our 10 meter visibility. He drifted out of sight, as did a school of 30-odd roundfaced batfish (*Platax teira*). We followed the slope, dotted with coral knolls, to 24 meters, then dropped down into a canyon. The Canyon was lined with huge boulders, and bottomed out at 32 meters.

**The Canyon
(a.k.a. The Toilet)**

Bottom formation	3
Visibility	1.5
Coral variety	1
Fish variety	2
Special	1
Total:	**7.5**

—*Wally Siagian*

AT A GLANCE
Candi Dasa

Geography:	Steep coral walls; underwater canyon
Access:	20–30 min by small outboard
Visibility:	Variable; poor to very good; 6–20 meters
Current:	Can be extremely strong, more than 5 knots
Coral:	Excellent coverage and variety
Fish:	Literally teeming with fish
Highlights:	Tepekong's Canyon, good chance to see pelagics
Other:	Very tricky currents, strong surge; uncomfortably cold

---

East Tepekong

Bottom formation	1
Visibility	1
Coral variety	1
Fish variety	2
Special	0
Total:	**4**

Gili Mimpang

Bottom formation	2
Visibility	1.5
Coral variety	1
Fish variety	1.5
Special	1
(Lots of sharks)	
Total:	**7**

—*Wally Siagian*

over a meter in length. Wally thought the fish we saw was an Australian potato cod (*Epinephelus tukula*), perhaps north for a quick vacation.

Groups of schooling fish hung in the current, which "gusted" occasionally to such speeds that I almost felt my mask was going to tear off. We hung on to outcrops, watching schools of rainbow runners, bigeye trevally, sleek unicornfish and little packs of Moorish idols. We occasionally shifted our position, disturbing a resident whitetip shark at one point, and a cubefish at another.

Each coral-covered pinnacle hosted firefish, which flicked their long dorsal spines in the current, and clouds of lyretail coralfish (*Pseudanthias squammipinnis*). These were all at our 5-meter decompression stop.

This dive was one of the best I have experienced in Indonesia. But it was far from easy. Conditions could well have postponed this dive until my time in the area had run out. And even for an experienced diver, this is a tricky dive. Wally doesn't call it "The Toilet" for nothing.

The teeming fish life makes it well worth whatever effort it takes, however. It is particularly easy here to get very close to normally wary fish. You might even see an oceanic sunfish, the strange *Mola mola*. Wally has seen one on three occasions in his more than 100 dives here.

East Tepekong

After one of our aborted attempts on the Canyon, Wally directed our *jukung* to the far eastern end of the island. We dropped into surging, cold water, and shivered as we descended. Visibility was restricted by the water movement to around 8 meters. And the surge was too strong to allow us to peer into the many caves—between 16 and 32 meters—as well as a 10-meter-long passage between several huge boulders

Above: *The little galatheid crab above was first found in 1985 by Wally Siagian at Tulamben, diving with Roger Steene at the time, at 30 meters on the slope past the wreck. A specimen was sent to Dr. Keiji Baba at Kumamoto University in Japan, and he described it—only the second discovered member of its genus—in 1994. It has been named after Wally:* Lauriea siagiani. *These attractive crabs can be found at a number of sites, always living in the outer folds of the barrel sponge* Xestospongia testudinaria.

Here, visibility increased to close to 20 meters and the fish life also increased considerably. So did the current, to 2.5–3 knots. Sometimes the current here swirls around the Canyon with a downward pull, leading to Wally's nickname for the place: "The Toilet."

The conditions that produce this unforgettable experience are usually strong swell from the north or northeast. If these are the conditions on the surface, do not dive the Canyon. Unless you want to be sucked down in a swirling current.

As soon as we entered the Canyon we saw a huge aggregation of sweetlips, 50 or 60 of them, hovering next to a pinnacle: Goldman's sweetlips, oriental sweetlips, and yellow ribbon sweetlips. Then we saw a very healthy looking grouper, well that appear to have fallen from the topside cliff.

We spotted a tuna, a fairly big grouper and a cuttlefish after we made our way down the slope to about 25 meters. The coral cover was good, including both stony corals and soft corals, and several blunt pinnacles sheltered reef fish in shallow pockets.

Fish huddled between overlapping layers of table coral, each irregular "shelf" holding several species. All this was fine, but the strong continuing surge, lack of visibility and cold water led us to surface before our air ran out.

Gili Mimpang

These same conditions plagued our dive on Gili Mimpang, a cluster of three little exposed rocks between Tepekong and the coast of Bali. Despite our wet suits, we were freezing. Descending to the 12-meter bottom, we disturbed a small blue-spotted stingray, and a much larger black-spotted ray. We swam against a slight current to the top of a wall around 30 meters, working our way around detached clumps of coral. About 10 minutes into the dive I was ready to quit, mainly because of the cold, but also because of the increasing current and the restricted visibility. I signalled to Wally and we headed up.

Around 18 meters we hit a thermocline, and life took a very definite turn for the better. Almost instantaneously, the water temperature increased 6°C. Fish life improved considerably as well, beginning with a docile star puffer, three easily spooked (as usual) reef white-tip sharks and several blue-finned trevally. A school of blue-lined snappers buzzed us from above.

As we stopped on top of a pinnacle at around 7–8 meters, a school of bignose unicornfish parted just enough to afford us a glimpse of a Napoleon wrasse on one side and several bumphead parrotfish on the other. A small school of longfin bannerfish accompanied us, from a safe distance, almost to the surface.

Back in the *jukung,* Wally said that had we not turned back, we could well have seen lots of large pelagics ahead. But I was well satisfied, and very happy to be warm and dry.

Below: *A yellow-headed moray eel* (Gymnothorax rueppelliae) *nestled among tube sponges. Bali.*

WALLY SIAGIAN

CEMELUK

Outstanding Variety of Fishes and Corals

Below: *A black-spotted puffer,* Arothron nigropunctatus, *has found the perfect resting place in the leather coral* Sarcophyton. *Bali.*

HELMUT DEBELIUS / IKAN

Divers on a tight schedule could dive Cemeluk in the morning, and the Tulamben wreck—just a few kilometers away—in the afternoon. But these are both excellent dive spots, so why rush? Cemeluk—sometimes called Amed—was hit hard by the coral bleaching caused by El Niño warming in the spring of 1988, particularly in the shallow areas, but recovery is progressing.

Cemeluk is just off Bali's main east coast highway. From the resort areas of the south, the highway passes through Klungkung, then Candi Dasa, then swings inland past Karangasem, skirting 1,175-meter Mt. Seraya, Bali's easternmost mountain. Just before it reaches the coast again, about 10 kilometers before Tulamben, a paved side road from the little town of Culik drops directly to the coast at Amed, 3 kilometers away.

From Amed, the paved road turns right and passes a long stretch of traditional salt works. Two kilometers from Amed, you're in Cemeluk, a fairly small bay with a beach of black, volcanic sand, crowded with dozens of colorful *jukung,* local outrigger fishing canoes powered by sails or small outboards.

Diving Cemeluk

The reef off Cemeluk curves around a rock outcropping just east of town. We took a *jukung* out into the bay, and dropped into a very slight current pushing us southeast along the reef. At about 8 meters we came down on an extensive spread of staghorn *Acropora* teeming with damselfishes and cardinalfishes. A short slope led to a coral wall, where we dropped to 43 meters, hanging there about 8–10 meters above the sandy bottom. The wall was magic.

Schools of fish of several species cascaded down the wall or took the electric stairs back up in orderly, two-way traffic. The numbers were staggering, the best we have seen in Bali and only rarely matched or surpassed to the east. The schools included black triggerfish, lots of bannerfish, black snappers, humpback snappers, pyramid butterflies, and countless others. Further off from the wall, the usual school of

Cemeluk

Teluk

Cemeluk

Reef

0   100

Meters (approx.)

200m

Deep slope

Large outcrops, covered with sea fans

Sand slope

Big gorgonian, concentration of fish (37m)

Large basket sponge

Beginning of the coral wall   29m

59m

48m

Shallow wall (Good for beginners)

18m   30m

8m

59m

9m   Sand slope   25m

Diving

9m

6m

Second coral wall   40m

Rocky overlook

Very good hard coral variety

Large table corals   12m

Black sand bottom (10m–15m)

N   30°

6m

Black sand beach

Hill climb

Snack stand, small pavilion, parking

River

Amed

Amlapura

Note: From parking area, bearing to the beginning of the wall is 30° from North as shown

---

yellowtail fusiliers kept an eye on proceedings.

According to Wally Siagian, my stellar dive guide, by beginning our dive towards the southeast part of Cemeluk Bay we left the best coral formations behind, although there were still impressive outcrops along our 200-odd-meter journey, covered with sponges, sea fans and crinoids. One sponge sheltered a small lionfish, and in another a well-camouflaged tassled scorpionfish would have passed unnoticed except for Wally's sharp eyes.

Towards the end of the dive, the dense growth of sponges and gorgonians created a tunnel between two of the outcrops. Inside, it was wall-to-wall with life. Large barrel sponges poked out from clearings in this forest. A couple of mean-looking Titan triggerfish eyed us with undisguised hate, but refrained from charging. A clown triggerfish approached, then fled. On a small sandy patch next to an outcrop, a little juvenile blue ribbon eel (the juveniles are black) stood his ground bravely.

The larger fish included a longnose emperor, a patrolling giant trevally, and several bluefin trevallys. Two very large tuna, both over a meter and in the 30–40 kilo range, shot by quickly. As we finished the dive, we saw a mismatched pair of Napoleon wrasse: a very large adult and a very small juvenile. Wally often sees reef white-tip sharks here, although we saw none on this day. Our visibility was around 10 meters, but can double under the right conditions. The area is calm year around with only very occa-

No Anchors!

Please remind your guide not to anchor at Cemeluk. It is easy enough for boats to wait without anchoring, and the coral cover here is so rich there is no place to put down an anchor without causing damage.

—Wally Siagian

AT A GLANCE

Cemeluk

Reef type: Coastal reef; flats, slope and wall

Access: Beach; 5 min by small boat

Visibility: Fair to very good, 10–20 meters

Current: Mild

Coral: Excellent; best hard coral variety in Bali

Fish: Excellent numbers, superb variety

Highlights: Density of fish on the deep wall; coral species just off beach sional surge and high current conditions.

A Dive from the Beach

A dive directly from the black sand and pebble beach at Cemeluk gave a very different perspective: smaller fish, but a great number and variety of corals. We had barely donned our fins and dropped to the less than two-meter depth when we saw a scattered group of orange-band surgeonfish (*Acanthurus olivaceous*), some 15 strong. Their bright orange marks are distinctive, and we had seen very few in previous dives.

Neon blue devils darted around, two parrotfish paddled furiously, and a graceful pair of Moorish idols swam into view. Two yellow-margined triggerfish were doing headstands while furously blowing at the sand hoping to uncover some worm or spiny thing to eat. A dozen striped convict tangs (*Acanthurus triostegus*), which we had not seen in Bali before, swam across our path. All this within 15 meters of shore!

Just a bit further out (we were heading due north) all life stopped, the sloping grey sand offering nothing until we saw crate-like enclosures holding bits of coral, an experiment conducted to determine coral growth in this environment. A few dozen meters beyond the crates, several scattered coral outcrops jutted up from the sand, little oases in the sandy desert.

From the outcrops we headed east at about 20 meters, crossing a stretch of grey sand bottom until we came to the reef wall, which follows the coast from this point. About 10 meters from the surface, the irregular wall started sprouting fan gorgonians and pastel trees of *Dendronephthya*. Tube sponges were numerous.

The reef here is topped by a relatively flat area, just 2–5 meters deep and 30 or more meters from the rocky shore.

The corals in the relatively small area between here and the sandy beach were heavily damaged by the warm episode in the spring of 1998. Many were bleached and killed. It will be interesting to watch the progress of recovery over the years.

Below: *An undulate or orange-striped triggerfish,* Balistapus undulatus, *takes shelter in a sponge. This speciman is a male. Bali.*

The *Liberty* Wreck, Bali's Most-visited Site

At first sight, the little village of Tulamben is rather uninviting. Its beach is a spread of black sand covered by smooth, fist-size rocks, the waterworn remains of rubble cast here by Gunung Agung's 1963 eruption. In the dry season, the countryside assumes a nondescript shade of brown.

Like all the north coast villages, there are no lush rice fields here—Gunung Agung and the other mountains steal the rain, which comes from moisture-laden air that blows in from the south. Thus South Bali is the island's rice bowl.

What brings people to Tulamben is not visible from above water, however. People wake up early, fight the snarled traffic from the tourist centers of the south and emerge from their *bemos,* groggy and cross, for only one reason: to dive the wreck of the *Liberty* at Tulamben.

The Liberty

Just 30 meters from the beach at Tulamben is a World War I–era cargo ship, broken up but impressively large, stretching along more than 100 meters of steeply sloping sand. The top of the wreck is just 3 meters underwater; the bottom is at 29 meters. (See map page 114.)

On January 11, 1942, this ship was hit by torpedoes from a Japanese submarine while crossing the Lombok Strait (See note at right). The damage was critical, but two destroyers hitched up to the ship and tried to tow it to the port at Singaraja. The wounded cargo ship was taking on too much water, however, and her crew ran the vessel up on the beach at Tulamben. There she stayed there until 1963. Local entrepreneurs stripped the boat of its cargo—one source says raw rubber and railroad parts—and were in the process of cutting her up for scrap when Gunung Agung exploded in 1963. The explosion was disasterous, killing thousands and destroying vast tracts of fertile riceland to the south. It also pushed the *Liberty* off the beach to its present location, in the process splitting the hull in two.

Welcoming Committee

Divers simply walk out from the beach, spit in their masks, and go. Sometimes the waves are up, churning up the sand and turning a suited-up diver into an ungainly creature. And the big smooth stones that serve as a beach are always hard on the feet—bring diving boots! Never mind these small indignities, however. This dive is most decidedly worth it. Wave action is

Tulamben Wreck	
Bottom formation	2
Visibility	1.5
Coral variety	1.5
Fish variety	2
Special	1
Total:	**8**

AT A GLANCE
Tulamben

Reef type:	*Liberty* wreck; wall
Access:	Beach; ship is 30 meters offshore
Visibility:	Fair to good, 12–15 meters
Current:	None or moderate, 1 knot
Coral:	Good growth of encrusting animals on wreck; fine coral on wall
Fish:	Superb variety, excellent numbers
Highlights:	Full moon night dive on wreck
Other:	Fish on wreck are regularly fed and quite tame; during midday, wreck can be crowded

Some notes on the *Liberty*

The Liberty was a U.S. Army cargo ship built in 1918 by the Federal Ship Building Company in Kearny, New Jersey. She was 395 ft. (120 m.) long, 55 ft. wide, and grossed 6211 tons. Despite her early date of manufacture, the ship had a turbine engine.

The Liberty is not, as is sometimes (Continued next pg.)

suggested, a Liberty class ship, which are piston-engined ships built during World War II.

At the time the Liberty was torpedoed, 4:15 a.m. on January 11, 1942, the ship was carrying materiél from Australia to the Philppines. The Japanese sub that torpedoed the Liberty, I-166, was itself sunk by the British submarine Telemachus off Penang, Malaysia, on July 17, 1944.

—Research by Bruce Watkins

strongest during the southeast monsoon, late June through August and again—but somewhat less—from late November through January.

As soon as you dump the air out of your BC and drop to the black sandy bottom, you know that you've made the right move. Right away you meet a colony of spotted garden eels (*Heteroconger hassi*), heads and bodies swaying in the current like plants in a breeze. Their tails remain in the sand as they snap plankton from the current. As you get closer the eels shoot back into their burrows, disappearing into the sand like an illusion. At this disturbance, goatfishes hit the sand, searching for juicy tidbits.

You look up and here comes the welcoming committee: several species of snubnose chubs, sweetlips, parrotfishes and a small army of fearless sergeant-majors, not so numerous elsewhere in Bali. These plucky little damselfishes swim right up to your face, to the point where you can even touch them. If you've brought a camera, excercise restraint. If you don't watch out, you'll shoot your whole roll before even reaching the wreck.

Electric blue neon damsels, darting around with a seeming inexhaustible store of energy, stand out vividly against the black sand and rocks. As I watched, their happy antics were interrupted. A hawkfish pounced,

Tulamben

Key to wreck inset

1. Door (9m)
2. Cannon (18m)
3. Juvenile fishes (18m)
4. Tunnel (8m–16m)
5. Tunicate wall (8m–18m)
6. Flashlight fish (21m)
7. Pillar house (14m–17m)
8. Boom with sweetlips (6m)
9. Cleaner shrimp station (17m)
10. Gorgonian overhang (18m)
11. Soft coral "desk" (7m)
12. Lone black coral (12m)
13. Sign to beach on stone
14. Best part of wreck (18m–29m)

Liberty wreck

Bearing to near end of wreck is 60° from North taken from two coconut trees closest to beach

0 10 20 30
Meters

Singaraja
Area of inset
Liberty wreck
Toilet

Parking lot
Palm Beach Paradise Hotel w/ dive shop
Good, shallow coral
35m
18m Bali Timur Hotel
Kantor Kepala Desa (Village headman's office)
Ganda Maju

TULAMBEN

Big gorgonian on corner (29m)
Deep slope
64m Basket sponges
35m 15m
35m Short overhang; the best spot
Sand slope Temple
Swimming Pool Salt-making operations
Hill climb
Large tree
To Candi Dasa

Reef
0   300
Meters

snatching a small damsel in a flash. A sudden jerk, the damsel's head disappeared, and the hawkfish resumed its motionless posture, looking for his next meal. Small groupers, cornetfish and trumpetfish, the odd parrotfish and a few morays inhabited patches of coral along our route.

The black sand bottom around the wreck makes an excellent background for fish photos—but be careful with auto-exposure cameras, as the meter will want to overexpose your shots. On and around the ship, carefully monitor your buoyancy. Bumping the wreck could lead to a nasty burn from a stinging hydroid, or even a more serious sting from a lionfish or scorpionfish. More likely, however, you will just damage the fragile organisms encrusting the ship. Move slowly and carefully. This is also the best way to get close to the fish.

On to the Wreck

The wreck of the *Liberty* lies parallel to shore on a steep sand slope. Part of the superstructure is within snorkeling distance from the surface. The hulk is broken into large chunks, and there are lots of big holes in the hull, making it easy to explore the vessel's innards. Don't expect to find any interesting mementoes inside, however. Remember, this ship was stripped while still on the beach.

The treasures of Tulamben are swimming in and around the wreck: hundreds of species of fish in good numbers, most having become semi-tame and used to divers. We saw several fairly large—a meter or so—specimens, but it is the huge numbers of medium-sized fish—30–80 centimeters—that make the wreck such an interesting dive. If you planned just one or two dives here, we guarantee you will regret not having more time.

Unfortunately, not everything

is perfect in Tulamben. When we dove there in late June, visibility was just 12–15 meters, and this seldom improves much.

Expert underwater photographers and marine biologists, men like Rudie Kuiter, John E. Randall and Roger Steene, dive Tulamben over and over, coming up with great shots and even new species. Australian Rudie Kuiter, author of the definitive guide to Indonesian reef fishes, estimates that some 400 species of reef fishes live on the wreck, which is also visited by perhaps 100 species of pelagics. These are remarkable numbers for an area just 100 meters long.

On our dives we never saw any sharks or other really big fish at Tulamben. There were a few good sized tuna, bonito, several 80-centimeter plus emperors, and jacks, Napoleon wrass-

Above: *A school of lunar fusiliers,* Caesio lunaris, *at the Tulamben wreck. Tulamben, Bali.*

Just off the beach in front of the Palm Beach Paradise Hotel and dive shop are some excellent shallow water corals, a site Wally calls Coral Gardens.

Coral Gardens

Bottom formation	1
Visibility	1
Coral variety	1.5
Fish variety	1.5
Special	1
(Easy beach dive)	
Total:	**6**

es pushing the meter mark, and one huge 80-centimeter scribbled filefish. On the sandy bottom next to the wreck, where I thought rays would abound, I saw only one small eagle ray, and a very large blue-spotted stingray. Both ducked for cover before I could say "Glenfiddich." We also saw a meter-long barracuda, but one of my dive partners, Wolfgang Bresigk of Baruna Water Sports, says a 1.5 meter barracuda regularly forages on the wreck.

Another dive buddy, Wally Siagian, saw a huge oceanic sunfish (*Mola mola*) close to the wreck, four times in a one-week span. On one of these occasions, he saw this most unusual fish being cleaned by several singular bannerfish (*Heniochus singularis*). Off to one side of the wreck Wally took us to visit a colorful black-spotted moray eel (*Gymnothorax melanospilos*), a beautifully marked animal with a yellow body and black markings. The eel lives at the base of a barrel sponge at about 40 meters.

A Swarm of Beggars

Arriving at the wreck, we stayed shallow and settled near the upper edge of one of the ship's large holds. The top of the open hold lies at around 5 meters, with its bottom at around 14 meters. The superstructure reaches to couple of meters of the surface.

It took a good ten minutes before the swarms of sergeant-majors, a couple of insistent crescent wrasses, and a dozen large bignose unicornfish all understood that we had no food for them and stopped bothering us. Fish here are often fed by divers or their guides, which is why they allow divers to get so close. Bananas, strange as this may seem, are their standard fare. Clearly nonplussed that we had not brought any food, the fish finally left us alone—but not before the sergeant-majors gave us a few nips.

Once the beggars left us alone, we were able to look over the swarms of fishes living on and around the wreck. Schools of several dozen golden and lined rabbitfishes hung almost motionless in 6–7 meters of water. Standing out like a sore thumb in this group, was an occasional big-eye emperor, or large red snapper. Below this group were bright pairs of coral and foxface rabbitfishes. These beauties were a bit nervous, and it took patience to get within good camera range.

Lone snappers and mixed schools of sweetlips also inhabited the shallow areas near the northeast corner of the wreck. We identified five species of sweetlips: clown sweetlips, Sulawesi sweetlips, striped sweetlips, Goldman's sweetlips, and, most numerous of all, the oriental sweetlips. These fish allowed us to approach to one meter.

Surgeonfishes were common, and inhabited various depths. We frequently saw yellowfin surgeonfish, orangeband surgeonfish, Thompson's surgeonfish, and clown surgeonfish. We saw a few orangespine unicornfish, with their curious mandrill-like faces, and a few male spotted unicornfish. Bignose unicornfish wandered the wreck in large schools, mostly consisting of drab females, but with an occasional bright blue courting male, his magnificent tail filaments undulating with each flip. These fish allowed us to get very close, and we saw them on every dive.

A variety of fairly large parrotfishes (40–75 centimeters) added color to every dive. With a bit of patience we could get to within a meter of the blue-barred parrotfishes, but the others—mostly palenose parrotfish and bullethead parrotfish—were more shy.

Small damsels were common, in particular golden damselfish.

These bold little animals frequently nipped us if we got too close to their home turf.

Butterflyfishes are not present here in overwhelming numbers. Perhaps the dearth of hard corals is responsible for this, as many butterflyfishes are polyp feeders, some relying completely on this source of nutrition. The vaguaries of memory have reduced the list to six: lined butterflyfish, raccoon butterflyfish, threadfin butterflyfish, Bennett's butterflyfish, spotnose butterflyfish and the Pinocchio-like longnose butterflyfish.

I had seen Titan triggerfish—a sometimes nasty animal with a distinctive "mustache" and loopy eyes—on many previous dives in eastern Indonesia, sometimes as many as a half-dozen in a single dive. They had always been very wary, never allowing me to get close. On the wreck, however, they were much more relaxed, allowing me to get within 1.5 meters. These were also among the largest I had seen, doing justice to the name "Titan."

Angelfishes were not particularly abundant on the wreck, but those that I saw here were among the largest specimens I have seen. We spotted blue-faced angels, blue-girdled angels, emperor angels and regal angels. None of these fellows shamelessly coddled up to divers to beg for food or out of curiosity, but kept a healthy distance from the human visitors. Moorish idols here shared the same trait; none was as bold as the similarly marked longfin bannerfish.

Groupers prowled around on every dive, including red-mouth groupers and white-lined groupers, although the real stars were the aptly named peacock grouper, and its even more colorful relatives: the coral grouper, the flagtail grouper, and the black-tipped grouper. The largest groupers we saw were the blotchy grouper, and the saddleback grouper, sometimes called the giant coral trout.

Sea Fans and Sponges

The encrusted wreck is mostly a community of opportunists: soft corals, sponges, gorgonians, hydroids, bryozoans, tunicates, bivalves and crinoids. It is still

Above: *An emperor angelfish,* Pomacanthus imperator, *on the wreck at Tulamben. Although the steel structure has not yet been much colonized by hard corals, it is heavily encrusted with soft corals, gorgonians and hydrozoans.*

Enoplometopus debelius: A Reef Lobster of One's Own

It was night, and 15 meters down I glided along the sloping reef in pitch black water. I could hear the noise of my bubbles much more clearly than during the day. A pair of cardinalfish swam into the beam from my lamp and, startled, fled at high speed. I had learned to find my way around this beautiful reef off Tulamben during the afternoon, and I was now looking for reef lobsters and other big crustacea as I always do on night dives.

I shone my light into every crevice and cave. Here it fell on dancing shrimps, and there on a marbled shrimp. I saw the brightly colored common reef lobster, *Enoplometopus occidentalis,* and snapped two pictures before it could hide. Suddenly the beam of my light came to rest on a patch of violet. I looked again, and made out the shape of a reef lobster, crouching in the coral rubble.

I could scarcely breathe as I adjusted the focus of the camera, for this species looked completely new to me. The entire body of the little 10-centimeter lobster

Above: *A gravid female* Enoplometopus debelius. *Author and photographer Helmut Debelius is a skilled aquarist, and has succeeded in spawning the lobsters in captivity.*

was sprinkled with small violet dots, an enchanting sight in the bright light. I snapped off three shots as the animal slowly backed up.

Quickly, I laid my camera aside and took a small net from my wetsuit and placed it behind the lobster. With my free hand I gently touched its pincers and, as I had expected, the animal dashed backwards into the net. "A shame for you," I muttered to the lobster, but when it comes to scientific aims, I have no mercy.

Later, my suspicions were confirmed: Dutch crustacean expert Prof. L.B. Holthuis examined the animal and said that it was a new species. He named it after me: *Enoplometopus debelius.*

The Reef Lobsters

Reef lobsters are beautiful, but rarely seen inhabitants of the holes and crevices of Indonesian reefs. In size and shape they resemble freshwater crayfish more than the common spiny lobsters of Indo-Pacific reefs. These omnivorous creatures emerge only at night, to feed on carrion, worms and anything else they can catch—even a sleeping fish.

—*Helmut Debelius*

Left: Enoplometopus debelius *in one of the author's tanks in Germany.*

much too soon for a really large accumulation of hard corals. In less than 30 years, however, great sections of the wreck's iron hull have been smothered in a bright encrustation of life.

Great sea fans, gorgonians up to 2 meters across, jut from the bow section. Several large trees of black coral (*Antipathes* sp.) grow here safe from the jeweler. Sponges, tunicates and hydroids crowd each other for a holdfast. In places, there are great aggregations of thorny oysters, their bright "lips" visible through parted shells. Crinoids cling to every stable growth—a sponge, a gorgonian—and unfurl their arms to the current. In one of the the shallower spots, a growth of hard plate coral has already reached over 3 meters.

The many "cleaner stations" around the wreck offer a great show. Fish line up to be cleaned by one of the small cleaner wrasses (*Labroides*). We saw both bluestreak and bicolor cleaner wrasses at work here. Some divers have actually succeeded in having the fish pick bits of food out from between their teeth—although this requires holding one's breath from a minute or so.

Night Dive on the Wreck

Daytime dives are extraordinary on the wreck, but a night dive, especially around full moon, will be among the most memorable dives you will make.

As we walked along the beach to the entry point, three local fishing outriggers sailed silently by in the moonlight. We waded out, took our bearings, and headed toward the wreck. As we approached the ship, we extinguished our lights. The large hulk loomed above us, a massive ghostly presence with the bright moon a distant pinpoint of light.

We kept our lights off for a bit. Each fin-stroke stirred up a twinkling trail of biolumines-

Above: *Closeup of a soft coral. Note the small goby in the background.*

cence. Peering into the dark hold of the wreck, we saw a magical show of zigzagging lights. These were the curious flashlight fishes (*Anomalops*), each possessed of a bioluminescent organ beneath its eye.

Many sections of the wreck provide the overhangs preferred by the large, bright orange polyps of *Tubastraea* and *Dendrophyllia*. These corals are best appreciated at night. At night one can also see crinoids crawling about in search of a new holdfast, or perhaps even swimming, their feathery legs opening and closing in the manner of a octopus. Sometimes when we trained our lights on the wreck, hundreds of red shrimp eyes stared back.

Here again, however, the fish are the real stars of the show. We saw a couple of unconcerned common lionfish, and a stunning spotfin lionfish. A large red parrotfish slept, secure in its mucous cocoon, under a shallow overhang. We approached a big map puffer, and several groggy unicornfish.

The most interesting fish we came upon was an absolutely huge barred filefish (*Cantherhines dumerilii*). I spotted the big fella at least 10 meters above me, sleeping under a large lacy plate of coral growing horizontally from the wreck.

My computer screamed its warning just as I made for this animal, but I paid it no heed. My

Tulamben Wall

Bottom formation	2
Visibility	1.5
Coral variety	1.5
Fish variety	1
Special	1
Total:	**7**

subject was sleeping in a tilted position. After a few shots, I pushed him a bit to correct his posture. He didn't particularly appreciate this, but obliged me anyway. I moved him into the open water. A few more shots, and he had had enough, charging straight for me. We photographers really are a pain.

A Popular Site

Tulamben is probably the most popular dive spot in Indonesia (and justifiably so), and during the daily rush, from about 11:30 a.m. to 4 p.m., an average of three or four groups of about a dozen divers each visit the wreck. The ship is big, however, and most of the groups just zip by. But serious divers seldom appreciate crowds, and novice divers, not having mastered buoyancy control, have the unfortunate habit of thrashing up clouds of sand with their fins.

Some of our best dives on Tulamben were in the early morning and late afternoon, before and after the crowds. The only way to do this is to overnight in Tulamben (see "Bali Practicalities" page 280, 285).

Staying overnight also takes a lot of the logistical headaches out of night dives, but be sure to stash a towel on the beach. The 10-minute walk back can be chilly. For day trippers, there's a shower at the toilet block on the beach, next to the dive site, but sometimes there is no water, and there can be long lines.

The Tulamben Wall

Should you want to take a break from wreck diving, there is a good coral wall beginning just off the eastern end of the beach. The rocky knoll southeast of town plunges straight down into the sea, and coral grows along its face. Be careful who you dive with—or what group you follow—as the fine gray sediment here is easily stirred up.

Just as we began our dive, heading down over sloping grey sand, a good sized barracuda cruised by—but that was the only big fish we saw during the dive. We soon found our wall: it has a nice overhang around the 18 meter mark, and drops to a sand bottom at just over 60 meters. We explored only to the 30 meter mark, following the ridge to its furthest extension. This wall does not host huge numbers of fish, but like the wreck has a tremendous variety.

At one point along the dive, Wally stopped at a shrimp cleaning station, manned by the candy-striped cleaner shrimp *Lysmata amboinensis.* Taking out his regulator and opening his mouth, he soon had two of the fellows working on the remains of his lunch. Others were eager for leftovers, but there are limits to Wally's breath-holding capabilities.

Large barrel sponges sprouted from the slope, and sponges in general were abundant here—tube sponges, vase sponges, and encrusting sponges. Once we left the wall, the coral grew only in small knolls.

The final part of the dive was a short glide over black sand. This environment, though it at first appears featureless, is home to many interesting animals, including skeleton shrimp, ornate ghost pipefish, and juvenile scorpionfish. If you have air left, take a close look.

The Tulamben Wall is known for rare species, including the comet (*Calloplesiops altivelis*), a beautiful fish with elaborate finnage and a false eye-spot. The posture and coloration of the comet mimics the spotted moray eel (*Gymnothorax meleagris*).

For the keen-eyed observer, new species are waiting here to be discovered. A few years ago science added a new fairy basslet to its list, *Pseudanthias bimaculeatus,* first discovered here.

PEMUTERAN

Good Diving and Comfortable Resorts

Pemuteran

It's a long drive from the Nusa Dua/Sanur/Kuta area to Menjangan, which adds up to a lot of time on the road for just a couple of dives. But there is an excellent alternative: stay in Pemuteran, which has several nice bungalow accommodations and several dive operators, including the pioneering Reef Seen Aquatics. Pemuteran is located just a few kilometers east of Menjangan on the north coast, on a little bay.

Reef Seen runs its own boat to Menjangan, but divers often prefer the closer locations. The latter are all just a few minutes away. There are five main dive spots, well explored by the operator, each worth several dives.

The dive center caters to small groups of divers, especially to those staying for several days, for whom discounts are available. Independent divers, not requiring a guide, can save a bundle on both day and night dives from shore. We highly recommend this dive business, developed by PADI instructor Chris Brown, a pro in all senses of the term, who also takes concrete measures to preserve the marine ecology.

The atmosphere in Pemuteran is quiet and pleasant, and the Pondok Sari Beach Bungalows and more upmarket Taman Sari are very nicely designed: The rooms are spare and decorated with natural woods and clean white sheets on the beds; the bathrooms are open to the sky, and feature dripping Japanese bamboo pipes and smooth black river pebbles. A very comfortable, and romantic place.

All the sites Chris Brown has pioneered off Pemuteran are small *takas*, or bank reefs. He is constantly investigating new sites, however.

The diving here is generally good year-round, with very occasional rough seas during the southeast monsoon, May–July. The very best times are from March to early May, and September through January. The rainy season, during the northwest monsoon from January to early March, usually brings heavy rain only in the late afternoon ar at night. Water temperatures almost always are around 28°–32°C. Visibility is good, but not as clear as Menjangan under the best of conditions. There is hardly any current, and this is a good site for beginners.

Napoleon Reef

"Napoleon Reef," is a flat-topped, underwater mound, about the size of a football field. At its shallowest, to bottom rises to about 5–10 meters of the surface. The reef is covered with sponges and corals, including great table-top

---

AT A GLANCE
Pemuteran

Reef type: Near shore banks and mounds

Access: Shore, or a few min by boat

Visibility: Good, 10–15 meters

Current: Very slight

Coral: Good numbers and variety; abundant soft corals

Fish: Good number, good variety

Highlights: Deep end of Napoleon Reef, occasional mantas

Other: Convenient dives, operator is pioneering new sites.

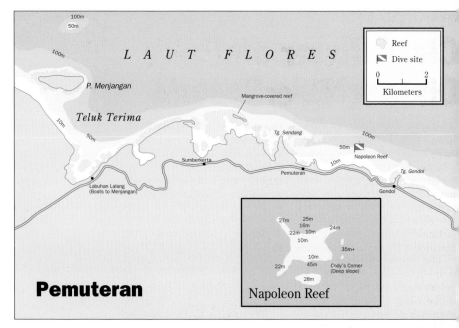

Acropora reaching a diameter of 5 meters. From the top, the profile follows a gentle slope to 35 meters, with very good invertebrate life. Two enormous barrel sponges serve as landmarks. Fish life is quite good. Large cuttlefish are often seen. Occasionally, manta rays appear to feed across the reeftop.

The southeastern point of Napoleon drops down to 35 meters, where there is an excellent deep reef with soft corals and whip corals, dubbed "Cody's Corner."

Close Encounters

"Pertamuan Dekat" (literally "Close Encounters") takes its name from the big fish here which allow—and even initiate—close encounters with divers: reef sharks, tuna, mackerel, barracuda and jacks, and an occasional large grouper or Napoleon wrasse. Even whale sharks have been seen here on occasion

Lebar Reef

At Lebar (literally "wide") Reef, steep slopes drop to flat sand at about 25 meters. Out over the sand, coral outcrops appear at 25 meters and again at 35 meters Both the reeftop and sides of the *taka* are covered with thickets o staghorn *Acropora*, some with colorful blue tips, interspersed with tabletops *Acropora* and far gorgonians.

Kebun Batu

Kebun Batu ("Rock Garden") is just a 5-minute snorkel from shore. Here a huge boulder rises vertically from about 18 meters to just 3 meters from the surface The rock, full of crevices and small, shallow caves, serves as a hotel to many fish. Elsewhere the substrate shows a mixture o sponges, hard and soft corals This is a very good night dive.

Kebun Chris

Kebun Chris ("Chris's Garden") is the dive operators current favorite site. Diving begins just 20 meters from his back door with hard corals starting at less than a meter's depth and continuing on down to about 10 meters This reef spreads continues for about 300 meters, parallelling the shoreline.

Clear Water off Bali's Distant 'Deer' Island

Menjangan Island—the name means "deer"—hangs just off-shore of the mountainous point in far northwestern Bali. Because the island is in a protected position, currents and wind-generate waves are rarely a bother, and the reefs here offer fine diving, particularly for beginning and intermediate divers. Occasionally, the water can be crystal clear—a snorkeler, distinct, 50 meters above you—and the rest of the time visibility seldom drops to less than 25 meters.

The island is part of Bali Barat National Park, a protected reserve area that encompasses much of Bali's little-populated western end. (See map page 125.) The drive from the resort areas of the south is at least three hours, the first hour through the thick traffic that envelops Denpasar like a fog.

Craggy Walls

The coral walls around Menjangan are vertical down to 30–60 meters, and then slope outward. The reef surface is particularly rugged: caves, grottoes, crevasses and funnel-like splits break up the coral wall, and the surface is textured with little nooks and crannies. Gorgonians of many kinds reach large sizes here, and huge barrel sponges are abundant. Soft corals blanket the colorful walls all the way down.

We found the variety of fish here to be somewhat inferior to other dive sites—we ask for a lot!—but the numbers are good and some of the fish are quite bold, as guides feed them regularly. We were blessed with a curious pack of half a dozen fully grown roundfaced batfish, and

two aggregations of bignose unicornfish. A few individuals from a large school of longfin bannerfish approached us, but the majority kept a discreet distance, as did the yellowback fusiliers, which accompany almost every dive in Indonesia.

Small boats ferry divers from the Nature Reserve dock at

AT A GLANCE
Menjangan

Reef type:	Walls, particularly rugged; wreck
Access:	30 min by boat from Labuan Lalang post
Visibility:	Excellent to superb, 25–50 meters
Current:	Very slight
Coral:	Very good numbers and variety; abundant soft corals
Fish:	Good number, only average variety
Highlights:	"Anker" wreck
Other:	Past 60 meters, can find the rare *Genicanthus bellus* here

---

Labuhan Lalang to Menjangan's small beach, where gearing up takes place in the sandy-bottomed shallows. The edge of the reef terrace is at 1–5 meters, and a V-shaped delta of sand points the way out to the edge.

Guides usually take their groups to the east (left) on their first dive—keep an eye out for a huge gorgonian at 18 meters—and down to 15–30 meters, and then back through the shallows (5–10 meters) on the way back. After a lunch on the beach, the group goes west (right). Here the wall has much more relief, and the guides send their boat to pick up divers at the end of their dive, returning them directly to the Nature Reserve dock at Labuhan Lalang.

On the second dive, we saw a couple of names carved into sponges. Please don't join the ranks of the morons.

The Anchor Wreck

Menjangan's western tip holds a deeper, but more interesting dive on an old wreck. The so-called "Anker" wreck is just off the coast, near a small dock and guardpost maintained by the Park Service (PHPA). (See map opposite.) The guardpost—"Pos II"—is about a 30-minute boat ride; our craft anchored about 75 meters from the beach at a point designated by our guide. (Note: few guides know the location of this wreck.)

We entered the water near the reef edge, and dropped some 5 meters through very clear water (more than 20 meters visibility) right onto the large coral-encrusted anchor of our sunken ship. Dropping over the reef edge, we followed a fairly steep slope with bits and pieces of wreckage and anchor chain down to 30 meters where the ship was resting, prow shoreward. Along the way, we saw a reef white-tip shark (sharks and rays are common here) and a few lizardfishes.

It seems obvious that the craft, probably a copper-sheathed sailor from the last century, tried to anchor just off the reef, broke the anchor chain, sunk and slid back to its resting place on the sloping sand bottom. It's a small ship, just 25 meters long, and its stern sits in 45 meters of water.

Flat rectangular sheets, perhaps copper sheathing material, lay in what had been the hold, which also contains an assortment of ceramic and glass bottles. These perhaps had contained *arak,* a powerful local booze distilled from palm wine that had been a major trade item of the last century. Miraculously, previous divers have not stolen all the bottles—yet.

There were fewer fish on the wreck than usual, according to my guide, but this was because a group of divers had just passed through. We saw several snap-

Below: *A dive boat off Menjangan Island.*

Menjangan Island

Reef
Dive site

0   1   2
Kilometers

MENJANGAN I.

358m
124m
100m
Tg. Bedak
Tg. Pasir
73m
Area of
detail below
169m
200m
90m
Tg. Batu
Licin
55m
100m
Teluk Terima
3m
Randung Agung
338m
Banyuwedang
"Reef Seen"
Dive Center
+ Singaraja
Prapat Agung ▲
Labuhan Lalang
Boats to Menjangan
Ferry to
Ketapang, Java
Gilimanuk
Teluk Gilimanuk

BALI   BARAT   NATIONAL   PARK

Sumberklampek

Key to inset

1. Pos II ranger hut; sand beach
2. Best diving route
3. Underwater cave (18m)
4. Pos I ranger hut; sand beach
5. Anchor wreck (7m)
6. Sand slope
7. Underwater bay; nice overhang
8. Diving route; best for snorkeling

277m
200m
124m
86m
"Bat cave"
100m
MENJANGAN I.
71m
52m
102m
160m
200m

Menjangan Island

---

pers, sweetlips, goatfishes, wrasses and Moorish idols. In the vicinity of the wreck, visibility dropped to just 10 meters, again perhaps because of the last group. Large gorgonians grow on the wreck as well as on the slope leading to it. The wreck and the area around it was dominated by soft corals. The sandy slope beyond the wreck was largely bare.

After less than 10 minutes, we decided to ascend a bit, partially because of the depth, but mostly because my guide had said earlier that the reef life was most abundant above, and a bit south of the wreck. He was certainly right. On our slow upward progress, diagonally to the slope,

we crossed a slow, orderly cascade of surgeonfish, broken up by two bright, terminal male filament-finned parrotfish, chasing each other at top speed.

Here, and in the shallows above, were more species of parrotfish than we have ever seen on a single dive. There were also many unicornfish, with the bluespine unicornfish being the most numerous. Several large and colorful bignose unicornfish tried hard to keep their harems under control, but on our approach, the ladies beat a hasty retreat into nearby minicaves. A large, spread-out school of longfin bannerfish was much less concerned with our presence.

The butterflyfishes were well

Menjangan

Wally Siagian rates the various sites around Menjangan Island from 6 to 7.

He figures the cave along the south coast (#3 on the map above) has perhaps the most interesting structure of any of the sites.

represented, especially the masked bannerfish (*Heniochus monoceros*). We saw a large pinnate batfish, and several small roundfaced batfish. Rabbitfishes, fairy basslets and damselfish were abundant. Perched on coral knobs and gorgonians were two species of hawkfishes, tiny falco hawkfish, and curious longnose hawkfish. From 20 meters on up, stretches of the coral face were cut with caves and narrow, vertical funnels. These offered refuge to soldierfishes and medium-sized groupers, including a couple of clownish polkadot groupers (*Cromileptes altivelis*). A pair of longnose emperors appeared against the dark blue sea background.

Back in the shallows—5–7 meters—our visibility returned to its original 20+ meters. Here we saw two red snappers, and a small school of blackspotted snappers. A pair of Clark's anemonefish, living in a beautiful green-tentacled anemone, challenged us to a brawl. The tentacles of this anemone (*Entactmaea quadricolor*) have strange, bulbous tips. Nearby, a tassled

scorpionfish did not defy anyone secure with the power of its venom. Moorish idols were unusually abundant, but shy.

Colorful Picasso triggerfish played hide and seek amidst the coral, and a large scribbled file fish seemed unconcerned as we closed in on him to within a half a meter for a photo. Two Titan triggerfish, intent on each other, took little notice of us, nor did a small patrol of bumphead parrot fish, following their meter-plus leader. But a school of black triggerfish seemed almost to wish us Godspeed. We reluctantly left our fantasy playground, out of film and almost out of air.

Getting to Menjangan

Most of the people who dive Menjangan sleep in the Kuta-Nusa Dua–Sanur tourist triangle. They are picked up around 7:30 a.m. by one of the dive operators with filled tanks, weights, any rented gear and box lunches already packed in the minivan. For the first hour or so of the three-hour ride, you might as well catch up on your sleep as the driver maneuvers out of the

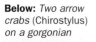

Below: *Two arrow crabs* (Chirostylus) *on a gorgonian*

heavy traffic surrounding Denpasar and continuing past the town of Tabanan. The next hour and a half are worth opening your eyes for, with wide spreads of terraced rice fields reaching to the sea on the left.

The road is a good one (it's the main Java–Bali highway) and the drivers are quite aggressive—if you get nervous at such things, stay out of the front seat. As you approach the town of Negara, the land becomes drier, and there are lots of coconut plantations producing copra. Past Negara, it's a half hour to Cekek, the headquarters of the Bali Barat (West) National Park, just 3 kilometers short of Gilimanuk, the ferry crossing to Java. Macaques, looking for handouts, line the road a bit before Cekik, and after the turnoff for the 12-kilometer stretch to Labuhan Lalang. Labuhan Lalang is a total of 125 kilometers from Denpasar.

At the boat landing, while you register with the park service—name, nationality, passport number—all your gear is unloaded from the minivan into a boat, big enough for six divers and all their accompanying gear.

While driving through west Bali, keep your eyes out for an unusual bird, endemic to this area. The Bali starling, or Rothschild's myna, (*Leucopsar rothschildi*) is a crested, snow-white bird with black on its wing-points and the tip of its tail, and a bright blue patch of skin around its eyes. Unfortunately, you will almost certainly not see one, as fewer than 100 are thought to remain here.

As a cage bird, Rothschild's myna fetches a very high price; there are many more now in captivity than in the wild. Do not be fooled if you see a white, crested myna with a black tail and wings. This is the black-winged starling (*Sturnus melanopterus*). It has much more black on it than the Bali starling, and the skin patch around its eyes is yellow.

It's just short of a half-hour ride to Menjangan, and on the way you can see three of Java's eastern-most volcanoes. As you approach Menjangan, keep a lookout for dolphins. Menjangan island is uninhabited—except, of course, by deer.

Below: *A troupe of common lionfish (Pterois volitans). These animals sometimes seem to travel in packs, lurking particularly around vertical formations like coral outcrops or shipwrecks.*

WALLY SIAGIAN

Exploratory Dives on Islands North of Bali

We left the port of Benoa, in Bali, at 2 o'clock in the afternoon, after a long wait for port clearance. We had chartered a boat and were bound for the Kangean archipelago, a cluster of small islands that lies 130 kilometers due north of Bali. These were to be exploratory dives, as there is no organized diving in the Kangean group. Our air would be provided by an on-board compressor.

Beneath the Kangean islands are huge reservoirs of natural gas that are expected to supply the energy needs of Surabaya, Indonesia's second-largest city.

Although north of Bali, the islands are part of the province of Madura, Java. Construction on the 130-kilometer pipeline has started, but the Kangean islands are still undeveloped, and as such, an idyllic destination for a small group of divers.

Leaving from eastern Bali, our course took us through the Lombok Strait, a particularly fickle stretch of water. We knew the strait was subject to strong currents, but we weren't prepared for the persistent monster our craft had to battle the first night—at sunrise, we were still within sight of Bali. Soon, however, our speed improved, and in another few hours we could see the islands ahead.

Arriving at Sepankur

Three waving men, balancing on what looked from our still distant position like a log, welcomed us to Sepankur island, right in the middle of the group. (See map opposite.) As they paddled closer, we realized they were in a small canoe. The men were hunting sea turtles, and one of the divers still wore his goggles.

Below: *A swarm of purple queens,* Pseudanthias tuka, *hovers over a very healthy section of Indonesian reef.*

These were homemade: disks of glass cut from the bottom of soda bottles fitted with pitch into sections of bamboo. The strap came from an old inner-tube.

We dropped anchor in a sheltered bay on the north of Sepankur. There were holding nets here filled with thousands of live sea bass, awaiting their fortnightly shipment to Hongkong. This was an unexpected bonus, as dinner was only a matter of swimming over to the nets, and choosing a fish from the keeper.

This was only one of many beautiful anchorages we discovered in the next four days as we sailed from island to island in this shallow sea. The dozens of small islands are inhabited by Muslim fishermen and their families, and in the evenings we would invite them aboard for conversation. The first night we found out about the crocodiles.

Apparently, a fellow villager who was poaching teak logs from the nearby Kangean Reserve had recently been attacked by a very large saltwater crocodile and severely mauled, dying of blood loss before proper medical attention could be found. We were also told that during the rainy season the crocodiles have been known to swim across to Sepankur and enter the holding nets, helping themselves to the Hongkong delicacies.

(Back in Bali a few months later, we heard that the crocodiles had been particularly active since our visit—there were reports of 10 deaths.)

Diving Sepankur

Our first dive at the southwest point of Sepankur was understandably a nervous one. Unfortunately, however, it was disappointingly uneventful. The greater part of the sea here is shallow, no deeper than 25 meters. On our first dive we explored a shallow (8.5 meter) sandy bottom with coral outcrops

around which we found blue-spotted stingrays, angelfish, goatfish and butterflyfish.

On our way back to the boat on the Zodiac, we met a fishing boat with more divers. These men were rigged in hookah outfits, with the air delivered by a hand pump on deck. They had had a successful day fishing for trepang and lobster, which they would sell on Kangean, the largest island of the group.

After this uninspiring beginning to our diving trip, we decided to snorkel any potential diving spots first. We headed for Saebus, a green, palm-fringed island surrounded by white sand beaches and inhabited by more friendly fishermen.

We took the Zodiac to the southwest "corner" of this elongated island and jumped in to snorkel the sandy slopes only 20–30 meters off the shore, immediately coming face to face with a group of four bumphead parrotfish, and a turtle.

We rushed back to the Zodiac, geared up, and descended. As we entered the channel between Saebus and Saur, the sandy bottom gave way to a fine white clay which, owing to the half-knot current, produced poor visibility—at times only five meters.

Huge coral knolls, each with dozens of different types of corals, and terraces of table corals were abundant. Again we saw many rays, angelfish, butterflyfish, parrotfish and wrasse. We gently drifted through the canyons made by the coral bommies. Our maximum depth was 20 meters and the gentle current made for an effortless drift back to the yacht.

Diving a Submerged Reef

We dived early the next day before the swell picked up and disturbed the sediment. We had gone back to the submerged reef we had navigated around the day before, on our way to Saebus, between Sepankur and Saur.

This bank reef was approximately 140 meters by 40 meters, and the local fishermen called it a "taka." At low tide it was only a meter below the surface, and extended down to a sandy bottom, ten meters below.

Coral cover was quite good, although we saw some evidence of bombing by the fishermen. As we descended, we frightened away a reef whitetip shark, and saw a large school of snappers. The variety and numbers of fish were amazing—butterflyfish, angelfish, surgeonfish and more.

Pangerang Island

On our navigational maps, the north coast of Pangerang Island was the next spot that had looked like potential diving. The visibility was great—25–30 meters. A sandy bottom at 18 meters rose to coral slopes alive with fish: firefish, blackspot snapper, fusiliers, bream, humphead bannerfish, six-banded angelfish and emperor angelfish. We swam close to a school of large bumphead parrotfish, came across numerous blue-spotted rays nestled under the edges of coral outcrops, and found a medium-sized turtle.

Sakala Island

Our time was running out, but we had just enough left to dive off the island of Sakala, the most easterly of the Kangean group.

Here we were on the edge of the Sunda shelf, and our dive site was once again on a bank, but much deeper than the others. Its top was at 16 meters, and its sandy slopes descended out of sight. This dive was quite different from our previous dives.

Visibility was 20 meters or more, and we saw many pelagic fish, particularly sharks—at least a dozen reef whitetip sharks, reef black-tips, and even a couple of gray whalers. Schools of mackerel and trevally patrolled the area. The reef was flat with few pinnacles, and very little live coral other than a few gorgonians. We surmised that it was unprotected and swept clean by currents.

Coming back from Sakala we hugged the coast of Sepanjang hoping for another quick dive, but we could only manage an exploratory snorkel as the water was too rough to take the loaded Zodiac out. We discovered a sight not unlike our first dives, only much deeper, perhaps 20 meters. The bottom formation was a flat sand terrace gently sloping out of sight, interspersed with low coral knolls at intervals of 20–30 meters. The knolls were alive with myriad reef fish, and we sighted an enormous spotted eagle ray, and two reef whitetip sharks. The visibility here was very good—25 to 30 meters.

A Wild Storm

We left the Kangean islands and headed back to Bali. Our trip was smooth and uneventful until sunset, when we sighted Bali. Then a strong wind blew up. We didn't reach land until dawn the following morning, 20 kilometers off course and drenched through by the waves that continually swamped our decks. It wasn't until we were well and truly out of the rough water that Eric, our captain, admitted it was the worst storm he had ever experienced in the Lombok Strait.

—*Cody Shwaike*

Exciting Runs to Points East

Serious divers looking for a real treat should sign up with one of the live-aboards operating out of Bali, and head east. There are several boats available (see "Bali Practicalities," page 288) and you can also charter.

One of the most promising is the new *Sea Contacts I,* operated by Larry Smith (see sidebar page 132), who is the most experienced dive cruise operator working in the islands. *The Sea Contacts I* is a 34-meter ship with six double-occupancy, air-conditioned cabins with ensuite bathrooms and a full set of diving facilities: Bauer K-14 and mariner compressors, dive gear and repair facilities, full GPS and navigation equipment, three Zodiac tenders, and a full video facilities.

Larry will be taking the *Sea Contacts I* to the Banda Sea, the Sangihe-Talaud archipelago north of Sulawesi, the Sangalaki area off Kalimantan, and the Komodo and Rinca area.

Other live-aboard operators working out of Bali include Grand Komodo Tours and Travel, the pioneers of the Komodo area, and Pro Dive Bali.

The great advantage of a live-aboard, of course, is that it gives you access to isolated dive sites. Some of the places I have dived in Indonesia cannot be reached by any other means. The Komodo area is covered in the next section, and the fine sites of the Banda Sea in the Maluku section. Here, however, I thought I would briefly mention some sites that can easily be reached by live-aboards running to or from Bali, and not very easily by any other means.

Taka Bonerate

Spread over 2,220 square kilometers in the Flores Sea south of Sulawesi, Taka Bonerate is the largest atoll in Indonesia, and the third-largest in the world. Only Kwajalein in the Marshall Islands (2,850 sq. km.) and Suvadiva in the Maldives (2,240 sq. km.) are larger. The 21 small islands of Taka Bonerate offer nesting areas for sea turtles, which thrive on the huge seagrass meadows.

The atoll rises sharply from the side of a submerged ridge,

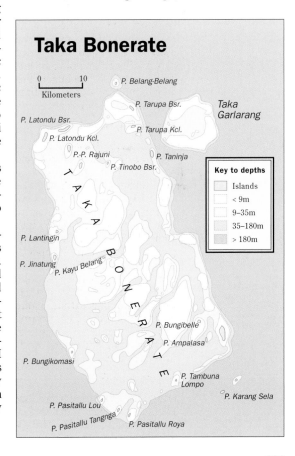

Taka Bonerate

0   10
Kilometers

P. Belang-Belang

P. Tarupa Bsr.

Taka Garlarang

P. Latondu Bsr.

P. Tarupa Kcl.

P. Latondu Kcl.

P.-P. Rajuni

P. Taninja

P. Tinobo Bsr.

T A K A

Key to depths

Islands
< 9m
9–35m
35–180m
> 180m

P. Lantingin

B O N E R A T E

P. Jinatung

P. Kayu Belang

P. Bungibelle

P. Ampalasa

P. Bungikomasi

P. Tambuna Lompo

P. Karang Sela

P. Pasitallu Lou

P. Pasitallu Tangnga

P. Pasitallu Roya

Larry Smith

Folks, meet Larry Smith. He has been in the business for more than 25 years, and has 12,500 dives under his weight belt. He has a deep bass voice, a red beard, and almost always a smile. Larry is built like a linebacker, the kind of man you want with you on a dark night in a dark alley—or underwater in an emergency.

Larry, from Longview, Texas, learned scuba diving under Doctor Blood—a.k.a. Captain Blood—a Ph.D. in chemistry, sea captain, inventor of polypropylene rope, and generally a figure of legend. During the next decade, Larry fueled his passion by opening a dive shop, combining teaching, commercial scuba work, and organizing dive trips to Mexico and Central America. He helped his good friend, gourmet chef Gladys Howard, set up a dive resort in the Caribbean's best dive location, Little Cayman.

After many years in the Caribbean, Larry became the dive director of the *Tropical Princess,* Indonesia's first live-aboard, cruising out of Biak, Irian Jaya. He fell in love with the country. He trained the *Princess's* crew from scratch, treating them like brothers, sharing the hard work and meals, and even the occasional drinking binge.

Not satisfied with the dive locations close to Biak, Larry looked at the charts and found Mapia atoll, 18 hours away. During the tidal change, Mapia's reef channel came alive with sharks, rays and other big fish, and it became a world-class dive location. He eventually left the *Princess,* and it has also stopped operation.

While working on the *Princess* Larry met Dewi, a pretty young woman from Central Java. The two married, and Larry passed to his wife his passion for diving.

Following his stint in the eastern part of the archipelago, Larry became the divemaster of the *Cehili,* a dive boat that ran seasonally along the Sangihe–Talaud islands north of Sulawesi, and the Banda Sea. When the *Cehili* stopped operations a year ago, Larry worked for Kungkungan Bay Resort on the eastern side of Sulawesi's northern peninsula and they benefited from Larry's prodigious talents. Now he is back running a live-aboard, the *Sea Contacts I* based in Bali. This ship will be running to Sangihe–Talaud and the Banda Sea, areas Larry knows intimately, as well as Sangalaki and Komodo.

Larry knows the charts, he knows the tides and conditions, and most of all, he knows the animals. He is, simply, the best.

2,000 meters down. Once a huge volcano, it has since subsided, leaving a wide ring of coral. The waters inside the atoll are magnificent turquoise, surrounded by the deepest blue imaginable. And they are rich: a survey found 158 coral species here.

Our dive started at 2–3 meters over the reef top, and then we swam out over the eastern outer wall of the atoll. Visibility was good to 30 meters, and the wall seemed to extend downward forever. The growth of coral and gorgonians was excellent, and schools of jacks cruised the wall. In the huge cuts and crevasses in the wall, we saw three giant groupers, Napoleon wrasse, turtles, lionfish and moray eels.

Unfortunately, as an overall dive site, Taka Bonerate suffers from having been extensively fish-bombed by itinerate fisherman. There are extensive seagrass beds here, which can be interesting for some divers, but only the outer edge of the atoll offers really good diving, particularly in the north.

Moyo Island

Moyo Island, some 250 kilometers from Bali, lies just off the north coast of Sumbawa. It's a good sized island, an irregularly shaped 40 by 10 kilometers with a maximum elevation of 600 meters.

I dove with Ian White, the PADI dive instructor at the Amanwana resort on Moyo. His is a very good operation, but at $500–$600 a night, the luxurious Amanwana is not for everybody. Ena Diving in Bali offers diving at Moyo as well, but live-aboards on their way to Komodo can do the same.

The best diving I found was at a series of five reefs, located far offshore of Moyo, called Pelagic Point. If you have the experience to handle currents, this area offers some excellent diving. Ian even saw a sailfish pass by two meters away from him on a deco stop here. This area is ideal for divers who relish a sense of discovery, as many areas on these reefs have hardly been explored.

Pelagic Point locations call for a quick drop to the bottom, at around 10 to 12 meters. The entries are well "upstream" of the current, but it's still necessary to dump all the air out of your BC and getting down fast so the current won't blow you by the reef.

On our first dive, we bombed down on a sloping area dotted with many large barrel sponges of many shapes, groupings and contortions. I have never seen such a profusion of barrel shapes, some with the large opening pointing sideways and downward, a sure sign of an area swept by a strong prevailing current.

We counted five sharks, white and black tips, with one bold one even buzzing by me at less than a half meter. This kind of action is only recommended to divers who have completely lost their fear of reef sharks. Aside from the big boys, there were out-standing schools of rainbow runners, good ones of fusiliers, surgeons, midnight snappers and pennant butterflyfish. Loose groups of redtooth triggers swarmed around, quickly heading for their holes at our approach.

The second dive on Pelagic Point offered something very different. We dropped down on a huge bed of garden eels and decided to wait patiently at one edge to see what would pop into our visibility. First, the normal sharks, two white tips and a blacktip, swam by to look us over. The garden eels were becoming accustomed to us, coming out of their burrows and swaying in the current. Then, just at the edge of visibility, a large, fat shape loomed out of the hazy underwater mist. It got just close enough, maybe ten meters, to make the positive identification that it was a grey reef shark.

All through the dive, five frisky blue trevally followed us, begging for attention while they buzzed various members of our gang of four. We never figured out why they were so friendly.

Below: *A school of yellow-backed fusiliers* (Caesio teres), *one of the most common schooling fishes seen in Indonesia.*

KAL MULLER

Introducing Nusa Tenggara

The islands east of Bali, running from Lombok in the west to Timor in the east, are called Nusa Tenggara, the "Southeastern Islands." These rough, dry and sometimes volcanic islands support a culturally diverse population of 10 million people.

Stretching 1,300 kilometers east to west, the islands lie just a few degrees south of the equator. One count yielded 566 islands, 246 of which were named and 42 inhabited. (See map page 138.)

The region is divided into three provinces: Nusa Tenggara Barat ("West"), including Lombok and Sumbawa, Nusa Tenggara Timur ("East"), including Sumba, Flores and West Timor, and Timor Timur (East Timor), which is a special province all by itself. The three provinces together cover 82,161 square kilometers, a little over 4 percent of Indonesia's total land area

Diversity of Cultures

Nusa Tenggara remained for the most part outside the great historical changes that swept through Indonesia, including the period of Indianization, from the 8th through the 15th centuries, and the later periods of Islam and European colonialism.

Only Timor had a trade product of interest: fragrant white sandalwood. For hundreds of years, the wood of the sandalwood tree (*Santalum album*) has been used in China, India and the Middle East for incense. The Portuguese were the first Europeans to reach Timor in 1515, but a century later the Dutch took over control of the trade.

Languages in at least 50 distinct groups are spoken by the people of Nusa Tenggara. The populations of Lombok and Sumbawa are Muslim, and because of a relatively long history of Portuguese colonial involvement in eastern Flores and Timor, the people of these areas are Roman Catholics. But in much of the rest of the region—and even in the areas where one of the modern religions holds sway—community religious life takes the form of animism and ancestral spirit worship.

The most spectacular cultural event in the region is the yearly Pasola in Sumba. In this dangerous celebration, the seasonal spawning of sea worms triggers a ceremonial, but very real spear fight between hundreds of mounted horsemen.

Volcanoes and Chalk Cliffs

Two geologically distinct island arcs make up Nusa Tenggara. The northern islands—Lombok through Flores and Alor—are volcanic, with jagged coastlines and rich soil. The southern islands—Sumba, Savu, Roti and Timor—were formed from uplifted coral limestone and sediment, and are dry and relatively barren.

Some 40 volcanoes have been identified in Nusa Tenggara, 25 of which are still active. The greatest eruption in modern history took place when Mt. Tambora, on Sumbawa Island, exploded on April 5, 1815. The blast produced 150 cubic kilometers of ash, far greater than that produced by the better-known explosion of Krakatau in 1883 (See "West Java" page 77).

The largest volcano in the islands is Mt. Rinjani in Lombok, which stands 3,726 meters, one

Overleaf: *An anemone shrimp,* Periclimenes holthuisi, *in the anemone* Heteractis magnifica. *Ambon, Maluku. Photograph by Jan Post, IKAN.*

Opposite: *A snorkeler with a whale shark,* Rhincodon typus. *These harmless, krill-feeding giants can be found seasonally at some sites in Indonesia. Indonesian fisherman call the whale shark ikan hiu bodoh, literally "stupid shark," because the animal has so little fight in it. Maumere, Flores. Photograph by Lionel Pozzoli, IKAN.*

of the highest points in Indonesia. Perhaps the most beautiful of Nusa Tenggara's volcanoes is Keli Mutu in south-central Flores, a trio of craters, each containing a differently colored lake.

The southern islands have no dramatic volcanoes, and are covered in dry scrub. The terrain of parts of Timor looks like Australian savannah. Limestone cliffs and beautiful white beaches ring some of these islands.

Most of the people of Nusa Tenggara, particularly in the western islands, subsist on rice, which is grown in wet "paddies" or *sawah*. But in the drier areas, corn, manioc and various tuber crops are grown. On Roti and Savu, among the driest parts of Indonesia, islanders depend on the drought-resistant *lontar* palm to give them nourishment through the dry season.

Rainfall patterns in Nusa Tenggara are quite complicated, and determined as much by local geographical conditions as by the seasonal monsoon winds. In general, southeast winds from May to July tend to bring wind and some rain to the south coasts of islands, and northwest winds from December to March bring rain to the north coasts. Prolonged rainfall is rare.

Plant and Animal Life

The islands of Nusa Tenggara form a biogeographical transition zone between the animals of Asia and those of Australia. This region is called Wallacea, in honor of Alfred Russel Wallace, a British naturalist who discovered the transition in types of wildlife here when he explored the islands in 1854–1862.

These dry islands are less rich in plant and animal life than the more densely forested islands of Borneo, Java and Sumatra to the west. Offshore, however, the islands teem with life, supporting some of the archipelago's richest reefs.

The region's most famous endemic species is the Komodo dragon (*Varanus komodoensis*), a huge monitor lizard found only on the tiny islands of Komodo, Rinca and a bit of west Flores. These fierce predators are the size of crocodiles.

—*David Pickell*

Diving on Lombok's Three Islands Resort

The three Gilis—Trawangan, Meno and Air—just off the west coast of Lombok, are beautiful little sandy islands that have become a favorite destination for sun-bathing, frisbee tossing and other low-impact seashore sports. The Gilis are close to Bali, and are particularly popular with young, European tourists.

Although all three islands are ringed by coral, the diving here is not exactly world class. The reef slope peters out into sand at a maximum of 25 meters, and the visibility hovers around 15 meters, just fair by Indonesian standards. Still, we saw a quite good assortment of fish life, including large trevally and sharks. Mantas are said to make an appearance here as well, albeit not often.

The coral is generally quite healthy around the Gilis, but unfortunately the authorities have not yet been able to put a complete stop to fish bombing. Still, the practice—which has lit-erally destroyed some Indonesian reefs—is now quite uncommon here.

AT A GLANCE
Gili Islands

Reef type: Coral slopes and sandy bottom, some wall

Access: 15 min by boat

Visibility: Fair, 15 meters

Current: Gentle, occasionally to 2 knots

Coral: Good variety and fair amount, some bombing damage

Fish: Fair to good variety and numbers

Highlights: Reef whitetip sharks and giant trevally at Takat Malang

---

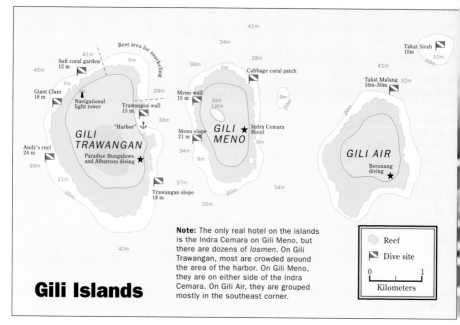

Note: The only real hotel on the islands is the Indra Cemara on Gili Meno, but there are dozens of *losmen*. On Gili Trawangan, most are crowded around the area of the harbor. On Gili Meno, they are on either side of the Indra Cemara. On Gili Air, they are grouped mostly in the southeast corner.

Gili Islands

The Gili sites are excellent for less experienced divers: most dives were in very calm water, no deeper than 18 meters. During two of our dives the current was slight, and in one it approached 2 knots, a little unsettling perhaps for a novice.

Much of the credit for the good diving here should go to Albatross diving, which pioneered five sites off Gili Trawangan, and Baronang Divers, which takes divers to sites north of Gili Air. Other operators take divers to the Gilis as well, but we recommend these two, which are headquartered on the islands themselves. In 1990 we had a series of really awful dives here arranged by other companies.

The best time to dive the Gilis is from late April to late August. We dove in late September, when the mid-day and late afternoon winds created some fairly choppy conditions—however the water was always smooth during the morning hours. Visibility averaged 15 meters. At the height of the northwest monsoon, late December–late February, big waves discourage all but

the most fanatic divers.

Gili Trawangan

Trawangan is the furthest west, and at 3.5 square kilometers, the largest of the three islands. Some 700 people live here, and the island is very popular with tourists. We found the best diving off the west coast, at two contiguous sites called, by Albatross, Andy's Reef and Giant Clam. (See map, this page.) While there were neither the absolute numbers of fish or species we have seen elsewhere in Indonesia, the marine life here was quite enough to make for interesting dives. And we can substantiate Albatross' claim of (almost) guaranteeing sharks in this area. We saw three reef whitetip sharks in one dive and five in another, with remoras in attendance. We were able to approach them to within 4–5 meters before our bubbles sent them off in a lazy retreat.

Andy's Reef and Giant Clam required just a 15-minute boat ride. We entered at some 100 meters from shore, dropped some 6–7 meters to spreads of staghorn coral, checked out the slope to 24 meters where flat sand began, then spent the bulk of the dive between 18 and 20 meters. Visibility was 15 meters.

The hard coral cover was decent, with tables, small domes and occasional pinnacles. One stretch showed heavy dynamite damage but elsewhere we saw only a few small bombed out spots. There was a very slight current, less than half a knot. Small channels of low coral and sand, cut parallel to the shoreline, were the favorite haunts of reef whitetip sharks. One dive ended conveniently on a coral pinnacle swarming with fish, just 5 meters from the surface. Another offered us a view of dead coral for our usual 3-minutes-at-5-meters stop before surfacing.

At Giant Clam, our guide took us to see the site's namesake, a *Tridacna gigas* more than a meter long. Such a large specimen is very unusual in this part of Indonesia. Our guide said that he has seen manta rays at this site on two occasions. We had to be satisfied with the mundane blue-spotted lagoon stingrays, plus a fair variety of reef fish.

We saw two quite impressive schools of fish: a packed mass of at least 200 blue-lined snappers (*Lutjanus kasmira*) in the shallows, and a bit deeper, a loose gathering of some 15 Goldman's sweetlips. We also saw schools of surgeonfish, small groups of bronze soldiers, and a very friendly cuttlefish.

Soft Coral Garden

This site is a drift dive along the north coast of Trawangan. The reef slopes to 25 meters where the coral gives way to grayish sand. We saw a lone tuna cruising this depth. During our dive, the current swept us along at a very healthy 1.5–2 knot clip.

There is little hard coral growth here, but the many gorgonians, sea fans and lacy soft corals well justify the area's underwater name.

Trawangan Slope

We sampled the east coast of Trawangan at night, drifting along the Trawangan Slope in a moderate current. This was definitely not a dive for beginners. At both entry and exit points we had to make our way from the beach over a low, wide, coral ledge. Boots are essential, and a steadying hand from a member of the Albatross staff was much appreciated. Albatross staffers, who had previously checked the strength and direction of the current, followed our progress from shore, and were helpfully on hand at our exit point.

The reef slope became flat sand at 20 meters, and the fish life—whether asleep, somnambulent or alert—was best at about 15 meters.

Below: *A young clown triggerfish,* Balistoides conspicillum. *This plucky species is among the most wildly patterned fishes on the reef.*

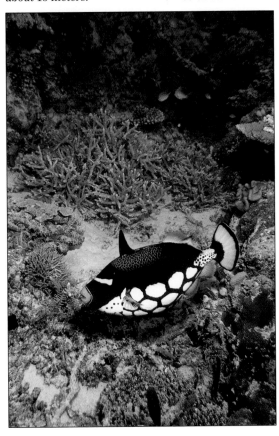

Gili Meno Wall

Gili Meno, the middle island, is home to about 350 people, and has the only real hotel of the three, the Indra Cemara. There is no fresh water here, and drinking water must be shipped in from Lombok.

The Gili Meno Wall is on the west coast, and is quite a nice reef, marred only by more than occasional fish bomb craters. The variety of reef fishes justified this site's claim as a good destination for beginning divers—easy and plenty to see.

From a shallow spread of staghorn *Acropora*, the terrain sloped to sand at 20–23 meters. A few isolated coral knolls rose from the slope, each harboring a mini-world of fish and invertebrate life. As one descended along the slope, more massive and thick-fingered hard coral gave way to carpets of soft corals, sponges and gorgonians. Two short sections of the wall were pocked with ledges and overhangs sheltering fish.

Gili Air

This island is the closest to Lombok, and the most populous, with 1,000 inhabitants. The beach circles the entire island, as does the coral, but the west coast in particular is quite barren. Just north of the island, however, at a site called Takat Malang, we had our best dive in the Gilis, better even than the West Trawangan dives. We counted 9 reef whitetip sharks, and 3 absolutely huge giant jacks (*Caranx ignobilis*).

The bottom is flat and featureless, but following some channels down around 30 meters, we found plenty of whitetip sharks.

Takat Sirah, our second dive, was anticlimactic. Some 15 minutes from Takat Malang, we dropped anchor and descended about 10 meters onto a dome-like bank of coral. Staghorn *Acropora*

forms large thickets on this coral bank that rises from the 20–25 meter sandy bottom. We saw anthias and hordes of damsels, but except for one Titan triggerfish, nothing bigger.

Dive Operators

Albatross, on Gili Trawangan, is the best outfit for dives off that island and nearby Meno. We found the guides reliable, knowledgeable and familiar with local conditions. Albatross's Bauer compressor is well-maintained, and while the guides do not use computers, they know their tables. Six regulator and BC sets are available for rent, along with basic snorkeling equipment.

Prior to dives, tanks and all gear are taken by cart the 500 meters or so to the dive boat's anchorage, so you have nothing to lug. Depending on the water conditions and the number of clients, Albatross uses one of three boats—a small speedboat, a long outriggered canoe, and a wide-hulled fiberglass.

All have 40hp outboards and plenty of space to suit up. A metal ladder provides easy exits. Boats and engines are well-maintained, and the helmsmen are capable.

During the short rides to the dive sites, if you like, the crew will assemble your gear for you. Two-way radios keep the boats in touch with the office on Trawangan and, from there, Lombok. The guide uses a buoy on all drift dives. Our boat was always close-by when we surfaced.

Our dives off Gili Air were arranged by Baronang Divers, named after the locally common rabbitfish. Baronang is basically a one-man show, run by Pak Sjahral Nasution. Nasution, a Batak from Sumatra, is a strong, well-trained diver who inspires confidence. Nasution spent 11 years in France, and speaks fluent French. He has a Bauer compressor, 30 tanks and 6 regulator and BC sets.

Little-Explored Reefs around Dragon Island

Komodo

Out of the corner of my eye, I caught sight of a shape moving steadily towards us. A *huge* shape. For a split second I thought: a tiger shark! Fear of this species—aggressive, and a known man-killer—lurks in the subconscious of every tropical diver. Then the apparition veered, displaying its side, decorated by a reassuring pattern of white spots.

This was a whale shark, the world's largest fish, and as gentle and peaceful as a whale. Suspended 20 meters down in the rich seas south of Komodo Island, this glorious, 6-meter-long animal glided by just a few meters from my face mask. Wow. My first sighting of this magnificent species ranks among the greatest thrills I have experienced in more than 1,000 dives in Indonesia.

World class diving

I saw this whale shark while diving in front of a sheer cliff on the south face of Kode Island, which almost fills a wide bay on the southernmost extension of Rinca Island, between Komodo and Flores. The north side of Kode faces a protected channel; the south faces the deep strait between Flores and Sumba.

Even without the whale shark, diving in the area around Komodo and Rinca is among the most exciting in the world. The boat halts just off great cliffs of black basalt, relentlessly pounded by sheets of blue water. Scattered rocks and outcroppings lie just offshore. Some of the pinnacles have an almost eerie look. Black and angular, and undercut at the base by the action of the seas, they look just like the statues at Easter Island. The surge and swirl of current visible at the surface is a bit daunting, but once you are down about 10 meters, things calm down considerably.

Underwater, the black cliffs continue, cut by huge chasms and in places split into huge, rectangular blocks, like undersea buildings. The black rock provides a dramatic backdrop to the colorful encrusting growth of gorgonians and soft corals, and the rugged terrain is unlike just about any other tropical reef in the world.

Healthy growths of hard corals—boulders, the tangled branches of staghorn coral, table corals and many other forms—decorate the occasional protected coves and the shallow tops of the undersea cliffs. On the sheer drop-offs, and in the caves and crevasses, the rock is covered by a solid mat of bright yellow cup corals, multi-colored gorgonians and countless varieties of soft

AT A GLANCE
Komodo

Reef type: Sloping reef, takas and walls

Access: Liveaboard, speedboat

Visibility: Variable, 2–30 meters; usually quite good

Current: From gentle to wicked (8+ knots), often around 2 knots

Coral: Excellent at the best sites

Fish: Very good to excellent

Highlights: Whale sharks, mantas, great underwater formations, profusion of interesting invertebrates

Komodo

coral. A photographer trying to steady himself with his left hand cannot find enough unoccupied space for even a single finger.

Dragons and Fierce Currents

Komodo island is most famous as the habitat of the Komodo dragon, the largest lizard extant. *Varanus komodoensis* is a varanid or monitor lizard—what the Australians call a "goanna"—an alert and agile predator and scavenger that can reach 2.5 meters in length and 125 kilos. Locally called *ora,* about 2,000 of the dragons inhabit Komodo and about 600 live on Rinca island. There are reports of a small population on Flores.

Komodo village is a stop-over on the ferry from Sape, Sumbawa to Labuhanbajo, Flores, and has become a very popular tourist destination. In the past, tourists would visit this dry, rocky island to watch the great beasts tear apart goats that have been hung at carefully monitored sites by the Indonesian Parks service. Today, the service has stopped the organized feeding, and the impressive animals can be seen

from a watering hole blind.

Labuhanbajo is a quiet little Muslim fishing village of about 3,000 people on an attractive harbor in northwest Flores. Because of tourist interest in Komodo's dragons, Labuhanbajo has enjoyed a small boom of late, with more *losmen* being built.

Geologically, Komodo and Rinca are part of Flores, separated from Sumbawa to the west by the Sape Strait. In the middle of the strait, the bottom drops to almost 300 meters. The many islands and relatively shallow seas between Flores and Komodo's west coast mean very fast currents at tidal changes.

By "fast" we mean more than 8 knots, which is a problem no matter how experienced a diver you are. Because of upwellings, it can also get very, very cold. Don't dive here with a super-thin, high-tech, pantyhose type suit. Bring a proper, thick suit. Even a hood wouldn't hurt.

Biological riches

The Komodo area offers just about every imaginable type of

diving, from current-swept sea mounds patrolled by groups of sharks, tuna and other big fish to dead-calm, colorful reefs alive with invertebrates and hundreds of colorful reef fishes. The water temperature varies from a chilly, upwelling-induced 22° C to 30°C bath water. Visibility ranges from a clear 25 to 30 meters in the horizontal plane, to a dismal 3 meters, where clouds of tiny fish and plankton allow only macro photography.

The underwater relief varies just as much: sheer walls, one of which we checked out to 70 meters, and it just kept going; caves, cracks and overhangs; slopes of varying angles; sea mounds; sand and mud bottoms.

The variety of marine life in the Komodo area rivals the world's best. There are deep seas both north and south of the narrow straits running between the little islands, and strong currents and upwellings bring nutrients and plankton, keeping everything well-fed, from tiny polyps right up to the sharks.

Unlike other areas of Indonesia, the reefs around the southern area of Komodo have suffered relatively little damage from the use of dynamite for fish bombing. Much of the area lies within the Komodo National Park, and local fishermen may only use lines and nets.

The shallow reefs between Labuhanbajo and north Komodo, extensively bombed in the past, are in the process of slowly recovering. This damaged sector covers perhaps 15 percent of the Komodo archipelago, and even here steep drop-offs and current-swept points offer good diving.

Exploration Diving

The Komodo area is not well explored, and we picked our dives based on a marine chart, advice from pearl divers and fishermen, and a good look at the above-water structure and water movement. These were real exploration dives, and in most places we jumped into water that nobody had ever dived before. Although this is exciting—and the kind of diving we like the best—it means that you have to take the good with the bad.

Some of our dives dropped us into water churned up by the winds and current, or over reefs that were empty of fish or had poor coral growth. Occasionally we miscalculated the current, and were swept in the wrong direction, over bare sand. One has to make the best of these experiences. There is almost always some redeeming feature.

For example, based on some information from local fishermen and our charts, we chose a lone rock in an island group just north of Rinca for a dive. When we descended, however, we found a sparse reef with very poor fish life. The visibility was okay, but there was nothing to see.

We were about to scrub the dive due to lack of enthusiasm when a flight of at least a dozen stingrays flapped off gracefully when we approached their sandy lair. Then we began to look at the bare sand, and found graceful sea pens, beautifully tentacled cerianthids, and a variety of other interesting animals.

In most of this area, however, particularly in the south, it is hard to go wrong. The whale sharks off both Kode and Motang Islands were the highlights of the trip, but even our typical dives in this area were excellent.

Diving the South

Conventional wisdom has it that December is the wrong time to visit Komodo, but in our experience this is not so. Although the rainy season is well on its torrential way in the western part of Indonesia, around Komodo the skies are usually blue and the tanning sun beats down. The seas are calm at this time, and there is enough of a breeze to cool down sunburnt bodies.

Because of the prevailing winds, in the middle of the summer when most people travel, the southern islands in the Komodo and Rinca area are inaccessible. The seas are just too rough. This is the time to dive the north. But in the winter, when wind and waves are stirring up the water

ED ROBINSON / IKAN

Above: *A spotted eagle ray,* Aetobatis narinari. *Unlike other reef-dwelling rays, these large animals—the wingspan can reach 2.3 meters—swim well above the bottom, and do not bury themselves in the sand.*

at the northern sites, head south.

In December—as well as late November and January—visibility is as good as it can get in such plankton-rich seas, 10–15 meters, and the coral growth and fish life in the south are nothing short of excellent.

Tala Island

Tala, a tiny, angular island in Langkoi Bay, just south of the southernmost part of Komodo Island, offers several excellent sites. The inner passage between Tala and Komodo proper is shallow, and ripping with current, but the southern point of the island has two adjacent sites: to the west, "The End of the World," a sheer wall of black rock that goes down well past 100 meters; to the east, "Colleen's Corner," a reef slope through rugged blocks of rock leading to a deepwater grove of wire coral.

On our first dive off Tala, the current at the point broke east, so we dropped in and went that way. We descended along a steep slope, full of coral-encrusted chunks of black rock, ending up in a strange forest of spiral whip coral on a sand bottom at 40 meters.

We were immediately greeted by a group of white-tip reef sharks, including one large and friendly individual who acted as if he had never seen a diver before.

We also encountered a turtle, and a very large reef ray finally got tired of our attentions and lifted slowly off the bottom. As we worked our way back up, we entered an area of reef that was very rich with damsels, anthias, butterflyfishes, and other colorful reef fishes.

At a point where a short tunnel led through a coral boulder, a large school of boldly patterned sweetlips gathered. We passed snappers, and several large schools of surgeonfish.

The rocky reef surface was everywhere covered with extensive carpets of bright cup corals. We surfaced near a little cove, graced by an incongruously white beach about the size of an apartment kitchen.

West of the point is a sheer wall of rock, broken up by some nice cuts, overhangs, and sandy shelves down to about 40 meters, and from there on a flat, black plane. Here we saw sharks, rays, morays and rich coral growth in the cuts and shelves. On one dive, a strange group of pelagic puffers conducted an elaborate series of maneuvers in the open water just off the wall.

The flat areas of the wall are covered with vast fields of orange cup corals, a beautiful effect against the dark rock. On one dive we followed the wall down to 70 meters, and although visibility was good, we never saw the bottom.

Pillarsteen

This site is identified by a tiny pinnacle, just off the southern tip of a small island east of Padar's southern point. In honor of its designation on our old Dutch map we call it "Pillarsteen"; on the British Admiralty chart, it is identified as "Pillar Rock."

The best plan—conditions willing—is to drop of the southernmost point of the pinnacle and head west. The structure here is wonderful, with huge chunks of rock broken up by caves and channels, canyons, and chimneys. The rugged underwater topography continues to 50–60 meters. There are good caves at

about 40 meters, and at 16 meters. Visibility, in the winter, averaged about 10–12 meters here.

The fish life is first rate, with large groups of medium-sized schooling fish, such as fusiliers, sweetlips and surgeonfish, as well as sharks, and a big *Mobula* ray. In areas, antipatharian wire corals grow out horizontally 4–5 meters from the rock, and the variety of soft corals and gorgonians here is excellent.

In places we saw sea apples, squat, plankton-feeding sea cucumbers that are unbelievably bright red and purple. This is a world-class site.

Heading east from the point, the structure is not as interesting, but there is a nice shallow area that makes a good safety or decompression stop.

Nusa Kode

Off Kode, we followed the coral-covered ridges down to 50 meters—this was our limit, as we were diving three times a day to explore as many sites as possible. The water was cold, a result of the upwelling of deep water

Above: *The scribbled filefish, Aluterus scriptus. This large (to 71 cm.) and weirdly marked fish can occasionally be seen on reefs throughout Indonesia.*

that also gives the area is biological richness. Visibility was 15 meters horizontal.

The shallows were very rich in fish life, particularly plankton feeders. Fork-tailed fairy basslets swarmed around the drop-offs in great orange and purple schools. Pairs of colorful butterflyfish foraged in the reef crannies for small crustaceans or coral polyps. Clown triggerfish, perhaps the most distinctively marked of all the reef fishes, staked out their territory along the face of the reef.

As soon as we got into the deeper waters a couple of white tip reef sharks swung around to give us a closer look. Sharks tend to be wary animals, but these approached us quite closely. Then we encountered a huge grouper, weighing perhaps 90 kilos. Red snappers, with bright yellow eyes, kept a wary distance. A highly esteemed food fish, the snapper has a right to be careful around mankind. Then a green turtle rowed by, soon followed by a huge school of narrow banded batfish, a rare sight.

And of course, at 20 meters, the whale shark. Only one thing kept this dive from being perfect: when the giant cruised by, I was working with my macrophotography set-up. I also dive with a Nikonos and 15mm lens, but I had already used up my film.

(On the next dive, off nearby Gili Motang, I was prepared when a whale shark cruised by. Unfortunately, even though I finned with all my might, I could not close in on the big fellah as much as I wanted. I squeezed off a few shots anyway.)

Gili Motang

The south face of Gili Motang, which sits between Flores and southern Rinca, blocking the Molo Strait, offers sites with good coral growth, nice bommies and chunks of rock, and seasonal pelagics like whale sharks and mantas. But our favorite site is in the north: "Apple Orchard."

This spot is literally covered with the colorful filter-feeding sea cucumbers called sea apples (*Pseudocolchirus violaceus*). These beautiful animals—deep blood-red or purple, and with contrasting white or yellow radial stripes—are rarely seen, and nowhere have we seen so many in one place.

The other invertebrates here—unusual nudibranchs, plentiful soft corals, strange, bright-blue compound stalked tunicates—rival temperate waters in their color intensity.

The site, working west from the tip of Motang's small northern peninsula, offers rich coral growth in the shallows at top, and then a nice rock slope down to about 25–30 meters. Visibility, like most of the area, varies, but is usually around 12 meters or so, plenty for the up-close experience the site offers. This is an excellent place for macrophotography.

The rugged Komodo Plus

In 1992 we did our first dives off the *Komodo Plus,* a 18-meter wooden boat designed to ferry tourists to Komodo Island. At that time, we had six tanks and rented a rough-looking but still functioning compressor from a defunct *trepang* gathering operation in Bima, Sumbawa. Short of lead for our weight belts, we fashioned serviceable weights from steel pipe fittings and bits of chain. Not particularly fashionable, but they worked.

While there are a few local pearl-diving boats taking clients to locations close to Labuhanbajo, most of the best dive spots were pioneered by the *Komodo Plus*, including those mentioned above.

The *Komodo Plus* is a newly built craft, designed and constructed in traditional Bugis style but with an interior fixed up for western tastes. Cruising speed, with a 105-horsepower engine, is up to 11 knots, depending on the mood of the seas, of course. As of this writing, the boat is the only live-aboard currently operating in this area. It is definitely not luxurious—there is no air-conditioning, for example—but it's comfortable enough. The six small double and six single bunks can accommodate a dozen or more people, but for divers, particularly those wielding cameras, six or eight is much better. The boat has two modern shower-toilets. The food is delicious, varied and plentiful.

When we last checked, diving equipment included two compressors, 30 tanks, weights, but only 1 complete set of rental gear. Divers should bring their own basic gear, but with sufficient notice, rentals for six sets can be arranged. Entry consists of a giant leap from the mother ship, and pickup is either by the *Komodo Plus* itself, or by a fiberglass dinghy powered by a 25hp motor.

The boat is operated by Grand Komodo Tours, based in Bali, and you should contact them for booking information (See Komodo Practicalities page 290.) The *Komodo Plus*'s home port is Sape, Sumbawa, because until the airport in Labuanbajo gets lengthened, Bima airport is a far more reliable way to get to the area.

Diving the North

The first dive we made in the area, some years ago, was off Komodo Island's Pantai Merah, literally "Red Beach." This site is very near the old dragon feeding station, and snorkeling and lunch here was a regular stop on most tour operators' schedules.

The snorkeling is excellent, over a healthy, shallow reef. Where we dove, however, was at the reef edge, where the bottom

drops down to 20 meters or so.

When we hit the water, the current was like a raging river. Out of the dozen divers in my group, half came right out and into the Zodiac. My partner and I headed straight down, where the current was a bit less strong and we could grab coral outcrops.

By the time we had the situation more or less under control and could take a look around, we were surrounded by thousands

Below: The spotfin lionfish, Pterois antennata, *displaying the eponymous spots on its pectoral fins. Bali.*

of fish of every color and shape, against a beautiful background of corals, gorgonians and sponges. Although worth the struggle, this was not a dive for someone who has just completed a resort course.

We dove in August, but the best weather for diving should be around late March through early May, and again from late September to early November, but there is often current here.

Above: A pair of firefish, Nemateleotris magnifica. *Firefish are skittish plankton-feeders that hover in pairs or small groups near the reef bottom. Flores.*

GPS Point

Bottom formation	2.5
Visibility	1.5
Coral variety	2
Fish variety	2
Special	1
(Lots of sharks)	
Total:	**9**

—*Wally Siagian*

Banta Island

Perhaps the best site in the North Komodo area, and dive guide Wally Siagian's personal favorite, is "GPS Point," a small bank reef just off the point of the easternmost of Banta Island's two north-facing peninsulas. The reef is most easily located using a Global Positioning Satellite receiver.

The top of this sea mound lies just 6–14 meters underwater, and it attracts lots and lots of fish. This is one of the very best sites to see sharks, and five species can be identified in a single dive. GPS Point is also often swarming with jacks, dogtooth tuna, and big schools of barracuda and surgeonfish.

Unfortunately, this site seems to have been discovered by shark fin hunters. On his last dive on the mound, Wally Siagian found several shark carcasses, sad dead bodies with their fins rudely hacked off. This is a common practice among shark-fin fishermen, who often pull in a shark, cut off its fins, and throw the still living animal back, as there is just not enough space on the boat to keep the rest of the animal. The fins are dried, but there is no easy way to preserve the rest of the animal.

The soft coral growth at GPS Point in particular is excellent, and the entire surface of the sea mound is richly overgrown with sessile invertebrates.

Strong currents often sweep the top of the mound, "gusting" to 3 knots or more. Things settle down around 25 meters or so, but this is not really a beginners' dive. Visibility here is variable, and can drop below 10 meters because of plankton in the water. It is usually clearer at depth.

Banta offers several other sites, including a protected bay in the southwest, "Alcyonarian Bay," which is quiet and rich with interesting soft corals and delicately structured hard corals, and "Banta Bommies"

Sabolan Kecil

Sabolan Kecil ("Little Sabolan") and its partner island, Sabolan Besar ("Big Sabolan") are north of Labuhanbajo, just a bit west of the large island of Seraya Besar.

Below: *A pair of fimbriated moray eels,* Gymnothorax fimbriatus, *curled in their lair. This relatively small (to 80 cm.) moray is primarily nocturnal.*

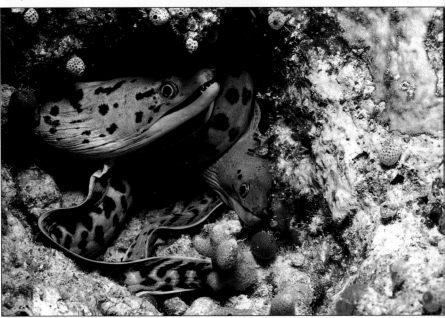

Just east of Sabolan Kecil, heading toward Sabolan Besar, are two sea mounds, a site called "Wally's Shark Bank." The first—and larger—of the two starts about 18 meters, and continues down to a sand bottom at 35 meters. The second is much smaller, and rises just 5–10 meters from the bottom.

Hard coral cover here is minimal, but there are lots of soft corals, and some very large gorgonians. The reason to dive here, however, is for the fish life, particularly sharks. Work your way down to the valley between the two mounds and pause for a while to watch the white-tips, silver-tips and black-tips.

The most exciting, particularly when the visibility is marginal, are the constantly circling and usually slightly irritated grays. If you don't make too much commotion—there is a large sponge you can hide behind—look out across the sand bottom here, and you will see a very large colony of garden eels.

Like just about everywhere around Komodo, conditions here vary widely, and visibility, especially near the top of the first mound, can be absolutely soupy from plankton. It always clears out as you get deeper, and once the visibility at depth was more than 25 meters.

Tatawa Island

A bit south and slightly west of Tatawa Island is a rocky islet called Batu Besar, literally "Big Stone," the location of a site called "Current City." East of the islet, as the name suggests, currents can regularly top 3 knots, making diving a bit of a headache. If the current is this strong along the East face, however, it is usually fairly calm along the West.

The west face of Batu Besar offers a series of steep drops to about 30 meters, and several nice coral caves. The soft coral cover is very good, and there are lots of fish, including large schools of sweetlips. Sharks are common here, as are turtles, and we have seen very large reef rays here.

Sebayur Kecil

We had another top rated dive off the north coast of Sebayur Kecil Island. Our entry point was 25 meters off a white sand beach. The beach is marked by a clump of three trees, and is next to the highest point on the island.

The reef top sits just 4–5 meters from the surface, and from here a nice wall, covered with corals and sponges, drops to a sandy bottom at 25–30 meters.

Underwater we headed east, then followed the reef as it curved south. Visibility was excellent, more than 25 meters. (Note: We also tried this site in the winter, and found visibility reduced to 1.5 meters). As we began our descent, we met a group of 5 Napoleon wrasse, and schools of striped bristletooth tangs. Reef fishes—puffers, butterflyfish, and others—were plentiful. We also spotted a very large giant grouper, but it quickly hid in a deep cave.

At one point we surprised an absolutely beautiful juvenile pinnate batfish, fringed with bright orange. This bright coloration is thought to mimic a toxic flatworm, affording the young fish some protection from predators. This one was not very confident, however, and peered out at us from a coral niche.

Another interesting site in this area is off a rock outcrop just west of about the middle of Sebayor Besar called Barusa Saha. The bottom here is just sand and coral rubble, but there are more stingrays here than just about anywhere else we have seen. A one point, a synchronized flight of more than a dozen of the animals took off from the sand, a very dramatic sight indeed.

Diving North Flores After the Earthquake

In the late 1980s, when the first edition of this book was released, the reefs off Maumere were universally considered among Indonesia's best. They particularly attracted underwater photographers, who built up portfolios of giant sea fans, and hundreds—even thousands—of species of fish.

But on December 12, 1992, disaster struck: an earthquake of 6.5 on the Richter scale, followed by tsunami waves. At Pulau Babi, the waves generated by the tsunami reached 7.9 meters, and at the shore of Maumere Bay, 4 meters. More than 2,500 people were killed, and the loss of boats, houses and businesses was devastating.

The epicenter of the quake was offshore to the north. The worst damage was on Babi Island, just north east of Maumere Bay, where the tsunamis killed well over 1000 people.

And if this were not enough, little more than a month later, on January 23, 1993, Cyclone Lena ripped through the Flores Sea, further tearing at Maumere's already shattered reefs.

Although the loss of life was chiefly a result of the tsunami waves, most of the damage to the reef was caused by the earthquake, which rocked the foundations of the reefal substrate, cracking larger coral heads and dislodging gorgonians and other clinging animals.

Visiting the area in the year after the earthquake, many divers stated that Maumere was permanently destroyed. On the other hand, author, biologist and underwater photographer Rudie Kuiter, who has done more diving here than just about anyone else, writes in a report he prepared after the quake: "Little has changed and in a way it is even more interesting. I would say that perhaps 10 percent of the outer drop-offs have suffered bad damage, but little on the coastal reefs."

We have not had the chance to revisit the site since September 1993, and the following text reflects our opinion at that time.

After the Damage

When we visited a year later, there was little evidence of damage on land. Massive infusions of aid and rebuilding have wiped out just about all evidence of devastation. But what about underwater?

Pamana Kecil

Our first dive, off the Pamana Kecil, was the best for big fellows. Even before beginning our descent, just as I peered below, two large dogtooth tuna cruised

AT A GLANCE

Maumere

Reef type:	Mostly steep walls, some vertical
Access:	Up to 2 hrs by boat
Visibility:	Good to very good, 10–20 m
Current:	Gentle at the coastal sites, can be strong (to several knots) around the islands
Coral:	Good at some sites
Fish:	Very good numbers of big fish at the best sites
Highlights:	Sharks and dogtooth tuna

Maumere Bay

by some ten meters beneath me. We descended in very good 15–20 meter horizontal visibility, down a sheer vertical wall which bottoms out around 60 meters.

Several white tip sharks checked us out from a respectful distance and a couple of gray sharks looked us over from a bit closer. A large school of good-sized jacks were hardly disturbed by our passage, remaining in a disciplined swirl within a meter or two away. Several white tips were resting on a ledge around 55 meters and I dropped for a closer look. Not far off, a large hammerhead cruised by.

Coming up under the admonishment of my computer, a large Napoleon wrasse headed the other way. At around 30 meters, we spotted a group of a half dozen large dogtooth tuna. Another pair of these toothy blokes followed us for the rest of the dive, often coming to within 4–5 meters. A guide spotted and grabbed a medium-sized green turtle, showing off the distressed beast until I took his photo so he would let it go.

While the big fish were exciting enough for anyone, the wall was disappointing: little coral growth and few reef fishes. Much of it was covered with a layer of sand, a condition we noted at other dive sites here. Our decompression step was enlivened by one of our guides spotting four small nurse sharks under a clump of large rocks.

Gosong Bone

The day's second dive, near the leading light buoy on Gosong Bone atoll, was disappointing. There were very few fish, coral growth was poor, and invertebrate life was almost absent. A couple of medium-sized schools of fusiliers and a large, wary puffer were the most interesting fish we saw on the dive.

We checked the vertical wall to 40 meters, especially along the 35 and 20 meter levels, but saw few reef fishes, even inside interesting-looking shallow caves and a swim-through passage. Visibility was quite good, in the 12–15 meter range, but the teeming life we remembered from previous years' dives was gone.

West Babi

My guide recommended good diving off Babi Island. This struck me as odd, because Babi bore the brunt of the tsunami, and was the single most devastated spot. We dove at the outer edge of the reef fringing the western coast of the island. Visibility was 7–12 meters, and current was slight. We dropped down a wall to about 40 meters (the wall continued to 50 meters) where the visibility improved to about 15 meters. A couple of giant fan gorgonians marked the 40 meter level.

Heading south, we saw a good cover of soft corals and sponges, along with medium to small gorgonians and patches of hard corals. Fish life was concentrated in several areas with good numbers and variety of snappers, along with a few emperors, damsels, parrotfishes and schools of yellow-tail fusiliers.

The underwater structure here used to be full of caves and depressions, and although a few of these remained, most had collapsed. Some areas were covered with the sandy deposit seen on other dives, but by and large, the scenery and life here was pretty much as I remembered from previous years. Only the top 10 meters was dead, and showed little evidence of regeneration. According to my guide, the other dive spots off Babi have simply been washed away.

Two dives off the south side of the islands blocking northeast Maumere Bay showed Maumere diving like its old, glorious, pre-earthquake days.

Maragajong

At Maragajong we anchored on the reef flat and swam against a fairly strong current over dead coral rubble to reach a vertical, 40 meter wall with good invertebrate cover, especially small soft coral trees and sponges, overhangs and small, shallow caves. Visibility was none too good, fluctuating from 6 to 10 meters. The current gusted to two knots, but most of the time it was a manageable, less than a knot.

The good growth lasted but about 100 meters before an underwater landslide marked our turnaround point. On the way back, rounding an outcrop, we were greeted with strong gusts of current and a plethora of fish: large, colorful parrotfish (*Scarus festivus*), a huge cloud of sergeant majors, an unusual school of emperors and the usual fusiliers. The mass of fish life was impressive but the current forced us to hang on to rocks to watch the show.

South Pangahbatang

Another dive to the east, off south Pangahbatang also started in a strong current. But here the reeftop was in top shape, the growth dominated by large leather corals. Visibility was not great (less than 10 meters) and the current gusted to 1.5 knots as we dropped along a slope to sand bottom at 27 meters, the

Above: A slipper lobster, Parribacus antarcticus, lodged in a small barrel sponge. In these small lobsters, the foremost pair of appendages have evolved into small, flat plates rather than the thorny antennae of the more familiar spiny lobster.

HELMUT DEBELIUS / IKAN

maximum for this dive.

A good-sized white tip shark was curious enough to come in fairly close, but there were too many of us (six) for its careful nature. Other white tips hovered in the current further off along with a couple of 2-meter grays and a black tip. While the shark aggregation was impressive, so were the soft coral trees, among the largest, most colorful and splendid we have ever seen.

We crossed a white sand trough, spotting a couple of good-sized tuna, a crocodilefish, several blue-spotted rays, a Napoleon and a lumbering bumphead parrotfish, perhaps part of a shadowy pack, at the very edge of visibility. At one edge of the sand, a mini-forest of garden eels disappeared during our approach, cautiously slithering out heads and part of their bodies after our passage.

One rocky area was speckled with many small bright yellow sea cucumbers, the only place we have seen them in a concentration outside of Kupang. A splendid dive indeed, in spite of the strong finning required by the current.

Wailiti Reef

On the far west side of Maumere Bay, where the full force of the tsunamis hit, diving was said to be good only below the 20 meter level, to where the slope stops at around 30 meters and blends into an almost flat sand bottom. We found the contrary to be true.

Except for a couple of blue spotted stingrays fish life was better further up: fairly good numbers and variety, but nothing outstanding by Indonesian standards. We noticed the common yellow-eyed black snappers (*Macolor macularis*), several *Phyllidia* nudibranchs covered with yellow-tipped bumps as well as a couple of nudibranchs.

The invertebrate scene was dominated by several fairly large gorgonians decorated with crinoids. The dive's highlight was a friendly cuttlefish, which allowed a very close encounter for several minutes before drifting off backwards, gently undulating. The reeftop was in very

MAUMERE   155

good condition at snorkeling depths.

Labuhan Tour

Labuhan Tour, off west Besar Island, also offered good shallow diving, to about 15 meters. On our way down the vertical wall, we saw a large Napoleon wrasse at about 15 meters, then very little life from 15 meters to the bottom, at 45 meters. On the return

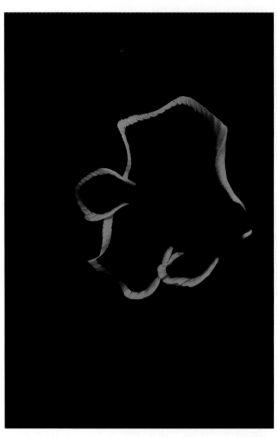

MIKE SEVERNS

Above: *A juvenile batfish* Platax pinnatus. *This is a very young individual, and it has not yet developed long dorsal and ventral fins. The coloration and movements mimic the toxic flatworms of the genus* Pseudobiceros. *Lembeh Strait.*

to the boat, between 10 and 15 meters, we found two large, colorful nudibranchs and a clown triggerfish, along with a good sized puffer hovering in a cave.

In the top 15 meters, coral growth, both hard and soft, was quite good. As we decompressed at 5 meters, a fat saddleback grouper (*Plectropomus laevis*) swam by below. This one must have been of record length.

Other Sites

We stopped at Waigete, on the coast due south of eastern Besar, but we saw little life down to 15 meters, except for a couple of octopus. Below, small soft corals grew well, along with sponges and a variety of tunicates, but except for a school of the common yellow-tailed fusiliers, fish life was poor.

We did not try three of the 11 spots which my guide said still offered good diving. These were Ray Lagoon/Shark Point where, he said, the coral is all gone and there is strong current, but big fish are often encountered. At Pamana Selatan, the topside coral is gone, but the lower levels are worthwhile, he said. This site also often has current, and choppy seas.

Wai Terang

At Wai Terang, where a sunken Japanese freighter from World War II lies close to the beach, the coral growth on the wreck is unaffected, according to my guide. Some parts of the wreck collapsed, but the fish life is the same as before.

When we dove there before, it was a difficult but excellent spot. Nowhere else have we seen so many lionfish (all *Pterois volitans*), in groups of four, six and even up to a dozen, including some huge old fellas. The wreck lies on its side, almost completely turned over, on a slope. Although depths range from 12 to 24 meters, there is no reason to use up your air on the deeper part of the wreck, as there is more than enough to see near the top. The ship is less than 100 meters from the beach.

The substrate here is a fine, gray sand that produces an instant smoke screen as soon as someone gets a fin within two meters of its surface—this is not a dive on which one wants to invite neophytes still struggling with their buoyancy control. On our first visit, we were in a group of a dozen divers who cut the 10–15 meter visibility to zero within five minutes. For our second dive on the wreck, we came as a group of three more seasoned divers, and carefully monitored our movements.

The silty bottom restricts coral growth, and there is none around the wreck. On the hull itself, however, we found small clumps of branching hard coral protecting tiny fish. A few sponges and lots of clams cling to the side of the hull, along with bunches of grassy whip coral. Several fat sea cucumbers crawled along the ship. Juvenile three-spot dascyllus (*Dascyllus trimaculatus*) found protection near the beautiful stinging sacs or acrorhagi of bubble coral, *Plerogyra* sp.

Although far from overwhelming, we found the fish life here quite adequate. In addition to the remarkable number of lionfish, a small cloud of anthias decorated the top of the lower hull and fat goatfish rooted in the silt. A dozen adult pinnate batfish appeared from the wreck, swam off into the haze, and then returned, as if they had forgotten something.

We also found a beautiful little blue and white juvenile emperor angelfish. Several groupers and wrasses wandered in and out of a large hole in the hull. The silt inside, however, prevented human exploration.

My dive buddies startled a large cuttlefish, and saw two moray eels posturing at each other with open mouths. Was it territorial defense or love?

Sea World

Diving in Maumere began in the early 1970s, when an Italian couple began operating Sea World. The original owners gave up the business, which was taken over by a local Roman Catholic foun-

RUDIE KUITER
Photographer and Author

Rudie Kuiter's knowledge of Pacific reef fishes and underwater photography is equaled by few others. At first, he comes across as a more handsome Charles Bronson, with a long lion's mane of hair and clear blue eyes. But there is nothing gruff or closed about this man—he is willing to share his endless knowledge of Indonesia's reef animals with peers and beginners alike.

After logging hundreds of dives in Indonesia—mostly in Maumere Bay and Bali—Kuiter authored *Tropical Reef-Fishes of the Western Pacific: Indonesia and Adjacent Waters*. His interest in this project began in 1985 with an invitation to survey the fishes of Maumere Bay for the Flores Sao Resort. In the process, he catalogued over 1,200 species, including a half dozen new to science. From 1990 to 1993, Kuiter organized the yearly underwater photo competition at the Sao Resort.

Kuiter's interest in fishes began in 1948, when at the mature age of five he started catching river fish with cotton and worm lures in his native Holland. His father built him a fish pond where Kuiter raised local species. After training in electronics and a two year stint in the army, he moved to Australia, his home since 1964. Today, he lives with his wife and children in Melbourne.

Within a month of his arrival in Australia, Kuiter was already taking a scuba course. A few years later, he began taking underwater photographs, using a housed Nikon F with a 55 macro. Kuiter's knowlege of electronics, with which he supported himself until 1979 (and on a self-employment basis since) has served him well in putting together his underwater gear and keeping it in working shape in the field.

Today, Kuiter works with 60 mm and 105 mm macro lenses mounted in an F4. The whole is contained in a custom housing which he has modified. He also tore apart two Nikon SB24 flashes—sophisticated units with active links to the camera's built-in computer and light meter—and rebuilt them according to his requirements. It is a one-off, state-of-the-art setup.

According to Alison, Kuiter's wife and the mother of red-haired Hendrik and blond Steven, Kuiter's success is due to his unbelievable powers of observation and endless patience as much as his technical skill. Alison Kuiter was already a keen diver and underwater photographer when she met Rudie in 1976.

— *Kal Muller*

This page, top:
*Paccagnelle's dotty-
back,* Pseudo-
chromis paccagnelle.

This page, bottom:
Chromodoris mag-
nifica. *Halmahera,
Maluku.*

Opposite: Bargibant's
seahorse, *Hippo-
campus bargibanti.*
This wonderful ani-
mal is a commensal

dation. Sea World still runs dive tours, but only about 15 percent of their clients dive.

Sea World owns a well-maintained Bauer compressor, but the operation has frequent troubles with their dive boat, and their rental equipment could stand to be upgraded.

New rooms have been added but unfortunately, these are rather unattractive, motel-style buildings. The existing beach-

of two species of gorgonian in the genus *Muricella,* here *M. plectana.* Discovered in New Caledonia by accident in July 1969 by Georges Bargibant (he was collecting gorgonians for the Noumea aquarium) it has since been found at several places in Indonesia.

side cottages are pleasant, although they certainly need some fixing up.

My sleep in one was disturbed by a scampering rat (I can handle that) and a huge spider by the light switch (not handleable, absolutely horrible). The food and service at the restaurant was excellent, however, and the staff is helpful and friendly.

While Sea World has no swimming pool, their beach is

nice. It is also a friendly, local place, where people will strike up conversations with guests in their limited English.

The real headquarters of diving in Maumere used to be the Flores Sao Resort, but this has not survived the loss of business associated with the 1992 earthquake and has closed.

Still Worth It?

Is it still worthwhile to travel to Maumere just for the diving? It didn't look too good to me in 1993, but that was six years ago. Rudie Kuiter, in 1993, writes:

"Earthquake damage is restricted to the drop-offs facing the epicenter and most coastal reefs show no damage at all... [T]he place now has a special interest to see how reefs are formed and regrown. It is now obvious that the caves and crevices which Babi is known for were formed by previous earthquakes."

Kuiter's opinion is that by the earthquake's 1994 anniversary a lot of soft coral will be back and in 4–5 years things will be the same as before. It will be interesting to see if this is the case. Scientists have noticed elsewhere that for some reason, reef recovery from natural disasters seems to take place much more quickly than recovery from damage caused by man. In fact cycles of storm damage in some areas seem to have a relationship to coral diversity, clearing monotypic stands of fast-growing branching corals, and giving other species a chance to take their place on the reef.

Magic
Mountain

A Rich Sea Mound
Swarming with Sharks

We were a kilometer off the western shore of Sumba Island, anchored in 15 meters of water atop a submarine mound. The green murky water was not at all inviting. The word 'ominous' even comes to mind. This mound is a famous fishing site, but the stories of easy strikes when trolling across the mound are always qualified with a caution about a second run—subsequently hooked fish are invariably eaten by sharks before they can be landed.

With this in our minds, we quickly descended the anchorline, and hugged the bottom as we accustomed ourselves to the 6–8 meter visibility. Following the contour of the plateau in a southerly direction, we dropped

of conflict and carnage, and hosted three obviously well-fed remoras. We were shadowed for an interminable five minutes before they relaxed and left us alone. Either we had moved outside their territory, or they had come to accept that we weren't a threat. With a collective exhalation of relief we turned our attention to the passing parade.

Magic Mountain

We've only rarely witnessed a concentration and density of fish-life as found on the site we dubbed Magic Mountain. In other areas of Indonesia, rich fishing grounds such as these would have been exploited and fishbombed to oblivion by local fisherfolk. But Sumba lacks the population demands of western Indonesia; neither does it have much of a fishing tradition.

The technology used here is primitive: fishermen paddle small dugout canoes no further than a kilometer offshore and fish with handheld lines. More organized exploitation is limited to the sporadic visits of turtle or shark boat.

The waters around Magic Mountain are rich in plankton, and consequently, in fish life. Schooling fish here are profuse: fusiliers, bannerfish, unicornfish, and triggerfish literally engulf a diver. Big predatory fish prowled the sea mound, jacks, dogtooth tuna and wahoo. Mackerel scad, smaller jacks, and rainbow runners swept by in schools.

Most impressive were the vast schools of barracuda, which in the daytime hover in groups of hundreds or thousands as a form of protection. Their giant

---

AT A GLANCE

Sumba

Reef type:	Sea mound, some slopes
Access:	15 min by boat
Visibility:	Poor to good, 6–15 m
Current:	Can be strong across the mound
Coral:	Good at some sites
Fish:	Very good numbers of big fish at the best sites
Highlights:	Lots of sharks, huge schools of barracuda, profuse fish life

---

onto a saddle at 20 meters and continued descending along the eastern wall.

There they were: five grey whalers swimming away, and then circling back, and these fellows were agitated! The leader of the pack was a plump, 2-meter-plus beast with a tatooed history

Magic Mountain

cousins, the great barracuda, were also around. While fewer in number, they definitely grabbed our attention.

At the top of the chain were the sharks, including the whalers, grey reef sharks, white-tips, and a solitary hammerhead shark.

The mound itself was rich in invertebrate life, including big barrel sponges, table corals, and bright soft corals. Much of the area was covered with orange cup corals, and green trees of *Tubastrea micrantha*. The variety of smaller reef fishes was excellent. We also saw the biggest sea snake we have seen anywhere: more than two meters long.

Sumba Reef Lodge

Magic Mountain can be explored easily in a morning of diving from Sumba Reef Lodge, on Tanjung Karoka about 20 kilometers south of Waikabubak, West Sumba. Sumba Reef Lodge is not solely a dive operation—it is a luxury resort that emphasizes outdoor activities. In addition to diving, horseback riding, trekking, sea kayaking, and deep sea fishing are also offered. But whatever you do, don't neglect to spend a few relaxing hours in the gigantic free-form pool whose edge leads to the horizon between heaven and the sea.

Meloba Bay

Sumba Reef also offers dive safaris to Meloba Bay, east of Tanjung Karoka. These are an adventure in their own right. Camp is pitched on a expansive white sand beach in a secluded bay with good snorkeling.

The diving in Meloba is not as exceptional as Magic Mountain. We found hard coral only in areas completely protected from the walls of water generated by the southeast tradewinds in July and August. The typical underwater profile was silty clay bottom covered with tough leather corals and coralline algae. The visibility was generally poor, and the bottom is quite shallow.

The pinnacles at the entrance to Meloba Bay were the exception to the norm. Here we found good visibility, depths to 30 meters, wonderful craggy rock formations, and lots of fish.

—*Cody Shwaiko*

Kupang

KUPANG

Big Fish, Top Service, and Great Night Dives

Kupang, located near the southwest tip of Timor Island in Indonesia, has started to acquire a well-deserved reputation in diving circles the world around. Other places in Indonesia also offer great diving, but in Kupang the dive business, called Dive Trek East, is well-run by two Aus-

tralians, and there are none of the language problems that can get in the way elsewhere.

The two men are well qualified. Donovan Whitford holds a PADI instructor's license, and his father is a dive-master. They have dived the area for the past four years, establishing dozens of proven dive locations, all within an hour's boat ride from Kupang. The operation has also pioneered Roti Island, as well as Alor.

While there is no specific dive "season" here, wind conditions put some of the locations out of reach from mid-January to early

March and sometimes in the June to August period. Visibility varies considerably, usually from 5 to 15 meters, but the suspended planktonic matter sustains a great diversity of both invertebrates and fishes. Little and medium sized chaps support the big fellas: sharks, Napoleon wrasses and big groupers (cod to Aussies), along with mantas, other rays and turtles.

It is very likely that you will see one or more of these on any one dive—and, with a bit of luck, all of them in a dive series. If the heavens really smile on you—as they did once on us—you could, on a single dive, see manta rays and a ride on a whale shark. No guarantees on this, of course.

Diving in Kupang

The Whitfords had developed 22 dive sites when we last visited, some of which are worth several repeats. Plans were to check out other spots, including sites where there are Japanese ships sunk by the Allies during World War II.

At least one of these wrecks lies in Teluk Pelikaan (Pelican Bay) on Semau Island. This is a Japanese fuel barge that was sunk by Beaufighters out of Drysdale on April 6, 1944, exploding in a "great ball of fire" according to one of the pilots. Visibility around the wreck is limited, but it is enough to see the encrusted barge. So far, nobody has been brave enough to enter.

For a variety of practical reasons, dives from Kupang are restricted to the area around the harbor, the northeast coast of Semau Island, and Kera Island, a

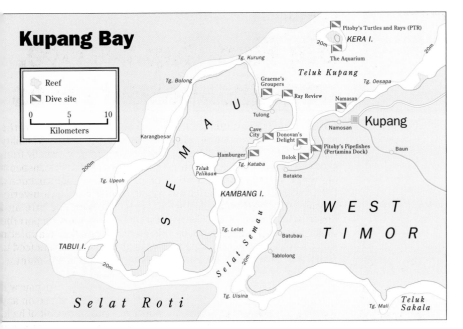

Kupang Bay

Legend:
- Reef
- Dive site

0   5   10
Kilometers

**Labels on map:**

Pitoby's Turtles and Rays (PTR)
KERA I.
20m
The Aquarium
Tg. Kurung
Teluk Kupang
Tg. Bolong
Graeme's Groupers
Tg. Oesapa
Ray Review
Namasan
Tulong
Kupang
Cave City
Namosan
Donovan's Delight
Karangbesar
Pitoby's Pipefishes (Pertamina Dock)
Baun
Hamburger
Bolok
Tg. Kataba
Teluk Pelikaan
Batakte
Tg. Upeoh
KAMBANG I.
SEMAU
WEST TIMOR
Tg. Lelat
Batubau
TABUI I.
Selat Semau
Tablolong
20m
20m
Selat Roti
Tg. Uisina
Tg. Mali
Teluk Sakala

---

low-lying, sand fringed island north of Kupang (see map above). It takes about 45 minutes to reach any of the locations on the Whitford's boat, a beamy 13.5-meter wooden craft powered by a 40hp outboard. The boat has a high tarp roof, and tanks are stored in an out-of-the-way spot. The boat draws very little water, so there could be a bit of spray bouncing around, depending on the wind.

The boat picks up clients at Tenau, the main harbor, at the bottom of a wide flight of stairs. Getting on and off can be a bit tricky somtimes, but there are always plenty of helping hands. The crew will get your dive bag aboard. On the way to the dive site, divers can either sit in the shade under the awning, or work on their tans out in the bow area. Fishing gear is usually available, if you want to troll on the way to the dive site.

Pulau Kera

Pulau Kera ("Monkey Island"), circled by a brilliant white sand beach, lies at the entrance of Kupang Bay. Dive Trek East has

a long-term lease on this little piece of paradise, and plans on building cottages here, and making it the base of their water sports operations, which include, in addition to snorkeling and diving, windsurfing, waterskiing, surfing, fishing and sailing.

"The Aquarium," a site off Kera's south coast, offers good diving, particularly for beginning divers. A shallow (2 meters) offshore sandbank ends at a coral wall that extends to about 12 meters before becoming a gently sloping sand bottom. Visibility varies considerably, but there are fair numbers and varieties of reef fish here.

"WTR," short for Whitfords's Turtles and Rays, is a site on the far side of Kera, and offers just what its name suggests. With the boat anchored offshore, we dropped some 20 meters and landed at the edge of the scattered coral formations that slope up to the island. We were right where the sandy bottom began in earnest, and it sloped gently into infinity. As soon as I neared the bottom, a startled blue-spotted stingray flew off, the first of at least a half dozen we spotted during the dive. We also discovered a very large black-spotted ray, (*Taeniura meyeni*), wedged under a maze of hard coral.

Some four or five turtles shot out of our way as we worked along at 20 meters. Then, just off our flight path, we caught another turtle, this one napping, with two striped remoras firmly attached to its back.

About halfway through the dive, a school of perhaps a dozen bumphead parrotfish rumbled in formation at the very edge of visibility. Our safety stop took place along a colorful spread of corals dense with small reef fish, right at the 5-meter level.

Semau Island

"Graeme's Groupers" lies about 100 meters off the beach at Semau where Teddy's and the Flobamor's cottages are located. The name comes from the unusual number of varieties of groupers (cod to the Aussies) that inhabit this reef. The reef extends from the shore in a very gradual slope, reaching 4–9 meters before the edge of a coral wall, which drops sharply to a sandy bottom at 30 meters.

Much of the hard coral growth here has been destroyed by extensive fish bombing here, but soft corals are present in fair numbers. The wall is pocked with shallow depressions and caves, some reaching back a meter or two.

True to the site's name, we identified a half-dozen species of groupers: blotchy, coral, flagtail, polkadot, saddleback and whitelined. These were all 20–30 centimeters, with an occasional fat 40-centimeter specimen. Cleaner wrasses worked their stations along the wall, servicing the groupers as well as longnose emperors, black-and-white snappers, sweetlips, dogface puffers and roundfaced batfish. We saw several large emperor and six-banded angelfish. Visibility never exceeded 10 meters.

"Ray Review" is a short distance east of Graeme's Groupers. The reef here is also wide and flat, dropping unevenly to a slightly sloping sandy bottom at 22 meters. Several detached coral pinnacles jut upward. Close to the sand bottom, we saw a half-dozen blue-spotted stingrays, which appear first as a pair of eyes, the rest of their bodies covered with fine sand.

Few fish inhabited the area, except for schools of black triggerfish. We also swam over a small forest of garden eels (*Heteroconger*) which disappeared at our approach.

"Cave City" is on the east coast of Semau, around the northeast tip and past the skeleton of the Japanese pier. The site is a coral wall more than a kilometer long, with at least a dozen good sites. The caves are the distinguishing feature here, some reaching back more than 5 meters. The reeftop, covered by 2–5 meters of water, drops off very close to shore to a sandy bottom, 20–40 meters below.

Hard coral growth is good, and we saw lots of gorgonians, some of them reaching several meters across. Soft corals grew in white tufts like wind-blown snow. On the very deepests sections of wall, we encountered bushy growths of antipatharian black corals.

In one cave we saw a school of yellow ribbon sweetlips, in another a large hawksbill turtle, and in others several species of groupers. Some of the animals swam back to the far dark corners of their homes before we could make an identification. Smaller caves were guarded by detachments of soldierfish.

We spotted two large, but skittish Napoleon wrasse (they are frequently sighted here). The waters near the wall were dominated by schools of black triggerfish, and we also spotted several gaudy clown triggerfish and small Picasso triggers. The six-banded angelfish we saw here were among the largest and fattest we had ever seen. As we ascended, we crossed paths with a school of tank-like bumphead parrotfish.

Visibility in the shallower waters was reduced to almost zero by hazy clouds of tiny fish. Below 20 meters, it was about average for this area.

Donovan's Delight

While flying into Kupang a while back, Graeme Whitford noticed a large, relatively shallow area in the Semau channel, fairly close to the main port. This looked promising to his trained eyes. His son Donovan embarked on a series of exploratory dives here, and was delighted after each one.

The site, marked by a navigational buoy, is now featured in all of Pitoby's dive series, and makes an especially good night dive. This is fine, fascinating diving indeed—with the usual caveat of poor to fair visibility. In our five dives here, it never sur-

passed 8 meters, and once it dropped to a really miserable 2–3 meters.

"Donovan's Delight" covers an irregular, oval shaped rise, more than 200 meters along its long axis. The reef top is 3–9 meters below the surface, and a vertical coral wall partially encircles the rise, dropping to a sandy bottom at 25–40 meters.

A fair variety and number of hard corals cover the top of the dome (there is some fish bomb damage, but it is not extensive) and soft corals are plentiful. The wall features several shallow caves.

During several dives here we saw sharks, both reef whitetips and reef blacktips, a number of large hawksbill turtles, and groupers up to 90 centimeters. Blue-spotted lagoon rays hide under table coral in the shallows or in the sandy bottom. Towards the ragged bottom of the wall, we saw clusters of sweetlips, emperor fish and puffers.

Groups of 10 to 20 roundfaced batfish patrolled the walls, and pairs of very large six-banded and blue-girdled angelfish wan-

Below: *A common lionfish (Pterois volitans) taking refuge in a sponge. Note that at least eight differently colored crinoids grip the edge of the sponge.*

Above: *A crown-of-thorns starfish (Acanthaster plancii). Outbreaks of this large, voracious coral-eating animal have occasionally proved ruinous for entire reefs. Do not handle these starfish, as their thorns can cause a toxic reaction.*

dered the reef face. Lionfish hovered near the top of the wall, including black morphs of *Pterois volitans.*

The wide, relatively flat reef top was ideal for safety stops. Several times we saw cuttlefish that would allow us to handle them gently. Large clusters of bright red anemones held their aggressive little guests.

There was, however, a strange absence of butterflyfish and damselfish here. In several areas we found small (5–8 cm.) bright yellow feather sea cucumbers, spread in a carpet over several square meters. We have seen these colorful animals in only a few other places, and nowhere in such numbers.

One afternoon dive, thanks to Donovan's keen eyes, we spotted more than a dozen species of nudibranchs.

Night Dive at Donovan's

A night dive at Donovan's Delight was one of the most fascinating hours of my life. I had hardly reached the shallow reef top and Donovan was already playing with an indignant puffer. Then he spotted three Spanish dancer nudibranchs (*Hexabranchus*), one of them with a silvery diamond pattern on its back.

The crinoids were hard at work, waving their feathery tentacles through the water. Following us around was the longest trumpetfish I have ever seen.

This fellow was so intent in participating in our fun that he kept bumping into me.

Sea urchins ambled around, some looking like World War I mines, others fuzzy balls, and still others with long, banded spines. Basket stars, creeping little bushes with agitated branches, clung to the high ground on coral and sponges, wherever there was a bit of room.

Ever alert Donovan spotted a large hawksbill turtle, tugged the sleepy giant out of its lair and tried to go for a joyride—but by then our turtle was wide awake and shot away at breakneck speed. In contrast, several cuttlefish and a squid were in a playful mood, allowing us to gently pet them. Our attentions caused one to change colors unbelievably fast, from a brownish red to barely spotted white and back again.

A fimbriated moray eel (*Gymnothorax fimbriatus*) nestled in the crack of a spread of red sponge, and the lionfish were out in force.

A great non-stop show all around—the only things we missed were the slipper lobsters and large bailer shells often seen on night dives here. Topside, a couple of swigs of Glenfiddich capped my best night dive ever.

Pitoby's Pipefishes

Just 10–15 minutes by boat from Donovan's Delight is Whitford's Pipefishes, a shallow dive off the Pertamina dock. The very irregular coral slope drops to 12–14 meters, but most of the action is above 10 meters. In addition to the pipefishes, we saw a good variety of small reef fish. A fine dive for beginners.

The namesake pipefishes are fascinating little creatures, much like seahorses with the kinks ironed out. We saw several network pipefish (*Corythoichthys flavofasciatus*), and several scribbled pipefish (*C. intestinalis*) in just 4–6 meters of water.

Manta Rays and still Little-Explored Diving

The western tip of Roti offers a fine underwater show. Walls of bright soft corals grow amid the rugged limestone formations of the island's coast. Fish life, particularly large and medium-sized species, is very good. Only the restricted visibility we encountered (8–10 meters) keeps the site from being world-class.

Roti is a small, dry island just off Timor's southwestern tip. In some areas dramatic white cliffs line the rugged coastline. Perhaps 100,000 people live here, tending small farms and fishing. The staple food of Roti—and Savu, further west—is the rich sap of the draught-resistant *lontar* palm, which is made into syrup, sugar and even a mild toddy.

The island capital is Ba'a, a town of 3,000 midway along the island's northern coast. (See map page 168.) Here, passable accommodations are available for visitors. Graeme and Donovan Whitford of Pitoby Water Sports in Kupang, the pioneers and only operators here, took us to Roti.

Batu Termanu

Batu ("Stone") Termanu is just a half-hour northeast of Ba'a. We puttered along coastline of mixed beaches and rugged chunks of raised coral in an open fishing boat, 8 meters long and powered by a 25 hp outboard. There are two sites at Batu Termanu, each marked by differently shaped stone pinnacle.

The closest and largest one, with a tip of sculpted limestone with two holes cut through it, is locally dubbed Batu Termanu Mai, the "female." Some 15 minutes further east, Batu Termanu Jantan, the "male," is less impres-

sive: a low, rounded rock with a detached, oval pinnacle. At high tide, only the pinnacle shows.

The vertical rock face of "Lady" Termanu continues a few meters underwater, and then a flat reef begins that slopes gently to a wall just 100 meters offshore. This wall drops vertically to 25–27 meters. It is almost completely covered with bright and pastel soft corals, yielding at the deeper end to green soft corals and stands of black coral.

As we began to explore the small caves in the wall, we were distracted by a large school of surgeonfish, followed by a quite large shark, heading down the wall. Just as the big fellow disappeared, a smaller reef whitetip appeared out of the gloom. He would not allow us to get within four meters, but he stuck around for at least 10 minutes.

Fish cascaded down and up the wall: schools of surgeonfish and unicornfish, groups of pinnate batfish, and big parrotfish.

AT A GLANCE
Roti

Reef type:	Slopes and drop-offs, often amid rocky outcrops
Access:	30 min to 4 hrs from Ba'a
Visibility:	Poor to fair, 8–10 meters
Current:	Generally mild
Coral:	Good growth and variety, particularly soft corals
Fish:	Variable; sharks and rays relatively common
Highlights:	Manta rays and good wall at Batu Termanu

Yellowtail fusiliers flashed by traveling horizontally. Below, sweetlips hung in small groups, and a large barracuda shot off into the darkness. Prides of lionfish—including a group of nine!—patrolled the reef wall. We drifted along the slight current, one-half to one knot, until our air was finished.

The seaward dive path from Batu Termanu Jantan—Christened "The Cathedral" by the Whitfords—leads through narrow passages between rocky outcrops. The bottom deepened gradually to 25–30 meters, the limit of our journey.

A reef whitetip shark monitored out our progress, but the highlight of the dive was a school of blackfin barracuda (*Sphyraena genie*). Discovered in the shallows, these 50–75 centimeter fish were almost friendly. During the deeper part of the dive, we saw two schools of jacks. We barely noticed the groupers, lobster and rainbow-hued parrotfish.

Termanu beach

The Whitfords have also pioneered another dive in the area of Termanu Mai, beginning from the beach. The reef starts close to shore, and soon one encounters a series of craters, 2–4 meters across, and 5–6 meters into the rock. The current turns these into swirling funnels, which are sometimes full of fish trapped by the outgoing tide. Further out from shore, great chunks of rock covered with soft corals lead to the near side of Termanu.

In this channel, at around 12 meters, I saw the grand spectacle of two manta rays, at least two meters across, gliding overhead. Later, at similar depth, a single manta cruised by overhead. Gently flapping his wings, he banked directly overhead. As he reached the limit of visibility, around 8–10 meters, he turned sharply and made another overhead passage, just two meters away. Two little remoras stuck to his smooth, wide belly. Donovan Whitford, who has dived here in April, May and August, has seen mantas every time.

Ndao Island

On a special arrangement basis, Dive Trek East offers a two-day,

West Roti

Laut Savu

Laut Timor

Batu Termanu Jantan
Batu Termanu Mai
Batu Termanu
Feapopi

DENKA I. KODI I.
Oelaba
Ba'a
White sand Tg. Sai beaches
Oelua
Nuse
Oele
NUSE
Tg. Tonga
Bone
Busalangga
North Ndao
Ndao
East Ndao
Mbueain
Seda
Mok
NDAO I.
DOO
Oebatok
Oenale
Oenitas
Batutua
Kuli
Oelasin
LAI I.
Surfing
Namberala
BATU TELU
Tungaun
Tudameda
Oeseli
Teluk Buka
MANUK
Oenggaut
Tg. Aras
Teluk Serdale
LANDU
BIBIK I.
Tg. Boa Boa
North Haliana
LIUNG I.
Dana
BATU HELIANA
South Haliana
DANA

Reef
Dive site
0   5   10
Kilometers

one-night trip from Ba'a to Ndao Island, a tiny island off the tip of Roti about 4 hours by boat from Ba'a. This is neither for fanatical divers, nor for tourists hungry for cultural events. It is a casual mix of interesting diving and contact with friendly people who seldom see foreigners in their midst.

Ndao Island is a dry, poor island that is the home of itinerant silver and goldsmiths. These men spend from March to November in Roti, Sumba, Flores and Timor, making jewelry out of old coins with simple tools.

We made the trip in August, but we recommend that you do so between September and May, as the June–August period has the strongest winds and worst waves. It was unseasonally calm when we went, but we were still drenched with spray on several occasions. We followed Roti's coast, past Nuse Island, and then out to the pristine beaches of Ndao. We checked in with the local authorities and walked around the village of thatch- and tin-roofed huts, all laid out on neatly swept sand.

Diving Ndao

Our marine chart showed a contour line at 50 meters just off Ndao's deserted northwest coast, so we decided to try a pioneer dive there. Despite the chart, the underwater profile turned out to be quite different. We descended to about 8 meters, then swam far out on a strong current over a very slight slope. The bottom reached only 25 meters, with detached outcroppings of coral rock covered with hard and soft corals, and the usual complement of reef fish. A couple of small reef whitetip sharks vanished as soon as we saw them, and a school of ringtail surgeonfish (*Acanthurus blochii*) drifted by. A large group of longnose emperors followed us for much of the dive. Visibility was poor, just 7–8 meters.

Our marine chart proved wrong again on our second dive, just in front of Ndao village. Instead of an 8 meter bottom, dropping very gradually to 16 meters, we went right down on a steep sand slope to 35 meters. The slope just kept going into the gloom. After a few patches of seagrass, the bottom was bare sand. Scattered here and there we saw cerianthids and strange-looking sea urchins sheltering tiny fish in their spines. In the shallows, we saw sea pens and several fat, long worms. Neither I nor my buddy had ever experienced such a dive—almost pure sand below, and menacing gloom ahead and on either side.

An Evening on Ndao

As dusk settled on Ndao, we bucket-bathed in the back of our host's house, then settled in to enjoy our home-stay. A supper of rice, vegetables and salted fish was followed by singing and dancing in the living room. An elderly gentleman played the *sasando,* a Rotinese string instrument made from bamboo and folded *lontar* palm leaves. While we were drinking *tuak,* the juice of the *lontar* palm, three little girls danced for us, decked out in beautiful wrappings of locally woven *ikat* cloth.

Although the people of Ndao originally came from Sawu, much of their culture—weaving styles, the *sasando*—has been borrowed from their near neighbors, the Rotinese. Very little of original Ndao culture is left, except gold and silver smithery.

After a night in very comfortable beds, complete with (unnecessary) mosquito netting, we woke to hot coffee, followed by a breakfast of rice, vegetables and chicken curry. We left early on the outgoing tide.

Nuse Island

Our boat cruised past Doo Island, deserted, and lined with

Above: *A terminal phase pale-nose parrotfish,* Scarus psittacus, *asleep in its mucous cocoon. This covering, which is secreted from the skin, is thought to block the parrotfish's scent from night predators. Mapia atoll, Irian Jaya.*

white beaches. We decided against a dive there. Continuing to Nuse Island, we motored past a small hamlet of Ndao fishermen and anchored off the north coast to try a dive. Just then we saw a manta ray breaching. Our crew said the large rays are often hooked by local fishermen.

Things didn't look too promising at first, however, as we dropped to scattered patches of coral. We went along a slope to 40 meters, where all life ceased. Returning to shallower depths, and more life, we spotted a large, light brown stingray keeping a wary eye on us. We approached carefully, however, and got to within an arm's length before it slowly drifted away.

Just about then my buddy grabbed me and pointed up. Holy cow! A huge manta ray hovered over us, turned slowly, and, with exquisite grace, flew out of our range of visibility. We came up in ecstasy, ready for the long tanning haul back to Ba'a.

Batu Heliana

The Whitfords have also pioneered some dive sites off southwest Roti, the southernmost extremity of Indonesia. We dove off both sides of Batu Heliana, a jagged pinnacle rearing up from the sea a short (15–20 minute) boat ride from Oeseli village. The sheer sides of the rock unfortunately do not continue underwater. There is no wall, only slop-

ing bottom, well-covered by soft corals. Here and there, detached coral blocks—at 10–15 meters— support good populations of reef fish and invertebrates. We saw two small reef sharks, a turtle and a stingray.

Off the southwest face of the rock, the only large fish we saw was a single golden trevally. We descended to 20 meters, but saw nothing of interest. The visibility was lousy, less than 8 meters. In the shallows, we discovered a good number of *Tridacna* clams, and the largest spreads of carpet anemones we had ever seen.

As we motored away, the engine's racket flushed out hundreds of flying foxes. These large fruit-eating bats are the only permanent inhabitants of the "island." Birds nest here as well, but only seasonally.

Large Dana Island has an inviting beach, but no one lives here. Its inhabitants were massacred several centuries ago, and their spirits keep out everyone except occasional deer hunters (the island teems with deer.) We worked our way around the island's northwest tip to a spot beyond the big waves, which broke in perfect tubes, enough to make any surfer drool.

We dropped 8 meters to the reef top, which was cut through with narrow surge channels. The reef sloped to 12 meters, then dropped sharply to 25 meters. Visibility was about 10 meters.

We saw a spotted grouper, a hawksbill turtle, and a 1.5 meter reef whitetip shark. Along the wall we saw a school of a dozen or more pinnate batfish, and a couple of large schools of fusiliers. A shadowy mass of surgeonfish, distinguishable only by the silhouette they cast, passed by at the limit of visibility. On other occasions, the Whitfords have seen huge specimens of almost every kind of tropical fish here, in excellent visibility. On this day I was not so lucky.

Eastern Indonesia's Dream Dive Sites

Experienced sports divers, a tough lot to satisfy, dream about this. Whence the site name: "Kal's Dream." We had it right in front of us, with ringside seats. Four good sized grey sharks circling us, then cruised back-and-forth while a black tip and a white tip made a brief appearance. At the same time two groups of tuna, each following by an absolutely huge leader cruised by just overhead, drifting off, returning for a closer look, then coming back again.

To one side a mere few hundred jacks swirled around our dive guide. A small group of yellowtail barracuda were dwarfed by one well qualified for its name of "great" barracuda. None of us had ever seen so many big fishes at the same time. We hung on in the gusting current, living a diver's dream.

Welcome to Alor, a small island north of West Timor, at the end of a little archipelago east of Flores. The dive locations here are absolutely world class. But for those divers who are concerned about creature comforts, better wait while. There is nothing here even close to star-rated accommodations, and it's going to be a long time before a luxury hotel rises on the shore of the long, narrow bay where Kalabahi, the little district capital, is located.

And the food is also strictly Indonesian: no burgers, juicy steaks or junk food. However, the local operator has now found a number of local restaurants specializing in seafood and their accommodation is at a new losmen that has spring beds and hot water. Not four-star, but fine.

Alor is still pretty much in the middle of nowhere, and getting there takes an effort. The three scheduled weekly flights from Kupang, the district capital, are often cancelled. The throbbing ferry is reliable, but takes 14 hours to get there from Kupang.

The bright spot, of course, is that there won't be any crowds. The the only operator based in the area is Dive Trek East, run by the father and son team of Graeme and Donovan Whitford in Kupang. Based on solid bookings, they make all the arrangements from Kupang to be ready to take you diving when you arrive in Alor. Dive Trek East is not a large outfit, and as they also run diving around Kupang and to Roti, booking ahead is essential.

We dove with the Whitfords, but live-aboards also now make the run, including Grand Komodo Tours and Travel, which has three years experience diving the area. See "Alor Practicalities," page 292.

The Alor locations—actually a

AT A GLANCE
Alor

Reef type:	Banks and walls
Access:	15 min–2 hrs by boat
Visibility:	Generally good, 12–20 meters
Current:	At some sites, 2 knots or more
Coral:	Very good coverage and varieties
Fish:	Superb numbers and varieties, particularly big fish
Highlights:	Sharks, giant grouper, sheer richness of fish life

series of sites in the Pantar Strait between western Alor and smaller Pantar Island—were pioneered in April 1993 by Donovan Whitford, who took a small group there from Perth, West Australia. Graeme, Donovan's father, had looked over the place when planning a pearl farm and thought that diving could be excellent. The Perth group, which had dived with Pitoby's in Kupang and Roti, wanted to try a new location on their island hopping trip to Bali. Alor was their first stop. Boy did they get lucky.

Kal's Dream

All the hassles are forgotten when you finally make the giant leap into the underwater world. At The Dream, aside from the big fellows, we also saw an incredibly huge mass of fish, either schooling or in loose aggregations: fusiliers, triggerfish, unicorns and surgeons and at least three species of snappers, all in the 40–70 cm range.

This giant, species-rich mass moved around the quiet leeward side of the sea, dominated by the big fellows. Aside from an unusually large concentration of large, eye-catching imperial angelfish, we did not even bother to look at the usual reef fishes.

What we did notice was that the surfaces of the substrate were completely covered with invertebrates, so grabbing a handhold in the current—which gusted up to two knots—always presented our ecologically oriented conscience with a dilemma. As we let go, with our air running low, a huge Napoleon wrasse passed by, seeing off his guests. We drifted fast during the decompression stop, but our boat was nearby when we surfaced, physically and emotionally drained.

Of course we could not leave well enough alone, and returned the next day for another dive at the same site. The current was even faster this time, and we lost an anchor trying to hook up the boat. We put in just a bit too far downcurrent, and had to kick hard to reach the sea mound, whose top portion comes to 8–10 meters of the surface.

A couple of gray sharks watched our struggles, but only with passing interest. By the time we grabbed hold and looked around, we saw that the previous day's show had changed, and we could not crawl over the top of the sea mound to the calmer side. There were no tuna around, and the 7 or 8 sharks which appeared throughout the dive quickly drifted out of sight.

But just ahead and above us, four absolutely huge yellowtail barracuda faced into the current, with barely a tail flick necessary remain in place. Hand over hand we managed to approach them to within a couple of meters before they moved off a bit.

We began an only partially controlled drift along the current-swept side of the sea mound, between 25 and 35 meters down, past a group of Napoleon wrasse, which eyed us curiously. There were at least eight of them of varying sizes, from 50 cm juveniles to huge grand-daddies, the largest concentration of these fish we had ever seen.

A school of at least 50 batfish flickered by, swam out of sight and returned twice for a closer look. One of our party spotted a sea snake heading for the depths from 35 meters and Moorish idols appeared in large numbers. Clouds of the two-hued blue triggerfish hovered over the outer edge of the mound.

With the current occasionally gusting to a mask-and-regulator–wrenching three knots, and no bare rock to hold on to, there was time to look over the invertebrate life, none of which managed to struggle to any height above 20 centimeters. The most abundant species we remember

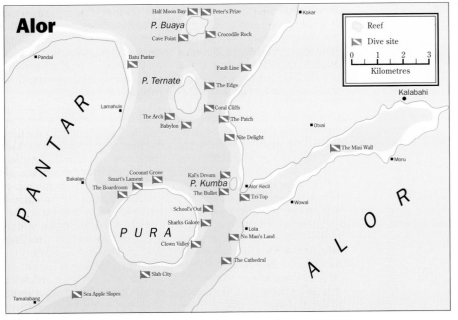

Alor

Half Moon Bay • Peter's Prize
P. Buaya
Cave Point • Crocodile Rock • Kokar
• Pandai
Batu Pantar
Fault Line
P. Ternate
The Edge
Kalabahi •
Lamahule
Coral Cliffs
The Arch
The Patch
Babylon
• Otvai
Nite Delight
The Mini Wall
• Moru
Coconut Grove
Kal's Dream
Bakalan
Smart's Lament
P. Kumba
The Boardroom
The Bullet • Alor Kecil
• Wowal
School's Out
Tri-Top
P U R A
Sharks Galore
• Lola
Clown Valley
No Man's Land
A L O R
The Cathedral
Slab City
Tamalabang
Sea Apple Slopes
P A N T A R

Reef
Dive site
0   1   2   3
Kilometres

were small sponges, soft coral trees and small, tightly packed colonial cup corals, normally nigh feeders but a few open ones with tiny yellow tentacles, searching for plankton.

Monster Grouper

On our third Dream dive we managed to get over the sea mound, found a quiet ringside seat at about 25 meters, and again witnessed the greatest show in the sea. If we missed the circling grey-shark formation of the first dive, others were bold enough to approach us closer than previously.

There were more big barracuda this time, and a breath-taking formation of four tuna, all over 1.5 meters, followed by a dozen or more smaller ones. But all of this paled when the main attraction showed up on the scene: an absolute giant, the mother of all groupers, 2 meters long if it was an inch, with a dark head and light grayish midsection.

These monster groupers are a tough lot, said to swallow whole spiny lobsters, sharks and possibly even pearl divers. The one we saw certainly looked capable of bullying just about anything it encountered, and could certainly swallow us for dessert. Even the largest gray shark gave it a wide berth. He checked us out from 3–4 meters, drifted off a bit, and returned for another look.

While we were holding still and keeping a wary eye on our fat monarch, three of the giant-sized tuna cruised around, often coming into close range, probably just curious, over and over. Deciding that the noisy intruders into his kingdom posed no threat, the grouper drifted off.

We left with our fish-story and bodies intact except for a few coral scrapes. Out of my 1000-odd dives, the three on the Dream are all in the top five. Nowhere else comes even close to the variety of huge fish: barracuda, tuna, shark, grouper.

The strong current that almost continuously sweeps the area brings nutrients to the invertebrates and small fishes, which become fodder for medium-sized fishes, which in turn are gobbled by the big ones. Don't miss this show.

Sharks Galore

For those put off by strong current, there's almost as good a show a quick ride away, off the coast of Pura Island, across a short stretch of sea from The Dream. Here we dove at the edge of the "Clown Valley" site where a previous group had spotted a giant grouper and several sharks. But instead of following our dive plan and heading north, we decided to go with the flow and drift south, in a gentle current, along the sloping profile.

Less than a minute after hitting the water, we were greeted by at least a dozen great barracuda, all in the meter-range. These were followed by a half dozen long, sleek barracuda. They were still at the edge of visibility when a swirling school of bigeye jacks surrounded us, finning rapidly with no apparent purpose. Later in the dive we were shadowed by even larger jacks.

About half way into the dive, at about 30 meters, we came to a ledge and stopped there for most of our remaining bottom time. In front of us was the shark show, with an occasional appearance by a giant-sized dogtooth tuna.

The dogtooth tuna, (*Gymnosorda unicolor*), is a sharp-toothed coral reef marauder which moves with a characteristic jerky tail beat. It can grow to over two meters in length and weigh 125 kg. Unlike most tunas, the dogtooth is primarily a reef dweller, preferring rough, current-swept areas which are also home to fast-moving, aggressive, requiem sharks. In Alor, you can get close enough to these tuna to see their large, conical teeth, set in a single row along each jaw. Also look for short pectoral fins, dark finlets and a prominent, wavy lateral line.

These tuna are voracious predators of fishes, especially planktivores. The body is without scales and the white flesh is of high quality. Due to this latter factor, the dogtooth tuna has been fished out under regular pressure in much of the Indo-Pacific. We hope you get to see them in Alor before they get fished out from there also.

While at any one time we saw "only" nine sharks, there must

Below: *Fishermen around Alor Island use rattan traps like this to catch fish on the reef.*

Above: *This young Alorese fisherman wears homemade goggles made of wood, pitch and salvaged glass chipped into circles.*

have been well over a dozen of them, all of very respectable size except for a couple of reef whitetips which seemed somewhat more at ease than usual, perhaps feeling a degree of protection from their bigger brothers. And some of the brothers were big indeed. Taking into account the hard fact that everything looks 30 percent bigger underwater, plus human beings' natural tendency to exaggerate—especially when telling shark stories—the 4 or 5 grey sharks in front of us were a good 2 meters long, and there were several reef blacktips almost the same size. The reef whitetips were a manageable 1.25 meters.

The show lasted a good while as we anxiously glanced at our computers and air gauges. Just before our instruments told us to get out of there, a curious pair of sharks appeared. They seemed joined in the forward-section of their bodies, like Siamese twins. As all of us confirmed this—it was unlikely to be a narcosis-produced vision. Perhaps it was the shark version of sexual foreplay.

The anti-climatic decompression stop was held in an almost solid carpet of anemones, interspersed with orange sponges and, in the shallower portion, with hydroids. Strangely, we saw no clownfish in any of the anemones. Back on board, excitely matching sightings and numbers, we dubbed the location "Sharks Galore."

Soon, we had something else to talk about. As we were motoring to Ternate Island from the south, a huge number of pilot whales broke the surface, some leaping and frolicking, accompanied by dolphins. We never came very close to the seething mass, but on another occasion Donovan led a group of snorkelers who were rewarded by underwater sightings of a half-dozen pilot whales which approach to within 5 or 6 meters. Our guide also snorkeled with these whales just off the entrance to Kalabahi Bay.

The Mini Wall

Tired from too much input and three-dive days, we had time only for one night dive. This was along the southern edge of Kalabahi Bay, about 10 kilometers from town. We entered off a pebbled beach, and headed parallel to the coast over rubble covered with an almost continuous carpet of crinoids. Some 30 meters of this, then a small wall, cracked in several places and pocked with shallow holes. The "Mini Wall" bottomed in sand at 7 meters.

Soft corals, sponges and invertebrates covered the wall, a solid, multi-hued mass of life. Several reef fishes were still swimming, but others slept, oblivious to the humans. The keen eyes of Donovan, my dive guide, picked out three exquisite little shrimp, along with several decorator crabs and two other species of colorful crabs, unidentified. A tiny cuttlefish, just 7–8 centimeters long, allowed us to play with it until it became tired of games and shot off in a cloud of ink, surprisingly large given its tiny body.

We saw nothing big, but there was plenty of that in the day dives. However, all the locals admired our bravery for diving at this location. The entry area is considered haunted, as access to it is by a path across a cemetery.

And there are many stories, unconfirmed, of a huge snake living in one of the caves under the wall. We checked carefully but no monster snake eyes were reflected in our lights. Just as well.

Walls and Sea Mounds

The dive locations explored up till now in this area are concentrated around the three islands lying between Alor and Pantar: Pulau Buaya in the north, Pulau Ternate in the middle, and Pulau Pura to the south. Most of the sites show an excellent wall profile, dropping to 50 or more meters and with a topside ledge perfect for the decompression stop. Many of the walls are pocketed with caves. Invertebrate life and reef fishes compare favorable—both in absolute numbers and species diversity—other top dive locations in Indonesia.

Some of the sites are "takas," or sea mounds, generally coming to about 8 meters or so of the surface. The steeply sloping bottom prevents convenient, up-current anchorage. There's no other choice: giant leap and down fast, finning like hell at an angle to the current to reach the nearest part of the sea-mound. Then it's hand-over-hand to the far side, and down to 25 meters for a ring-side seat. We can't really say how rich these mounds are in invertebrate and small fish life, as we were always too busy watching all the big ones. In general, however, on both walls and *takas*, the Pantar Strait is very rich.

Of the normally seen tropical reef fishes, we saw unusual concentrations of longnose emperors, red-tooth triggers, surgeonfish and unicorns, emperor angels, and snappers. The latter two species showed up several times in close to unbelievable concentrations. Of the larger fellows, sharks showed up on almost every dive, usually the harmless, and rather skittish reef whitetip. Less frequent but still common are the great barracuda, Spanish mackerel and schools of big eyed jacks.

Visibility varied from a good 12 meters to—rarely—an excellent 40 meters in the horizontal plane. Most locations are suitable for even neophyte divers, with no current and plenty of action. However, the best spot to see really big fish, Kal's Dream, requires some experience, because of the strong current usually encountered.

Dive Trek East

Dive Trek East is based in Kupang, the capital of Nusa Tenggara Timur Province. Access to Kupang is easy, via several daily flights from Bali. The Whitfords arrange everything from airport pickup to seeing your final flight off back to

Bali or to Darwin, Australia. Donovan Whitford, a PADI dive instructor, is the only dive guide available. Young but with plenty of experience, and always cheerful and pleasant, he can adapt dive series to match experience and interest.

The dive boat currently used is a new 13.5 meter by 3.5 meter traditional timber vessel, much the same as is locally used as an inter-island ferry. It has been modified by the Whitfords to include such comforts as a toilet, diving ladders, and an exhaust muffler—things the local crews don't seem to bother with on their boats.

It has a large raised bench-height area in the center for laying out dive gear and cameras, and a large tub of fresh water is provided for rinsing cameras after diving.

The boat can accommodate 14 divers and the roof is a huge sundeck, a great place from which to watch the sunsets, which are spectacular here.

The usual dive routine calls for leaving the hotel after breakfast, around 8 am, and a short minibus ride to Kalabahi harbor where the alighting divers are invariably greeted with yells of "Hello Meeester!" from the kids and young hotbloods showing of their English skills.

The boat takes about 45 minutes to reach the first and most famous dive site, "Kal's Dream." There are several sites in this area, and from this point, no dive sites are further than a surface interval away. As the boat does not return until the day's diving is over, lunch, afternoon tea and coffee, and hot soup for after night dives are all kept on board.

Donovan personally plans and accompanies all dives. While there are areas of strong current at Alor, there are also many excellent dive sites where current is not a factor. In each case, Donovan plans the diving based on the experience levels of each member of the group, and according to what they would like to see.

It is usually possible to dive three times a day, and for real enthusiasts, a night dive on top of this. The days are tiring, but exciting.

Below: *The fish and invertebrate life of Indonesia is still little-explored. Below is the first photograph ever taken or photographed of the Banggai cardinalfish,* Pterapogon kauderni, *a fish that has since become something of a star among marine aquarists. Kal saw the unusual fish while snorkeling, and shot it with a Nikonos. This cardinalfish lives among diademnid sea urchins in shallow, sandy areas in the Banggai Islands off Sulawesi, the only place it has ever been found. When he saw Kal's photographs, ichthyologist Gerald R. Allen thought it might be a new species, but when he collected it and researched the archives, he found it had been named in 1933.*

Introducing Sulawesi

The contorted island of Sulawesi lies in the middle of the archipelago's sweep, north of Flores and reaching almost to the Philippines. Formerly—and on some maps, still—called the Celebes, the island offers some of the most stunning scenery in all of Indonesia, both above and below water.

The people of Sulawesi are culturally diverse, ranging from the cosmopolitan Bugis of Ujung Pandang, Sulawesi's largest city and the hub of eastern Indonesia, to the traditional Toraja of the highlands.

Shaped by Fire

The island took its unusual shape about 3 million years ago, when a chunk of land that had split from western New Guinea and drifted eastward (Sulawesi's eastern and southeastern peninsulas) collided with a volcanic island that had formed along a fault line east of Borneo (the south and the northern peninsula). The force of collision spun the two islands and left them joined in the middle.

The great majority of Sulawesi's 227,000 square kilometers is higher than 500 meters. The province has 17 active volcanoes, concentrated in North Sulawesi and in the Sangihe Islands. In the past few years, Lokon near Manado and Siau Island's Karangetang have been the most active.

Exquisite Reefs

Because of its unique shape, no part of the island is more than 100 kilometers from the sea, and Sulawesi has a whopping 6,000 kilometers of coastline. More than 110 small offshore islands are also part of the Sulawesi group. Most of this coastline is ringed with reef.

Although too disturbed to be of interest to divers, the 16,000 square kilometers of reef off Ujung Pandang supports one of the most productive fisheries in the world. In the north, the near pristine reefs off Manado are famous for their sheer walls and abundance of fish life.

Perhaps the best diving in the island remains inaccessible: the Togian Islands in Tomini Bay, famous for displaying in a very small area every known type of coral reef; Taka Bone Rate, southeast of Selayar Island in the south and the third-largest atoll in the world (see map page 182); and the Tukang Besi Islands off southeast Sulawesi, rumored to have moved Jacques Cousteau—who recently passed through Indonesia—to declare them the finest diving site in the world.

Because it straddles the Asian and Australian biogeographical zones and offers a wide range of habitats, Sulawesi has a great number of endemic species. Discounting bats, fully 98 percent of the island's mammals are found nowhere else. Among the most unusual of these are the babirusa—literally "pig deer"—a wild pig with huge, curving tusks; the rare anoa, a water buffalo the size of a dog; and the tiny tarsier, a big-eyed primate the size of a hamster. Some 34 percent of the non-migratory birds—88 species—are endemic.

Famous Entrepôt

Although the Gowanese and Bugis developed their own writing systems, adapted from an Indian alphabet, the early texts

Overleaf: *A long-nosed hawkfish, Oxycirrhites typus, in a gorgonian. This little predator keeps a lookout from its perch, and then swoops down and 'hawks' small crustaceans. Bunaken group, Sulawesi. Photograph by Mike Severns.*

Opposite: *A colubrine sea snake, Laticauda colubrina, pokes its head (lower right) behind a sponge in search of food. Too slow to snatch a swimming fish, these snakes must corner their prey in tight crevices or feed on spawn. This species, with leather much smoother than its terrestrial brethren, is heavily collected in the Philippines, where it supports a very large snakeskin industry. Though not in the least aggressive, the colubrine sea snake is quite venomous and should not be harassed. Bunaken group, Sulawesi. Photograph by Mike Severns.*

Sulawesi

Laut Sulawesi

See knockout below for continuation of Sangihe Islands

SIAU I.

TAGULANDANG I.
BIARO I.
BANGKA I.

North Sulawesi
(Sulawesi Utara)
Manado
Amurang   Bitung
Tondano

Tolitoli

Limboto   Kotomobagu

Gorontalo

Teluk TOGIAN Is.
UNA UNA I.
Tomini   TOGIAN I.   WALIABAHI I.   Laut Maluku
BATU DAKA I.   TALATAKOH I.

Donggala

Palu   Ampenan
Teluk Poso   Tg. Pangkalaseang

Poso   Luwuk

Gimpu   **Central Sulawesi**   PELENG
Uwekuli   (Sulawesi Tengah)   BANGGAI I.
Tentena   BANGKULU I.

South Sulawesi   BANGGAI Is.   KARAKELANG I.
(Sulawesi Selatan)   TALAUD
Mamuju   Teluk   ISLANDS
Wotu   Sorowako   Tolo   SALIBABU I.
Rantepao   KABARUANG I.

Palopo   D. Towuti   SANGIHE I.
Majene   **Makale**   Cimpu   SANGIHE
Pinrang   Rapang   Southeast Sulawesi   ISLANDS
Pare-   Singkang   Kolaka   **Kendari**   SIAU I.
Pare   Teluk   WOWONI I.
Watansopeng   Bone   (Sulawesi Tenggara)   TAGULANDANG I.

Watampone   Raha   Continued
Maros   Sinjai   MUNA   BUTON I.   from above

Ujung   KABAENA I.   WANGIWANGI I.
Pandang   Jeneponto   Baubau   KALEDUPA I.
   TUKANGBESI   TOMEA I.
SELAYAR I.   ISLANDS   BINONGKO I.
Benteng

TAKA
KAYUADI I.   BONE   Laut   0   100   200
   RATE
TANAH JAMPEA I.   ATOLL   Flores   Kilometers
BONE RATE Is.   KALAOTOA I.

Selat Makassar

The Dutch arrived at this time, and quickly muscled the Portuguese out of the spice trade. Although Holland used force of arms to insist that sellers accept low prices, spices continuted to "escape" to Makassar, where sellers got a fair return. To save their monopoly, the Dutch fought the famous "Battle of Makassar," defeating Gowa by allying with the Bugis.

The People of Sulawesi

Among the 11.5 million people living on Sulawesi are dozens of ethnic groups, of which the Bugis, Makassarese and Mandarese of the south, the Minahasans of the north, and the Torajans of the interior are the best known.

The Muslim Bugis have always been famous seafarers, and their distinctive wooden *pinisi*—schooner-shaped boats now fitted with diesel engines—still serve as the vehicles for much of the inter-island cargo carried around the archipelago.

The people of Manado and the Minahasa region in the north are predominantly Christians, having converted during the early 19th century. Good relations with the Dutch led to the region being blessed with schools and other perquisites of colonial favor.

The most famous of Sulawesi's ethnic groups among visitors are the Toraja, who live in the beautiful highlands north of Makale. The Torajans' tall, sway-backed *tongkonan,* or ancestral houses, graced by huge stacks of water buffalo horns, are the archipelago's most distinctive architectural feature.

Even Torajans working in the big cities of western Indonesia return home for an important funeral of one of their kinsmen. At these grand events, in which the entire community participates, hundreds of very valuable water buffalo are slaughtered.

are concerned chiefly with myths of origin and royal genealogies. Until the Europeans arrived in the 16th century, little is known of the island's history.

The Portuguese pioneered the European trade route to the Spice Islands, and Makassar (now Ujung Pandang) was a regular stop on the route from Malacca to the nutmeg and clove islands of Maluku. At the time, the Gowanese and Bugis sailed the monsoon winds as far as Australia in search of trepang and other sea products.

The king of Gowa petitioned the Portuguese for missionaries, but these never arrived. The proselytizers of Islam were more responsive, however, and by the early 17th century South Sulawesi—both the Gowanese and the Bugis—had become a Muslim stronghold.

World-Class Walls and Outstanding Fish Life

Divers, from neophytes to those who have dived all the world-famous spots, have nothing but praise for the reefs surrounding the small islands in Manado Bay. These are very steep, pristine coral walls. In good weather, visibility on Bunaken Island's drop-offs is typically around 25 meters, very good for Indonesian waters. At some sites, and when the current is up, this can drop to 12 meters because of plankton.

The reefs here are basically untouched. Little damage from fish bombing is visible, in part because the reefs are so steep, and drop off so near the shore. Nor have there been enough divers here to tear up the sites, although some Bunaken sites are looking a bit worn. In 1989, thanks to the efforts of Loky Herlambang, founder of Nusantara Diving Centre (NDC), the pioneering dive operator here, 75,265 hectares of underwater area around Bunaken, Manado Tua, Siladen, Montehage and Nain islands became a national marine reserve: Taman Nasional Laut Bunaken–Manado Tua.

North Sulawesi and the islands in the Bunaken group face the Sulawesi Sea, which reaches more than 6 kilometers. Even on the short boat rides to the dive sites, one passes over more than a kilometer of water covering a trench that separates the islands from the mainland. Nutrient-rich water from these depths sweeps across the islands' reefs.

The variety of marine life here is excellent; the surfaces of the walls are crowded with hard and soft corals, whip corals, sponges, and clinging filter-feeders like crinoids and basket stars. Huge schools of pyramid butterflyfish (*Hemitaurichthys polylepsis*) and black triggerfish (*Odonus niger*), and clouds of anthias swarm around the reef edge and the upper part of the wall. Sharks, schools of barracuda, rays, moray eels and sea snakes—particularly the black-and-grey–banded colubrine sea snake (*Laticauda colubrina*)—are relatively common here.

Beginners like the ease of the conditions. There is usually very little current, and the boats anchor right on the edge of the walls. Experts appreciate the fact that most operators keep groups small: four to seven people.

The Bunaken–Manado Tua reserve features some dozen-and-a-half dive sites. Most are concentrated off the south and west coasts of Bunaken, a low, crescent-shaped coral island completely surrounded by a steep fringing reef. Adjacent Manado Tua—"Old Manado"—

AT A GLANCE
Manado

Reef type: Steep coral walls

Access: 45 min to 1.5 hr by boat

Visibility: Fair to very good; 12–25 meters

Current: Usually gentle; at some sites to 2 knots or more

Coral: Excellent condition and variety, particularly soft corals

Fish: Good numbers and excellent variety

Highlights: Pristine walls; sheer number of species; interesting wreck

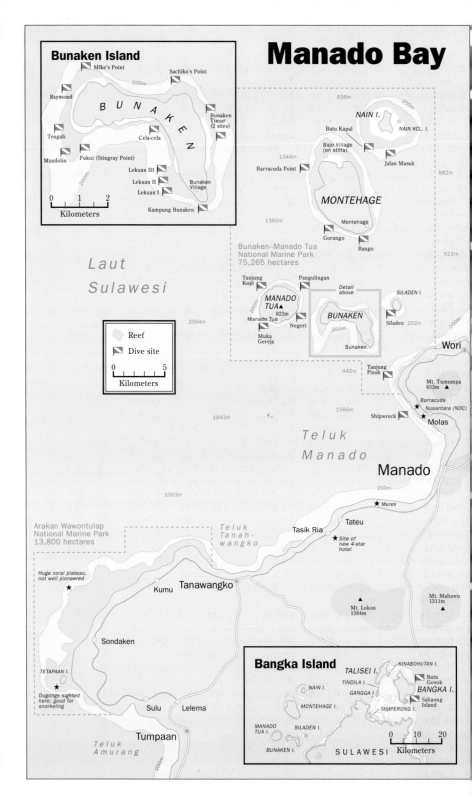

Manado Bay

Bunaken Island

Mike's Point
Sachiko's Point
Raymond
B U N A K E N
200m
Bunaken Timur (2 sites)
Tengah
Cela-cela
Mandolin
Fukui (Stingray Point)
Lekuan III
Lekuan II
Lekuan I
Bunaken Village
200m
Kampung Bunaken

0   1   2
Kilometers

936m
NAIN I.
200m
Batu Kapal
NAIN KCL. I.
Bajo Village (on stilts)
Jalan Masuk
Barracuda Point
882m
MONTEHAGE
522m
Montehage
1344m
1360m
Gorango
Bango

Bunaken–Manado Tua National Marine Park 75,265 hectares

Laut
Sulawesi

2064m

Tanjung Kopi
Pangulingan
Detail above
SILADEN I.
MANADO TUA ▲ 822m
BUNAKEN
Manado Tua
Siladen 252m
Negeri
200m
Muka Gereja
Bunaken

| Reef |
| Dive site |

0   5
Kilometers

446m
Tanjung Pisok
Wori

Mt. Tumumpa 653m ▲
Barracuda
1843m
1566m
Nusantara (NDC)
Shipwreck
★ Molas
Teluk
Manado

Manado
1563m
200m
★ Murex

Arakan Wawontulap National Marine Park 13,800 hectares
Teluk Tanah-wangko
Tasik Ria
Tateu
★ Site of new 4-star hotel

Huge coral plateau, not well pioneered
★
Kumu
Tanawangko
Mt. Mahawu 1311m ▲
Sondaken
Mt. Lokon 1584m ▲

TETAPAAN I.
★

Dugongs sighted here; good for snorkeling
★
Sulu
Lelema
Tumpaan
Teluk Amurang
200m

Bangka Island

KINABOHUTAN I.
TALISEI I.
TINDILA I.
Batu Gosok
NAIN I.
GANGGA I.
BANGKA I.
MONTEHAGE I.
Sahaong Island
TAMPERONG I.
MANADO TUA I.
SILADEN I.
0   10   20
BUNAKEN I.
SULAWESI
Kilometers

is a volcano, a well-shaped cone reaching 822 meters. Three other islands complete the group: tiny Siladen, a stone's throw northeast of Bunaken; Montehage, the largest of the islands, north of Bunaken; and Nain, a tiny island north of Montehage surrounded by a large barrier reef. (See map at left.)

Bunaken Island

The reef is good all the way around Bunaken, and the 6-kilometer-long island features no fewer than 13 dive sites. Bunaken is the centerpiece of the reserve, and with careful observation, on this one island you could probably see the majority of coral reef fishes found in Indonesia.

All the sites are similar in that they feature steep walls of coral, pocked with small caves, and buzzing with small and medium-sized reef fish. Good coral growth usually extends down to 40–50 meters, and in the deeper parts of the wall one can see sharks, large rays and Napoleon wrasse. The current is usually gentle, perfect for a slow drift along the face of the wall, although it can occasionally come up in the afternoon.

Lekuan I, II and III. The most frequented site on Bunaken is a three-pronged coral wall in front of Lekuan Beach. Here your chances are very good of seeing Napoleon wrasse, turtles, bumphead parrotfish, scorpionfish and lionfish, and on the reef edge, swarms of anthias.

The Lekuan sites offer little current and clear water, and are perfect for beginners. They are popular for night dives as well.

Here—and everywhere else in the Manado Bay area—watch out for the stinging hydroid *Aglaophenia*. This "sea nettle" looks like a pinkish or brownish fern, and when brushed by unprotected skin causes a burning sensation.

Kampung Bunaken. This site, in front of Kampung ("Village") Bunaken on the island's southeastern tip, offers much the same underwater scenery as the Lekuan sites. However, the shallow reef flat here has suffered the most damage of any around the island, thanks to its proximity to the village.

Bunaken Timur. The two sites called "East Bunaken," barely separated from each other, feature a more sloping profile than the sites on the south and west of the island. Here we discovered turtles, Napoleon wrasse, and some sleeping reef whitetip sharks.

Sachiko's Point. Named after a Japanese tour leader, this steep wall is prowled by big fish, including large tuna, and turtles. The soft coral growth here is particularly good, and there are nice caves around 30 meters. The current is often quite strong at Sachiko's Point.

Mike's Point. Named for photographer Mike Severns (whose work appears in these pages), the profile here features wall and a pinnacle. The coral growth—including large, showy gorgonians—is very good. This site is particularly rewarding at depths of 30 meters or more. The point is sometimes swept by strong currents, and one can occasionally see sharks, and large schools of jacks. Pelagic visitors such as yellowtail tuna also call on Mike's Point.

Raymond. This is a wall, with good hard and soft coral growth and some nice whip corals. Fish life is good, including Napoleon wrasse. Colubrine sea snakes are particularly common here, both on the reef flats and in the reef itself. *Laticauda colubrina* is sometimes called the amphibious sea snake, and it spends more time ashore than most of its brethren. Although not aggressive, the snakes are poisonous and should not be harassed, although the guides

Above: *A school of blackfin barracuda (Sphyraena genie). Groups of these swift predators can be seen at several locations around the Bunaken group.*

and crew members often round one or two up for photographs. Strong "gusts" of current can sometimes be felt here, both horizontal and vertical. Don't panic, just hang onto the coral rock if necessary until it passes.

Tengah. This site, which means "middle" or "midway," is about in the middle of Bunaken's western reef face. This spot and nearby Mandolin are known for large schools of yellowtail fusiliers. One can also see an occasional turtle or shark here.

Mandolin. Just south of Tengah, this site also offers schooling fusiliers, and good coral growth. The wall here is best at depths of 30–35 meters.

Fukui Point. This site, also called Stingray Point, has a stepped profile: the reef top is at 2–4 meters, and then slopes down with several short, but steep, drops. It is known for its rays, of course, as well as turtles, barracuda and a couple of good-sized *Tridacna* clams.

Cela-Cela. This site, in the crook of the reef along the south face, offers many of the same charms as the popular Lekuan

sites. Good coral growth and fish, and mild currents.

Siladen. There is one regular site off the small island of Siladen, just 2 kilometers northeast of Bunaken. The wall is steep down to about 35 meters, and coral growth—particularly soft corals—is good. Siladen is a good place to see big pelagic fish, and the largest stingrays in the reserve.

Manado Tua

"Old Manado" is a dormant volcano jutting up just west of Bunaken. The two best sites are wall dives, on the west coast.

Muka Gereja. This site, in front of the church, is a steep wall with vertical canyons cut into it. Coral growth is good, and there is a nice cave at 20 meters. Sharks, barracuda and Napoleon wrasse are common.

Tanjung Kopi. "Coffee Cape" is also a wall, and offers sharks—usually reef whitetips, but with an occasional hammerhead—and barracuda. The cape is often swept by strong currents.

Negeri. A decent wall, with caves and good soft corals.

Pangulingan. This site, on the northeast of the island, has a sloping profile. There are nice shelf corals here, but the current can be very strong and there are few fish. It is best at 35 meters.

Montehage and Nain

Montehage is a large, flat island north of Bunaken. A community of Bajo fishermen has built a village on stilts in the shallow estuarial back reef area north of the island. The dive sites are off the west and south, which is fringed with a wide, shallow reef flat, much of it exposed at low tide.

Bango. The profile here is slope, then wall. Soft coral growth is good, and there are some caves. Scorpionfish are easy to find here, and Napoleon wrasse and sharks are common.

Gorango. The name of this site means "shark" in the local dialect, and these can usually be seen here. The reef profile is a steep wall to 40 meters.

Barracuda Point. This is a steep slope from 5 meters to about 20 meters, then a sheer wall to more than 30 meters. Schools of barracuda can be seen here, as well as sharks—at a shallower depth than at most sites—Napoleon wrasse, and bumphead parrotfish. Occasionally, huge tuna appear here.

Nain is a tiny island, but is surrounded by a wide lagoon filled with patches of reef, and a barrier reef. The people living on the island have cut a path through the reef just wide enough for their canoes. The island features two dive sites, both on the outer edge of the barrier reef.

We didn't dive Jalan Masuk ("Entryway"), but were told the scenery was the same as Batu Kapal, which we dove twice.

Batu Kapal. This site, literally "Stone Boat," is a slope down to 42 meters to a coral outcrop shaped like a boat (hence the name). A narrow canyon begins here that plunges way, way down. A couple of European dive instructors in our group went down to 90 meters (on a single tank) into the canyon to look at some big jacks under an overhang. A light and a depth gauge exploded. (This is not recommended for beginners. These

Below: *A red-spotted blenny (Istiblennius chrysospilos) pokes its clownish face out of a hidey hole. This fish is relatively common in quite shallow water, but only the sharp-eyed will see it, as the red-spotted blenny grows to just 10 centimeters and rarely shows more than its head.*

MIKE SEVERNS

two were used to diving in the Mediterranean, where dives to 60 meters are common.)

There is some bomb damage on the reef flat, but the rest of the coral is pristine. We saw sharks, big tuna and Napoleon wrasse. We also saw large groups of parrotfish, and at the reef top one of the guides found a couple of the strange crocodile fish (*Cymbacephalus beauforti*).

Tanjung Pisok

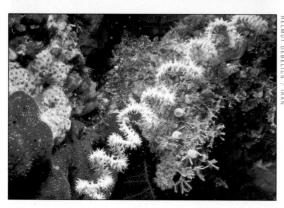

The dive at Cape Pisok is just off the mainland, some 15 minutes motoring from Molas Beach. The profile begins with a gentle slope, and then becomes a wall. Tanjung Pisok is one of the best places to see blue ribbon eels (*Rhinomuraena quaesita*), slender and gaudy relatives of the morays. The animals are quite shy, and guides and a great deal of tact are required to see them. One can also see blue ribbon eels

in relatively shallow depths at some of the Bunaken sites. There are barracuda at Pisok, including an occasional big one, and—particularly in the afternoon—squid and sharks.

The Manado Wreck

A steel-hulled German merchant ship, which sank on February 22, 1942, lies in the mud just 5 minutes from Molas beach. The wreck makes a fine break from wall diving. It might take the crew a few minutes to find it, as there is no buoy—if the local fishermen knew its location, they would soon catch all its fish.

Loky Herlambang of NDC found the wreck in 1980 while diving for trepang to try to make ends meet at his fledgling diving club. The harbormaster's office has no records of the ship. It has been discovered to be German, and when Loky first found it there was a machine gun and belts of ammunition on the foredeck. (Long gone now.)

Once the wreck is found, the crew drops anchor and you follow the line down, as visibility is usually lousy here. The wreck lies on a sandy slope, at 25–40 meters. The twin screws of the 60-meter ship are still intact.

The hull is largely undamaged, but you can enter the wreck through several openings on the deck. Bring good underwater lights! Most of the cargo space is easily accessible, but the engine room is tricky. Following the ladder (towards the stern) down the first couple of meters is easy, but to get through the narrow passage, you must remove your BC and tank. The engines and pistons are in good shape, as is one of the two electrical gauges. Move very slowly: perhaps a half-meter of fine sand and mud fill the compartment. A few careless strokes of your fins and you won't be able to see your hand in front of your face.

Because of the depth and the

generally murky water (8–10 meters at best), there is little hard coral growth here. But there are plenty of giant black coral bushes, and some gorgonians and feather stars. Fish are not normally abundant. We saw a reef whitetip shark, a bright yellow trumpetfish, a large puffer, angelfish, some butterflyfish, Moorish idols, and small schools of sweetlips and snappers.

Our favorites were a beautiful and shy juvenile pinnate batfish (*Platax pinnatus*), and an adult roundfaced batfish (*P. tiera*) that seemed to be living in the wheelhouse. If you ask your guides ahead of time, they might find and point out to you two unusual species in the wreck: banded pipefish (*Doryrhamphus dactyliophorus*) and the longsnout flathead (*Platycephalus chiltonae*).

As this is a fairly deep dive, be aware of your depth times or check your computer, and keep a close watch on your air supply to allow for a decompression stop. Usually the crew will hang a spare tank and regulator at 5 meters, but this is really a precaution, and you shouldn't count on it. If you want to have a look inside the ship, we suggest you make two dives: one to get acquainted with the wreck, and one to explore inside.

Nusantara Diving Centre

North Sulawesi's reefs are becoming internationally famous, and credit can only go to two men: Hanny Batuna and Loky Herlambang. Hanny was free-diving with the Bajo as a young man, which began his interest in the underwater world. He wanted to join the navy, but his father forced him to study medicine. Loky was studying biology at Bandung, Java when he read Jules Verne's *20,000 Leagues Under the Sea*.

Loky was in Manado collecting marine ornamentals and pursuing a girlfriend when he got the idea to found Nusantara Diving Centre in 1975. After a visit in 1977, Loky was encouraged by John E. (Jack) Randall, Curator of Ichthyology at the Bernice P. Bishop Museum in Hawaii. Randall supported his efforts to promote recreational diving in the Bunaken Island group.

In the early 1980s he met Hanny, and the two quickly became associates in the Nusan-

HELMUT DEBELIUS / IKAN

tara Diving Centre (NDC).

They started a program of conservation among the local fishermen. In 1982, the local government declared the Bunaken–Manado Tua area a protected zone (as well as the Arakan–Wawontulap area southwest of Manado), and the federal government made them both marine parks in 1989. In recognition of his conservation efforts, Presi-

Above: *A half-grown pinnate batfish,* Platax pinnatus, *in the wreck just off Molas Beach. The ship, which sunk during World War II, lies on a soft bottom, 25–40 meters underwater.*

dent Soeharto awarded Loky the prestigious Kalpataru Environmental Award in 1985.

In the early '80s, business suffered as an unscrupulous French dive agent sent numerous clients to dive, but refused to pay NDC. With the business at this low point, Hanny lost interest, but Loky stayed on. From a trickle of clients in the early '80s, he slowly built the business to the thriving state it is in today.

Murex

In 1980, Hanny bought a sea-side property south of Manado as a weekend family house, and a fish farm. He continued to dive with many expatriate friends, who eventually convinced him to get back into the dive business. He had moved his family house to the location in 1987, and in the same year started Murex, short for Manado Underwater Explorations.

Diving Bunaken

Although there are many operators in the area now, there are three in the area that can be con-

sidered pioneers: NDC, which is the oldest; Murex, which many divers consider to be the best managed; and Barracuda, which also has its partisans, although some consider the service to be inconsistent. Some people are also fans of the newer operations have sprung up as well, most of them associated with new resort hotels.

The dive process is similar at all three of the main dive resorts. Divers depart around 9 am, and reach Bunaken or the other sites in the area in 30 minutes to an hour and a half, depending on the remoteness of the site and the boat's engine.

Bungalows have now been built on Bunaken Island itself, and this operator offers convenient shore diving. We are not supportive of this move.

Building even a small operation in the middle of what is according to the Indonesian government a nature reserve seems to us to be, at best, misguided, and do not recommend divers encourage this kind of thing by staying on the island.

Below: *The decorated dartfish,* Nemateleotris decora. *Pairs of these beautiful little dartfish can be found hovering over sandy patches, where they pluck plankters and small crustaceans from the water. Bunaken Island, 40 meters.*

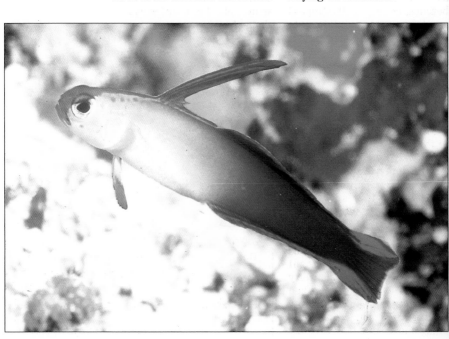

BANGKA

Good Diving and a Fine Boat Ride North

Divers, snorkelers or just visitors interested in a scenic boat ride will enjoy the day trip to Bangka Island, on Sulawesi's northernmost tip. Scuba diving off Bangka was pioneered by Dr. Hanny Batuna of Murex and this outfit offers a delightful trip to Bangka—with the option of going or returning overland.

As you leave mainland Sulawesi from Murex, just north of Manado, Lokon and Mahawu volcanoes are at your back, and the island of Manado Tua looms large, often cloud-wreathed, with low-lying Bunaken in the foreground. The dive boat cruises past several scenic islands, and the mainland looks fine too.

Soft Coral Gardens

Bangka Island, of contorted bays and hills, has a few white-sand beaches, but mostly the tropical vegetation grows right down to the sea. Jagged pinnacles stick out of the waters off southern and southeastern Bangka, and it is here that Dr. Batuna, the owner of Murex, pioneered some outstanding dive locations.

The rugged scenery continues underwater. The tips of some of the jagged pinnacles don't make it to the surface, while others shoot a few meters into the air. The spread and variety of soft corals here is truly outstanding and at some drop-off points, the swarms of fish cascade about as in a wind-driven snowstorm.

There are also a few big fellas around: we spotted a decent sized shark, several hefty Napoleon wrasse and a dozen large barracuda with unusual yellow tails. Some small sharks hid under the table coral. Visibility was good, 10–15 meters, but because the current often picks up here—to 2 knots or more—the site is best for more experienced divers.

Fish for Hong Kong

We took lunch under a shelter on a sandy beach in a deep bay. There was good snorkeling here as well. But dismaying was the sight of a floating house in the bay with large attached nets. This operation used nets and lines to capture live groupers—particularly *Cromileptes altivelis*—and Napoleon wrasse. These were kept in a live well, and periodically shipped to Hong Kong, where they command a very high price at the table. When we revisited the site in 1996, the operation was thankfully shut down. Uncommon and beautiful animals like the Napoleon wrasse should be left alone.

For the way back to Manado, you have a choice: a scenic one-hour drive back from the mainland village of Likupang, or the boat ride back the way you came.

AT A GLANCE
Bangka

Reef type: Pinnacles, coral slope

Access: 1.5 hr by boat

Visibility: Fair to good; 10–15 meters

Current: Usually some, occasionally to 2 knots or more

Coral: Good; outstanding soft corals

Fish: Good numbers and excellent variety

Highlights: Sharks, barracuda, soft corals

Diving the Rich Waters of the Lembeh Strait

The busy port of Bitung, the main shipping harbor for north Sulawesi, seems an unlikely choice for a dive center. Yet just north of the port, in the straight formed by Lembeh Island, is some of the finest diving in North Sulawesi.

Lembeh Island—long, narrow and parallel to the coast of Sulawesi—creates a calm channel, protected from both the northeast and southwest monsoons. Prevailing currents through the area are also concentrated by the strait, bringing a rich supply of plankton, and since Lembeh Island and the coast of Sulawesi offer many different habitats—sandy bays, craggy volcanic outcrops, and mangrove—a wide variety of animals settle out of the plankton stream here. As a result, the waters are unusually rich, both in numbers of animals and in diversity.

Because they are so full of plankton, the waters here are not particularly clear, with visibility generally ranging around 10–15 meters. And there are no pow-

dery white sand beaches here, the protection of the island and the volcanic rock yielding only gravelly black strips of sand. But for divers interested in rare and unusual animals—sea horses, mandarinfish, squid and octopus, sea spiders, snake eels, strange crabs and shrimp, nudibranchs, scorpionfish—this is one of the best sites in the world.

As testimony to the richness and uniqueness of this area, in 1994 a National Geographic Explorer film crew chose the area to shoot a special on venomous reef animals.

The only dive operator here is Kungkungan Bay Resort, a U.S.-operated hotel on a little bay of the same name in the village of Tanduk Rusa, five kilometers by twisty road north of Bitung. The site—a former coconut plantation—is quiet, and isolated, and the tasteful cottages are constructed of the attractive grainy wood of coconut trees.

Most of the sites here were first found by local boat captain Engel Lamakeki, and during his tenure as divemaster at the resort, Larry Smith added several more, including two new wrecks. None of the strait's top sites is more than about 30 minutes away by boat.

Batu Angus

Batu Angus, at the northern end of the strait on the Sulawesi side, is the site of an old lava flow, hence the name, which literally means "burnt rock." Here rough chunks of black, volcanic rock enclose a quiet area that looks like the mouth of a river.

Underwater, the site is a large bowl, just 10 meters deep and

AT A GLANCE
Bitung

Reef type:	Slopes, pinnacles, wreck
Access:	5–30 min by boat
Visibility:	Fair to good, 10–15 meters
Current:	Very little inside the strait
Coral:	Very good, especially soft and black corals
Fish:	Good numbers, excellent variety
Highlights:	Wreck, sheer richness of species

Lembeh Strait

Batuangus
▲1134m

Tanjung
Batu Angus Batu Angus

Saudara
1365m
▲

Angel's Window

Reef

Dive site

Kungkungan
Bay Resort
Tanduk Rusa ■ Kungkungan Bay

0   1   2
Kilometres

Aertembaga
BITUNG ●

Mawali
wreck

Gririan

P. Susulina

Tg. Merah
Beting Pasir

10m

P. Dua

about 50 meters across. The entire area, completely protected from current, is covered in finely branched and thin leafy corals. There is literally not a single square inch that isn't covered. It is dead calm, beautiful, and as fragile-looking as crystal.

There are no big fish in here, but the variety of smaller species is very good. And this is one of the few places where one can easily see the reclusive and beautifully patterned mandarinfish (*Synchiropus splendens*) as well as tiny, colorful coral gobies. Batu Angus is also a fine spot for snorkeling.

Mawali Wreck

This wreck, a sunken Japanese freighter from World War II, lies just across the strait from Kungkungan Bay, a ten-minute boat ride away. The coral-encrusted ship lies on its side between 17 and 30 meters. This wreck is in very good condition,

The wreck is beautifully encrusted with crinoids, black coral trees and soft corals. The boom sticks straight out sideways, and in this area huge schools of fish gather. On one dive we saw a group of at least a hundred full-grown batfish, and schools of small silversides the size of a house.

Moray eels hide in iron crevices, and it seems at times that every encrusted lump is a scorpionfish of one species or another. Within the groove of an overgrown iron spool we found two large octopus, perhaps interrupted in a private moment.

The owners of the wreck, however, are a pride of lionfishes. Groups of 6 or 10 are always out, and at times as many as 40 of these calmly majestic animals gather together.

Kungkungan Bay

Some of our favorite dives were right out in front of the resort itself, beginning under the pier at the southern end of the beach-front, and working our way north. Night dives are especially nice here, and no cold boat ride to get between a tired diver and his or her glass of whisky.

The richness of the waters here can be seen beginning right under the dock, where you can see Henshaw eels, buried in sand up to their evil-looking teeth, several species of *Actinodendron* anemones, some with their commensal shrimp, cerianthids, sea spiders, crabs, cuttlefish and octopus. How often, for example, does one find beautiful red gorgonians growing on a wooden dock pier, or crinoids in—literally—six inches of water?

Working our way along the good coral in just 2–4 meters of water, we saw scorpionfish, octopus, the strange little bobtail squid *Euprymna,* which look like big green bumblebees, unusual nudibranchs, and crabs—including the beautiful demon hermit crab *Trizopagurus,* whose striking red-and-yellow–striped body is flattened so it can take advantage of cast-off cone shells, with their long, narrow openings.

Angel's Window

This is an excellent location to find frogfish—anglerfish, to some. Sure enough when I dove there, my guide found one for me within about twenty minutes. The beast's black, globular body was sprinkled with silvery sand-like specks as it waited, motionless, propped on its pectoral fins between two sponges. The frogfish was not camouflaged by color, but by holding perfectly still, it was difficult to see.

The site's name comes from a swim-through, at about 25 meters. The passageway, about four or five meters long, is festooned with gorgonian fans. With careful buoyancy control, so as not to bust up the scenery, I finned through. On the other side—surprise—four Napoleon wrasse greeted me.

Kungkungan Bay Resort

The Kunkungan Resort's luxurious, but tasteful bungalows opened in late 1994. An architecturally interesting two-tiered lobby and dining room, built out over the water, offers western cuisine and a few local dishes, although the latter are invariably underspiced. The buildings are constructed of coconut wood.

Although they're all still working on their English, the staff are friendly, and a joy to be around. The setting is quiet and breezy, and, well, salubrious.

Below: *A frogfish and a scorpionfish share an encrusted pinnacle on the Mawali wreck in the Lembeh Strait.*

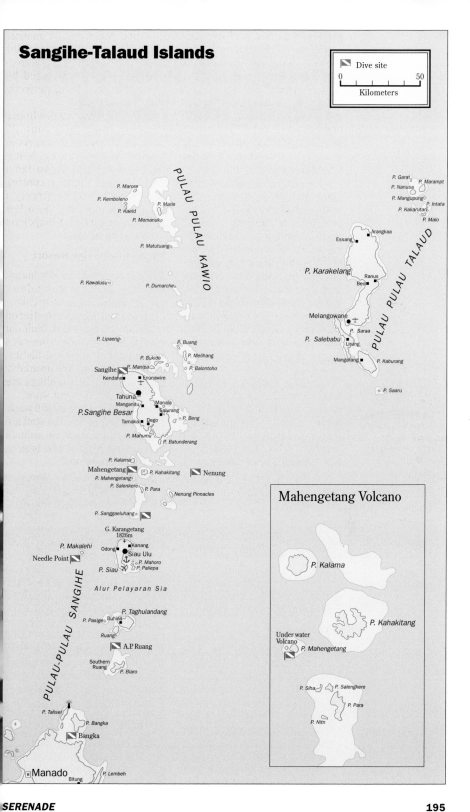

Sangihe-Talaud Islands

Dive site

0 — 50
Kilometers

PULAU PULAU KAWIO

P. Marore
P. Kemboleno
P. Kaeld
P. Marie
P. Memanuko
P. Matutuang

P. Kawalusu
P. Dumarche

P. Garat
P. Nanusa
P. Marampt
P. Mangupung
P. Intata
P. Kakarutan
P. Malo

Essang
Arangkaa

P. Karakelang
Ranus
Beo

PULAU PULAU TALAUD

P. Lipaeng
P. Buang
P. Bukide
P. Melihang
P. Manipa
P. Balontoho

Sangihe
Kendahe
Enunawire

Tahuna
Manganitu
Manala
Salurang
P.Sangihe Besar
Tamaka
Dego
P. Beng
P. Mahumu
P. Batunderang

Melangowane
P. Saraa
P. Salebabu
Lirung
Mangarang
P. Kaburang

P. Saaru

P. Kalama
Mahengetang
P. Kahakitang
Nenung
P. Mahengetang
P. Salenkere
P. Para
Nenung Pinnacles

P. Sanggaeluhang

G. Karangetang
1826m
P. Makalehi
Odong
Kanang
Siau Ulu
Needle Point
P. Mahoro
P. Siau
P. Paliepa

Alur Pelayaran Sia

P. Taghulandang
P. Pasige
Buhias
Ruang
A.P Ruang
Southern
Ruang
P. Biaro

P. Talise
P. Bangka
Bangka

Manado
Bitung
P. Lembeh

Mahengetang Volcano

P. Kalama

P. Kahakitang

Under water
Volcano
P. Mahengetang

P. Siha
P. Salengkere
P. Para
P. Nitn

Serenade

Diving the Ring of Fire in Sangihe-Talaud

It looked like any other midwater reef, until we dropped onto it. The top of the reef was flat and featureless with a telltale yellow cast—and it was steaming with strings of tiny bubbles.

The coral substrate was covered in yellow and yellow and brown algae, strange colors not often encountered beneath sea. We dropped over the reef edge and descended down a rocky rubble slope following a cleft in the structure to a sandy bottom 40 meters below. This sandy plain was alive with a forest of black coral in every color imag-

AT A GLANCE
Serenade

Reef type:	Slopes, pinnacles, walls
Access:	Liveaboard
Visibility:	Variable; 8–15 meters
Current:	Often tricky, and strong
Coral:	Usually very good
Fish:	Excellent numbers and variety
Highlights:	Underwater volcano, sheer profusion of life at most sites

inable. This was a cruise unlike any other I had ever been on.

MV Serenade

We were abroad the *MV Serenade,* a 25-meter wooden motor vessel operating in the seas to the north of Sulawesi, between Manado and Mindanao in the Philippines. It is one of two liveaboard dive boats operating in this area, both run by Murex. The *Serenade* was built locally in 1992, is manned by a local crew and is capable of a cruising speed

of 9 knots. There are four air-conditioned double cabins on the top deck and four additional cabins with shared facilities down below. The optimal dive group is ten, but larger groups can be accommodated if required.

We had boarded the *Serenade* the evening before in Manado and motored all night to our anchorage at Makalehi Island, near Siau Island in the Sangihe group. Dawn broke while we were still at sea, and we awoke to the sight of a volcano belching smoke ahead of us, dolphins breaching to starboard and a rainbow billowing to port.

Needle Point

The first dive was on the southeastern point of the island: three finger rocks pointed the way to the coral outcrop—underwater, a vertical wall dropped 65 meters to a white sand bottom. This dive—and all our dives in the area—were marked by very capricious current, one minute flowing in one direction and the next completely reversing itself, or worse, sucking unwary divers down. My dive buddy said he didn't remember much about the wall—he was too busy watching his bubbles go down!

We dubbed this site "Needle Point" as it was literally covered in bushes of white needle coral (*Seriatopora hystrix*). The fish life was prolific, featuring schools of unicornfish, snappers, fusiliers and butterflyfish.

Mahengetang

Due north was Mahengetang, the site of the submerged volcano. Some 200 meters west of the island, separated by a shallow saddle, are two cones at just four meters depth. Though the surface was at the mercy of wild currents—our boat spun around the anchorline in a 180-degree arc twice, in just 10 minutes—we encountered little current below. The undersea panorama was captivating. Everything was tinged in sulphurous tones of yellow, hard and soft coral included.

Everything seemed larger than it should have been, or more numerous. It was a magical landscape. There might be better diving in Indonesia, but surely nothing quite like this.

Drowned Village

The most mysterious site was on on Sangihe, north of the capital of Tahuna. The weather had turned overcast and misty, the perfect backdrop for our search for a lost village.

The information we received was scanty and anecdotal. We surmised that the village had slipped into the sea in a landslide associated with the cataclysmic earthquakes that occured in 1963 throughout Indonesia.

A rainstorm had made the waters murky, and we descended the anchorline to a clay bottom at 40 meters. Black corals were abundant, but this wasn't what we were looking for. We ascended along silt-covered terraces, reminiscent of rice paddies. It was beginning to look like a wild goose chase and then, at 25 meters, we found a horizontal tunnel, then a makeshift door, then some obviously fabricated stone blocks. A strange scene.

Nenung Pinnacles

The port of Tahuna, nestled in a deep and narrow bay, was our anchorage until just before dawn of the following day, when we motored to the pinnacles of Nenung. The setting was dramatic: craggy rocks riddled with caves and veined with the telltale rust of iron oxides; hillcrests cov-

ered in tenacious scrub; swarms of terns startled into flight by the sound of our engine.

The dive site at the southernmost of the pinnacles is named after Michael Aw, a photographer and our guide on this trip. Currents were strong, and we had to circle the southernmost of the pinnacles repeatedly, in opposition to the current, to drop divers in squads on the south face. The strategy was to empty BCs, drop fast, and grab hold.

We found two plateaus, then a gentle slope to white sand at 50 meters. There was good soft coral growth, and around the northeast, where the current picked up, huge schools of fish.

Ruang Island

We were wondering how the diving could possibly get any better, and then we went to Ruang, a dormant volcano that last erupted in 1956. The southern coast is a intriguing mosaic of verdant greens contrasting with the black bleakness of volcanic rock.

After a series of dives off south Ruang, we baptized site "Basilica," as its structure and carpeting of life inspired the wonder and awe of a baroque cathedral. Sponges were arrayed in all shapes, sizes and colors; crinoids came in every color. The fish life was fantastic: sharks, a giant grouper, dogtooth tuna, and huge schools of barracuda.

—*Cody Shwaiko*

Above: *A bubbling vent of the underwater volcano at Banua Wunu, just west of Mahengetang in the Sangihe group.*

Atolls, Wrecks and a Diversity of Corals

Although not as famous or well-developed as the North Sulawesi sites, South and Central Sulawesi offer a trove of little-explored diving gems. Among the more notable are the Spermonde Archipelago off Ujung Pandang, Tanjung Bira and Selayar, the Tukang Besi Archipelago in Southeast Sulawesi, and the Togian Islands, nestled in Tomini Bay. The infrastructure for mass or luxury diving in these areas is not yet developed, but for those interested in exploratory diving, these are the places to go.

AT A GLANCE
South & Central Sulawesi

Reef types: Fringing reef slopes and walls, atolls, wrecks
Access: Speedboats, fishing boats
Visibility: Fair to excellent
Current: Moderate to strong, particularly during tidal flush
Coral: Excellent
Fish: Variable numbers, great diversity
Highlights: Kapoposang, Tukang Besi atolls, Taupun (Togians)

Ujung Pandang

The 16,000-square-kilometer Spermonde Archipelago off Ujung Pandang offers over 150 reefs within easy reach of the capital city of South Sulawesi. Home of the famous Makassarese and Bugis seafaring peoples, this archipelago, although heavily fished, ranks at the top of marine biodiversity surveys for eastern Indonesia.

The Spermonde offers a wide range of exciting dive possibilities— among them numerous fringing reefs with average to spectacular coral formations in 5–20 meter depths, three underexplored WWII wrecks in 20–40 meter depths and world-class wall diving along the shelf edge at Kapoposang Island, which has recently been gazetted as a marine park .

Although the fish life here has been heavily exploited, the reefs are generally in good shape and they boast over 300 species of hard coral, easily one of the highest diversity counts in the world for an area of this size. Coral buffs in particular should check out the west side of Bone Tambung, a tiny fishing village 14 kilometers offshore Ujung Pandang. This particular reef has an unusually well-developed reef flat with luxuriant coral growth in 2–6 meters depth. The very gradual western reef slope is interrupted by several sand terraces which are frequented by spotted eagle rays; huge cuttlefish are also commonly spotted here. Other mid-shelf reefs which afford similar diving possibilities include LumuLumu, Badi, and Bone Lola.

Wreck-diving enthusiasts will not be disappointed as this area was the site of numerous WW II skirmishes between Japanese and American forces, and the Makassar Dive Center offers trips to three of the better-preserved wrecks: a Japanese destroyer, a Japanese supply vessel, and an American fighter plane. Other wrecks rumored to exist in the area include a WW II bomber and a minesweeper.

For those who require sharks

for an adrenalin rush, deep dives along the shelf edge at Lanyukang Island (a wall which starts at 30 meters) or the wall at Kapoposang are guaranteed thrillers. The Makassar Dive Center has pioneered numerous dive sites along the extensive 200-meter-plus dropoff at Kapoposang. This is one of the few sites in the Spermonde where large fish are still relatively common—large grouper, Napoleon Wrasse and bumphead parrotfish on the wall nearest the island, and giant trevally and Spanish mackerel on the seaward side of the dropoff. The lagoon on the northwest side of the island is a true jewel. The protected waters have nurtured delicate coral formations which are absoutely stunning.

The best months for diving are April–June and September–November. Try to avoid the northwest monsoon (November–March), as the weather and seas can be very rough.

There is only one dive operator in Ujung Pandang—the Makassar Diving Center, locally known as POPSA—however, several travel agents and hotels offer day and overnight trips to the islands for snorkelling/picnicing. If you are of an independent mindset and can speak Indonesian reasonably, you can rent gear/tanks from the Makassar Diving Center and arrange a trip of your own by chartering a wooden speedboat from Pak Laut (literally, "Mr. Ocean") on the beach across from Fort Rotterdam. Talk to Pak Laut to arrange Sahid as your boatman, who has extensive knowledge of the reefs.

Bira/Selayar

At the southeastern tip of the southwest leg of Sulawesi lies Tanjung (Cape) Bira, and below it, the long narrow island of Selayar. This area, which has been slated for major tourism development, offers enthusiasts some

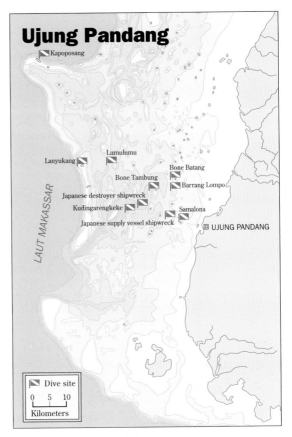

excellent exploratory diving.

Tanjung Bira is a very dry peninsula of uplifted fossil coral, with no freshwater river input. This feature, combined with the very deep waters of the Makassar Strait, makes for outstanding visibility year-round, and a plethora of marine life, including dolphins, mantas, large pelagics, and the ever-present sharks.

The diving around Bira itself is on nice fringing reefs, but most outstanding by far are the sheer walls of Pulau Kambing (Goat Island), a stark slab of rock rising out of the ocean between Bira and Selayar. The coral cover and fish life here can be fantastic. The east coast of Selayar is said to have some of the most stunning beaches in Indonesia, with diving to match. A glance at the nautical charts for the area would seem to affirm this: the mountains plunge abruptly to the beach, creating spectacular waterfalls which cascade into white sand coconut groves, with further drop-offs into the deep blue only a couple of meters from the shore.

Tukang Besi Archipelago

Just off the southeastern tip of Sulawesi lies one of the undiscovered jewels of Indonesian diving, the Tukang Besi islands.

Named for the ironsmiths on the southernmost island of Binongko, this remote archipelago had Jacques Cousteau and members of the *Calypso* raving during their visit in the mid-1980's. Rising deep out of the Banda Sea, these islands boast all three of the major coral reef formations — atolls, fringing reefs, and a single barrier reef off the island of Wangi.

In addition, the four major islands of Wangi, Kaledupa, Tomea, and Binongko ("WaKaToBi") are very interesting in that they have been formed by geologic uplift of fossil coral terraces, evident in the step-like appearance of these islands from afar. A stroll through any of these islands reveals fascinating fossil reef formations, including the occasional giant clam or nautiloid shell.

The four big islands are populated, inland by the Butonese, and at the ocean edge by the Bajo people ("sea gypsies"). The Bajo have thinned the fish populations on the fringing reefs, but there is still some excellent diving near the islands, especially the steep dropoffs around Binongko and Hoga.

But the real draw of this area are the many scattered atolls, most of which are inaccessible to the Bajo's dugout canoes for seven months of the year. Standouts include the Ndaa, Kapota, Koromaha, Moromaho, and Koka atolls. The fish populations here are as dense as any in Indonesia. The corals, both hard and soft, are fantastic.

The entire area serves as a cetacean thoroughfare, and night dives along the walls here are absolutely breathtaking. The entire wall bursts into vivid color as the Tubastrea and soft corals "bloom", and the diversity of in-

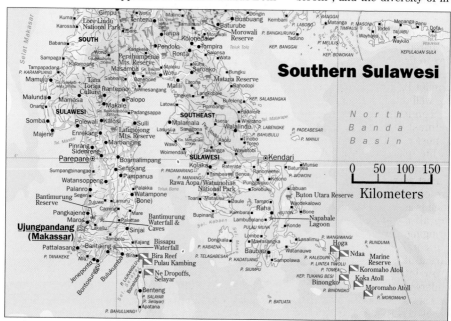

Southern Sulawesi

vertebrates (crustaceans, nudibranchs, pencil urchins, etc) is bewildering. During two months of diving there, we encountered dugongs, sperm and pilot whales, spinner and bottlenose dolphins, coconut crabs, maleo birds, and orcas.

Currently, this area is completely inaccessible to divers except through a new operation called Wakatobi Divers on the small island of Tolandono. (See "Sulawesi Practicalities," page 299). The Tukang Besi archipelago is now slated for development as a National Marine Park, but the area is mostly unknown.

One can also sometimes dive here by joining an expedition by Operation Wallacea, a non-profit venture supported by Hongkong Bank and the Indonesian government. Operation Wallacea brings in dive volunteers, trains them in rapid ecosystem assessment techniques, and then takes them on two to four-week expeditions to assess the status of the reefs and fish populations. This data is used to help formulate management plans for the parks.

Togian Islands

For those who are interested in true exploration diving and are prepared to endure a tough journey to find it, the Togians are a must. These islands located in Tomini Bay in Central Sulawesi are well worth the journey.

Tomini Bay, reputedly the calmest bay in the world, is almost completely surrounded by the spidery arms of Sulawesi, which means relatively flat seas almost year-round and spectacular cyan-blue visibility. The islands are renowned for displaying all major reef formations (fringing, barrier, and atoll) and the corals here, safe from the threat of heavy wave damage, grow into beautifully delicate underwater forests.

Large schools of barracuda, big-eyed jacks and other pelagics are common around the outer reefs of Taupun, Taipi and the southeast of Batudaka and Togian. Hawksbill turtles and even dugongs are spotted among the many islands.

Of the six dives we did here, Taupun was unquestionably our favorite. The dropoff here is quite topographically complex and offers numerous small caves and crevices teeming with cryptic fish and crustaceans. Two large dog-toothed tuna continually buzzed us during the dive, and a huge eagle ray, apparently lulled into a dreamy glide by the bath-calm water, literally bumped into us before shooting off into the deep. A platoon of 20 large longtoms in flank formation hovered motionless near the surface, and butterfly-like clouds of anthias alternately swam into the slight current to feed, and then darted back into the reef framework for shelter. The ocean was so flat that the dense coral gardens of the reef flat were reflected down to us from the surface, creating the surreal impression of being surrounded by coral above, below and to the side. A banded sea krait kept us company during our safety stop, rounding out a truly unforgettable dive.

The Togian islands themselves are stunning. Scores of densely-forested rocky islands rise out of the placid water to create endless idyllic bays; a sea-kayaker's dream. Small pods of dolphins cruise the channels between these islands, and the sound of their spouting is one of the few disturbances to the mountain lake tranquility of the place. Reefs fringing the islands in these bays are poorly developed, but interesting for their abundance of gorgonians and soft corals. Avoid diving the reefs outside of the bay mouths during ebb tide, as quite strong currents flush the bays and temporarily reduce visibility drastically.

—*Mark Erdmann*

Sangalaki

Mantas, Turtles, and a Strange Jellyfish Lake

The outline of a huge shape slowly emerged from the gloom. A shot of adrenaline whacked me as I made out a set of slowly flapping wings. At five meters the manta snapped into focus, enormous and black all over. Normal mantas are dark on top with a white belly. The black mantas are the largest of the many that hang around Sangalaki Island, off the east coast of Kalimantan, Indonesian Borneo.

The mantas around Sangalaki seldom reach their maximum 6 meter size; the larger ones averaging some 3.5 meters across.

AT A GLANCE
Sangalaki

Reef type: Walls and slopes
Access: 1 hr by boat from Derawan
Visibility: Seasonal; 5–15 meters
Current: Modest
Coral: Very good
Fish: Excellent numbers and variety
Highlights: Mantas, jellyfish lake at Kakaban Island

But what they lack in size, they make up in numbers—on a clear, sunny day, during the April –October season, up to a hundred have been seen on a single dive. They tend to feed near the surface in currents of about 1.5 knots, so to enjoy this show divers only have to descend 5 meters and go with the flow.

Since Sangalaki opened for sports diving in April 1993, every client has seen mantas, with the exception of three members of a small group who were there in early January. Others, in the same group did see some, so very occasionally manta sightings could be a matter of luck. During the local rainy season, which starts around November–December and ends around late March, the visibility sometimes falls to 5–8 meters, but it does not stay this lousy all the time during the wet season—all it takes is a few days of sunshine for visibility to improve.

Even in restricted visibility, there's plenty to see. Circumstances brought me to Sangalaki in mid-January for five days' diving—not the ideal time for clear waters. But the diving was still so good that I wanted to extend my stay a few more days which, unfortunately, was impossible.

Diving Sangalaki

Every dive at Sangalaki was worthwhile, revealing something unusual for me. One of my guides, Yien-Yien, has identified over 40 species of nudibranchs along with at least six colorful flatworms. She pointed out couple of dozen nudis and four flatworms during our dives. My other guide, Jon, spotted three species of barracuda during one of our night dives, along with sleeping flounders, a nesting Titan triggerfish (about the only marine organism I fear—but only in daytime) and lots more. One day dive brought a huge grouper into view, on another we found a pair of unusual pink leaf-fish. Friendly cuttlefish abound. Polka-dot groupers (*Chromileptes altivelis*) are common, as are scorpionfishes.

By top-Indonesian standards, we found fish life somewhat lack-

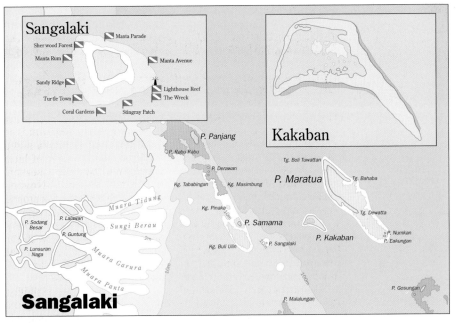

Sangalaki

ing—good but not excellent. Schooling fish were only occasionally seen: spotted rabbitfish, batfish, snappers, fairy basslets, glassfish and cardinals. On the other hand, both hard and soft coral cover is excellent, showing no dynamite damage. A few overturned blocks of table coral were perhaps due to careless diving by the abundant green turtles.

Development of Sangalaki

Borneo Divers' building of a 5-star PADI facility on Sangalaki deserves unstinted praise. This top-rated dive operator opened the island of Sipadan several years ago, after an extensive program of explorations searching for a world-class location. Sipadan surpassed all expectations and, with extensive marketing, drew demanding clients from the USA and Europe. But the superb diving also drew other operators to Sipadan with now far too many bodies — divers and support staff — for the small island's fragile ecology.

So Borneo Divers' search began all over for another dive location. It took a couple of years to find Sangalaki and to check out its potential. Then, having learned their lesson from Sipadan, Borneo Divers, along with their Indonesian partners, obtained the exclusive rights to develop the island's potential: no other operators allowed. Following the strictest ecological guidelines possible, ten two-bed wood bungalows were built with all the required support facilities.

After scarcely a year of operation Borneo Divers' Indonesian partners, who were loosing money in other businesses, were forced to pull out. The dive operation shut down, but Borneo Divers found another partner and plans ot reopen diving on Sangalaki.

Derawan Island

Derawan Island, about an hour's boat ride from Sangalaki, also offers diving and tourist facilities—and at the time of this writing, the only access to Sangalaki. Just over 1,000 people live on 2.5-square-kilometer Derawan, most of them of the Bajau ethnic group. These former sea nomads and occasional pirates started settling down in the area in the late 19th century.

While the diving is not as good on Derawan as it is at Sangalaki, the scuba facilities, a part of the Bhumi Manimbora complex, seem well run by two PADI-trained divemasters from Bali. (We didn't have the chance to dive with them). The compressor and equipment looked well-kept.

The nearby dive spots are passable and, although the boat ride is a bit long, the operator can take you diving on Sangalaki, Kakaban, and other sites.

For diving with this outfit, you make reservations at their dive shop, the Derawan, at the Benakutai Hotel in Balikpapan, then fly on a small Merpati plane to Tanjung Berau via Samarinda. The operator will pick you up at Tanjung Berau and whiz you over to Derawan by speedboat. (See "Sulawesi Practicalities" page 300).

Tourism started on Derawan in 1987 and most foreign visitors, usually Europeans, visit the island in July and August. But so far, no crowds, so it's unlikely that accommodations will be full.

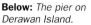

Below: *The pier on Derawan Island.*

A new resort with cottage-style rooms facing the white-sand beach should be open by the time you read this, and there are two inexpensive *losmen* on the island. There is also the possibility of homestays.

A newly started yearly Pesta Laut ("Sea Festival") starts on November 4 and runs for four days. Featured events include: diving, competition swimming, spear and line fishing and a "marathon" around the island. During the evening, songs and traditional dances entertain guests—who so far are few indeed, due to a lack of publicity.

Sea Turtles

Green sea turtles love, breed and lay their eggs on several of the small islands off the northeast coast of Kalimantan. Sangalaki is their island of choice, a genetically imprinted home turf, programmed when the baby turtles hatch and make that first mad dash for the sea. About 20 years after birth, the green turtles (*Chelonia mydas*) return to their home island measuring well over a meter in length, and weighing

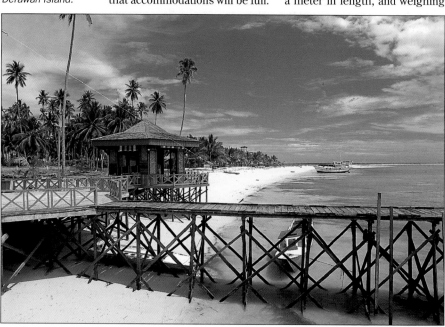

some 90 kilograms.

They breed just off the island, then the females crawl ashore at night, laboriously dig a large hole in the sand, lay an average of 70 fertilized eggs, cover the nests with sand and drag themselves back into the sea. This procedure is repeated three to five times during the female's fertile season, which occurs every two or three years after sexual maturity.

Depending on the ambient temperature, the eggs hatch in 50 to 65 days. The baby's sex is also temperature-determined: if the nest temperature is above 27° C, all the eggs develop as females, if colder, all males. Most of the babies perish in that first clumsy run to the sea, as birds and other predators gobble up the helpless little fellows. Estimates of the hatchlings' survival rate suggest that perhaps 2 percent make it to adulthood.

Until Borneo Divers developed the site, Sangalaki was a famous turtle egg gathering site. In 1991, some 1.5 million eggs were taken from the nests on the various islands, about half of these from Sangalaki. Using the 2 percent survival estimate, that meant 30,000 fewer adult turtles every year.

When they opened Sangalaki, Borneo Divers found the perfect way to stop the collecting. The turtle egg concessions are awarded through a bidding process, and Borneo Divers simply bought the concession for Sangalaki. This was a rather expensive solution, however, and on April 1, 1993, they paid $50,000 to insure that not more eggs would be taken from the island.

Even better, the dive outfit hired the men who had previously made their living by robbing the nests. One of these men, Pak Tambuli, the doyen of turtle-egg gatherers, had been at this job since before World War II. Now well into his 70s, (he doesn't know exactly how old he is) the still vigorous old man gathers data on the turtles. Walking around the island each day, guided by the turtle tracks in the sand, he counts the number of nests made the previous night. He keeps track on a long leaf or piece of scratch paper. He also tracks how many nests hatch each day. This information is entered into the resort's computer to build a long-term record.

Borneo Divers further helped the laying mother turtles by following a minimum necessary electric light policy at night to prevent the disorientation of the females when they return to the ocean. The technique works. During my five nights on Sangalaki, when some 50 nests were dug every night, anywhere from one to four nests were made within a few meters from my cabin—with one nest just outside my front porch.

Be sure to bring a flashlight to prevent stumbling into a nest when returning at night from the central lobby to your cabin, or when you have to answer a call of nature. Watching the turtles dig their nest and lay their eggs is a unique experience for Sangalaki's visitors.

And, of course, you will see them underwater. The turtles here are not as diver-friendly as those on Sipadan, a well-known dive site north of Sangalaki, off the coast of Sabah, Malaysian Borneo, which have had several years to get used to the human bubble-machines. But we had several brief but intimate encounters with the green turtles during our dives.

Kakaban Island

Less than a half hour away in one of the dive boats, Kakaban Island offers an excellent wall dive with a vertical, cave-pocked drop to a bit over 50 meters. There might be some current here, but basically this is an easy dive for expe-

Above: *Sangalaki is one of the most favored green turtle (Chelonia mydas) nesting areas in the region. Unfortunately, a taste for their eggs and—in Bali—a market for the meat threatens these animals.*

rienced divers.

We saw many schooling surgeons and snappers, along with barrel sponges and, at depth, large gorgonian fans. Other divers here have spotted reef white-tip sharks, grays and—on one occasion—a bone-chilling 5-meter hammerhead. The topside decompression stop alone is worth the dive, with excellent coral cover, swarming with colorful fairy basslets.

But Kakaban has a much more unusual dive site. A brackish lake fills much of the central part of the island, slightly above sea level, with a salt concentration only about two-thirds that of the ocean. The lake holds many species of marine life, some very new to science. There are hundreds of stingless jellyfish, of four different species, pulsating along on the surface and at various depths. (See "Kakaban" opposite.)

There are just eight species of fish, all of them small, but they are unusually unafraid of divers. We watched some fish dive into the soft muck at the lake bottom for what we supposed were tasty

tidbits. Others would follow some of the divers who, with less than perfect buoyancy control and careless finning technique, stirred up great clouds which settle very slowly. Fish enter these clouds, we suppose for minimorsels.

We also saw tunicates, small, colonial bivalves, nudibranchs, a land snake, the unusual jellyfish-eating white Kakaban anemone, at least three species of sea cucumbers, sponges, and two kinds of crabs, These crabs were the only animals in the lake which we could call skittish.

The lake is ringed by thickly encrusted mangrove roots, and the slopes at the lake edge are covered in Vegetation includes heavily encrusted mangrove roots at the lake's edge and a thick, bushy growth of *Caulerpa* on the slopes and covering some sections of the bottom profile.

It's an easy, 10-minute walk to the lake along a wide trail hacked out of the vegetation. The trail leads past a hut used by some copra makers, who temporarily live on the island to gather and dry coconuts.

Kakaban: A Biological Paradise

Kakaban, a low, limestone island off the coast of eastern Borneo, holds a fascinating surprise: a brackish lake literally alive with jellyfish.

"The lake is totally unique—a biological paradise," said Canadian marine ecologist Dr. Thomas Tomascik, who together with his wife Anmarie has been studying Kakaban. "It teems with jellyfish and other marine creatures, yet is isolated from the sea. You really must see it for yourself to appreciate it."

According to Tomascik, the famous jellyfish lake in the Palau Islands—the only other known example—is a biological desert compared to Kakaban.

Kakaban Island is a coral atoll that has been uplifted by geological forces, turning the lagoon into a land-locked lake. The 5-square-kilometer lake, surrounded by a 50-meter ridge, occupies most of the interior of this uninhabited island, which has been declared a government nature reserve.

The Tomasciks hope to solve the mystery of how the lake's plants and animals are able to survive in this isolated system. The lake has no outlets, but fresh saltwater continually seeps in from below, mixing with trapped rainwater. The salinity averages 24–26 parts per thousand, considerably less salty than normal sea water.

The seepage from outside seems insufficient to sustain the abundance of life in the lake, and most likely the lake operates as a more or less closed system, with nutrients being produced and recycled in its own waters.

From the surface Kakaban looks like a typical freshwater lake, but below there is an abundance of colorful marine life. The shoreline is fringed with a tangle of mangroves. Their sturdy roots, as thick as a human arm, are cloaked with sponges, seaweeds and tunicates. Visibility is around 10–12 meters, and the lake is at most 11 meters deep.

Although not a particularly diverse ecosystem, the lake's unique ecology and the unusual associations between organisms make it a fascinating subject.

The dominant animals in the lake are jellyfishes, of which two species are particularly abundant. In the deeper areas, a species of rhizostome jelly forms such dense concentrations that it's like swimming in a kettle of jellyfish soup. Fortunately they do not usually sting. Another species, the upside-down jelly, literally carpets the bottom in parts of the lake.

One of the most unusual animals in the lake is an as yet undescribed species

ROGER STEENE

of pure white anemone which, in the absence of more usual planktonic prey, feeds on jellyfish. Jellyfish that blunder into its tentacles are immobilized and summarily devoured.

Eight species of fish have been identified here. A cardinalfish (*Apogon lateralis*) and goby (*Exyrias puntang*) are by far the most abundant, and in the absence of large fish predators these are totally fearless. Another of the lake's five gobies is a new species of *Cristatagobius* with an unusual cock's comb.

—*Gerald R. Allen*

Introducing Maluku

The islands of the Moluccas—Maluku in modern Indonesian—were the first in the archipelago to capture the imagination of the Europeans. Not for their beauty, although these thousand-odd islands, with powder-white beaches, swaying coconut palms, and constant, lazy sunshine certainly fit most northerners' definition of paradise. The Europeans came in search of one of the world's most coveted commodities—spices.

The Spice Islands

In the 16th century, cloves, nutmeg and mace were literally worth their weight in gold in Europe. When the 18 men aboard the *Victoria,* the only survivors of Ferdinand Magellan's original expedition of 230 men and five ships, hobbled home with their load of just over a ton of cloves, they all became rich men.

From the beginning of the spice trade—Chinese sources make reference to cloves as early as the beginning of the common era—until the Dutch planted cloves on Ambon Island, every clove in the world came from the tiny islands of Ternate and Tidore, just off the west coast of Halmahera (see map page 212). All the world's nutmeg—and the even more precious mace, which comes from the bright red aril that surrounds the nutmeg "nut"—came from the tiny, and isolated, Banda Islands.

Today, Indonesia grows more cloves in Sulawesi than in Ternate or Tidore, and nutmeg and mace is produced in Grenada, in the Caribbean. The early European explorers would no doubt be shocked to find out where most of the world's cloves end up today: in *kretek,* the ubiquitous Indonesian clove cigarets.

The People of Maluku

Maluku no longer attracts much attention. The old Dutch forts sit crumbling, and ancient Portuguese armor and gold pieces have become heirlooms to be passed down by families through the generations. Other than Ambon—a city of 275,000 and the center for communications in the three provinces of Maluku—and Ternate, the islands have only scattered small population centers.

Most Moluccans are fishermen and farmers. Because many of the sandy islands do not support rice, they rely on manioc, taro and sweet potatoes as staples, with fresh fish for protein.

In the interiors of Seram, Halmahera and some of the other large islands, people who trace their genealogies back further even than the arrival of the first Malays live lives relatively untouched by the modern world.

Two Island Arcs

The islands of Central and South Maluku are made up of two parallel, but differently formed, island chains. The outer arc of islands—continuing from Timor through Leti, the Babar Islands, the Tanimbars, the Kei Islands and then around through Seram and Buru—is made of calcareous rock, the remainder of ancient reefs. The inner arc—continuing from Flores and the Alor archipelago to Wetar, the Damar Islands, and ending in the isolated Banda archipelago—is part of Indonesia's "Ring of Fire," a string of volcanic islands that

Overleaf: *A view of Gunung Api in the Banda Islands, sitting in splendid isolation in the middle of the Banda Sea. Photograph by Kal Muller.*

Opposite: *Pearl oysters hanging from an underwater fence. The oysters are cultivated in this way until they are large enough to form pearls. Then they are shipped off to one of the many Japanese-run pearl farms where they are seeded and left to grow pearls. This is Bobale Island, off the east coast of Halmahera's north peninsula. Photograph by Helmut Debelius, IKAN.*

mark the edge of a crustal plate.

North Maluku is quite separate. Halmahera Island, shaped like a miniature Sulawesi, was formed, like its larger neighbor, when two long islands were joined together by the forces of continental drift. The western side of the island, including tiny Ternate and Tidore, is volcanic; the eastern side is a mixture of limestone and other rock.

Underwater Riches

The sea was never low enough to allow land crossings between all the islands of Maluku, and the animal life of the islands reflects this: although there are few mammals, birds and insects have done well on the islands. The birds are varied and beautiful—kingfishers, lories, parrots and, in the Aru Islands, the legendary birds of paradise.

According to 19th century naturalist Alfred Russel Wallace, the fishes of Maluku are "perhaps unrivaled for variety and beauty by those of any one spot on earth."

Unfortunately, diving in the region is currently limited to the Banda Islands and a very new operation in Ambon. One can only dream of what the diving is like in the Gorom and Watubeli Islands, or the small islands in the Kei group, seasonally washed by rich upwellings from the depths of the Banda Sea.

—David Pickell

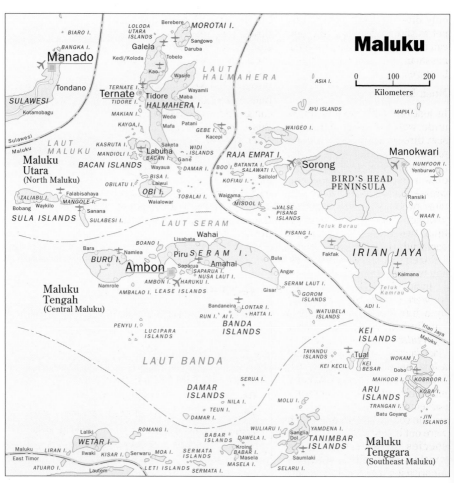

Fine Diving in the Central Moluccas

In the Ambon and Saparua areas, aficionados can find dive sites that are truly world-class. Scuba has just begun here, and the divers who have experienced the area have been trying hard to keep it secret. Sorry chaps, here is the lowdown.

Our summer dives off Ameth village on Nusa Laut island rate the very highest marks, particularly for the number of big fish seen there. Divers have asked Tony Tomasoa, currently the only dive operator in the area, not to spread the word. But you can't blame Tony. He is a businessman, and has no objections to more clients.

Nusa Laut

In just one and one-half hours underwater off Nusa Laut, we saw: three gray reef sharks of 1.5 meters; three large turtles, including one of over a meter; a dozen enormous Napoleon wrasse, including one school of four; two very impressive giant groupers; two large dogtooth tuna; two black-spotted rays; a barracuda of more than a meter; a dozen longnosed emperors; and two huge reef lobsters.

In addition to the big fellows, we were enveloped at one point by a huge school of fearless longfin bannerfish (*Heniochus diphreutes*). We saw a school of black jacks (*Caranx lugubris*) and a few giant jacks (*C. ignoblis*); several large schools of unicornfish; and a school of Thompson's surgeonfish.

The colorful crowd of reef fish were out in force. We counted 12 species of butterflyfish, six species of angelfish, and saw Moorish idols, snappers, rainbow runners, and more. This is really a rich site. Some divers have reported spotting the rare, lumbering dugongs here.

But the big ones are not guaranteed at this location. Our initial dives at Nusa Laut were in May, when visibility was nothing to brag about, around 10–15 meters. As a very general rule, the top visibility in the Ambon/Lease area lasts from September through November.

The northwest monsoon blows on and off from May through August, bringing occasional showers and rough seas for a few days. The southeast monsoon lasts from May through August, with long, heavy rains and wind-driven seas which can go on for weeeks. But during this time, the north shores are still diveable.

June is the area's wettest month, averaging some 650 millimeters over 24 rainy days. Diurnal tides are between 2.2 and 2.3 meters. Usually (but not always) the fish life is best seen during the rising tide.

AT A GLANCE
Ambon and Lease

Reef type: Walls and slopes

Access: 30 min to 1 hr by speedboat

Visibility: Fair to excellent, 10–13 meters; depending on the season

Current: Moderate or none

Coral: Some areas quite good

Fish: Excellent at the best sites

Highlights: Huge arches, possibility of large fish at several sites

Lease Islands Diving

Although we found our initial dives at Ameth village the very best in the Ambon/Saparua vicinity, this was probably due to plain dumb luck. There are many other excellent locations. For diving around Saparua, Nusa Laut and Molana islands, it is the most convenient to stay at the Mahu Diving Lodge on the east shore of Tuhana Bay, north Saparua Island. The center is owned and operated by Tony Tomasoa's Daya Patal Tour and Travel, based in Ambon. This travel agency can handle all your logistics and diving.

While the dive operation on Mahu was not a professional one, help was on its way in early 1994. The dive guides speak very little English but the capable boatmen know the locations well. Speedboats powered by twin 40 hp outboards whisk divers to sites.

Ameth and Akon

Ameth village on Nusa Laut faces a small bay filled with sand and coral that is exposed at low tide. The reefs off this village, as well as those off Akon, further south along coast of Nusa Laut, offer fine diving. (See map below.)

The people of Ameth and Akon take good care of their reefs, allowing no fish bombing. Before diving here, the operator must ask the villagers' permission, which is easily obtained upon payment of a very reasonable users' fee. (This is included in the package prices already paid by the guests.)

Dives at Ameth begin off the reef edge, which drops vertically to sloping sand at 40–60 meters. The far ends of the site are coral and sand slopes. (See map page 218). Corals—both hard and soft—are abundant in areas, but not overall. But sponges grow here in unusual numbers.

During some dives in May and July, the big fish life here was tremendous. But dives off Ameth in late January offered nothing big except for a panic-stricken reef white-tip shark, a couple of Napoleons, a few barracuda and the odd tuna. Of course, this wouldn't have been too bad if we had not remembered the previous dives here.

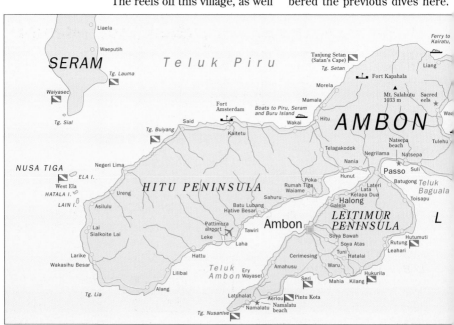

Also, January visibility was much better, in the 25–30 meter range.

The next time we dove we stuck to the areas marked 5 and 6 on the map on page 218, and at slack tide. Here we found a large (well over 100) mixed aggregation of snappers and chubs, drifting along at 15–20 meters near a huge school of surgeons. Sand flats at 15 meters sprouted miniforests of garden eels, patrolled by Titan triggerfish.

The coral knoll (6 on the map) was decorated by two very large soft coral trees at its base which, from the seaward side, opens into a swim-through featuring two schools of cardinalfishes. A long decompression stop was rewarded by excellent coral cover at 3–5 meters, with many damselfish and outrageously colorful small wrasses.

During our two dives off Akon we encountered visibility of more than 30 meters. The wall drops from the fringing reeftop, at 2–6 meters, straight down to 50–60 meters. The wall is full of shallow caves and has several ledges.

A huge arch marks the end of the dive—one could also start here, depending on the current. The top of this arch forms a continuation of the reef edge, at about 6 meters. At its highest, the inner arch reaches to about 12 meters below the surface, with a width varying between 6 and 12 meters.

The arch encloses an approximately oval-shaped opening, 5 meters high and 15 meters wide. The bottom profile slopes through the arch, then drops vertically in ledges from to more than 40 meters. The body of the arch, especially the underside of the "roof," is full of small pockets, along with thickets of soft coral trees, barrel sponges growing at crazy angles and daisy cup corals. Try it at night, when the polyps open to feed.

The bulk of the wall section that we dove off Akon had the usual invertebrates and reef fishes. With one notable exception: a cape-like projection into the sea, at about 20 meters, where the current picked up from 1/4 knot to occasional gusts of one knot. From the sheltered side of the cape we observed a very large aggregation of curious medium-sized fishes, mostly snappers and unicorns.

Molana Island

South Molana is a good dive, off a flat reef which extends south of the island. The reef slops very gradually from 3-4 meters to the drop-off at 10-20 meters. From this edge, a wall drops vertically to flat sand at 40 meters. The wall face is full of caves, ledges and large depressions, with soft corals and a few gorgonian fans. Reef fish variety was quite good, highlighted by three humphead parrots. The topside deco stop offered spreads of staghorn coral. A few snappers came up from their normal, slightly deeper habitants and several small schools of yellow-striped goatfish. Our dive here offered 25–30 meters visibility, and no currents, although a slight downcurrent often runs from the reeftop to the depths. We saw none of the sharks said to be present in numbers according to locals.

The profile at Southeast Molana is similar to that on the island's south side, but the reeftop is higher, 2–6 meters, and less extensive. The wall, with less relief, bottoms out to sand at 30 meters. Fish life was slightly better here than on the other sides of Molana, with schooling fusiliers, a large school of bannerfish near the lower end of the wall and a big, lonely barracuda patrolling the shallows. The topside showed good cover of hard and soft corals.

Pombo Booi

A small islet just east of the southwest peninsula of Saparua Island goes by the name of Pombo (local name for pigeon) Booi (the name of the nearest village. The site is also sometimes called Mamala.

We found the fish life here better than Molana—excellent species variety and very good numbers. The most noticeable species included painted sweet-lips, snappers, yellow- and blue-streak fusiliers, long-nosed emperors, angels and Titan triggerfish. And a fair-sized black-tipped reef shark, along with a large Napoleon wrasse.

There were lots of tunicates and spreads of leather corals, along with a normal variety of soft corals. We dove in a slight current, and reached a sand bottom at 35 meters. The dive spot has many outcrops, some with caves and swim-thoughts.

We had an excellent night dive in Saparua Bay at a nearby location. Highlights include numerous Spanish Dancers, hermit crabs, and octopus. Depths vary from 4 to 12 meters. We also saw many urchins—at least five different species—all with mean sets of spines, so be careful at night. This location is only known to and dived during the cruises of the live-aboard *Pindito*. (See page 228.)

Nusa Tiga

The three tiny islands at the westernmost end of Ambon Island are called, simply enough, Nusa Tiga ("Three Islands"). We anchored for the night at Asilu-lu, on the far western tip of Ambon's Hitu Peninsula, and after obtaining permission from the traditional ruler of the area, headed out to dive the area.

We started both dives off the west coast of Ela Island, following the reef north on the first dive, south on the second one. The reef profile was a slope of 45 degrees, well-covered in diverse species of coral. Several large schools of black triggerfish (*Odonus niger*) checked us out, and moray eels weaved menacingly out of several holes.

We saw fusiliers, a very large aggregation of unicornfish (at least 70 individuals) and a small group of sweetlips. Clown and Titan triggerfish patrolled the reef, and we counted a dozen species of butterflyfish.

At depths of 15 to 25 meters we saw several large bamboo fish traps, belonging to the Butonese fishermen who maintain a few huts and a prayer house on Ela Island.

Diving Ambon

The Ambon Dive Centre, which opened in early 1994, seems like a good bet to see the best of the nearby underwater world. The operator has two NAUI dive masters, one Indonesian, the other English. Sony, with hundreds of dive around Ambon, knows the best dive spots and guarantees good, year-round dives, shifting locations according to weather conditions. Laura handles walk-in clients and promotions as well as escorting guests. It is a professionally run outfit.

The Centre is based in Namalatu, near the Leitimur Peninsula's southwest tip. Namalatu is about a half-hour's drive, along the shore of Ambon Bay, from the city. It is a pleasant trip once you're out of city traffic. From there, the operator's 9-meter fiberglass dive boat, powered by twin 40 hp outboards, whisk divers to various locations.

During the northwest monsoon, from around September to March diving is generally along the south coast; during the southeast winds, about May through August, diving is better on Ambon's northern areas, along with west Seram.

The maximum length of the boat rides is two hours, usually much less. If the seas are a bit rough for the speedboat ride from Namalatu to the north, clients are taken overland to Hilu, where the operator maintains a base camp and the speedboat waits. The Centre plans to buy a 15-meter wooden ship, with a rubber dingy, for diving at further out locations.

There are a wealth of attractions among the Centre's 30-odd tried-and-true dive spots. The sites feature a variety of profiles, some with spectacular underwater formations: arches, caves, bubbling sand, chimneys, and vertical walls.

Fish life is always good, but it takes luck to see the area's most

Above: *Cuttlefish can sometimes be coaxed into allowing a diver to touch them. Although molluscs, they have a very large repertoire of behaviors, and like their relatives, squid and octopus, can be among the most entertaining animals encountered on the reef. The cuttlefish's "cuttlebone" is a porous calcareous structure that helps the animal with buoyancy control.*

Ameth
1. Very nice coral slope; many juvenile fish
2. Small wall; lots of grottos
3. Opening in reef; good for anchorage
4. Wall to 60m; many holes
5. Wall to 25m, then sandy terrace
6. Coral knoll, top at 8m; soft corals
7. Sand slope; jacks, hammerhead shark at 25m

CORAL SLOPE

SAND SLOPE

WALL

Red-roofed church

0   100
Meters

Coral covered with sand; exposed at low tide

Ameth village

spectacular denizens: big tuna, sharks, manta and eagle rays, Napoleon wrasses, schools of humphead parrots, barracuda. The real show-stoppers, according to the guides, are absolutely huge groupers, described to us as "VW Beetle–sized."

Of course, none of these can be guaranteed on any one dive. But in one of the locations, several species of big morays are always lurking in their caves. A strange blue-colored dart goby (a species which is usually red) can be occasionally spotted. Octopus sightings are frequent.

Night diving, just in front of the Centre's base at Namalatu, can be rewarding indeed, with Spanish dancer nudibranchs and lots more. It can be so good in fact, that the liveaboard *Cehili's* divemaster, Larry Smith, says he has had his best night dive ever here. (And Larry Smith has more than 11,000 dives).

Amboina Diving Club

If you speak at least some Indonesian, and you want to dive with the locals try the Amboina Diving Club. The club was founded in 1988 and has 20 active members. Most are businessmen, so they practice their sport only on Sundays and holidays. But the club owns two dive boats and there are guides—who speak minimal English—available with a bit of advance notice. The club offers two-dive day

trips to 11 locations off the outer periphery of Ambon, with the cost depending on the distance from the harbor. While none of the dive spots are world-class, most are quite decent, and the club knows the area very well. We tried two locations with one of their guides.

Waimahu, off the southwest tip of Leitimur, looked good—it si on the cape and there was current flowing—but turned out to be quite ordinary. It was a beach entry and we swam out by following long, narrow gaps in the dead reef.

At first we dipped into a half-knot current, following a slope to about 30 meters, then returned in shallower water. Visibility was fair at 15 meters, and the coral was undamaged by fish-bombing. But fish life was rather scarce: sharks, sometimes sighted here, kept well out of sight when we dove.

Our second dive, at Pintu Kota ("City Gate") was much better. We followed the dive boat's anchor line to about 25 meters and a Napoleon wrasse was waiting to greet us. Following the sea bed at the lower edge of a ridge, we soon arrived at a huge arch, some 10 meters high and 15 meters wide: the City Gate.

Two species of jacks, including some big ones, came by to check us out, the more curious approaching to within a meter. A school of surgeonfish and a bunch of fusiliers guarded one side of the arch, and a white-tip shark patrolled the far side.

We ascended up a couple of submerged ridges sprouting an almost-solid carpet of small, tapering orange sponges covered with bumps and interspersed with purple-laced *Polycarpa* tunicates. A moray slithered out of its lair, curious but not aggressive. Stopping at 8 meters on the ridge-top, we hung on in a half-knot current to decompress a bit. An excellent dive.

BANDA ISLANDS
Pristine Reefs and Many Pelagic Fish

The Banda Islands are one of Indonesia's top destinations for divers. Both experts and beginners will enjoy themselves here, as the diving ranges from the shallow lagoon between Banda Neira and Gunung Api to the vertical walls of Hatta Island, the most easterly in the group.

The variety and numbers of fish are both excellent; the chances here are always good to see several big animals of a meter or more: reef sharks, Napoleon wrasse, turtles, rays and groupers. Schools of medium sized fish, and the usual kaleidoscope of small reef fish in the shallows are all here in abundance. The reefs we saw were pristine, with no signs of fish bombing damage. Currents were negligible at the sites and times we dove.

Banda has two dive seasons—one centered around April, the other in October. The months before and after these are usually quite good also, but any more than that is a matter of luck. The off seasons bring high waves and relatively turbulent seas, usually December/January during the northwest monsoon, and early June through August for the southeast monsoon.

But, with enough time and patience, one can enjoy good diving even off-season, as there are always breaks in the weather. Visibility, however, remains restricted to 10–20 meters off season, reaching 30–40 meters only around the ideal months.

Staying in Banda

Diving is available only to guests staying at one of Des Alwi's hotels, although this is hardly a problem. Des Alwi is Banda's most famous son, and a tireless promoter of his islands. While Mohammed Hatta and Sutan Sjahrir—two of the leaders of Indonesian independence—were exiled in Banda, they became mentors to the young Des Alwi, who later entered the world of diplomacy and business.

AT A GLANCE
Banda

Reef type:	Vertical walls, and some slopes
Access:	5 min to 1.5 hrs by speedboat
Visibility:	Fair to excellent, 10–20 meters in the off season; up to 40 meters during the best months
Current:	None or moderate, to 1.5 knots
Coral:	Excellent, undamaged reefs
Fish:	Excellent numbers and varieties at the best sites
Highlights:	Pristine, sheer walls and great number of fish off Ai and Hatta

After a quarter of a century, he returned to his native islands, and there applied himself to building up the infrastructure and the economy, and raising the profile of the little islands in the Indonesian nation and in the world. He is extremely knowledgeable about the history and culture of his islands.

The cost of diving—boat, tanks, weight belts—is quite reasonable, and if there are just two people diving, there are good spots near Banda Neira to keep boat costs down. For trips further out, it's easier on the wallet to form groups of 4 to 6 divers.

Although there are a few BCs and regulators for rent, we suggest, as always, that you bring your own equipment, including lights for night dives. The boatmen know the good dive spots, but there are no dive masters.

Non-divers need not worry about boredom: the snorkeling is good in the lagoon right off Banda Neira, there are tennis courts, and jaunts can easily be arranged to ruined forts and nutmeg plantations. Although the Bandas are not the ideal place for children, attentive hotel staffers will look after them as they jump off seaside diving boards, swim in calm waters, or watch the sharks, fish and turtles in two coral enclosures in the lagoon.

Sonegat

You could start diving the day you get to Banda, as the flight from Ambon arrives in the early morning. The nearest site for a decent dive is just five minutes by boat from the hotels. It is in the *sonegat*—"sea arm"—between Banda Neira and Gunung Api, just offshore from a little seaside house owned by Des Alwi.

The dropoff here is steep, and the wall extends down 25 meters to a grey, sandy bottom. The wall is cut by vertical clefts, and is overgrown with huge patches of cabbage coral. There were few fish around, but a good-sized dogtooth tuna cruised by, and we saw some of the beautiful blue-girdled and emperor angelfish.

Keraka Island

Pulau Keraka—"Crab Island"—is just a few minutes further out, and protects the north entrance of the Neira–Gunung Api sea passage. A nice sandy stretch on the north coast is perfect for a picnic. We started our dive just off the south shore, descending some 18 meters down a mini-wall covered with hundreds of large blue-and-yellow tunicates (*Polycarpa* sp.).

Swimming to the east, we rounded Keraka's tip, where there is a lighthouse, and started along the north face. Just as we turned the corner, we met a huge grouper, who examined us unhurriedly. At 10 meters we encountered a good assortment of reef fish, and a school of half-

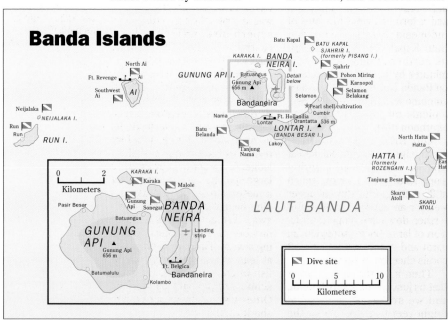

Banda Islands

LAUT BANDA

Dive site

0   5   10
Kilometers

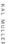

meter-long barracudas, hanging out like hoodlums deciding on their next move.

Sjahrir and Batu Kapal

Just off the northern tip of Lontar Island is Sjahrir (formerly Pulau Pisang, "Banana Island"), recently renamed for Sutan Sjahrir, one of Des Alwi's childhood mentors and a former Prime Minister of Indonesia. Sjahrir Island, and Batu Kapal—"Boat Stone"—off its northern point, are just 20 minutes by boat from the hotels on Banda Neira. These two sites combine well for a morning dive, a picnic on the beach, and an afternoon dive.

Our first dive was off the north edge of Batu Kapal, and at first we encountered a boring slope leading to a sandy trench at 25 meters. This did not auger well for an interesting dive. But further down the slope a profusion of large barrel sponges, fan coral and a good variety of soft corals cheered us up.

Then a meter-long grouper met us just off the sandy bottom, and we swam into a cloud of bright reef fish, notable for the profusion of butterflyfish. The best was just ahead: two enormous, rounded coral pinnacles, reaching to around 10 meters of the surface. From 30 meters depth, the bottom dropped down out of our range of vision. The variety and number of fish swimming around or lurking in the caves in these towers of coral was overwhelming. This was a superb dive, marred only by restricted visibility, 10–12 meters. (This was early June.)

The afternoon dive, off the south coast of Sjahrir, started well. A steep coral slope dropped us down to a resting black-spotted stingray at 22 meters. He let us approach quite close before trying to hide under a shallow ledge. As we started our ascent, a large spotted eagle ray, well over a meter across, buzzed us, flapping by just two or three meters away. We also saw an unusual number of triggerfishes, including several Titan triggerfish, and at least six species of butterflyfish in good numbers, including schools of pennant bannerfish. Other divers have reported reef sharks in this area.

Above: *The strange crocodile fish, Cymbacephalus beauforti. This creature, which here looks a perfect match for the algae-covered coral boulders, lies in wait for any small fish or crustacean to wander within range of its prodigious mouth. Mapia atoll, Irian Jaya.*

Sjahrir Island
(formerly Pisang Island)

60m
40m 8m 15m
25m
BATU
KAPAL I.
Batu Kapal

Tg. Garam

Rocks

Reef

Dive site

0   100   200

Meters

Belakang
Sjahrir

10m ▲ *SJAHRIR*

▲ 35m   ▲ 15m

*Teluk
Pisang*
Note: Reef flat of
Pisang Bay is
exposed at daily
low tides.

▲ 20m

▲ 10m

Pisang Bay

Rocks

Village

Tg. Mantutu

The diving on Sjahrir is off Batu Kapal Island, and off the reef edge of Pisang Bay. **Batu Kapal.** Slope, then sandy bottomed trench at 25 meters. Two large coral outcrops north of the island are dense with fish, including great swarms of butterflyfish. **Pisang Bay.** The reef profile is a coral slope down to about 35 meters. There is the usual array of reef fishes here, as well as a large number of rays.

Gunung Api

The last major explosion, in May 1988, killed of most of the offshore coral formations around Gunung Api, but amazingly spared many sponges. Some corals are beginning to grow back, but by and large the seascape remains bleak. There are no walls off Gunung Api. The bottom slopes gradually to 30–35 meters, where life peters out.

It is startling to see bright reef fishes in such a barren seascape. We saw a fair number of colorful individual species, including clown triggerfish, a bright yellow trumpetfish and some sweetlips. Huge schools of fusiliers cruised the area, and we spotted a few small dogtooth tuna. The stars of the show were a fat, 90-centimeter-long grouper, and an eagle ray a meter-and-a-half across.

Lontar Island

The outer edge of Lontar Island, which represents part of the rim of a sunken caldera, offers several good dive sites, of which we visited two.

Selamon Belakang. We dove off Selamon Belakang (*belakang* means behind), so named because it lies across the island from Selamon village. The dive was superb from the start, as we descended down a steep dropoff split by a vertical cleft and covered with coral. The wall extended down to 45 meters.

We stopped at 30 meters, finding an unusual barrel sponge—huge, and with three openings. We encountered gorgonians and black coral trees. The wall held an unusually large concentration of lionfish, including a black-and-white juvenile who seemed very interested in the intruders. Visibility was 20 meters, very good for this time of year.

We swam north through a good variety of reef fish, with unusual numbers of Vlaming's unicornfish and schools of black triggerfish. The wall was interrupted here and there by sand falls. The dive's highlight was a bumphead parrotfish, a crusty old giant of almost a meter.

Batu Belanda. This site—literally "Dutchman's Stone"—is at the opposite end of Lontar Island. Here we found a good wall, this one ending with sloping sand at 30–35 meters. The drop featured many barrel and tube sponges, and small caves and cracks which offered refuge to abundant fish. The fish were varied and plentiful: a school of snappers, large emperor and blue-girdled angelfish, wrasses by the dozen, a large pinnate batfish, and numerous bannerfish.

Hatta Island

We rode in the newest of the Hotel Maulana's 8-meter open

Ai, Hatta and Run Islands

Ai Island

Tg. Kelip
❹
Parigi
❻ Fort Revenge
Ai Village
Tg. Nama
Nama
Tg. Keli
❺
AI
136m ▲
Batu Dua
Tg. Besar
❸
❷
Tg. Batu Udang
❶
Tg. Goranga

0   1
Kilometers

1. Wall to 70m; caves at 25m and 35m; schools of jacks, sharks sometimes; after bare of fish
2. Wall to 45m; large gorgonians; terrace at 7m–12m with coral outcrops
3. Wide terrace to edge, wall to 45m; barrel sponges, soft corals
4. Wall continues, terrace narrows; fishermen here
5. Wall to 50m; clefts, cracks, overhang at 35m; huge gorgonians—largest seen in Banda
6. Wall breaks up; spurs and sand falls

Hatta Island
(formerly Rozengain)

Hatta village
Tg. Kenari ❹ ❸ ❷ ❶
Tg. Salamasa
Mt. Hari 140m ▲
Tg. Pulu
HATTA
Semerad
Batulobang
Tg. Pohon Pinang
Tg. Besar
❺ ❻ ❼
Tg. Buton
❽ ❾
❿
SKARU ATOLL
⓬ ⓫

0   1
Kilometers

1. Vertical wall to 60m; many grottoes
2. Wall to 30m–40m; soft corals on 5m shelf
3. Wall to 30m–40m
4. Coral slope; very good hard corals plus lots of fish, including sharks, if the current is strong.
5. Wall to 40m; distinctive formations, many gorgonians—most anywhere in Banda
6. Very nice overhang at 27m; gorgonians
7. Coral terrace at 10m; coral knolls to 10m; huge schools of fish
8. Wall to 35m
9. Sandy slope with terrace at 20m; pinnacles
10. Wall to 30m–40m
11. Many pelagics at point; current picks up
12. Sandy slope at 12m; coral outcrops to 6m

Banda Islands

BANDA NEIRA I.
Batuangus
BATU KAPAL
SJAHRIR I.
Ai
AI
GUNUNG API I.
Batuangus
NEIJALAKA I.
Lontar
Bandaneira
Run
RUN I.
Nama
LONTAR
(BANDA BESAR)
Hatta
HATTA I.
NEIJALAKA I.
❷ Tg. Timbal
Tg. Tenusan

0   5   10
Kilometers
LAUT BANDA

Sand and coral exposed at low tide
Tg. Robin
Reef exposed at low tide
Tg. Soawor
Tg. Tuledan

Run Island

1. Coral slope to 35m; many coral spurs, clefts and overhangs, all dusted with white sand
2. Sand slope, 45°, with coral knolls; good dive for beginners

Tg. Cincin Seleman
Run Village ❶
Tg. Lenore
RUN
Waynero beach
Tg. Sehee
Tg. Nuret
Mt. Tanah Merah ▲
▲ 188m
Tg. Gandulang
Reef always submerged
Tg. Waynero

0   1
Kilometers

fiberglass dive boats—powered by twin 40hp outboards—to Hatta Island, about 25 kilometers by sea from Banda Neira. Because of the calm seas, usual for October and November, the trip took just 50 minutes.

Hatta is a recent name for the island, bestowed in honor of Mohammed Hatta, one of the founding fathers and the first vice-president of Indonesia. History buffs will recall the island's

Above: *Nudibranchs,* Polycera *sp. (above) and* Chromodoris bullocki. *Polycera was photographed in Bali, and Chromodoris, Flores.*

old name, Rosengain, a British possession at the time when control of the Banda spice trade was still disputed.

Skaru Atoll. Our first stop was the Skaru atoll, a barely submerged reef a few hundred meters off the southern point of Hatta. (See map page 223.) The atoll is completely underwater, and is only visible from a distance because of the waves breaking over it.

The sea was milky with a whitish sediment more commonly found here during the *panca roba* season in July and August. The conditions lingered because of an errant weather pattern associated with the El Niño effect, which irregularly every few years brings warmer water temperatures to the East Pacific off the coast of South America. The promised visibility of 30–40 meters usual in October and November has thus eluded us.

We began our first dive at the western end of the north edge of the atoll, as the site provided protection from the southeast swell and took advantage of a slight current running east. We dropped onto a coral slope that quickly became a wall, ending in a sandy bottom 35 meters below. During the first part of the dive we encountered many sandy terraces at around 20 meters, and the wall reached 45 meters before ending at the eastern reach of the north edge.

At the point, the current quickened to 1.5 knots, and we encountered a multitude of schooling fish. We perched on a coral outcrop and watched the passing parade of unicornfish, fusiliers, jacks and rainbow runners for a good ten minutes. In the course of the dive, we also saw some giants: a reef whitetip shark almost two meters long, two dogtooth tuna, a Napoleon wrasse, and a hawksbill turtle.

At this point the wall ended, and we passed over a sloping terrace of fine white sand, here and there broken up by coral knolls. In this area we found colonies of garden eels (*Heteroconger hassi*), and a prolific assortment of butterflyfish, angelfish (including the blue-faced angel, *Pomacanthus xanthometapon,* which has a very spotty distribution and is not often seen), triggerfish and schools of sergeant-majors.

Tanjung Besar. Our next dive was off the south coast of

Hatta itself, east of a point called Tanjung Besar ("Big Cape"). The wall was sheer, and ended in white sand at 40 meters. Its surface was honeycombed with small grottos and overhangs—at times we felt ourselves in a hanging garden, due to the unusual variety of soft coral dangling from the roof of the grottoes. We saw more gorgonians here than anywhere else in Banda.

This was a perfect environment for moray eels, and we found them in abundance. No sooner would we find one, but another would slither out—invariably right next to our faces!

A gentle current bore us east, past large schools of fish riding thermoclines up and down the wall. We decompressed on a coral terrace at 12 meters. This flat was studded with huge coral outcrops, each reaching almost to the surface. The "plain" was swarming with schools of snapper, fusiliers and unicornfish. The colors and variety of forms of the hard and soft corals here were outstanding.

Northeast Hatta. Our third dive was off the island's north coast, near Hatta village. Although the reef formation was virtually the same on every dive, this area is different in that we encountered many coral spurs, interspersed with falls of fine, white sand. The deepest wall here extended down 60 meters.

Halfway through our dive we encountered a very strange sight: a white object that looked like one of the margarine sculptures one finds in the restaurant of a fancy hotel. We descended to a sand terrace at 30 meters to investigate, and what we found was the whitened corpse of a Napoleon wrasse. Closer inspection revealed that a chunk of flesh was missing from behind the cranial hump. We surmised that this individual had been bested in a territorial dispute.

Just then, two enormous Napoleons buzzed us, an unusual display for such normally shy creatures. We were amazed that the corpse was intact, especially as we had seen two sharks earlier in the dive. From its white color, we judged the body had lain here for at least three days. It was fascinating to observe this monster at leisure, and at such close proximity. The strong teeth are intimidating, and combined

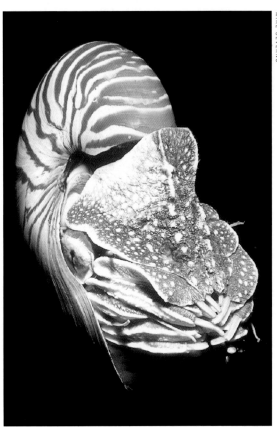

MIKE SEVERNS

with the animal's thick lips, one can see how it so easily dispatches the hard-shelled and thorny crustaceans and echinoderms that are its preferred prey.

Later, we told Des Alwi what we saw, and he had another explanation. There is, he said, a small green shrimp capable of poisoning the Napoleon wrasse.

For our second dive, we continued along the same formation,

but heading east from the northwest corner of the island. We found a 45 degree coral slope that continued down to 30 meters. Here we spent a few minutes playing with a large stingray, and then explored the reef.

Twenty minutes into the dive, the reef profile once again changed into a wall. We were back into the earlier formation, and found the dive to be much the same. There was an abundance of semi-pelagic predators, including dogtooth tuna, a giant jack and a school of bluefin jacks (*Caranx melampygus*), and kingfish (*Carangoides*).

Ai Island

Together with Hatta, this island offers Banda's best diving. Both the north coast and the southwest of Ai are ringed with flawless coral walls, dropping in one place to 70 meters. The walls are rugged and full of caves, just the kind of habitat that harbors fish. Some of the gorgonians are the biggest we have seen.

The highlights go on and on: a fat grouper, pushing a meter-and-a-half; a school of more than 300 Heller's barracuda; a couple of meter-long chevron barracuda; a lobster with a body the size of a man's thigh; endless schools of fusiliers; a longnosed emperor close to a meter, the maximum for its species; a group of spotted sweetlips, with one close to its maximum 70 centimeters; many unicornfish; an abundance of clown triggerfishes, and Titan triggerfishes within sight the entire dive; a large school of pyramidal butterflyfish; turtles; and moray eels.

North Ai. Along the north coast, the wall drops to 50 meters at the northwest point—where there is a large overhang—and then to 30–40 meters until it breaks up near Ai village. At this point, coral ridges alternate with sand filled clefts, and huge swarms of fish congregated. Perhaps it was the shifting warm and cold currents flowing here that attracted the fish.

Southwest Ai. The southwest area features perhaps the best wall in all of Banda, with good growth to 70 meters. Growing on wide terrace on the west coast were tube and barrel

Below: *Smaller species of barracuda such as these* (Sphyraena genie) *often school during the day as a form of protection. The shifting shapes of these schools—balls, spirals, rings—are fascinating. At night the fish separate, and prowl the reef individually.*

sponges, and great quantities of soft coral in red, beige, purple and orange hues.

This site gets a perfect 10 from dive guide Wally Siagian, which is high praise indeed. The richness of fish life, the sheer drop-off, the caves and fissures in the rock, and the overwhelming richness of life here compares only to the very best sites in South Komodo, in the Pantar Strait, and a few dive sites on the isolated islands of the Banda Sea, reachable only by live-aboard.

Run Island

The furthest dives from Banda Neira are off Run Island and tiny Neijalaka, a companion island off its northern point. In moderately choppy seas, it took an hour-and-a-half to reach Run.

The British once claimed Run Island, and it remained a hold-out against the Dutch, who controlled the rest of the archipelago, until 1667. In this year the Dutch and the British tried to consolidate their holdings. Britain gave the Dutch Run, and the Dutch gave the British New Amsterdam—or, as it is now called, Manhattan.

Run. The coral wall on the coast off Run village was somewhat disappointing. While there were shallow caves and clefts in the wall, the coral spreads were poor and covered in a layer of fine white sand. Reef fish were moderately abundant at 15–25 meters, and we spotted one turtle and a couple of fairly large barracuda. The best of the dive came at 3–5 meters, snorkeling depth: two big barracuda, a 90-centimeter Napoleon wrasse, and four huge parrotfish.

Neijalaka. We followed with a dive off the north coast of this tiny island, attached to Run by a wall of coral exposed at low tide. The gently slope had only isolated coral heads, and the fish were notable for their scarcity. Only a pair of barracuda, some 80 centimeters each, saved this dive from total disappointment.

We even surfaced early for lack of enthusiasm. We had been told that Japanese divers favored this site, which we found very strange indeed.

—Kal Muller and Cody Shwaiko

Above: *A school of lunar fusiliers, Caesio lunaris. Fusiliers are among the most common schooling fish seen in Indonesia.*

Luxury Diving in the Wilds of the Banda Sea

One of the huge groupers had been expected sooner or later—two top dive masters had assured me that four of these beasts regularly patrolled the reef off tiny Koon Island at the far eastern edge of the Banda Sea. Yet, even with forewarning, the first sight of the chap sent a rousing rush of adrenaline through my system.

For the past few minutes, a huge school of big-eyed jacks—well over a thousand of them—had welcomed me as one of their own. A cautious approach had been rewarded by the school opening up slightly to allow me in their midst. Thousands of unconcerned eyes stared at me as the fish slowly finned by, within touching distance.

I took a few photos, and enjoyed the dream-like spectacle for a while, then drifted slowly out of the school to observe them from the nearby reef. As they shifted away, the huge grouper appeared just behind them, a shepherd keeping a close eye on its flock.

A full two meters long and with the bulk to match, the giant grouper clearly dominated this kingdom. As it slowly vanished into the sea, my second rush of adrenaline of the past quarter hour slowly subsided.

Diving off a Pinisi

With a group from Switzerland, we had been diving off the *Pindito,* a beautiful, well-designed, wooden boat built along the lines of a *pinisi,* traditional Sulawesi-style trading schooners which, for the past three centuries, have dominated the inter-island trade in Indonesia.

Today, the *pinisi* no longer set sail with holds full of exotic products like bird-of-paradise feathers, pearls, sandalwood, tortoise shell, damar pitch (for fine varnish) or trepang. They are now all equipped with diesel engines, and they move more mundane bulk cargo: lumber, cement, packaged foods, and household utensils.

The schooners retain the handsome, classical lines of the sailing ships, however, which is why the *Pindito*'s builders stuck to the traditional design. The few modifications were to allow for eight air-conditioned double cabins, and all the other creature comforts required by demanding clients. And, of course, a professional setup for scuba diving. Indeed, the ship's name is an acronym created from the phrase: *pinisi* dive tourism.

Built in South Kalimantan, part of Indonesian Borneo, the 40-meter, 230-ton ship is the pride and joy of its Swiss designer and general manager, Edi

AT A GLANCE
Pindito

Reef type: Vertical walls and steep slopes

Access: Live-aboard

Visibility: Good to very good, 15–25 meters

Current: Variable, usually some

Coral: Rich, pristine reefs

Fish: Superb numbers and varieties at the best sites

Highlights: Sheer mass of schooling fish, huge groupers, curiosity and tameness of the fish at the most isolated sites

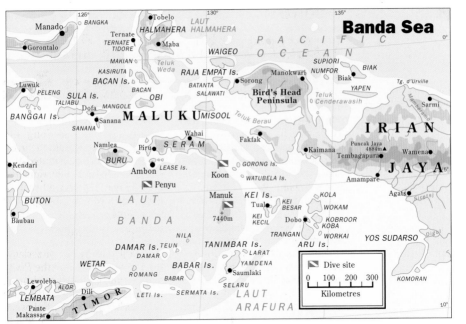

Frommenwiler.

Since April 1992 Frommenwiler has taken divers and adventurers into the most remote part of the Moluccas. He has settled into his adopted country, marrying a pretty Javanese woman and becoming the proud father of a baby boy.

The *Pindito* takes divers to sites in the Banda Sea, and when the weather shifts, to the Raja Empat Islands off Irian Jaya's Bird's Head Peninsula. We accompanied the ship during a Banda Sea run.

Cruises to Raja Empat take divers to sunken World War II Japanese fighter aircraft in the Sorong area, some excellent dives off tall offshore pinnacles, and—from April to September—some lucky clients are taken to one of the very few known nesting beaches of the giant leatherback sea turtles.

Koon Island

During our 10-day dive cruise on the *Pindito,* we checked out a couple of dozen locations pioneered by Peter, the on-board dive instructor, and Frommen-

wiler. Visibility was generally good, but not really excellent due to the plankton in the water, ranging from 15–25 meters. Most of the reefs were drop-offs and steep slopes around isolated islands. All were top spots, but the best of the best was, undisputedly, Koon Island.

Giant groupers are really something to see, but it was a combination of underwater spectacles that made our dives on Koon among the very best among more than 1,000 dives in Indonesia. Never have we seen so many huge schools and aggregations of various fish species.

In addition to the big-eye jacks, we saw large groups of batfish, bright yellow sailfin snappers and yellow-eyed midnight snappers, barracuda, longnose emperors, bannerfish, blue-fin jacks, unicornfish, painted sweetlips, and blue triggerfish. While on other dives I have seen one or two of these species in schools or large, loose groups—except for the sailfin snappers and the painted sweetlips—at Koon the diversity and numbers were overwhelming.

Reef sharks were conspicuous by their absence—except for a string of five (or was it six?) large white-tips, swimming by in single file, heads and tails almost touching, a formation I had never before witnessed. Other unusual marine life included many large groupers of a half-dozen species, all in the 60 centimeter to 1 meter range. And, of course, plenty of reef fishes of various kinds and the occasional turtle and sea snake.

Our next plunge was one of those once-in-a-lifetime experiences, reserved by Neptune only for divers who are patient and extremely well behaved (or are lucky enough to have booked on the Pindito). Visibility was nothing to brag about, around 15 meters at the surface and a bit better further down. My buddy and I had decided to go deep at first, take a quick look and then come up to where the fish life is more abundant.

We dropped in near the edge of the sloping reef and quickly made our way to where the vertical wall began. Right then we froze: one of the giant groupers decided to check us out. Slowly finning back and forth just out of decent photo range, the big fella must have decided that we were a harmless curiosity and drifted in for a closer look, stopping just a couple meters away. This was one big, big fish.

Video whirling and camera clicking like mad, our giant grouper seemed happy enough to pose until we had our visual fill. By then, we had spotted a huge school of batfish below and dropped a bit for a closer look. We needn't to have bothered—apparantly we piqued their curiosity, too, and they came up to check *us* out.

With our computers ready to edge into decompression mode, which is strongly discouraged by the *Pindito*'s divemaster, we slowly ascended to around 15 meters. This turned out to be the perfect ringside seat for the upcoming show.

From this vantage point, we watched schools of at least seven species, plus small groups of individuals of a dozen more species, a combined mass of fish that was truly breathtaking.

Night Diving

The walls turn into a night-time fish hotels, many species sleeping off their daytime labors, relatively safe from nocturnal predators—but not from the lights and gazes of divers. Species that would never allow a close-up daytime look blissfully sleep with open eyes, unaware of divers being far inside their private territory and zone of comfort.

One of these, a high-bodied grouper close to a meter in length, had put on impossibly colorful pajamas, bright and strongly patterned, but we could not even find it in any of the fish identification books on board the *Pindito*.

Our lights also brought out the bright yellow and orange polyps of the cup corals, along with the strong colors of soft coral trees. And crustaceans, seldom seen in daytime, were busy foraging: a slipper lobster here, several hermit crabs there, unconcerned by our bright lights.

It is probably tiny Koon Island's position which accounts for its almost incredible mass of fish life. It is the southernmost and final island in the little archipelago connected by very shallow waters to the southeast tip of large Seram Island.

These shallows end in a very extensive reef flat, about 15 kilometers long and 3–4 kilometers wide. Koon perches near the edge of this reef, very close to the Gorong Islands, but separated from them by deep waters: over 600 meters.

The eastern extremity of

Koon's reef, where we dove, is wide and flat. Its shallow areas, from 3 to 10 meters, are dotted with coral outcrops reaching close to the surface, each a wonderland of fish and invertebrates.

Sand flats alternate with the outcrops, and the rest of the underwater landscape is filled with hard and soft corals. We saw almost no fish-bombing damage on this reef.

The gently sloping reef leads to a wall, which begins at 10 to 30 meters. After that, a sheer drop to 50–70 meters. The wall is full of small and medium-sized caves, some reaching way back into the reef—and large ledges and overhangs. Upwellings and currents bring plankton and necessary nutrients to the bottom of the food chain, which sustains the great mass of fish found here.

The Pindito

The *Pindito* operates most efficiently, but the dive schedule is flexible in the face of unforseen circumstances: unseasonal weather, lost baggage, guests hitting the bottle a bit too hard,

something new in a dive location. The normal routine—if tremendous, world-class dives can be called normal—calls for two daytime dives plus one at night.

The suiting-up routine has been well thought out, and there's plenty of space for it. The crew brings filled tanks from the compressor area in the stern of the boat to the wide front deck where large open baskets hold the clients' dive gear. Everyone puts on his or her own BC and regulator, then the crew carries the tanks down wide ladders—one on the port side, the other on starboard—to the three waiting Zodiacs.

After a briefing by the divemaster, the clients step down the ladders for the short ride (usually 5 to 10 minutes) to the dive site. Two safety rules apply: no diving deeper than 40 meters, and a maximum of 60 minutes bottom time. The ship always anchors far enough away from the reefs to prevent damage.

Our cruise on the *Pindito* was one of the most exciting and enjoyable ones we have ever taken. The all-wood ship looks

Below: *A pair of Holthuis's shrimps* (Periclimenes holthuisi) *in what looks to the editor like the mimic anemone* Phyllodiscus sp. *This anemone is a very strange species in the intra-order Boloceroidaria. One form mimics hard coral, as seen here, and other forms mimic branching algae, or algae-covered substrate (currently, it is taxonomically unclear whether they are separate species or all forms of* P. semoni). *This is a fairly large anemone, 25 cm across, and delivers a blistering sting that not only hurts but leads to necrosis of the flesh. It has been called the "Hell's fire sea anemone," and is said to be even worse than the* Actinodendronids.

CODY SHWAIKO

and feels great. Solid, top-quality ironwood below the waterline, *meranti* for the deck, and fine wood paneling elsewhere.

The crew of 15, while speaking little English, is as cheerful and efficient as we had sailed with in Indonesia. The ever-varied meals were healthy and delicious. The atmosphere in the dining-room and lounge area was always cordial. With the main

Above: *Jacks sweeping past a gorgonian. The best of the Banda Sea sites are famous for huge schools of jacks and other fish.*

engine well muffled, and electric motors on the compressors, noise was never a problem.

The only weakness in the boat's design is that, since the *Pindito* is engine-powered, she draws only 2.7 meters, resulting in more pitching and rolling in heavy seas than deeper-keeled craft. But because the ship's routes are planned with monsoon winds in mind, wave-

induced rocking should not be a problem.

Manuk Island

The shark just appeared all of a sudden in my camera frame. Focus, shoot. Focus, shoot. Exultation. Yahoo! It was a common white-tip reef shark, notoriously difficult to photograph, unless baited, which some of us consider grossly unsportsmanlike.

White-tips barely qualify as sharks, and normally flee in panic at the sight of a diver. But not this one; curious and fearless, that's all. And not dangerous at all. Only divers unused to sharks try to swallow their regulators when they see the beasts.

Eyes glued to the viewfinder, I had tried to keep calm and concentrate on technical matters. This was not easy: the viewfinder kept filling with fish species which usually have a fear of strange, burbling creatures in their vicinity.

But off Manuk Island, some inbred, genetic molecules seemed to be missing, resulting in fearless fishes, and not just fearless, but downright curious. Not all species—the angelfish in the shallows were a bit flighty, and a group of jacks, heading straight for us, turned back after getting to within a few meters.

But the rest—focus, and click. The golden rule for underwater photography is "the closer, the better" and it was all too easy to follow here. In fact, the damn things kept getting *too* close. Now that's a complaint you don't often hear from underwater photographers.

The Galapagos Islands are the best known of those few rare places that are so isolated that the animals have no mortal fear of man. It is unlikely that more than a handful of humans visited the Galapagos before the mid 19th century, when Charles Darwin put these Ecuadorian islands on the map of general human knowledge.

Now, the presence of too many tourists threatens the ecology of the Galapagos. That's definitely not the case for Manuk Island. Occasionally, a few fishermen from the Banda Islands spend several weeks here, catching and salting tuna and snapper. But the often rough seas, and lack of freshwater on the island severly limits their stay.

Manuk is quite isolated. The closest landfall—and just another tiny island—is Serua, almost 100 kilometers to the southwest. Serua, together with Nila and Teun, were evacuated by the Indonesian government in the 1970s because of unpredictable volcanic activity.

The closest inhabited island, Hatta of the Banda group, lies over 110 kilometers to the northwest. The seas around Manuk are deep: just 10 nautical miles from the island the bottom drops to 3,000–4,000 meters; a bit further it drops to 6 kilometers.

An Isolated Volcano

Manuk Island is the easternmost active volcano in a long chain that sweeps through Indonesia, beginnning in Sumatra and including Java, Bali, Lombok, Sumbawa and Flores, before reaching the southwestern edge of the Banda Sea.

Here, beginning at Wetar Island, the volcanic chain of small islands sweeps through deep waters in a graceful arc, including Romang, Damar, Teun, Nila, Serua and Manuk, then heading northwest to end at Gunung Api in the tiny Banda group. This volcanic chain marks the boundary of a tectonic plate.

Aside from a bit of smoke, we saw little volcanic activity on Manuk during our visit. A few of us climbed the island volcano, reaching the 285-meter peak. Two fishermen led the way, hacking through patches of tropical vegetation with *parangs* (the Indonesian machete). The bare suggestion of a trail swept steeply upward, forcing us to pause several times to catch our breath. We caught occasional glimpses of large rats, common on the island.

As we left the line of vegetation, the sky filled with birds, mocking our laborious, sweaty progress. Light blue sky and dark blue ocean filled the rest of the breath-taking panorama, making the climb worth every drop—and there were many—of sweat.

We saw two species of boobies, one with a dark head and yellow feet, the other blue-beaked with a white head and reddish feet, and frigate birds, including a few breeding males with huge swollen red necks.

Frigate birds are the pirates of the air. Terrible fishermen themselves, they wait until a boobie catches a fish, and then, in mid-air, force it to regurgitate its catch.

The top of Manuk, covered with volcanic rocks, showed several very hot fissures, some with yellow sulfur deposits. A large, deep, but inactive crater and a broken rim, face south. Eventually we had had enough. Delicious showers and cold beer were waiting on the *Pindito*. We descended in record time.

Our fishermen guides were also happy. Aside from an unexpected tip, they had gathered a couple of dozen bird eggs for supper. Occasionally, they also eat the birds, which are easy enough to catch: walk up to them, grab one, and wring its neck. We preferred the meal waiting for us on the *Pindito*.

Diving North Manuk

Our first dive, off north Manuk, was good but not really spectacular. We saw lots of sea snakes, many of them coming to within a few centimeters of us, then loosing interest. They are of no dan-

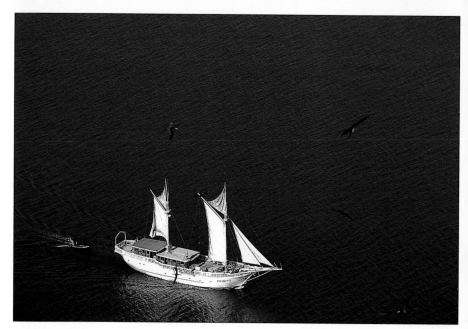

ger to divers. While their venom is very strong, and can easily kill a man, they rarely bite. And when they do, they often don't deliver their venom. (Apparently the venom takes some time to produce, thus the snakes don't use it unless they really have to.)

The only human fatalities we have heard of from sea-snakes are fishermen who net their catch, then sort through the writhing mass, bare-handed. The banded sea-snakes of Manuk displayed a pattern and coloration we had not seen elsewhere in Indonesia.

The coral formations were good, showing no fish-bomb damage. Lots of large barrel-sponges dotted the seascape, but we only saw one large school of fish. This was the only hint of the tremendous second dive, described above, which is definitely one of the best single dives of my career.

The highlights of that night's dive were the still foraging sea snakes, and several interesting gastropods, including a rare cowry and a seldom-seen tun shell (*Tonna perdix*) of unusual

size. This latter was, as is its habit, moving at break-neck speed (seeking other gastropods) but over hard coral, not usual sandy preying grounds.

Karang Pekelo

The fish show at Karang Pekelo, a site off southcentral Seram Island, was almost overwhelming. Even as we were descending we were greeted by a couple dozen long, sleek rainbow runners, a lone torpedo mackerel (*Scomberoides lysan*) and several good-sized tunas.

At about 12 meters, just above the reef top, we were mobbed by a huge school of big-eye jacks, dashing about with no apparent purpose, stopping, and then darting off again at breakneck speed. Visibility was a very good 20–25 meters.

A few couples, one the normal silvery color, the other completely dark except for a small white dot at the very tip of its dorsal fin, around the school with quick gyrations of their own, in perfect unison and often in physical contact with one another—a frantic mating dance, perhaps. The school vanished quickly but returned several times during the course of the dive.

We dropped down the reef face to sand at 30–35 meters, with a few scattered coral outcrops on the flat substrate. Upon arrival, a school of unicorn filefish (*Acanthurus monoceros*) finned by, a species we had never seen before.

Then, some 20 meters away, we distinguished a familiar species, the yellow-eyed puffer (*Arothon immaculatus*) but instead of just one we were looking at a most unusual school of about 50 individuals.

Warned by our computers that bottom time was up, we rose to the 20 meter level and settled in for a ringside seat at the fish parade: big-nosed unicornfish, surgeonfish, yellow- and bluestreak fusiliers, and red snappers. We never identified the fish in the biggest school, which kept parading back and forth. They were snappers of some kind, but with dirty-looking, mottled gray-brown bodies in need of a good scrubbing.

A couple of very obvious, and big, black jacks (*Corax lugubris*) finned by, but our attention was riveted on a giant grouper: 2 meters long of it was an inch. Other big boys included several very large Napoleon wrasses, and a couple of bumphead parrotfish.

But for one of our dive companions, none of these was the dive's highlight. At one point in the dive, a big gray reef shark made straight for her, fast, stopping only at the cardiac-arrest distance of a meter. There it took a good hard look at her, turned around, and left behind one very upset lady. A stiff drink back on board miraculously restored her powers of speech.

Schooling fishes of many species enliven all of Indonesia's better dive locations. During a typical dive, two or three schools put in a brief appearance, and quickly vanish. But only a very few dive locations literally swarm with masses of fish. Karang Pekelo, discovered only in late 1993, is one of these fantastic places.

Other Sites

While we have seen the highlights of a single *Pindito* cruise, other routes also feature exceptional diving. This includes a small group smack in the middle of the Banda Sea and well over 200 kilometers away from the Banda Islands.

These "lost" mini islands are divided into two small groups, and are so little known they go under various names, either the Lucipara Islands or Pulau Tujuh ("Seven Islands").

Four islands close to each other are shown on maps as Maisel; just a bit off, three more are called Shilpad or Penyu (this last means "turtle"). The northernmost of the tiny dots is referred to as Bingkudu or sometimes as Penyu.

Nesting turtles can be found throughout the group. the Lucipara Islanders catch green turtles, and sell them to traders who take them to Bali, where the meat is very popular, particularly in a ritual dish called *ebat,* in which raw turtle meat is pounded together with many spices into a paste. Turtles are expensive, and ironically, it's the new, tourist-derived wealth in Bali that is threatening sea turtles throughout Indonesia. South Bali's appetite for sea turtles is said to now reach 40,000 a year.

Underwater in Lucipara, there are fine dropoffs with excellent hard corals and black corals. There is nothing unusual in the fish life there, except that common species grow much larger than normal, close to or surpassing record lengths.

Introducing Irian Jaya

Irian Jaya is one of the last really wild places on earth. Although a few roads have been laid that lead a bit inland from some of the population centers on the coast, parts of the interior of the western half of New Guinea, an almost continent-sized island, are still shrouded in mystery. Even today, the flight maps used by pilots working the highlands for Protestant missions and mineral exploration contain large areas marked: Relief Data Incomplete.

Fewer than 2 million people live in Irian Jaya's 410,660 square kilometers. The largest city and capital of the province is Jayapura, a buzzing town of 170,000 on the north coast near the border with Papua New Guinea, which neatly cuts the island in half. Modern Jayapura boomed after World War II, based on infrastructure laid by U.S. General Douglas MacArthur, who began his famous island-hopping strategy from here.

Irian Jaya was not relinquished by Holland at the same time as the rest of the former Dutch East Indies, and did not formally become part of Indonesia until 1969. The territory was dubbed Irian Jaya—"Victorious Irian"—in the early 1970s.

The transition was far from smooth, and local rebellions by spear-wielding warriors and an independence movement, the Organisasi Papua Merdeka (OPM) —"Free Papua Movement"—haunted the changeover. There is little OPM activity today, but the government keeps a large military presence in the province, and many areas are still off-limits to tourism.

Linguists do not agree on how many unique languages are spoken in Irian, although most estimates hover around 250. The island's indigenous people, called Papuans, are dark-skinned and have kinky hair, and trace their ancestry back to before the expansion of the Malays through Indonesia.

An Impenetrable Island

The interior of Irian is craggy and mountainous—Puncak Jaya, at 4,884 meters, is the highest point between the Himalayas and the Andes—and to reach it from the coast one must cross thick swamps and forests. The rivers of the north are so full of oxbows that running them doubles or triples the overland distance to the interior. In the south, treacherous tides—changing the water level in rivers even 100 kilometers inland—conspired against explorers.

Until American explorer Richard Archbold flew over the Baliem Valley in 1938, and saw the neat little compounds and sweet potato fields of the Dani, these people had lived in their valley isolated from contact with any outsiders for some 10,000 years. Today, the Dani are Irian's most famous ethnic group. Their numbers have grown to about 70,000, and Wamena, a small town in the Baliem Valley and the de facto capital of Dani country, has been attracting several hundred visitors a month.

Farmers and Artists

Famous warriors in the past, today the Dani are simply farmers, living in thatch and wood huts and raising their staple sweet potatoes and pigs in the

Overleaf: An undersea ledge, encrusted with cup corals. These corals extend their bright yellow tentacles to snare plankton only at night. Mapia atoll. Photograph by Kal Muller.

Opposite: A pink clownfish, Amphiprion perideraion, in front of its host anemone, Heteractis magnifica. Because the anemone is partially contracted, its bright column is visible. Bunaken Island, 3 meters. Photograph by Mike Severns.

salutary climate of the 1,500-meter-high Baliem Valley. Despite 40 years of Protestant missionaries, many Dani are unregenerate in wearing their *kotekas,* or penis gourds.

If the Dani are the most famous of Irian's peoples, the Asmat are the most notorious. Living in the hostile tidal swamps of the south coast, ritual head-hunting had in the past been the centerpiece of Asmat culture.

This fact made international headlines in 1961, when Michael Rockefeller, the young son of then-governor of New York Nelson Rockefeller, disappeared after trying to swim ashore when his boat capsized. Whether or not Rockefeller was actually eaten by the people of Otsjanep has fueled many speculations, but has never been determined.

Rockefeller was visiting the Asmat to collect their art, among the most powerful and respected in the world. Huge war shields, canoe prows and several-meters-long *bisj* poles, decorated with abstract and heavily expressionistic figures, display the kind of raw energy that modernist Euro-pean painters treasured in their collections of "primitive" art.

Rich, Unexplored Waters

Cenderawasih—"Bird-of-Paradise"—Bay and the islands off New Guinea's western tip hold some stunning, unexplored reefs. Currently, only Irian Diving in Sorong (see "Irian Jaya Practicalities" pg. 307) operates in the region. The outfit takes divers to World War II–era wrecks and other fine sites in the Sorong area, in the Raja Ampat islands, and in Dore Bay.

South of Irian is the shallow Arafura Sea, which until perhaps just 10,000 years ago connected New Guinea to Australia. The coast here is silty, and fringed with brackish rivers and stands of mangrove and casuarina.

Bintuni Bay, cut deep into the Bird's Head Peninsula, offers one of the largest and most unmolested mangrove swamps in the world. Athough such habitats are not a paradise for divers, they play an important ecological role in developing the larval stages of fish and crustaceans.

—*David Pickell*

World-Class Wrecks and Pioneer Diving

At first I did not believe the wreck dive stories of Max Ammer, the tough but personable young Dutchman and Pacific World War II expert who has set up Irian Diving in Sorong, on the westernmost tip of Irian Jaya, and Manokwari, on the other end of Irian's Bird's Head. I do now: if you're a wreck diver or a World War II buff, Irian Diving can satisfy your wildest dreams.

Max runs ten trips a year, out of Manokwari or Sorong. The Sorong trips operate out of one of three base camps in the Raja Ampat islands, and the Manokwari operations run out of a base camp on an island in Cenderawasih Bay. Space fills quickly, so book as soon as you can.

Finding the Wrecks

Max trained as a para-commando in the Dutch army and as a machine-tool operator, and his practical and mechanical dexterity comes in handy in setting up and operating a dive business in the middle of the worst spare-parts supply area of Indonesia.

He used to make a very good living in Europe by customizing Harley Davidsons for clients, some with a propensity for drinking and profanity he did not always appreciate. His love for beautiful machines expanded from Harleys to World War II motorcycles and jeeps and other memorabilia for collectors.

With a family who used to live in Indonesia, seeking World War II remains in the Moluccas and Irian Jaya seemed natural enough. On his first trip to Morotai Island, the last Allied island stepping-stone before the recon-quest of the Philippines, Max picked up enough vintage Coca Cola bottles to pay for his trip several times over again.

During the course of drifting around, he also found many downed fighters, including six of the nine Dutch-piloted P40's lost in Indonesia. But Max's most valuable find in Indonesia was his wife, Anita Ammer Matahari. She is the real boss of Irian Diving, running the office and, as Max says, "without her, there would be no business."

AT A GLANCE
Irian Diving

Reef type: Vertical walls, lagoon channels, caves, platform reefs.

Access: By boat from base camps

Visibility: Very good to excellent, 20–45 m

Current: Moderate, excellent for drift diving

Coral: Very good variety and numbers

Fish: Very good variety and numbers

Highlights: Snorkeling with dolphins near the Wai base camp; white-tip sharks under a P47B wing; finding new wrecks untouched/complete

Consulting military archives, opened thanks to his chutzpah, he started looking underwater around Irian. So far, he has discovered about 65 shipwrecks, mostly Japanese transports, and some 35 aircraft, the majority U.S.-made P47 Thunderbolts and P38 Lightnings—the much flimsier, if more maneuverable, Japanese aircraft have pretty well disintegrated since the war.

He deserves a medal just for being able to operate in the face

Sorong

Depth	Ship/Aircraft	Description
❶ 12m	ship	broken up
❷ 16m	ship	~65m long
❸ 5m	2 ships	~25-30m long
❹ 15m	ship	~60m long
❺ 20m	B24	broken up
❻ 0/15m	ships	7 ships
❼ 4m	Jap. aircraft	"Oscar"
❽ 15m	several ships	
❾	reported aircraft	2 engines
❿	reported ship	big
⓫	reported ship	medium
⓬	reported ship	medium
⓭	reported ship	big
⓮ 20m	ship	~90m long
⓯	reported aircraft	broken up/2 engines
⓰	reported aircraft	1 engine
⓱	reported ship	big

◤ Dive site
⚓ Ship location known
⚓ Ship location reported
✛ Aircraft location known
✛ Aircraft location reported
⬡ Good area for diving reefs

0   2.5   5
Kilometers

given general instruction by Max. The rooms are very simple: the floor covered by a mat, then a mattress with sheets and pillow under a mosquito net. I had some of the best nights' sleep of my life in these rooms.

The first camp seen by divers out of Sorong lies a few minutes by speedboat from the Jefman Island airport. Matan Island, with a beautiful spit of white sand beach and a slight rise in the middle, has all the charm of a tropical dream: the ideal place to decompress after the many hours of flying from wherever. Guests are welcomed by the ever-hungry Flippy the cassowary, who never seems to get its fill of bananas, or for that matter anything else.

The main base camp, on Wai Island, was chosen for several very good reasons: a fine white-sand beach encircling the whole island, no insects, a huge resident colony of fruit bats, two resident sea-eagles, the wrecks of three P47 Thunderbolts just offshore, and the very good possibility of snorkeling with dolphins and manta rays. Reason enough?

The compressor, often busy filling tanks, has been relegated to a spot far enough away that you really have to listen to pick up its sounds. An open-sided thatched room, with chairs and padded benches off the jetty and over the turquoise lagoon makes for a fine late afternoon or early morning spot for viewing this tropical paradise.

The view will even be better at the other camp in the area, on Kri Island, which lies about 45 minutes north by speedboat, close to Waigeo Island. Here Max plans on building cabins right over the shallow offshore waters, moving the accommodations from the beach. From the back of this camp, a rough trail leads up the sides of a steep hill to a viewing platform built by the local Irianese for stunning

of an often stifling Indonesian bureaucracy. Before being able to dive off Manokwari, he has to report to seven different sets of authorities. But he does this with a smile and good humor, and the officials have come to accept him and his divers—even if they don't understand very well why foreigners don't stick to Bali, where the beer is cold and the nightlife is hot. Most Indonesian officials in Irian would give a leg and an arm to be able to transfer to Bali.

The Base Camps

Each of the four camps includes accommodations for a 12 guests, plus room for the staff, kitchen and dining room, a ladle-bath and a toilet. All of the solid, waterproof, thatch-covered buildings were erected by local Irianese builders whose foremen were panoramic viewing across the sparkling waters to Wai Island, with the large and mountainous Batanta and Salawati islands in the background. The half-hour sweaty climb is best done in the cool early morning hours.

The fourth camp is located on Nusorou Island in the large Cenderawasih Bay, off the north central Irianese coast. While the location is ideal for diving, the logistics are complicated, and the local government officials have not been very helpful to the operation, unlike their counterparts in the Sorong area.

The Shipwrecks

With limited time available, it was impossible to check out all the dive sites pioneered by Irian Diving. For the best shipwreck diving, Max advises aficionados to join one of his trips out of Manokwari, where the visibility is much better than in the Sorong area.

The Cross Wreck This Japanese ship lies some 150 meters off the Mansinam Island beach where a huge white cross marks the arrival of the first Christian missionaries to Irian Jaya. Easy location, shallow depth of 18 meters, excellent coral cover and proximity to a rich slope, this wreck tops the list of favorites in Manokwari Bay.

It took Max many dives to check out all the nooks and crannies of the Cross Wreck. The anchored ship had been sunk when it took a direct bomb hit through the front deck just behind the anchor winch. The explosion from the inside blew off the nose of the ship, opening it up like a can. Because of the copper railings, and large size of the engine in relation to the 35-meter length of the boat, Max speculates that this was a fast, lightly armed Navy patrol craft.

I was fascinated by all the gadgets and gauges in the engine room, as well as the ship's communications room with its switchboard and telegraph. On the rear of the ship, what are probably two rows of depth charges points to anti-submarine capabilities. A front hold contains small arms and machine gun ammunition, according to Max.

	Depth	Aircraft/Ship	Description
❶	38m	P47B	complete/intact
❷	25m	P47B	complete/intact
❸	3m	P47B	broken up
❹	15m	Ammo. ship	broken up
❺		reported aircraft	
❻		reported ship	
❼	20m	reported aircraft	
❽	40m	reported aircraft	
❾	15m	reported aircraft	
❿	40m	reported aircraft	

Dive site
Ship location known
Ship location reported
Aircraft location known
Aircraft location reported
Good area for diving reefs

0   10   20
Kilometers

Waigeo-Batanta

WAIGEO
GAM
P. FRIWIN
P. SAONEK
P. KOH
Base Camp "Mansuar"
P. MANSUAR
Base Camp "Wai"
P. MANSFIELD
P.WAI
P DAJANG
P. JAREFFI
BATANTA

Manokwari-Doré Bay

Pacific Ocean

Manokwari

Wosi

Pasir Putih

Airport

P. LEMON

Sowi

P. MANSINAM

DORÉ BAY

	Ship/Aircraft	Description
❶	Shinwa Maru	ship on side ±120m(L),16m(W),–16 to –32m(D)
❷	Ship	–16m on side ±60m(L)
❸	Ship	–15m straight up on white sand ±40m(L)
❹	Ship	–12/–20m straight up on slope ±40m(L)
❺	Ship	–15m straight up on slope ±40m(L)
❻	Ship	–35m
❼	Reported ship	
❽	Reported aircraft	(2 small aircraft, 1 bigger aircraft)
❾	Reported ship	"big"
❿	Reported aircraft	(2 Japanese aircraft)
⓫	Reported ship	"big"

L = length
W = width
D = depth

0 1 2
Kilometers

Mudi

◥ Dive site
⚓ Ship location known
⚓ Ship location reported
✛ Aircraft location known
✛ Aircraft location reported
〰 Good area for diving reefs

As though all this were not enough, the slope from the wreck up to Mansinam Island is perfect for your deco time. At first glance, this area seems to have no redeeming features: sand strewn with plastic bags and other thoughtful decorations. But careful looking reveals an incredible number of critters: on just one dive we saw two octopus, three leaf fish, four devil fish, and two mantis shrimp, one of them looking like an albino. Max and his guides are experts at spotting these guys, so all you need is a macro-setup to snap very impressive shots.

Pasir Putih wreck. Quite similar to the Cross Wreck, this is also very probably a coastal patrol craft. It too was anchored when it took a direct hit directly in front of the mast, blowing the bow sections to smithereens.

The remaining chunks of the front end lie detached five to fifteen meters in front of the body of the ship. There might well have been a light bow cannon, but no trace remians.

She lies upright on a slope ranging from about 20 to 25 meters, still in very good shape, especially its railings and superstructure. The very first swim along the top of the ship shows several large sake bottles along with a couple of naval lanterns— and right away we are grateful that the boat is deep enough to keep out local souvenir hunters. Max, of course, prohibits any souvenir-taking.

Shinwa Maru Max tracked down this large wreck thanks to the ship's bell, which had been salvaged many years ago by the Dutch marine corps detachment stationed in Manokwari. The Japanese characters revealed the name of the vessel, which means "good spirit."

The 3328-ton freighter was sunk on November 21, 1943 by B29 bombers based in Darwin, Australia. One of them scored a direct hit, blowing a huge hole in the starboard bow area, insuring a quick sink and thus leaving the rest of the large, 120-meter long ship intact. She lies on her left side, 200 meters off the beach, on a sand bottom at 33 meters.

The cargo of goodies is nothing short of amazing: long coils of rubber hoses, perhaps for hard-hat diving, two hard-hat diving helmets, a tracked vehicle perhaps for laying cable; gas masks, many large coils of cable, construction materials, telegraph machines, big round and mysterious objects, perhaps mines or depth charges.

Sorong wrecks The visibility for diving in the Sorong shipwreck are is not great in the best of times, and when I visited in late February was even worse than usual. On the wrecks here, all near Sorong itself, I had two to seven meters visibility, about half of the normal. Two of our wreck dives here were on single ships while another, at Pulau Dofior, was on a series of five smaller ships probably scuttled by the Dutch to prevent them from being used by the Japanese.

Down below, there is only fair fish life, with some lobsters and a moray or two. But the soft coral trees are outstanding, swaying in the surge which also pushes and pulls divers a bit.

World-class Coral Sites

Dozens of excellent dive sites lie just a few minutes away from the two main Sorong area base camps. We dove on three on them, doing follow-ups on them to experience different conditions. As elsewhere, the numbers and sizes of the fishes are in almost direct proportion to the current: the more, the bigger and merrier. Even at slack tides, with no current whatsoever, the fish life was very good.

While the mix varies, you can expect to see very large schools of sweetlips, bannerfish, sur-geons, snappers, fusiliers, emper-ors and batfish, along with the usual reef fish. You'll see at least two schooling species of bar-racuda, milling jacks, bumphead parrotfish, solitary Napoleon wrasse and some giant groupers. Sharks are common, including the weird and lethargic tasseled wobbegong. Eagle rays, mantas and turtles round out the show.

Dive profiles are down to the 30 meter range although more experienced divers might want to have a quick look below to check out if any of the bigger boys are around. The hard and soft corals are healthy and profuse.

Unique Experience

The experience offered by Irian Diving is not for everyone. Although there are easy dives with no current, it's not really worth coming this far for begin-ner divers. We highly recom-mend this outfit for those who do not require luxurious accommo-dations, but expect truly pristine and unexplored wrecks and reefs. Sign up early if you are one of these divers.

Below: *One of the many wrecked World War II aircraft dis-covered by Max Ammer in the waters near Manok-wari, Irian Jaya.*

Overleaf: *A swarm of striped eel cat-fish,* Plotosus linea-tus, *on a shallow reef on Bunaken Island. Photograph by Ed Robinson, IKAN.*

KAL MULLER

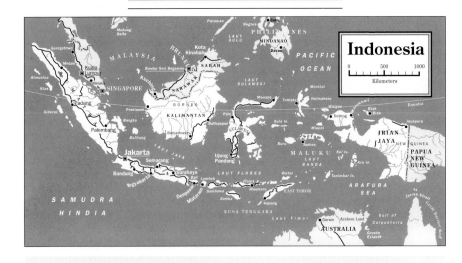

Indonesia at a Glance

The Republic of Indonesia is the world's fourth largest country, with 203 million people. The vast majority (88%) is Muslim, making this the world's largest Islamic country. More than 400 languages are spoken, but Bahasa Indonesia, a variant of Malay, is the national language.

The nation is a republic, headed by a president, with a 500-member legislature and a 1,000-member People's Consultative Assembly. There are 27 provinces and special territories. The capital is Jakarta (pop. 9.3 million). The archipelago comprises 2 million square km of land distributed over 17,508 islands.

Indonesia's gross national product comes from oil, textiles, lumber, mining, agriculture and manufacturing, and the country's largest trading partner is Japan. Much of the population still makes a living through agriculture, chiefly rice. The unit of currency is the rupiah, currently volatile, but about Rp7,500 to US$1 (12/98).

Historical overview. The Buddhist Sriwijaya empire, based in southeastern Sumatra, controlled parts of western Indonesia from the 7th to the 13th centuries. The Hindu Majapahit kingdom, based in eastern Java, controlled even more from the 13th to the 16th centuries. Beginning in the mid-13th century, local rulers began converting to Islam.

In the early 17th century the Dutch East India Company (VOC) founded trading settlements and quickly controlled the Indies spice trade. The VOC went bankrupt in 1799, and a Dutch colonial government was established.

Anti-colonial uprisings began in the the early 20th century, when nationalism movements were founded by various Muslim, communist and student groups. Sukarno, a Dutch-educated nationalist, was jailed by the Dutch in 1930.

Early in 1942, the Dutch Indies were overrun by the Japanese army. Treatment by the occupiers was harsh. When Japan saw her fortunes waning, Indonesian nationalists were encouraged to organize. On August 17, 1945, Sukarno proclaimed Indonesia's independence.

The Dutch sought a return to colonial rule after the war. Four years of fighting ensued between nationalists and the Dutch, and full independence was achieved in 1949.

During the 1950s and early 1960s, President Sukarno's government moved steadily to the left, alienating western governments. In 1963, Indonesia took control of Irian Jaya and began a period of confrontation with Malaysia. On September 30, 1965, the army put down an attempted coup attributed to the communist party. In the so-called "year of living dangerously" that followed, several hundred thousand people were killed as suspected communists.

General Suharto formally became president in 1968. His administration encouraged Western and Japanese investment, and the nation enjoyed three decades of steady economic growth. But in May 1998, facing charges of corruption and with the rupiah collapsing, Suharto stepped down, leaving his unpopular vice-president, Bacharuddin Jusuf Habibie, in charge.

MISS YOUR LOVED ONES BACK HOME?
PUT YOURSELF IN THE PICTURE WITH 001

When you're far away from home, nothing brings you closer to loved ones than a phone call. And it's so easy with 001. Indosat offers International Direct Dial to over 240 countries. Plus, you save 25% during discount hours on weekends*, and around the clock on national holidays and weekends. Call today, and share the good times!

IDD = 001 | COUNTRY CODE | AREA CODE | TELEPHONE NUMBER

From Hotel = HOTEL ACCESS CODE | 001 | COUNTRY CODE | AREA CODE | TELEPHONE NUMBER

001 IDD **NUMBER ONE ◎ INDOSAT**

* For information, call 102.

1 Java

2 Sumatra

3 Bali

4 Nusa Tenggara

5 Sulawesi

6 Maluku

7 Irian Jaya

Practicalities

TRAVEL ADVISORY, TRANSPORTATION, PRACTICALITIES

The following sections contain all the practical information you need for your journey. **Travel Advisory** provides background about traveling in Indonesia, from the economy and health precautions to bathroom etiquette. **Transportation** is concerned exclusively with transportation: getting to and traveling around Indonesia. It is followed by a handy **Language Primer** and a list of **Indonesian Dive Terms**.
The **Area Practicalities** sections focus on each destination and contain details on transport, accommodations, dive operators, dining and services. These sections are organized by area and correspond to the first half of the guide.

Indonesia
North Sulawesi
MANADO

Dive
ATTRACTIONS

NUSANTARA DIVING CENTRE

MOLAS BEACH, PO. BOX 1015
MANADO 95242 - INDONESIA
PHONE   : +62 - 431 - 860638 & 863988
FAX NO : +62 - 431 - 860368 & 854668
E-MAIL : ndc@mdo.mega.net.id
WEB   : http://mdo.mega.net.id/ndc/cover.htm

Discover Tropical Underwater Paradise

Wir informieren Sie gerne auf Deutsch

YOS DIVING CENTRE & MARINE SPORT
PADI Dive Resort

BALI
Lombok & Sumbawa

We serve you exclusively ✓

Daily Diving Tours • Dive Safari around BALI
Dive Box (w/o Accommodation) • Dive to SUMBAWA & LOMBOK
PADI Dive Courses • Introductory Scuba Diving
Breathaking Dive to Gili Tapekong
Don`t miss Romantic Dive Trips to Nusa Penida Island

Our Fleet ✓

2 X 200 HP Catamaran (1 Unit)
2 X 115 HP Powerboats (3 Units)
115 HP Speedboats (2 units) • 21 m Sailing Yacht (1 Unit)
2 X 40 HP Long Boats (3 Units)

Our Team Speaks ✓

Indonesian • Japanese • English • German • Dutch

HEAD OFFICE:
YOS Diving Centre & Marine Sports
Jl. Pratama 106x, **Tanjung Benoa**
Nusa Dua - Bali
Tel: (+62 - 361) 773774, 775440, 752005
Fax: (+62 - 361) 752985
Email: yosbali@indosat.net.id

BRANCH OFFICE:
YOS Diving Centre PONDOK SARI HOTEL
Pemuteran Village - North West Bali
Tel/Fax : (+62 - 362) 92337

DIVING AUSTRALIA

The first book of its kind, *Diving Australia* presents the continent's top dive sites in one easy-to-use book. Join our expert dive guides and world-class photographers as they take you on a fantastic underwater journey around this huge, diverse island continent. More than 200 superb photographs and lots of practical information.

ISBN 962 593 104 X

DIVING INDONESIA

This book is the result of hundreds of dives, thousands of kilometres of plane and boat travel (and weeks without a cold beer). Author and photographer Kal Muller's enthusiasm for the sport shines from every page as he invites you to explore Indonesia's dazzling underwater realm with him.

ISBN 962 593 314 X

DIVING SOUTHEAST ASIA

A truly unique book written by expert divers which tells where all the top dive spots in Southeast Asia can be found. Each site is mapped, photographed and described in minute detail. Details of dive facilities, prices, accommodation, transportation and the best times to visit are all given.

ISBN 962 593 312 3

BIRDING INDONESIA

This book is a "must" for the serious birder. Written by the world's leading authorities on Indonesian birds, it is packed with travel information and a complete checklist of Indonesian birds.

ISBN 962 593 071 X

SURFING INDONESIA

Another "first" from Periplus—the first surf guide to the world's largest archipelago. Author Leonard Lueras and his team of gonzo board-riders take you along thousands of miles of deserted shorelines, stopping at some of the best surf spots in the world. This book is very detailed, with maps, action-pumped photos and travels tips to get you there and back.

ISBN 962 593 313 1

SURFING AUSTRALIA

Capturing the adventurous spirit of Aussie beach culture, this guidebook shows the reader how to find and surf Australia's hottest beach, reef and point breaks, and get away from it all. Filled with invaluable travel tips, the book also explores Australia's surfing history, characters and the unique surf lifestyle which has inspired and entertained the world.

ISBN 962 593 322 0

PERIPLUS ACTION GUIDES

Periplus Action Guides are available at bookshops, surf shops and travel stores around the world. If you cannot find them where you live, please write to us for the name of a distributor closest to you:

USA/UK/Europe:
Tuttle Publishing
RR1 Box 231-5 North Clarendon, VT 05759-9700, USA
tel: 1-802-773-8930 fax: 1-802-773-6993

Asia-Pacific:
Berkeley Books Pte. Ltd.
5 Little Road, #08-01, Singapore 536983
tel: 65-280-1330 fax: 65-280-6290

Java 1
Sumatra 2
Bali 3
Nusa Tenggara 4
Sulawesi 5
Maluku 6
Irian Jaya 7

Travel Advisory

TOURIST INFORMATION

Overseas, you can contact the Indonesian embassy or consulate, or one of the following **Indonesia Tourist Promotion Board** offices: **ASEAN and Southeast Asia,** 10 Collyer Quay #15–07, Ocean Building, Singapore 0104. ☎ (65) 5342837, 5341795, fax: (65) 5334287. **Australia & New Zealand,** Level 10, 5 Elizabeth Street, Sydney NSW 2000, Australia. ☎ (61 2) 2333630, fax: (61 2) 2333629, 3573478. **Europe,** Wiesenhuttenstrasse 17, D-6000 Frankfurt/Main 1, Germany. ☎ (49 169) 233677, fax: (49 169) 230840. **Japan & Korea,** Sankaido Building, 2nd Floor, 1-9-13 Ahasaka, Minatoku, Tokyo 107. ☎ (81 3) 35853588, fax: (81 3) 35821397. **North America** , 3457 Wilshire Boulevard, Los Angeles, CA 90010-2203. ☎ (213) 3872078, fax: (213) 3804876. **Taiwan & Hong Kong,** 66 Sung Chiang Road, 5th Floor, Taipei, Taiwan. ☎ (886 2) 5377620. fax: (886 2) 5377621. **United Kingdom, Ireland, Benelux & Scandinavia,** 3-4 Hanover Street, London W1R 9HH. ☎ (44 171) 4930334, fax: (44 171) 4931747.

The **Directorate General of Tourism** in Jakarta has brochures and maps on all Indonesian provinces: Jl. Kramat Raya 81, PO Box 409, Jakarta 10450. ☎ (021) 3103117/9, fax: (021) 3101146.

Local government tourism offices, *Dinas Pariwisata*, are generally only good for basic information. More useful assistance is often available from privately run (but government approved) **Tourist Information Services**. Be aware that many offices calling themselves "Tourist Information" are simply travel agents.

VISAS

Nationals of the following 45 countries do not need visas, and are granted visa-free entry for 60 days upon arrival.

Argentina	Iceland	Philippines
Australia	Ireland	Saudi Arabia
Austria	Italy	Singapore
Belguim	Japan	South Korea
Brazil	Kuwait	Spain
Brunei	Liechtenstein	Sweden
Canada	Luxembourg	Switzerland
Chile	Malaysia	Taiwan
Denmark	Maldives	Thailand
Egypt	Malta	Turkey
Finland	Mexico	United Arab
France	Monaco	Emirates
Germany	Morocco	United Kingdom
Greece	Netherlands	United States
Hungary	New Zealand	Venezuela
Norway		

Be sure to check your passport before leaving for Indonesia. You must have at least one empty page to be stamped upon arrival and the passport must be valid for at least six months after the date of arrival. For visa-free entry, you must also have proof of onward journey, either a return or through ticket. Employment is strictly forbidden on tourist visas or visa-free entry.

Visa-free entry to Indonesia cannot be extended beyond two months (60 days) and cannot be converted to any other kind of visa.

A visa is required in advance for all other nationals or arrivals at minor ports.

Upon arrival you will be given a white embarkation/disembarkation card to fill out. Keep this card with your passport as you must present it when leaving the country.

Other Visas

The 2-month, non-extendable tourist pass is the only entry permit that comes without a great deal of paperwork.

A social visa, usually valid initially for 4–5 weeks, can be extended for up to 3 months. You must have a good reason for spending time in Indonesia (relatives, language study) and you must have a sponsor who will assume financial responsibility for you. The process can take weeks and extensions are at the discretion of the immigration office where you apply.

A business visa requires a letter from a company stating that you are performing a needed service for a company in Indonesia. It is valid for up to one year, but you must leave the country every 4 months. This is not intended as an employment visa, but is for investors, consultants, or other business purposes. You are not to earn money in Indonesia on a business visa.

Two other types of visas are available: the temporary residence card (KITAS) for research, formal study or employment, and the permanent residence card (KITAP). Both are difficult to get.

When dealing with the authorities, be on your best behavior and dress appropriately.

Customs

Narcotics, firearms and ammunition are strictly prohibited. The standard duty-free allowance is: 2 liters of alcoholic beverages, 200 cigarettes, 50 cigars or 100 grams of tobacco.

There is no restriction on import and export of foreign currencies in cash or travelers checks, but there is an export limit of 50,000 Indonesian rupiah.

All narcotics are illegal in Indonesia. The use, sale or purchase of narcotics results in long prison terms, huge fines and death, in some cases. Once caught, you are immediately placed in detention until trial, and the sentences are stiff, as demonstrated by Westerners currently serving sentences as long as 30 years for possession of marijuana.

FOREIGN EMBASSIES & CONSULATES

All foriegn embassies are in Jakarta:

Australia Jl. H.R. Rasuna Said, Kav. C/15-16, ☎ 5227111.

Austria Jl. P. Diponegoro No. 44, ☎ 338090.

Belgium Jl. Jend. Sudirman, Kav. 22-23, ☎ 5712180.

Brunei Darussalam Jl. Jend. Sudirman, Kav. 22-23, ☎ 5712180.

Canada Wisma Metropolitan I, 15th Floor, Jl. Jend. Sudirman, Kav. 29, ☎ 5250709.

China Jl. Jend. Sudirman, Kav. 69, ☎ 714596.

Denmark Bina Mulia Bldg., 4th Floor, Jl. H.R. Rasuna Said, Kav. 10, ☎ 5204350.

Finland Bina Mulia Bldg., 10th Floor, Jl. H.R. Rasuna Said, Kav. 10, ☎ 516980.

France Jl. M.H. Thamrin No. 20, ☎ 3142807.

Germany Jl. Raden Saleh 54-56, ☎ 3849547.

Greece Jl. Kebon Sirih No. 16, ☎ 360623.

India Jl. H.R. Rasuna Said No. S-1, ☎ 5204150.

Italy Jl. Diponegoro 45, ☎ 337445.

Japan Jl. M.H. Thamrin No. 24, ☎ 324308

Malaysia Jl. H.R. Rasuna Said Kav. X/6/1-3, ☎ 5224947.

Myanmar Jl. H. Agus Salim No. 109, ☎ 3140440.

Mexico Wisma Nusantara, 4th Floor, Jl. M.H. Thamrin No. 59, ☎ 337479.

Netherlands Jl. H.R. Rasuna Said, Kav. S-3, ☎ 511515.

New Zealand Jl. Diponegoro No. 41, ☎ 330680.

Norway Bina Mulia Bldg. I, 4th Floor, Jl. H.R. Rasuna Said, Kav. 10, ☎ 5251990.

Pakistan Jl.Teuku Umar No. 50, ☎ 3144009.

Papua New Guinea Panin Bank Centre 6th Floor, Jl. Jend. Sudirman No. 1, ☎ 7251218.

Philippines Jl. Imam Bonjol No. 6-8, ☎ 3149329.

Singapore Jl. H.R. Rasuna Said, Block X Kav. 2, No. 4, ☎ 5201489.

South Korea Jl. Gatot Subroto, Kav. 57-58, ☎ 5201915.

Spain Jl. Agus Salim No. 61, ☎ 331414.

Sweden Bina Mulia Bldg. I, Jl. H.R. Rasuna Said,

Kav. 10, ☎ 5201551.

Switzerland Jl. H.R.Rasuna Said B-1, Kav. 10/32, ☎ 516061.

Thailand Jl. Imam Bonjol No.74, ☎ 3904055.

United Kingdom Jl. M.H. Thamrin No.75, ☎ 330904.

United States of America Jl. Medan Merdeka Selatan No. 5, ☎ 360360.

Vietnam Jl. Teuku Umar No. 25, ☎ 3100357.

Passport Loss

If you lose your passport, it will be difficult to get new documents to leave the country unless you have the proper official forms from the police. Always keep a photocopy of your passport, visa and driver's license separate from the originals. You can then prove your identity in case of theft or loss.

When theft occurs, report to your consulate. Verification of your identity and citizenship takes two or three weeks and involves going to the local immigration office.

WHAT TO BRING ALONG

When packing, keep in mind that you will be in the tropics, but that it can get cold in the mountains. Bring wash and wear, light cotton clothes that absorb perpiration. (Synthetic fabrics are really uncomfortable in the tropics.) A medium-weight sweater or wind breaker is also a must, as is a light rain jacket with a hood. Don't bring too much, as you will be tempted by the great variety of inexpensive clothes available here. If you visit a government office, men should wear long trousers, shoes and a shirt with collar. Women should wear a neat dress, covering knees and shoulders, and shoes.

For those wanting to travel light, a *sarong* purchased upon arrival in Indonesia ($5–$10) is one of the most versatile items you could hope for. It serves as a wrap to get to the bath, a beach towel, pajamas, bed sheet, towel, etc.

Indonesians are renowned for their ability to sleep anytime, anywhere; so they are not likely to understand your desire for peace and quiet at night. Sponge rubber **earplugs** are available from pharmacies in the West or from the in-flight airline toiletry kit. Many consider them the most important 4 grams they carry.

Tiny **padlocks** for use on luggage zippers are a handy deterrent to pilfering hands. Some come with combination locks. **Flashlights** may come in handy, although these can be easily purchased locally.

Bring along some **pre-packaged alcohol towelettes** (swabs). These are handy for disinfecting your hands before eating, or after a trip to the *kamar kecil* (lavatory).

Rural Indonesia may not have Western-style department stores, so for things like **contact** lens solutions, dental floss, tampons, sunscreen, and insect repellent, if you think you might need them, pack them.

Passport photos may come in handy for applications/permits (for parks) or even as gifts.

On your travels you will meet people who are kind and helpful, yet you may feel too embarrassed to give money. In this kind of situation a small gift is appropriate. Chocolates, biscuits, pens, stationery from your hotel, even your T-shirt with foreign designs are appreciated.

CLIMATE

In general, Indonesia experiences two yearly seasons of monsoon winds: the southeast monsoon, bringing dry weather (*musim panas*— dry season), and the northwest monsoon, bringing rain (*musim hujan*—rainy season). Often the changing seasons can bring the time of high waves (*musim ombak*).

The **rainy season** is normally November to April, with a peak around January/February, when it rains for several hours each day. The rain is predictable, however, and always stops for a time, when the sun may come out. Before it rains, the air gets very sticky; afterwards it is refreshingly cool. Some areas are inaccessible during the rainy season and flights are even more unreliable.

The **dry season**, May to October (especially June to August), is, generally, a better time to come. Humidity is down and nights can be cool. This is the time to climb mountains or visit nature reserves; when wild bulls go in search of water and sea turtles lay eggs more often. This nice, neat picture is interrupted in Maluku province, where local effects alter weather patterns, and in areas where the rain shadow of mountains changes seasonal patterns. We have tried to give the best local times for diving in each relevant section.

The seas are more predictable. July and August are the best times to navigate off the north coast. January to March and June to October are the dangerous months for sailing off the south coast.

Tides in Indonesia average between one and three meters. The only place in the country with really big tidal fluctuations is the south coast of Irian Jaya, where the shallow Arafura Sea rises and falls 5 meters or more.

TIME ZONES

There are three time zones in Indonesia. The westernmost time zone, Western Indonesia Standard Time (including Sumatra and Java), is Greenwich Mean Time (GMT) +7 hours. Central Indonesia time (Bali, Nusa Tenggara and Sulawesi) is GMT +8, and Eastern Indonesian time (Maluku and Irian Jaya) is GMT +9.

MONEY

Prices quoted in this book are intended as a general indication. They are quoted in US dollars because the rupiah is currently very unstable, so prices stated in US dollars are more likely to remain accurate.

Standard **currency** is the Indonesian *rupiah*: Notes come in 50,000, 20,000, 10,000, 5,000, 1,000, 500 and 100 denominations. Coins come in denominations of 1,000, 500, 100, 50, 25, 10 and 5 rupiah. In stores, small change is often replaced by candies.

Banking

It is best to carry travelers' checks of two leading companies as sometimes, for mysterious reasons, a bank won't cash the checks of a company as well known as, say, American Express. U.S. dollars—checks and cash—are accepted in all banks which deal in foreign exchange, as are Australian dollars and (usually) Japanese yen, Deutsche marks, French and Swiss francs. Carrying cash is not a good idea. Aside from the possible loss, banks won't take the bills unless they are in perfect condition.

Moneychangers and banks accepting foreign currency are found in most tourist areas. State banks are open from 8am–3pm, Monday to Friday. Private banks open also on Saturday until 11am. The bank counters at major airports offer competitive rates. Bank lines in town can be long and slow; the best way around it is to arrive promptly at opening time.

Get a supply of Rp1,000 and Rp500 notes when you change money, as taxi drivers and vendors often have—or claim to have— no change for big bills. When traveling in the countryside, Rp100 notes are also useful.

Carrying **cash** (US$) can be a handy safety precaution, as it is still exchangeable should you lose your passport. Indonesian banks and money changers only accept foreign currency that is crisp and clean. Also large denomination bills— particularly the US$100—receive the best exchange rate at money changers.

Major **credit cards** may be accepted in some shops and hotels, but they often add a 3% surcharge. Most cities have at least one bank at which cash advances can be made. Visa and MasterCard are the most frequently accepted.

There are no exchange controls and excess *rupiah* (bills only) can be freely reconverted at the airport.

Tax, service and tipping

Most larger hotels and restaurants charge 21% tax and service on top of your bill. Tipping is not a custom here, but it is appreciated for special services. Rp1000 per bag is considered a good tip for roomboys and porters. Taxi drivers will want to round up to the nearest Rp 500 or Rp 1,000.

When tipping the driver of your rental car or a *pembantu* (housekeeper) of the house in which you've been a guest, fold the money and give it with the right hand only.

OFFICE HOURS

Many government offices have converted to a five-day work week and are officially open Monday to Friday, 8 am to 4 pm, but if you want to get anything done, be there by 11 am. In large cities most private businesses are open 9 am to 5 pm. Shops from 9 am to 9 pm. In smaller towns shops close for a siesta at 1 pm and re-open at 6 pm.

COMMUNICATIONS

Mail

Indonesia's postal service is reliable, if not terribly fast. *Kilat* express service is only slightly more expensive and much faster. *Kilat khusus* (domestic special delivery) will get there overnight. International express mail gets postcards and letters to North America or Europe in about 7 days from most cities.

Kantor pos (post offices) are in every little village, generally open Mon–Thurs 8am–2pm, Fri until 11, Sat until 1pm. Main post office in bigger cities are open daily (except Sunday) 8am–8pm.

Hotels will normally sell stamps and post letters for you, or you can use private postal agents to avoid hassles. Look for the orange *Agen Kantor Pos* (postal agency) signs.

Telephone and Fax

Long distance phone calls, both within Indonesia and international, are handled by satellite. Domestic long distance calls can be dialed from most phones. To dial your own international calls, find an IDD (International Direct Dial) phone and dial "001" or "008," otherwise you must go via the operator, which is far more expensive.

A magnetic debit (*kartu telpon*) phone card can be purchased at hotels, post offices and many other outlets. This is used on card phones which are increasing in popularity, eliminating the need for small change.

If your hotel has no IDD link you have to go to the main telephone office (*kantor telepon*), use a silver card phone (*kartu telpon*) and pay an un-inflated rate or use a private postal and telephone service: *Wartel* (*warung telekommunikasi*)/*warpostel/warparpostel*. These small "telecom shops" are all over Indonesia and fast becoming the most convenient way to call international (you avoid hotel price hikes). They are often run by well-trained, efficient staff and offer fast IDD services at near standard rates. Open daily from 8am to 10pm or 11pm. Prices per minute are about $2.30 to the Americas and $3.10 to most European countries. Night rates are lower.

International calls via MCI, Sprint, ATT, and the like can be made from IDD phones using the access code for your calling card company. Recently, special telephones have been installed in Indonesia's airports with pre-programmed buttons to connect you via these companies to various countries.

Faxes and can be sent and received at *wartel* offices and most main post offices.

Courier Services

Some big international courier outfits operate in Indonesia, along with some domestic ones. DHL Worldwide Express and LTH Worldwide Courier Service are probably the most reliable.

ELECTRICITY

Most of Indonesia has converted to 220 volts and 50 cycles, though a few places are still on the old 110 lines. Ask before you plug in if your are uncertain. Power failures are common in smaller cities and towns. Voltage can fluctuate considerably so use a stabilizer for computers and similar equipment. Plugs are of the European two-pronged variety.

HEALTH

Before You Go

Check with your physician for the latest news on the need for malaria prophylaxis and recommended **vaccinations** before leaving home. Frequently considered vaccines are: Diphtheria, Pertusis and Tetanus (DPT); Measles, Mumps and Rubella (MMR); and oral Polio vaccine. Gamma Globulin every four months for Hepatitis A is recommended. For longer stays many doctors recommend vaccination to protect against Hepatitis B requiring a series of shots over the course of 7 months. Vaccinations for smallpox and cholera are no longer required, except for visitors coming from infected areas. A cholera vaccination is recommended for travel in outlying areas, but it is only 50% effective.

Find out the generic names for whatever prescription medications you are likely to need as most are available in Indonesia but not under the same brand names as they are known at home. Get copies of doctors' prescriptions for the medications you bring into Indonesia to avoid questions at customs. Those who wear spectacles should bring along prescriptions.

First Aid Kit

A basic first aid kit should consist of aspirin and multivitamins, a decongestant, an antihistamine, disinfectant (such as Betadine), antibiotic powder, fungicide, an antibiotic eyewash, Kaopectate or Lomotil, and sunscreen. Also good strong soap, perhaps Betadine or other antiseptic soap. Avoid oral antibiotics unless you know how to use them. For injuries, make up a little kit containing Band-aids and ectoplast strips, a roll of sterile gauze and treated gauze for burns, surgical tape, and an elastic bandage for sprains. Also very important are Q-tips, tweezers, scissors, needles and safety pins. Keep your pills and liquid medicines in small unbreakable plastic bottles, clearly labeled with indelible pen.

Hygiene

Hygeiene cannot be taken for granted in Indonesia. Away from the tourist areas few places have running water or sewerage. Most water comes from wells, and raw sewerage goes into the ground or the rivers. Tap water is not potable and must be boiled.

Most cases of stomach complaints are attributable to your system not being used to the strange foods and stray bacteria. To make sure you do not get something more serious, take the following precautions:

☛ Never drink unboiled water from a well, tap or *bak mandi* (bath tub). Brush your teeth only with boiled or bottled water, never with water from the tap or *bak mandi*. Bottled water is available everywhere and usually called "Aqua", which is the most popular and reliable brand name.

☛ Ice is made in government regulated factories and is deemed safe for local immunities. Confirm that the ice is made from boiled water before relaxing with an ice drink.

☛ Plates, glasses and silverware are washed in unboiled water and need to be completely dry before use.

☛ Fruits and vegetables without skins pose a higher risk of contamination. To avoid contamination by food handlers, buy fruits in the market and peel them yourself.

☛ To *mandi* (bathe) two or three times a day is a great way to stay cool and fresh. But be sure to dry yourself off well and you may wish to apply a medicated body powder such as Purol to avoid the nastiness of skin fungus, especially during the rainy season from November to April.

Exposure

Many visitors insist on instant sun tans, so overexposure to the heat and sun are frequent health problems. Be especially careful on long boat rides where the roof gives a good view. The

Telephone Codes

From outside Indonesia, the following cities may be reached by dialing 62 (the country code for Indonesia) then the city code, then the number. Within Indonesia, the city code must be preceded by a 0 (zero).

City	Code	City	Code
Ambon	911	Mataram	364
Balikpapan	542	Medan	61
Banda Aceh	651	Merauke	971
Bandar		Metro	725
Lampung	721	Mojokerto	321
Bandung	22	Nusa Dua	361
Banjarmasin	511	Padang	751
Banyuwangi	333	Palangkaraya	514
Batam	778	Palembang	711
Belawan	619	Palu	451
Bengkulu	736	Pare-Pare	421
Biak	961	Pasuruan	343
Binjai	619	Pati	295
Blitar	342	Pekalongan	285
Bogor	251	Pekanbaru	761
Bojonegoro	353	Pematang-	
Bondowoso	332	siantar	622
Bukittinggi	752	Ponorogo	352
Cianjur	263	Pontianak	561
Cilacap	282	Parapat	625
Cipanas	255	Probolinggo	335
Cirebon	231	Purwakarta	264
Cisarua	251	Purwokerto	281
Denpasar	361	Sabang	652
Gadog	251	Salatiga	298
Garut	262	Samarinda	541
Gresik	31	Sekupang	778
Jakarta	21	Semarang	24
Jambi	741	Serang	254
Jember	331	Sibolga	731
Jombang	321	Sidoarjo	319
Kabanjahe	628	Sigli	653
Karawang	267	Situbondo	338
Kebumen	287	Solo	271
Kediri	354	Sorong	951
Kendal	294	Sukabumi	266
Kendari	401	Sumbawa	
Klaten	272	Besar	371
Kota Pinang	624	Sumedang	261
Kotabaru	518	Surabaya	31
Kutacane	629	Tangerang	21
Kuala Simpang	641	Tapak Tuan	656
Kudus	291	Tarakan	551
Kupang	391	Tasikmalaya	265
Lahat	731	Tebing Tinggi	
Lhok Seumawe	645	Deli	621
Lumajang	334	Ternate	921
Madiun	351	Tulung Agung	355
Magelang	293	Ujung Pandang	411
Malang	341	Wates	274
Manado	431	Wonosobo	286
Manokwari	962	Yogyakarta	274

cooling wind created by the boat's motion disguises the fact that you are frying like an egg. Wear a hat, loose-fitting, light-colored, long-sleeved cotton clothes, pants, and use a good-quality sunscreen (bring a supply with you). Do not wear synthetic fibers that do not allow air to circulate. Tan slowly—don't spoil your trip. Drink plenty of fluids and take salt.

Cuts and Scrapes

Your skin will come into contact with more dirt and bacteria than it did back home, so wash your face and hands more often. Cuts should be taken seriously and cleaned with an antiseptic like Betadine or Dettol, available from any pharmacy (*apotik*). Once clean, antibiotic powder (*Sulfanilamide*) or ointment, both available locally, should be applied. Cover the cut during the day to keep it clean, but leave it uncovered at night and whenever you are resting so that it can dry. Constant covering will retain moisture in the wound and only encourage an infection. Repeat this ritual after every bath. Areas of redness around the cut indicate infection and a doctor should be consulted. At the first sign of swelling it is advisable to take broad spectrum antibiotics to prevent a really nasty infection.

Not every mosquito bite leads to malaria, but in the tropics a scratched bite or small abrasion can quickly turn into a festering ulcer. You must pay special attention to these things. Apply calamine solution or Tiger Balm—a widely available camphorated salve—or some imitation thereof to relieve the itching. For light burns, use Aristamide or Bioplacenteron.

Diarrhea

A likely traveling companion. In addition to the strange food and unfamiliar micro-fauna, diarrhea is often the result of attempting to accomplish too much in one day. Taking it easy can be an effective prevention. Ask around before leaving about what the latest and greatest of the many remedies are and bring some along. Imodium is locally available as are activated carbon tablets (Norit) that will absorb the toxins giving you grief.

When it hits, it is usually self-limiting to two or three days. Relax, take it easy and drink lots of fluids, perhaps accompanied by rehydration salts such as Servidrat (local brands are Oralit and Pharolit). Especially helpful is water from the young coconut (*air kelapa muda*) or strong, unsweetened tea. The former is an especially pure anti-toxin. Get it straight from the coconut without sugar, ice or food color added. When you are ready, bananas, papayas, plain rice, crackers or dry biscuits, and *bubur* (rice porridge) are a good way to start. Avoid fried, spicy or heavy foods and dairy products for a while. After three days without relief, see a doctor.

Not all bouts of diarrhea mean dysentery. If you contract the latter, which is much more serious, you must seek medical help. Do this if your stools are mixed with blood and pus, are black, or you are experiencing severe stomach cramps and fever. If no medical help is available, try tetracycline and Diatab, effective for bacillary dysentery. If you feel no relief in a day or two, you have the more serious amoebic dysentery which requires additional medication.

To prevent stomach problems, try to eat only thoroughly cooked foods, don't buy already peeled fruit, and stay away from unpasteurized dairy products. For constipation, eat a lot of fruit.

Intestinal Parasites

It is estimated that 80 to 90 percent of all people in Indonesia have intestinal parasites and these are easily passed on by food handlers. Prevention is difficult, short of fasting, when away from luxury hotel restaurants and even there are no guarantee. It's best to take care of parasites sooner rather than later, by routinely taking a dose of anti-parasite medicine such as *Kombatrin* (available at all *apotik*) once a month during your stay and again when you get on the plane home.

If you still have problems when you get back, even if only sporadic, have stool and blood tests. Left untreated, parasites can cause serious damage.

Mosquito-Borne Diseases

Malaria is a problem in some parts of Indonesia. The disease accounts for a sizeable percentage of the country's total mortality, and is nothing to be irresponsible about.

Malaria is caused by a protozoan, *Plasmodium*, which affects the blood and liver. The vector for this parasite is the *Anopheles* mosquito. After contracting malaria, it takes a minimum of six days—or up to several years—before symptoms appear.

If you are visiting rural Indonesia, you *must* take malaria pills. Do not think that pills offer complete protection, however, as they don't. A virulent strain of malaria has recently become dominant particularly in Nusa Tenggara. If you are pregnant, have had a splenectomy or have a weak immune system, or suffer from chronic disease, you should weigh carefully whether the trip is worth the risk.

Chloroquine phosphate is the traditional malaria prophylactic, but in the past 10–15 years, the effectiveness of the drug has deteriorated. Deciding on an appropriate anti-malarial is now more complicated. There are actually four forms of malaria: *Plasmodium vivax*, which is unpleasant and can lie dormant for 50 years or more, but is rarely fatal to healthy adults; *P. melariae*, which is the least serious variant; *P.*

ovale, which is rare in Indonesia; and *P. falciparum*, which can be quickly fatal. *P. falciparum* is dominant in parts of Indonesia.

Malaria pills. As a prophylactic for travel, take two tablets of Chloroquine (both on the same day) once a week, and one tablet of Maloprim (pyrimethamine) once a week. Maloprim is a strong drug, and not everybody can tolerate it. If you are planning on taking Maloprim for more than two months, it is recommended that you take a folic acid supplement, 6 mg a day, to guard against anemia. [Note: The anti-malarial drugs only work once the protozoan has emerged from the liver, which can be weeks after your return. You should continue on the above regimen for one month after returning.]

There is now widespread resistance to Chloroquine in Irian. Mefloquin (such as Larium) seems to be the most commonly used prophylaxis now. It has been shown effective, although unpleasant side effects have been demonstrated for it as well. Mefloquine is also very expensive, about $3 a tablet. However, it can be a lifesaver in cases of resistant *falciparum* infection.

These drugs are not available over-the-counter in most western countries (or, indeed, even behind the counter at most pharmacies), and if you visit a doctor, you may have trouble convincing him of what you need. Doctors in the temperate zones are not usually familiar with tropical diseases, and may even downplay the need to guard against them. Do not be persuaded. Try to find a doctor who has had experience in these matters.

You can also buy Chloroquine and Maloprim over-the-counter in Indonesia, for very little (a few dollars for a month's supply). Maloprim, however, may still be difficult to find. [Note: there is a non–chloroquine based drug sold in Indonesia called Fansidar. This drug is not effective against the resistant strains of *P. falciparum* and not for use as a prophylaxis.]

The antibiotic Doxycycline can also be used as a prophylaxis for short-term stays (2-6 weeks): 100 mg. once a day with food, starting 2 days before arrival and continued through 4 days after departure of the malarious area.

Treatment. Malaria in the early stages is very hard to distinguish from a common cold or flu. A person infected may just suffer from headache and nausea, perhaps accompanied by a slight fever and achiness, for as long as a week until the disease takes hold. When it does, the classic symptoms begin:

1) Feeling of intense cold, sometimes accompanied by shaking. This stage lasts from 30 minutes to two hours.

2) High fever begins, and victim feels hot and dry, and may vomit or even become delirious. This lasts 4–5 hours.

3) Sweating stage begins, during which the victim perspires very heavily, and his body temperature begins to drop.

The classic fever/chill pattern is more likely to occur with people who are not taking prophylaxis. Those on prophylaxis will have stronger "flu" symptoms (aches, nausea, headache).

If you think you have malaria, you should call on professional medical help immediately. A good medical professional is your best first aid. Only if you cannot get help, initiate the following treatment:

1) Take 4 Chloroquine tablets immediately.

2) 6 hours later, take 2 more Chloroquine tablets.

3) The next day, take 2 more.

4) The following day, take 2 more.

If the Chloroquine treatment does not cause the fever to break within 24 hours, assume the infection is the very dangerous *P. falciparum* and begin the following treatment immediately:

1) Take 3 tablets (750 mg) of Mefloquine (Larium)

2) Six hours later, take 2 more tablets (500 mg) of Mefloquine.

3) After 12 hours—and only if you weigh 60 kg (130 lbs) or more—take one more tablet (250 mg) of Mefloquine.

The other mosquito concern is **dengue fever**, spread by *Aedes* sp., which bites in the morning and early afternoon, especially during the rainy season. The most effective prevention is not getting bitten (there is no prophylaxis). Dengue fever symptoms are headache, pain behind the eyes, high fever, muscle and joint pains, and rash, appearing between the third and fifth days of illness. Within days, the fever subsides and recovery seldom has complications. The more serious variant, dengue haemorrhagic fever (DHF), which can be fatal, may be the reaction of a secondary infection with remaining immunities following a primary attack.

Cases of **Japanese encephalitis**, a viral infection affecting the brain, have occured recently and are added cause to take protective measures against mosquito bites.

Prevention. Malaria, dengue fever, and Japanese encephalities are carried by mosquitos. If you don't get bit, you don't get the diseases.

1) While walking around, use a good quality mosquito repellent, and be very generous with it, particularly around your ankles. Wear light-colored, long-sleeved shirts or blouses and long pants. (Effective insect repellent may be hard to find, so bring some from home.) Any chemical repellent container deet (diethyl toluamide) should be applied with caution and never to the face. Application to clothing can be more effective. A local non-chemical solution is citronella mixed with eucalyptus oil (*minyak gosok, cap tawon*).

2) While eating or relaxing in one spot, burn mosquito coils. These are those green, slightly brittle coils of incense doped with pyrethrin. They last 6–8 hours and are quite effective. You will get used to the smell. (If you are worried about

inhaling some of the poison they contain, re-read the classic symptoms of malaria above.) In Indonesia, the ubiquitous coils are called *obat nyamuk bakar*. Double Rabbit is one of the more relizble brands. (There are brands which do not contain pyrethum, so are ineffective.) In some places where there is electricity, there is a smokeless repellent with a similar ingredient that is inserted into a unit plugged into the wall.

3) While sleeping, burn *obat nyamuk* and use a mosquito net. Some hotels have nets, but not many, and you should bring your own. If you set a couple of *obat nyamuk* coils going in strategic places when you go to sleep you will be protected. Remember that mosquitos like damp bathrooms—where few people bother to light a mosquito coil.

AIDS & Hepatitis B

Surprise! **Safe sex** is also a good idea. Documentation, awareness and education is just beginning. Another area of concern is the Hepatitis B virus which affects liver function and is only sometimes curable and can be fatal. The prevalence of Hepatitis B in Indonesia is the basis for international concern over the ominous possibilities for the spread of HIV virus, which is passed on in the same ways.

Medical Treatment

Pharmacies—*apotik*—carry just about everything you might need. You can readily get malaria pills here, and an excellent anti-bacterial ointment called Bacitran. Tiger Balm is available everywhere in Asia, and it is excellent for itching bites and muscles pains. Mycolog is a brand of fungicide sold in Indonesia. Oral rehydration salts are usually sold in packets to be mixed with 200 ml of (clean) water. Outside the larger cities, it's nearly impossible to purchase medicines or first aid supplies.

In the larger towns there are decent government hospitals (*rumah sakit*) and medicines are widely available. Smaller villages only have government clinics (*puskesmas*), which are not equipped to deal with anything serious. Your hotel or *losmen* will probably be able to find you doctor who speaks English.

Doctors and health care are quite inexpensive by western standards, but the quality leaves much to be desired. (At least they're familiar with the symptoms and treatment of tropical diseases, however, which is something your family doctor might have a real tough time recognizing back home.)

Consultations with doctors are very cheap in Indonesia, usually about $5–$8 for general practitioners, $8–$15 for specialists. If you check into a hospital, get a VIP room ($20–$30 for everything—including doctors' fees—but not medicines) or a somewhat cheaper "Klas I" room. The cheaper hospital rooms and wards tend to get less attention from the medical staff. Government hospitals, at provincial capital and district level, have improved considerably since the late 1980s.

Misuse of antibiotics is still a concern in Indonesia. They should only be used for bacterial diseases and then for at least 10 to 14 days to prevent developing antibiotic resistant strains of your affliction. If an injection or antibiotics are prescribed, be sure it's necessary. Ensure syringes have never been used before or better yet, buy your own disposable from an *apotik* (pharmacy) and take it to the clinic.

Emergency Medical Assistance

Even in the big cities outside of Jakarta, emergency care leaves much to be desired. Your best bet in the event of a life-threatening emergency or accident is to get on the first plane to Jakarta or Singapore. Contact your embassy or consulate by phone for assistance (see below). Medivac airlifts are very expensive ($26,000) and most embassies will recommend that you buy insurance to cover the cost of this when traveling extensively in Indonesia.

Check your health insurance before coming to make sure you are covered. Travel insurance should include coverage of a medical evacuation to Singapore and a 24-hour worldwide phone number as well as some extras like luggage loss and trip cancellation.

Two good insurers are AEA International, a Singapore-based outfit that offers world-wide medical evacuation insurance, and the nonprofit Divers Alert Network (DAN) which offers low-cost secondary insurance for divers.

AEA International The Americas: ☎ (206) 340-6000, Fax: (206) 340-6006; Asia: ☎ (65) 338 2311, Fax: (65) 338 7611; Europe: ☎ (33-1) 53-05-05-55, Fax: (33-1) 53-05-05-56; Australia: ☎ 61 (2) 9372–2468, Fax: 61 (2) 9372-2494.

E-mail: info@aeaintl.com

Web: www.aeaintl.com

This is a seasoned outfit that has been providing emergency services in the region for more than a decade. They combined with International SOS Assistance early in 1998. AEA offers individual and corporate insurance packages, with worldwide coverage.

AEA maintains 24-hour alarm centers throughout the world. The two in Indonesia are:

Bali ☎ (0361) 227-271 Frederika Nault
Jakarta ☎ (021) 750-6001 Jim Williams

Divers Alert Network (DAN) Peter B. Bennett Center, 8 West Colony Place, Durham NC 27705 USA. Membership services: 800/446-2671.

Web: www.dan.ycg.org

This well-known U.S.-based non-profit has been providing medical advice in the case of diving injuries, researching diving medicine, and promoting diving safety for a long time. They are often the first organization called by local emergency personnel in the case of a diving accident. The organization publishes the bimonthly *Alert Diver*, which is distributed to members. DAN offers yearly membership for US$29, and three different insurance packages for an additional US$25 to US$35 a year. We highly recommend DAN membership and insurance. The organization maintains a medical information line for questions about diving health and problems (919/684-2948; 9am–5pm U.S. Eastern Time) and a 24-hour-a-day hotline for dive emergencies: 919-684-8111.

DAN Southeast Asia–Pacific 49a Karnak Road, P.O. Box 384, Ashburton, Vic. 3147, Australia. ☎ 61-3/9886-9166, Fax: 61-3/9886-9155; Emergencies: 61-3/9828-2958. The Australian-based Southeast Asia branch of DAN.

FOOD AND DRINK

Drink lots of fluids. The equatorial sun takes out a lot from you and dehydration can be a serious problem. Symptoms are infrequent urination, deep yellow/orange urine, headaches.

Tap water in Indonesia is not potable and it should be brought to a full boil for ten minutes before being considered safe. Indonesians are themselves fussy about drinking water, so if you're offered a drink it is almost certainly safe.

Most Indonesians do not feel they have eaten until they have eaten rice. This is accompanied by side dishes, often just a little piece of meat and some vegetables with a spicy sauce. Other common items include *tahu* (tofu), *tempe* (soybean cake) and salted fish. Crispy fried tapioca crackers flavored with prawns and spices (*krupuk*) usually accompany a meal.

No meal is complete without *sambal*—a fiery paste of ground chili peppers with garlic, shallots, sugar, and sometimes soy sauce or fish paste. Fruit, especially pineapple and papaya provide quick relief for a chili-burned mouth.

Cooking styles vary greatly from one region to another. The Sundanese of West Java are fond of raw vegetables, eaten with chili and fermented prawn paste (*lalab/sambal trasi*). Minihasan food in North Sulawesi is very spicy, and includes some interesting specialties: fruit bat wings in coconut milk, *sambal* rat, and dog. In the more isolated parts of the archipelago, the food can be plain, and frankly, quite dull.

In most Indonesian restaurants there is a standard menu of *satay* (skewered barbequed meat)—most common are *ayam* (chicken) and *kambing* (goat), *gado-gado* or *pecel* (boiled vegetables with spicy peanut sauce) and *soto* (vegetable soup with or without meat). Also common are Chinese dishes like *bakmie goreng* (fried noodles), *bakmie kuah* (noodle soup) and *cap cay* (stir-fried vegetables).

In most larger towns you can also find a number of Chinese restaurants on the main street. Some have menus with Chinese writing, but usually the cuisine is very much assimilated to local tastes. Standard dishes, in addition to the *bakmie* and *cap cay* mentioned above, are sweet and sour whole fish (*gurame asem manis*), beef with Chinese greens (*kailan/caisim ca sapi*), and prawns sauteed in butter (*udang goreng mentega*).

Indonesian fried chicken (*ayam goreng*) is common and usually very tasty—although the local -grown chicken can be a bit stringy. Then there is the ubiquitous *nasi goreng* (fried rice); the "special" (*istimewa*) comes with an egg on top and is often served for breakfast.

There are restaurants everywhere in Indonesia that specialize in food from **Padang**, West Sumatra. This spicy, and very tasty cuisine has a distinctive way of being served. As many as 15-20 different dishes are displayed in the glass case in front of the restaurant. You tell the waiter what you want and he sets a whole stack of the little dishes in front of you. At the end of the meal, you are charged for what you have eaten and any untouched plates are put back in the case.

As tempting as fresh vegetables may be, avoid eating garnishes or raw salads unless the veggies are air-flown/imported.

The beers available in Indonesia are Bintang and Anker, both brewed under Dutch supervision and rather light (perhaps appropriately for the tropics). With electricity such a precious commodity, however, in out-of-the-way places the only way to quaff it cold is to pour it over ice.

Fruits

Tropical fruits here are plentiful and delicious. The undisputed king (at least among Indonesians) is the *duren* or durian, a large, thick-husked fruit full of a creamy flesh that is very rich, very strong-smelling, and certainly unlike anything else in the world. If you get a chance, you must try durian. Other unusual fruits include *salak,* a palm fruit which looks like a large garlic covered with brown snakeskin and has crisp segments that taste like a cross between an apple and a walnut, and *manggis* (mangosteen), which is pure heaven hidden within a thick purple-brown cover. The juicy white segments almost melt away. *Rambutan*, a relative of lychee, has soft spiny "hairs" (*rambut*) on its soft shell. The season varies for these juicy delights, and can be frustratingly short. Bananas, apples, tangerines, papaya, pineapples, pomelos (*jeruk Bali*), starfruit (*blimbing*), guava (*buah biji*), and watermelon are found year round.

Warung (Street Stalls)

Restaurant kitchens do not necessarily have healthier food preparation procedures than roadside *warung*. The important thing at a *warung* is to watch and judge whether or not the cooks inspire confidence. Beware: *warung* rarely have a supply of running water.

The first portion may not fill you up, so a second portion can be ordered by saying *"Tambah separuh"* (add half portion). But only the price is halved. The amount of food is more like three-quarters. Finish off with a banana and say *"Sudah"* (I've had plenty, thank you). The seller will total up the prices of what was served you and ask you how many *krupuk, tempe,* etc. you added; so keep track. The total will come to between Rp1000 and Rp2,500 (50¢–$1.25).

Vegetarianism

Say *"saya tidak makan daging"* (I don't eat meat), *"tidak pakai ayam"* (without chicken) or *"tidak pakai daging"* (without meat). Dietary restrictions are very acceptable and common due to the various religious and spiritual practices involving food. However, finding food that truly has no animal products is a problem. Often meals which appear to be made exclusively of vegetables will have a chunk of beef or chicken in them to add that certain oomph. *Tempe* (fermented soy bean cake) and *tahu* (tofu) are common sources of protein.

SECURITY

Indonesia is a relatively safe place to travel and violent crime is almost unheard of, but petty crime is on the upswing. Pay close attention to your belongings, especially in big cities. Use a small backpack or moneybelt for valuables: shoulderbags can be snatched. Bags have been snatched by thieves on motorbikes, so be vigilant. Be especially wary on crowded *bemos,* buses and trains; this is where **pick-pockets** lurk. They usually work in groups and are very clever at slitting bags and extracting valuables without your noticing anything.

Be sure that the door and windows of your hotel room are locked at night, including those in the bathroom, as thieves are adept at sneaking in while you are asleep. Big hotels have **safety boxes** for valuables. If your hotel does not have such a facility, it is better to carry all the documents along with you. Make sure you have a photocopy of your passport, return plane ticket and travelers' check numbers and keep them separate from the originals.

ADDRESSES

The Indonesian spelling of geographical features and villages varies considerably as there is no form of standardization that meets with both popular and official approval. We have seen village names spelled three different ways, all on signboards in front of various government offices. In this guide, we have tried to use the most common spellings.

There are three overlapping and concurrent address systems for any given location: old street name and number, new street name with new numbers, and *kampung* (neighborhood) name with block numbers. Every town now has its street named after the same national heroes, so you will find Jalan Jendral Sudirman (General Sudirman Street) in every city throughout the archipelago.

The names with the new house numbers are the preferred designations for postal purposes. However, when tracking down a hotel address you may find that the old street names, the *kampung* names, or local landmarks more helpful. You will also find number 38 next to number 119 and the streets referred to by different names, such as Jalan Diponegoro (an Indonesian hero), Jalan Abdi Dongo (from local history) or Gajahan Gang II (the *kampung* name and alley number).

Finding Your Way

Westerners are used to finding things using telephone directories, addresses, and maps. But in Indonesia, phone books are incomplete, addresses can be confusing and maps little understood. The way to find something is to ask.

To ask for directions, it's better to have the name of a person and the name of the *kampung*. Thus "Bu Murni, Jetis" is a better address for asking directions even though "Jalan Kaliwedas 14" is the mailing address. Knowing the language helps here but is not essential. Immediately clear answers are not common and you should be patient. You are likely to get a simple indication of direction without distance or specific instructions. The assumption is that you will be asking lots of people along the way. Begin by asking three people. Usually two point toward the same general vicinity. Proceed, then ask again.

Maps are useful tools for you, but introducing them into discussions with Indonesians may cause more confusion than clarity. More than likely the north arrow on the map will be turned to real north before a reading. Periplus Travel Maps provide detailed and accurate maps of all major tourist destinations.

CALENDAR

The Indonesian government sets national holidays every year, both fixed and moveable dates. The fixed national holidays on the Gregorian calendar are the International New Year, Jan. 1; Independence Day, Aug. 17; and Christmas, Dec. 25. The Christian Good Friday, Easter Day, and Ascension Day, the Balinese new year, Nyepi, and the Buddhist Waisak are also national holidays. These holy days and all the Muslim holy days are based on the moon, so confusion results in attempting to extrapolate several years ahead.

Official Muslim holidays in Indonesia:

Idul Fitri The end of the Muslim fasting month, Ramadan, also called Lebaran.

Idul Adha The day of Abraham's sacrifice and the day that the haji pilgrims circle the Kaaba in Mecca.

Hijryah The Islamic New Year, when Muhammad traveled from Mecca to Medina.

Maulud Nabi Muhammad SAW Muhammad's birthday.

Isra Mi'raj Nabi Muhammad SAW When Muhammad ascended on his steed Bouraq.

The 12 lunar months of the Muslim calendar are, in order: Muharram, Safar, Rabiul Awal, Rabiul Ahir, Jumadil Awal, Jumadil Ahir, Rajab, Sa'ban, Ramadan, Sawal, Kaidah, Zulhijja.

The Muslim calendar begins with the Hijriah, Muhammad's flight to Medina, in A.D. 622 according to the Gregorian calendar. Early A.D. 1996 corresponds to A.H. 1416. The Muslim calendar is a lunar calendar (354 or 355 days) and gains 10 or 11 days on the Gregorian calendar (365 days) each year.

ETIQUETTE

In the areas of Indonesia most frequented by Europeans, many are familiar with the strange ways of Westerners. But it is best to be aware of how certain aspects of your behavior will be viewed. You will not be able to count on an Indonesian to set you straight when you commit a *faux pas*. They are much too polite. They will stay silent or even reply *tidak apa apa* (no problem) if you ask if you did something wrong. So here are some points to keep in mind:

☞ The left hand is considered unclean as it is used for cleaning oneself in the bathroom. It is inappropriate to use the left hand to eat or to give or receive anything with it. When you do accidentally use your left hand then say *"ma'af, tangan kiri"* (please excuse my left hand).

☞ The head is considered the most sacred part of the body and, hence, the feet the least sacred. Avoid touching people on the head. Go for the elbow instead. Never step over food or expose the sole of your foot toward anyone.

☞ As it is impolite to keep one's head higher than others, it is appropriate to acknowledge the presence of others by stooping (extending the right arm, drooping the right shoulder, and leaning forward) while passing closely by someone who is sitting.

☞ Pointing with the index finger is impolite. Indonesians use their thumbs (palm turned upward, fingers curled in) or open palms instead.

☞ Summoning people by crooking the forefinger is impolite. Rather, wave downward with a flat palm face down.

☞ Alcohol is frowned upon in Islam, so take a look

around you and consider taking it easy.

☞ Hands on hips is a sign of superiority or anger.

☞ Indonesians don't blow their noses. Keep a handkerchief handy.

☞ Take off your shoes when you enter someone's house. Often the host will stop you, but you should go through the motions until he does.

☞ Don't drink or eat until invited to, even after food and drinks have been placed in front of you. Sip your drink and don't finish it in one gulp. Never take the last morsels from a common plate.

☞ You will often be invited to eat with the words *makan, makan* ("eat, eat") if you pass somebody who is eating. This is not really an invitation, but simply means "Excuse me as I eat."

☞ If someone prepares a meal or drink for you it is most impolite to refuse.

Some things from the west filter through to Indonesia more effectively than others and stories of "*free sek*" (free sex) made a deep and lasting impression in Indonesia. Expect this topic to appear in lists of questions you will be asked in your cultural exchanges. It is best to explain how things have changed since the 1960s and how we now are stuck with "*saf sek*."

Keeping Your Cool

At government offices like immigration or police, talking loudly and forcefully doesn't make things easier. Patience and politeness are virtues that open many doors in Indonesia. Good manners and dress are also to your advantage.

ACCOMMODATIONS

A hierarchy of lodgings and official terminology has been set by the government. A "hotel" is an up-market establishment catering to businessmen, middle- to upper-class travelers and tourists. A star-rating (one to five stars) is applied according to the range of facilities. Smaller places with no stars and basic facilities are not referred to as hotels but as *losmen* (from the French *logement*), *wisma* (guesthouse) or *penginapan* (accommodation) and cater to the masses and budget tourists.

Prices and quality vary enormously. In the major cities that don't have many tourists, such as Jakarta, Surabaya and Medan, there is little choice in the middle ranges and you have to either pay a lot or settle for a room in a *losmen*. In areas where there are a lot of tourists, such as Bali and Yogya, you can get very comfortable and clean rooms with fan or air-conditioning for less than $20 a night. In small towns and remote areas, you don't have much choice and all accommodations tend to be very basic.

It's common to ask to see the room before checking in. Shop around before deciding, particularly if the hotel offers different rooms at different rates. Avoid carpeted rooms, especially without air-conditioning, as usually they are damp and this makes the room smell.

Advance bookings are necessary during peak tourist seasons (July to August and around Christmas and New Year). Popular resorts near big cities are always packed on weekends and prices often double, so go during the week when it's cheaper and quieter.

In many hotels, discounts of up to 50% from published rates are to be had for the asking, particularly if you have a business card. Booking in advance through travel agencies can also result in a lower rate. Larger hotels always add 21% tax and service to the bill.

Bathroom Etiquette

When staying in *losmen*, particularly when using communal facilities, don't climb in or drop your soap into the tub of water (*bak mandi*). This is for storing clean water. Scoop and pour the water over yourself with the ladle/dipper provided.

If you wish to use the native paper-free cleaning method, after using the toilet, scoop water with your right hand and clean with the left.

This is the reason one only eats with the right hand—the left is regarded as unclean. Use soap and a fingernail brush (locals use a rock) for cleaning hands. Pre-packaged alcohol towelettes may make you feel happier about opting for this method. But don't throw the towelettes down the toilet.

Bring along your own towel and soap (although some places provide these if you ask).

Staying in Villages

Officially, the Indonesian government requires that foreign visitors spending the night report to the local police. This is routinely handled by losmen and hotels, who send in a copy of the registration form you fill out when you check in. Where there are no commercial lodgings, you can often rely on local hospitality. But when staying in a private home, keep in mind the need to inform the local authorities. One popular solution is to stay in the home of the local authority, the village head (*kepala desa*).

Carry photocopies of your passport, visa stamp and embarkation card to give to officials when venturing beyond conventional tourist areas. This saves time, and potential hassles, for you and your host.

Keep in mind that people in many rural parts of Indonesia have had limited experience with foreigners to date and are still learning how to share their homes with you. Villagers in rural Indonesia do not routinely maintain guest rooms. Things like soft beds, cold drinks and electricity are luxury items, and it is not guaranteed you will find someone who speaks anything other than Indonesian or the local language. They will, however, offer you the best they have and you should graciously return that respectful treatment. Paying a modest fee ($5) for a meal and a bed is appropriate and polite.

If a cash arrangement has not been pre-arranged, you should leave a gift appropriate to local needs—sugar, salt, biscuits, mirrors, small clasp-knives, clothing, cigarettes, or D-cell batteries for radios in remote villages. These gifts will be deeply appreciated. Send prints of any photos you take of your hosts.

SHOPPING

Be extremely cautious when buying antiques, works of art or other expensive objects, especially in the tourist areas. Most are reproductions, though very good ones and cheap to boot!

Handicrafts are produced all over Indonesia, and even if a good selection is available in hotels and tourist areas, it can be fun to seek out craftsmen in the villages (though often it's not cheaper unless you are very good at bargaining).

Bargaining

The secret here is not to care, or at least appear not to care. Some merchants are very upfront about giving prices that are about the minimum of what they want to sell an item for (*harga pas:* fixed price), but the trader who expects the buyer to bargain is more commonplace. A general rule of thumb is to aim for half the asking price by opening with an offer lower than that. The 50% rule is by no means universal and many sellers will only come down by 20%. On the other hand, in tourist areas, vendors will often ask 10 times or more the reasonable selling price, so don't feel shy about offering them 10% of the asking price.

More often than not the deal is closed in a ritual in which you cheerfully thank the merchant for their time and take steps towards the next stall or the door as the case may be. At this point keep your ears pricked for the *real* final offer of the seller and either thank them again and move on or return and claim your prize. If your final price is accepted it is a major breach of etiquette not to consummate the purchase.

In any event, staying cheerful and good humored will not only be more fun but can make a huge difference in the final price. This isn't just about money; it's also the nature of the interaction. And, yes, you should pay a bit more than an Indonesian would. That's the way it works.

Souvenirs

The best place for souvenir-shopping is Bali. The traveler's problem is how to lug around what is brought for the rest of the trip. While the most common souvenir items, hand-woven traditional cloths, are relatively light, they do take up some space. Carvings and other handicrafts are available in many areas, but Indonesia is not, as it is sometimes imagined, rich in craft everywhere. Particularly in some of the areas where divers frequent—coastal and lightly populated—the villages are populated by fishermen and copra farmers who do almost no craftwork.

SHIPPING & FREIGHT

Shipping goods home is relatively safe and painless. Items under one meter long and 10 kg in weight can be sent via most postal agents. All the packing will be done for you at minimal charge, although it's always advisable to keep an eye on how it's done. Buy insurance.

Larger purchases are best sent by air or sea cargo. Fowarders will handle the whole process for a price, from packing to customs. Some retailers may also prepared to send goods if purchased in quantity.

Air cargo is charged by the kilogram (10 kg min), and can be costly. Sea cargo (min. one cubic meter) is around $350 to the US or Europe and takes about 60 days. Insure your shipment: sea insurance is about 2.75% of the claimed value.

When shipping cargo, you are responsible for clearing customs back home and for the transportation from the port of entry to your destination. This can cost up to $500 so cargo is only economical for large purchases.

PHOTOGRAPHY

Indonesians generally enjoy being photographed. However, if you are in doubt or the situation seems awkward, it is polite to ask. Some religious activities, eating, and bathing are inappropriate subjects.

Beware of the strong shadows from the equatorial sun. Late afternoon and, especially, early morning, provide the most pleasing light and the richest colors. The only way to deal with the heavy shadows in midday is to use a fill flash.

The heat and humidity of the tropics is hard on camera equipment. Be particularly careful when moving equipment from an air-conditioned room to the muggy outdoors. Moisture will condense on the inside and outiside of the camera, Wait until it evaporates; don't be tempted to wipe it off. Also, watch the location of your camera bag and film. Temperatures in hot cars or on boats can be searing.

In general, stick with reliable equipment you are familiar with and bring extra batteries.

Photographic Supplies

Some 35mm Fuji and Kodak film is widely available in Indonesia, including color print film from ASA 100 to 400 and Ektachrome and Fujichrome 100 ASA daylight transparency film. In larger towns you can also buy Fuji Neopan 100 ASA black-and-white negative film and Fuji Velvia. Kodachrome is unavailable here, nor is there any processing available for Kodachrome. Print and E-6 slide processing is generally quite inexpensive, but the quality can vary widely so experiment before turning over all your precious rolls of film for processing, and consider processing the more important ones elsewhere.

PROTECTED SPECIES

Indonesia is home to more than 500 animal species—more than anywhere else in the world. It also has the greatest number of endangered species in the world. Establishing an effective environmental conservation program is a formidable project. The government with the help of private conversation agencies, such as the World Wide Fund for Nature and the Nature Conservancy, is working to create a viable network of national parks and nature reserves where fragile ecosystems and threatened species can be protected. Two of these national parks, Ujung Kulon in West Java (home to the world's most endangered large mammal, the Javan rhino) and Komodo in the Lesser Sundas (home to the Komodo dragon) have been declared World Heritage Sites by the World Conservation Union.

There are strict laws and severe penalties for trade in endangered species. The appendices of the Convention on International Trade in Endangered Species (CITES) lists more than 200 protected species of Indonesian mammals, birds, reptiles, insects, fish, and mollusks—including orangutan, parrots, cockatoo, crocodiles, tortoises and turtles, birdwing butterflies, and black coral. Visitors should be aware of the fragility of Indonesia's natural environment and not contribute to any further degradation of it.

TOURS AND TRAVEL AGENTS

Hiring your own vehicle for a private tour naturally allows you much more flexibility. An AC vehicle with a driver/guide costs anywhere from $30 up to $60 per day, all inclusive. The guides on both types of tours do expect tips, however be aware that they also get a 20%–40% commission on any of your purchases in the large souvenir shops along the way.

Travel agencies offer a variety of tours with knowledgeable, multilingual guides. If your time is limited, it may be best to entrust your schedule to an agency and let them handle all the arrangements.

Refer to area practicalities for local tours.

Transportation

GETTING AROUND IN INDONESIA

This advisory gives you an overview of the wide range of travel options available during your stay in Indonesia. A comprehensive run-down of travel services enables you to plan your way around the island according to time and budget. More specific details for each area you will be visiting can be found in the relevant Practicalities sections.

Prices are in US dollars, unless otherwise stated. Prices and schedules are given as an indication only as they change frequently according to the season. Check with a travel agent prior to departure for the most up-to-date information.

GETTING TO INDONESIA

You can fly direct to Indonesia from just about anywhere. Most people traveling from Europe and the US arrive on direct flights to Jakarta, while those coming from Australia usually go first to Bali. The main international entry points are Soekarno-Hatta airport in Jakarta, Ngurah Rai airport in Bali, and Polonia airport in Medan. There are also non-stop flights from several Asian cities, including Singapore, Hong Kong, Taipei, Seoul, Nagoya, Fukuoka and Osaka.

Jakarta's Soekarno-Hatta airport is served by many international airlines, with over a dozen flights a day from Singapore alone. A cut-price alternative from Europe or the US may be to get a cheap flight to Singapore and buy an onward discount ticket to Jakarta from there: the cost of these can be as low as $75 single, $150 return. An excursion fare return ticket from Singapore to Bali with stops in Jakarta and Yogyakarta, good for a month, is available in Singapore for around $300. Buy through travel agents—check the classified section of the *Straits Times*. [Note: an onward ticket ensures visa-free entry upon arrival in Indonesia.]

Direct flights also connect Jakarta with many major cities in Asia and Europe. Air fares vary depending on the carrier, the season and the type of ticket purchased. A discount RT fare from the US costs from $1,000–$1,200 and from Europe costs $800–$1,200; about half that from Australia or East Asian capitals. Garuda Airlines now has a direct flight from Los Angeles that flies non-stop via Honolulu to Denpasar.

Air tickets from Batam and Bintan are also inexpensive. These Indonesian islands just off the coast of Singapore can be reached via short ferry hops from Singapore's World Trade Centre (Batam) and the Tanah Merah Ferry Terminal (Bintan). Ferries to Batam cost $13 single, $21 return, and to Bintan $35 single, $45 return.

Garuda offers a visit pass to foreigners purchasing outside of Indonesia. A minimum of three coupons can be purchased for $300. Additional coupons are $100 each, up to 10 coupons. One coupon is valid for one flight and you can not return to a destination already covered. If the flight is not directly to your intended destination, you are charged one coupon per stop. This program is good value for long-haul travel within Indonesia, Medan to Jakarta for instance or Bali to Biak, which otherwise is quite costly.

TRAVELING IN INDONESIA

Having arrived in Indonesia, your choices for onward travel depend, as always, on time and money. In many ways, Indonesia is an easy place to get around. Indonesians are, as a rule, hospitable, good-humored, and willing to help a lost or confused traveler. The weather is warm, the pace of life relaxed, and the air is rich with the smells of clove cigarettes, the blessed durian fruit and countless other wonders.

However, the nation's transportation infrastructure does not move with the kind of speed and efficiency that Western travelers expect, which often leads to frustration. Bookings are often difficult to make; flights and reservations are sometimes mysteriously canceled.

It is best to adjust your pace to local conditions. What seems like nerve-wracking inefficiency is really so only if one is in a hurry. If you have to be somewhere at a particular time, allow plenty of time to get there. Check and double-check your bookings. Otherwise just go with the flow. You can't just turn off the archipelago's famous *jam karet*—"rubber time"—when it's time to take an airplane and turn it on again when you want to relax. You will get there eventually.

Peak periods around the Christmas/New Year holidays and during the June to August tourist season are the most difficult. It is imperative to book well in advance and reconfirm your bookings at every step along the way. Travel anywhere in Indonesia during the week

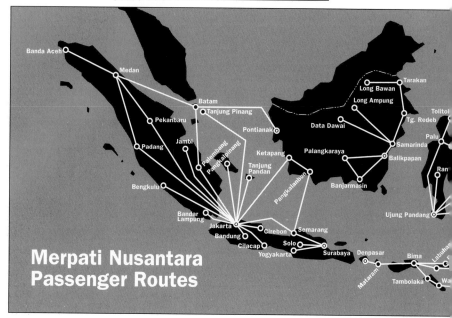

Merpati Nusantara Passenger Routes

prior to the Islamic Lebaran holiday is practically impossible. Find a nice spot and sit it out.

The golden rule is: things will sort themselves out. Eventually. Be persistent, of course, but relax and keep your sense of humor. Before you explode, have a *kretek* cigarette, a cup of sweet coffee, or a cool glass of *kelapa muda* (young coconut water). Things might look different.

Planning an Itinerary

The first thing to do to be easy on yourself andn ot to plan an impossibly tight schedule. Things happen slowly here, so adjust yourself to the pace. Better to spend more time in a few places and see them in a leisurely way, than to end up hot, hassled, and hurried. You'll see *more* this way, not less.

Wherever you are, keep in mind that the tropical heat takes its toll and you should avoid the midday sun. Get an early start, before the rays become punishing (the tropical light is beautiful at dawn). Retreat to a cool place after lunch and go out again in the afternoon and early evening, when it's much more pleasant.

AIR TRAVEL

The cardinal rule is book early, confirm and reconfirm often. If you are told a flight is fully booked, go to the airport anyway and stand in line. While Garuda's booking system is computerized, the other local airlines' are not, and bookings evaporate at the last minute all the time. However it is rare that flights are completely full. Always keep the following points in mind:

➜ It's practically impossible to get a confirmed booking out of a city other than the one you're in. You can buy a ticket and it may say you have a booking, but don't believe it until you reconfirm with the airline in the city of departure.

➜ Reconfirm bookings directly with the airline office in the city of departure between 24 and 72 hours before your flight, particularly during peak tourist seasons and Indonesian holidays. Your seat may be given away if you reconfirm either too early or too late (or not at all).

➜ Make bookings in person, not by phone.

➜ Get written proof or computer printout of bookings. Note the name of the person who gives it to you so you can hold them responsible if you're later told you don't have one.

➜ Note the computer booking code or PRN (passenger record number). Names have a tendency to go astray or be misspelled. Concrete proof of your booking is essential.

➜ If your name isn't on the computer try looking under your first or middle names as these are frequently mistaken for surnames.

➜ If you are told a flight is full, ask to be put on the waiting list, then go to the airport about two hours before departure and check the waiting list. Hang around the desk and be friendly to the staff and you will probably get on the flight. A tip will sometimes, but not always, help.

➜ There are usually alternate ways of getting from point A to B. Search them out.

➜ Generally, students (12–26 years old) receive a discount of 10%–25% (show an international student ID card) and children ages 2–10 pay 50% of the regular fare. Infants not occupying a seat pay 10% of the regular fare. Ask the airlines or

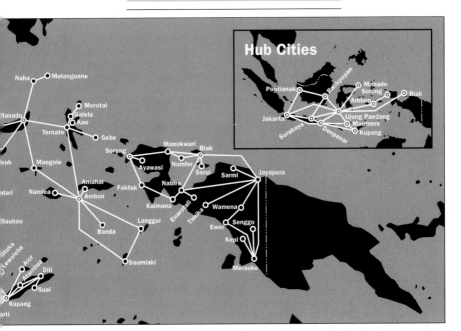

travel agent.

Garuda Indonesia's flagship airline has been in business since 1946. It serves all major cities in Indonesia and at least 38 international destinations. They fly only jets, mainly wide-bodies, and the service is reasonably good.

Head office is at the BDN Building, Jl. MH Thamrin, No. 5 (☎ [021] 2300925, Fax: [021] 334430). Sales counters also at the Borobudur Hotel (☎ [021] 2310023, Fax: [021] 2310448, Hotel Indonesia (☎ [021] 2300568, fax: [021] 2300870, and the ITC Building, Blok D 1-5, Jl. Arteri Mangga Dua (☎ [021] 2600238, fax: [021] 2600244). A small Garuda office at Wisma Dharmala Sakti, Jl. Sudirman 32, is open 24 hours (☎ [021] 2512286, fax: [021] 2512276).

Merpati A Garuda subsidiary, with a domestic network serving more than 160 airports throughout Indonesia. Merpati (literally "pigeon") flies smaller jets, turboprops, and propellor-driven aircraft: Boeing B-737's, McDonnell Douglas DC-9's, Fokker VFW F-28's, Fokker F-27's, Canadian DeHavilland DHC-6 "Twin-Otters," and the Indonesian-built Casa Nusantara CN-235's and CN-212's.

Merpati is not known for its punctuality, its service or its safety, but the airline does at least connect towns and villages across the archipelago, in some cases landing on a grass airstrip in a highland village of only 100 people that would take days to reach by any other means. Consider yourself lucky that you can even fly to these places.

Merpati's standard baggage allowance is 20 kg. for economy class, but some of the smaller aircraft permit only 10 kg. (after which excess baggage charges of $1/kg. begin to apply).

Main office: Jl. Angkasa 2, Jakarta. ☎ (021) 4243608, 6548888; fax: (021) 4246616, 6540609.

NOTE: Travel agents often give cheaper fares than airline offices and are easily found. The best for ticketing are **Pacto** Jl. Surabaya 8, Menteng, Jakarta, ☎ (021) 3487447 and **Vayatour** Jl. Batutulis 38, Jakarta, ☎ (021) 3800202, fax: (021) 3455252.

Departure Tax

Airport tax for departing passengers is Rp17,000 for international routes and Rp8,800 for domestic flights.

SEA TRAVEL

There is four times as much sea in Indonesia as land, and for many centuries transportation among the islands has been principally by boat. Tiny ports are scattered all over the archipelago, and the only way to reach many areas is by sea.

To travel by boat, you need plenty of time. Most ships are small, and are at the mercy of the sea and the seasons. Think of it as a romantic journey, and don't be in a hurry.

Pelni (Pelayaran Nasional Indonesia) the national passenger line, has 10 large ships (some 70 ships total) criss-crossing the archipelago carrying up to 1,500 passengers each. These boats travel on fixed schedules and the first and second class cabins are comfortable.

Many of the older vessels look like floating trash cans, but the new German-built passen-

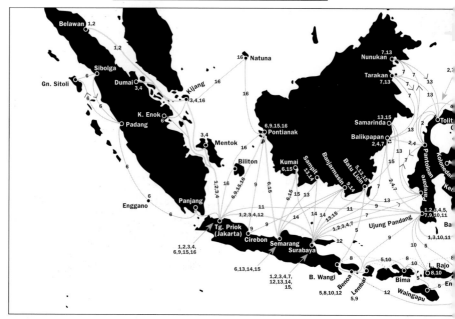

ger ships are modern and comfortable. (See route map previous page for destinations served.) Fares are fixed, and there are up to 5 classes, with different numbers of people sharing each cabin, and different service.

Head office: 5th floor, Jl Gajah Mada 14, Jakarta 10130. ☎ (021) 384 4342, 384 4366; Fax: (021) 385 4130. Main ticket office: Jl Angkasa 18, Kemayoran ☎ 421 1921. Open in the mornings.

There are a myriad of other options. Rusty old **coastal steamers** ply the eastern islands, stopping at tiny ports to pick up copra, seaweed and other cash crops and deliver commodities like metal wares, fuel and the occasional outboard motor. You can book deck passage on one of these ships in just about any harbor, for very little money. If you do, stock up on food—you will quickly tire of the rice and salt fish that the crew eat. Bring a waterproof tarpaulin and a bag to protect your gear. You can often rent bunks from the crew, to get a comfortable night's sleep.

Crowded **overnight ferries** connect smaller islands. Use your luggage to stake out a spot early, and bring a straw mat to lie on. It is usually best to stay on deck, where the fresh sea breezes keep your spirits up. Below deck tends to be noisy, verminous and smelly.

Small **perahu** can be rented in many areas for day trips upriver, around the coast, or to neighboring islands. These can be hired by the hour or by the trip, to take you snorkeling, sightseeing or birdwatching. Outboard motors are expensive in Indonesia, and tend to be small. Inspect any boat carefully before hiring it, as some craft are only marginally seaworthy. See if the boatman can rig up a canopy to block the blazing sun or the occasional cloudburst.

TRAVEL OVERLAND

By Train

Train travel (across Java and Sumatra) can be very cheap, depending on the class. The problem is that first class trains travel at night (you don't see much), and anything less than first class on long journeys is crowded, noisy, hot, and uncomfortable. Still, you can stretch your legs, walk through the train, sit on the back step and watch the tracks stream out from under you.

First class is good, but first class tickets do not always guarantee a seat when you get on the train. (In this case, see the station master for a hassle and eventual refund.) If your budget requires economy travel, purchase a second or third class ticket, spread a *sarong* out and sleep under the seats, not in the aisles, as vendors will tread over or spill things on you.

Tickets normally have to be bought at the station on the day of departure (go early in the morning!) or in the case of night express trains, the day before. Authorized agents also sell tickets. During major Indonesian holiday periods, better forget it: take a plane or a bus, or better still, stay put.

Between major cities there is only a single line, dating from Dutch times, and delays are common as a result. Trains traveling in opposite directions have to wait for one another; if one is late or breaks down, the whole system is thrown out of whack, which happens often.

Alternate Kelimutu route
(between Kupang and Dili)

On the Road

Road conditions in Indonesia have improved dramatically over the past years, but traffic has also increased and driving is a slow and hazardous affair.

Fully loaded trucks, with marginal brakes and drivers going for broke anyway; full-size buses, one and three-quarters lanes wide; small public minivans, stopping anywhere and with no warning for passengers; the occasional private car; scores of motorcycles, most of them small two-stroke affairs, usually piled with goods or, at the hands of a young hotshot, screaming along at full throttle; horse-drawn passenger carts; *becaks*, bicycle rigs that carry passengers in a cart in front; bicycles, with perhaps some children fore and aft, and almost always piled with produce, or perhaps fighting cocks in their cages; and, of course, pedestrians of all ages, all compete in what is at times a crazy battle for tarmac, where the biggest and fastest rule.

Rental cars and motorcycles are available in many major cities, and a number of different types of buses run cheap and regular services.

Night Express Buses—*bis malam*

The preferred mode of transportation for Indonesians, these buses operate only at night. Available in a wide variety of classes: from the public *patas* air-conditioned with reclining seats (crowded, run by the army) to the ultra-luxurious "Big Top" buses that run from Jakarta (these have seats like business class airline seats).

The better buses have a bathroom and arctic air-conditioning: the other reason you brought a sweater. The key to successful *bis malam* trips is sleep.

Most buses are fitted with televisions and show movies whether you want them or not, often followed by music. You are likely to be the only one who is annoyed by the volume, but a cheerful suggestion that the music be turned off (*dimatikan*) will at least get it turned down to the point where earplugs can block out the rest.

These buses leave in late afternoon and go all night, and often well into the next day. When *bis malam* cross from island to island, they go on the ferry. Tickets are sold at the bus terminal, or by agents, and there are usually a number of different buses going your way. Shop around, to see what you are getting.

Local Buses

The major advantages of these rattling buses is that they are extremely cheap, run every few minutes between major towns, and can be picked up at the terminals or any point along their routes. This is also their biggest disadvantage: they stop constantly.

The seats are very small, both in terms of leg room and width. You and your bag may take up (and be charged for) two seats. This is fair. But be sure you're not being overcharged for not knowing any better. The key is to know better. Ask someone what the proper fare is before getting on. A few words of Indonesian are indispensable to be able to ask for directions.

Larger towns have city buses charging nominal fares, usually Rp300 (15¢). Flag them down wherever you see them. The catch is knowing which one to take as there are no maps or guides.

Express Minibuses—"travel" or "colt"

These come in two varieties: old and hot (sit by a window and keep it open) and the newer, much revered, L300 van with air-conditioning. Even the L300 gets a lot of engine heat, and at midday can still be sauna-like: especially if the air-conditioning is broken and the windows shut.

These 8 to 11 passenger vans connect major cities and deliver you right to your destination. They sometimes also pick you up. They usually travel during the day, though on longer routes they travel at night like the *bis malam*.

Local Minibuses—*bemo*

These non air-conditioned vans ("colt" or "*bemo*") are the real workhorses of the transport network, going up and down even relatively impassable mountain tracks to deliver villagers and produce all over the island. Regular seats are supplemented by wooden benches, boosting the capacity of these sardine cans to 25. And there is *always* room for more.

There are standard fares but these are flexible to account for how much room you and your bag are taking up. Ask someone before flagging one down if you are concerned by the potential Rp100 price gouging. Flag one down on any roadside. You can also charter one to most destinations. Just say "charter" and where you want to go, then bargain for the fare in advance.

Chartering a Car or Minibus

This can be the best way to handle a land tour as you have the freedom to stop whenever things look interesting and the flexibility to try out some less traveled routes. This can also be an economical alternative if you can fill up a van. The minibus can take up to 7, but you need extra space if you are to be in it for a few days, so 5 passengers is generally maximum.

Some asking around will quickly give you an idea of where to hire a driver and what the local going rates are for a specific excursion or longer itinerary. A full day of driving one-way will cost from $50 to $80 and a five-day trip around $300. Much of this is for fuel, so distance is a major factor. Most of the rest goes to the owner of the vehicle, and only a tiny percentage left for the driver. It is understood that you will pay for the driver's meals and accommodation both while he is with you and on his journey back home. A tip of Rp5,000 per day is also appreciated if the driver is good.

The quality of both the driver and the vehicle will figure heavily in the enjoyability of your trip so don't be shy about checking both out before striking a deal.

Metered Taxis

Metered taxis are becoming increasingly common in major cities, not just Jakarta. If the taxi is equipped with an argometer, then the driver should be using it. Insist on this when you get in the taxi. Otherwise, you may end up paying twice the metered amount. If the driver claims that the meter is broken, then get out and flag down another one.

Driving On Your Own

Driving in Indonesia is not for the faint-hearted. At first glance the unwritten driving rules of Indonesia seem like a maniacal free-for-all. It is only later that the subtle hierarchy (truck vx. car: you lose) and finesse (2-centimeter tolerances) become evident. Vehicles and creatures of every size, shape and description charge onto the road out of nowhere. The traffic is horrendous on the main highways. Drive slowly and carefully. Road construction sites are not marked and few cyclists have relectors for use at night. The condition of road networks has considerably improved in recent years, however, and driving off the beaten track is one of the best ways to explore the territory. check your fuel gauge regularly as there are few gas stations away from the main roads. Small roadside fuel shops indicated by a "premium sign, sell gasoline for the bit more than the Pertamina stations.

A valid international license is required for driving cars and motorbikes. Insurance is not compulsory, but strongly recommended. You can get a policy from most of the rental companies and travel agents. Check the condition of the car before signing the contract. Beware: vehicles are usually rented with an empty tank. More important than the agency you rent from is to check and test-drive the car before renting.

Indonesian Language Primer

Personal pronouns
I *saya*
we *kita* (inclusive), *kami* (exclusive)
you *anda* (formal), *saudara* (brother, sister),
  kamu (for friends and children only)
he/she *dia* they *mereka*

Forms of address
Father/Mr *Bapak ("Pak")*
Mother/Mrs *Ibu ("Bu")*
Elder brother *Abang ("Bang"* or *"Bung")*
  Mas (in Java only)
Elder sister *Mbak* (in Java only)
Elder brother/sister *Kakak ("Kak")*
Younger brother/sister *Adik ("Dik")*
Note: These terms are used not just within the family, but generally in polite speech.

Basic questions
How? *Bagaimana?*
How much/many? *Berapa?*
What? *Apa?* What's this? *Apa ini?*
Who? *Siapa?* Who's that? *Siapa itu?*
What is your name? *Siapa namanya ?*
(Literally: Who is your name?)
When? *Kapan?*
Where? *Di mana?*
Why? *Kenapa? Mengapa?*
Which? *Yang mana?*

Civilities
Welcome *Selamat datang*
Good morning (7–11am) *Selamat pagi*
Good midday (11am–3pm) *Selamat siang*
Good afternoon (3–7pm) *Selamat sore*
Goodnight (after dark) *Selamat malam*

Goodbye (to one leaving) *Selamat jalan*
Goodbye (to one staying) *Selamat tinggal*
Note: Selamat is a word from Arabic meaning "May your time (or action) be blessed."
How are you? *Apa kabar?*
I am fine. *Kabar baik.*
Thank you. *Terima kasih.*
You're welcome. *Kembali.*
Same to you. *Sama sama.*
Pardon me *Ma'af*
Excuse me *Permisi*
(when leaving a conversation, etc).

Numbers
1	*satu*	6	*enam*
2	*dua*	7	*tujuh*
3	*tiga*	8	*delapan*
4	*empat*	9	*sembilan*
5	*lima*	10	*sepuluh*
11	*sebelas*	100	*seratus*
12	*dua belas*	600	*enam ratus*
13	*tiga belas*	1,000	*seribu*
20	*dua puluh*	3,000	*tiga ribu*
50	*lima puluh*	10,000	*sepuluh ribu*
73	*tujuh puluh tiga*		

1,000,000 *satu juta*
2,000,000 *dua juta*
half *setengah*
first *pertama* third *ketiga*
second *kedua* fourth *ke'empat*

Time
minute *menit* Sunday *Hari Minggu*
hour *jam* Monday *Hari Senin*
(also clock/watch) Tuesday *Hari Selasa*
day *hari* Wednesday *Hari Rabu*

Pronunciation and Grammar

Vowels
a As in father
e Three forms:
  1) Schwa, like the **e**
  2) Like **é** in touch**é**
  3) Short **è**; as in b**e**t
i Usually like long **e** (as in Bal**i**); when bounded by consonants, like short **i** (h**i**t).
o Long **o**, like g**o**
u Long **u**, like y**ou**
ai Long **i**, like cr**i**me
au Like **ow** in **ow**l

Consonants
c Always like **ch** in **ch**urch
g Always hard, like **g**uard
h Usually soft, almost unpronounced. It is hard between like vowels, e.g. *mahal* (expensive).
k Like **k** in **k**ind; at end of word, unvoiced stop.
kh Like **k**ind, but harder
r Rolled, like Spanish **r**
ng Soft, like fli**ng**
ngg Hard, like ti**ngle**
ny Like **ny** in So**ny**a

Grammar
Grammatically, Indonesian is in many ways far simpler than English. There are no articles (a, an, the).

The verb form "to be" is usually not used. There is no ending for plurals; sometimes the word is doubled, but often number comes from context. And Indonesian verbs are not conjugated. Tense is communicated by context or with specific words for time.

week	*minggu*	Thursday	*Hari Kamis*
month	*bulan*	Friday	*Hari Jum'at*
year	*tahun*	Saturday	*Hari Sabtu*
today	*hari ini*	later	*nanti*
tomorrow	*besok*	yesterday	*kemarin*

What time is it? *Jam berapa?*
(It is) eight thirty. *Jam setengah sembilan*
  (Literally: "half nine")
How many hours? *Berapa jam?*
When did you arrive? *Kapan datang?*
Four days ago. *Empat hari yang lalu.*
When are you leaving?
  Kapan berangkat?
In a short while. *Sebentar lagi.*

Useful words

yes *ya*   no, not *tidak, bukan*
Note: *Tidak* is used with verbs or adverbs; *bukan* with nouns.

and	*dan*	better	*lebih baik*
with	*dengan*	worse	*kurang baik*
for	*untuk*	this/these	*ini*
from	*dari*	that/those	*itu*
good	*baik*	same	*sama*
very good	*bagus*	different	*lain*
more	*lebih*	here	*di sini*
less	*kurang*	there	*di sana*
to be	*ada*	to be able to	*bisa*
to buy	*membeli*	correct	*betul*
to know	*tahu*	wrong	*salah*
big	*besar*	small	*kecil*
to need	*perlu*	to want	*ingin*
to go	*pergi*	to stop	*berhenti*
slow	*pelan*	fast	*cepat*
to wait	*tunggu*	to continue	*terus*
to	*ke*	at	*di*
old	*tua, lama*	new	*baru*
full	*penuh*	empty	*kosong*
quiet	*sepi*	crowded, noisy	*ramai*
few	*sedikit*	many	*banyak*
cold	*dingin*	hot	*panas*
clean	*bersih*	dirty	*kotor*
entrance	*masuk*	exit	*keluar*

Small talk

Where are you from? *Dari mana?*
I'm from the US. *Saya dari Amerika.*
How old are you? *Umurnya berapa?*
I'm 31 years old.
  Umur saya tiga pulu satu tahun.
Are you married? *Sudah kawin belum?*
Yes, I am. *Yah, sudah.*
Not yet. *Belum.*
Do you have children? *Sudah punya anak?*
What is your religion? *Agama apa?*
Where are you going? *Mau ke mana?*
I'm just taking a walk. *Jalan-jalan saja.*
Please come in. *Silahkan masuk.*
Please sit down. *Silahkan duduk.*

Hotels

room	*kamar*	bed	*tempat tidur*
towel	*handuk*	bedsheet	*sprei*
bathe	*mandi*	bathroom	*kamar mandi*
hot water	*air panas*		

Where's a losmen? *Di mana ada losmen?*

cheap losmen *losmen yang murah*
good hotel *hotel yang baik*
Please take me to... *Tolong antar saya ke...*
Are there any empty rooms?
  Ada kamar kosong?
Sorry there aren't any. *Ma'af, tidak ada.*
How much for one night?
  Berapa untuk satu malam?
One room for two people.
  Dua orang, satu kamar.
I'd like to stay for 3 days.
  Saya mau tinggal tiga hari.
Here's the key to the room.
  Ini kunci kamar.
Please call a taxi.
  Tolong panggilkan taksi.
Please wash these clothes.
  Tolong cucikan pakaian ini.

Restaurants

to eat *makan*   to drink *minum*
drinking water *air putih, air mimun*
breakfast *makan pagi, sarapan*
lunch *makan siang* dinner *makan malam*
Where's a good restaurant?
  Di mana ada rumah makan yang baik?
Let's have lunch. *Mari kita makan siang.*
May I see the menu?
  Boleh saya lihat daftar makanan?
I want to wash my hands.
  Saya mau cuci tangan.
Where is the toilet? *Di mana kamar kecil?*
fish, squid, goat, beef, chicken
  ikan, cumi-cumi, kambing, sapi, ayam
salty, sour, sweet, spicy (hot)
  asin, asam, manis, pedas

Shopping

cheap *murah*   expensive *mahal*
Please, speak slowly.
  Tolong, berbicara lebih pelan.
I want to buy... *Saya mau beli...*
Where can I buy... *Di mana saya bisa beli...*
How much does this cost? *Berapa harga ini?*
2,500 Rupiah. *Dua ribu, lima ratus rupiah.*
That cannot be true! *Masa!*
That's still a bit expensive. *Masih agak mahal*
May I bargain? *Boleh tawar?*
Is there a discount? *Ada diskon?*
Thanks, I already have one/some...
  Terima kasih, saya sudah punya ...

Directions

here	*di sini*	there	*di sana*
near	*dekat*	far	*jauh*
inside	*di dalam*	outside	*di luar*
map	*peta*	street	*jalan*
north	*utara*	south	*selatan*
east	*timur*	west	*barat*
central	*pusat*	middle	*tengah*
left	*kiri*	right	*kanan*
straight	*terus*	turn	*belok*

I am looking for this address.
  Saya cari alamat ini.
How far is it? *Berapa jauh dari sini?*
Which area? *Daerah mana?*

DIVE
INDONESIA WITH THE PROs

PRO DIVE
BALI

UNDERWATER ADVENTURES

Diving in Bali is definitely an amazing and unique experience! Bali has a range of dive sites you can explore on day trips or safaris, easily made from Kuta, Nusa Dua and Sanur. You will discover an abundance of magnificent marine life, gorgonian fans, coral beds and bombies. You can also experience the wonders of turtles, sharks and mantas..... sights sure to make your diving memorable! Drop off walls, the wreck of the USS "Liberty" and exhilarating drift dive locations are home to all of this. Once one has had a taste of Bali you're guaranteed to return.

PH 62 361 286336 FAX 62 361 288756
Email **prodivebali@bali-paradise.com**

LET'S GO DIVING

PRO DIVE
SURABAYA

Imagine life beneath the sea exploring the calm, clear waters of East Java -The Forgotten Island of Indonesia. You can dive the coral reefs, swim with whale sharks, drift dive or experience the remote Indian Ocean, all from the city of Surabaya. Learning to dive is safe, fun and easy. Our highly qualified instructors teach internationally recognised dive courses and will show you the magic of this underwater world. Pro Dive has 25 years experience teaching people to dive and enjoying the splendours beneath the sea.

PH 62 031 5464236 FAX 62 031 5462644
Email **prodive@rad.net.id**

PRO DIVE
KOMODO

HOME OF THE DRAGONS

Diving in the Komodo area is among the most exciting in the world. The area offers just about every imaginable type of diving, from sheer walls, caves and overhangs, to sea mounds and sandy bottoms. The underwater sea life varies just as much, patrolled by groups of sharks, tuna and other pelagic fish, reefs of beautiful soft and hard corals, all inhabited by thousands of colourful reef fish. The highlight of diving in this area is most certainly the whale sharks, reef sharks and manta's. PRO DIVE KOMODO is based in the Puri Bagus Komodo resort, Flores. The new resort offers 3 star accommodation in this undisturbed paradise. A truly unforgettable experience.

PH 62 0361 286336 FAX 62 0361 288756
Email **prodivebali@bali-paradise.com**

PADI DIVE CENTRE

1 Java PRACTICALITIES

Jakarta, with its 9.3 million people, is the center of Indonesia's government and commerce. It is beyond the scope of this book to give a complete description of all the lodging and transportation possibilities there. If you are going to be in Jakarta, you will need a good guidebook. Instead, this section offers practical information relating to diving Pulau Seribu and West Java.

Prices in US dollars.

City code for Jakarta: 021.

DIVE OPERATORS

There are many dive operators in Jakarta who take divers to Pulau Seribu and the West Java sites. Here are a few of the most reliable:

Aquasport Jl. Bangka Raya 39A, Kel. Pela, Jakarta 12720. ☎ 7199045; fax: 7198974. Contact: Vimal Lekhraj.

Active PADI 5-Star IDC Center located in new premises, with a large retail area, 3 classrooms and their own 4m-deep swimming pool. A very professional, reliable full-service facility (as is their affiliate, Divemasters Indonesia), offering snorkeling and diving equipment sales, rentals and servicing. The shop is very modern and well-stocked. They offer the full range of PADI courses—evening and daytime—in five languages (English, French, Dutch, German, Indonesian), including a host of specialities, such as wreck diver and underwater photographer, and at least twice a year, PADI Instructor Development Courses with related instructor-level training. Also stockist of PADI materials. They offer dive trips to Pulau Seribu nearly every weekend and special charters throughout the year.

Divemasters Indonesia Jakarta Hilton International Hotel, Indonesian Bazaar Shop 31, Jl. Jend. Gatot Subroto, Jakarta 10002 Indonesia. ☎ 5703600 ext. 9037, 9006; fax: 7198974, 4204842. Contact: Vimal Lekhraj.

This outfit is the country's largest dive specialist. They are a PADI 5-Star Dive Center; a professional, reliable, full-service facility. Apart from offering a full range of PADI courses, they are Indonesia's largest equipment retailer, handling US Divers, Seaquest, Tabata, Underwater Kinetics, Bauer, Poseidon, Sea and Sea and others. Snorkeling and diving equipment sales rentals, servicing, and diving equipment repair seminars. They offer dive trips to Pulau Seribu nearly every weekend and special charters throughout the year. They can also tailor-make dive trips to your needs. They have their own custom catamaran, which is available for charter.

Jakarta Dive School and Pro Shop Jakarta Hilton International Hotel, Indonesia Bazaar Shop 32, Jl. Jend. Gatot Subroto, Jakarta 10002 Indonesia. ☎ 5703600 ext. 9008, 9010, fax: 4204842; Telex: 46673, 46698 HILTON IA. Contact: Andre Pribadi.

They organize dive trips to Pulau Seribu, Bali, Manado, Flores and Ambon. PADI 5-star training facility. Also fills, equipment sales, rentals and repairs, and u/w photography.

Laut Dive Indo Club House Cilandak Sport Centre, Jl. Tb. Simatupang Arteri Cilandak, Jakarta 12014. ☎ 7504963 ext. 109, 129; fax: 7504969. Contacts: Jono Sugiyanto or Slamet.

This is a new business, and comes recommended by Jakarta expats as offering reliable service and very competitive rates. While they specialize in dive trips around the Jakarta area, especially Pelabuhan Ratu—where you really need a dive-master familiar with the currents—Laut Dive Indo also runs trips to Indonesia's top dive locations. Young, enthusiastic owner. Certification available, including PADI and SSI.

Stingray Dive Centre Gedung Mangal Wanabakti, Wisma Rimabawan 2d floor, room 4, Jl. Jend. Gatot Subroto, Jakarta Indonesia. ☎ 5703245, 5703264; ☎ /fax: 5700272. Contact: Andy or Hendro

PADI instruction, dive equipment sales and servicing and rentals. They are familiar with many dive spots throughout Indonesia, and have several scheduled departures every month to dive locations near and far. Contact them for a very extensive list of dive trips.

WEATHER

Diving is generally best during the dry season, which varies but generally takes place March through November. The very best time is from May to September.

Pulau Seribu

These islands are a favorite place for Jakartans to spend a weekend, so book ahead. Ferries depart daily around 7 am from the Ancol Marina. The trip takes about 2.5 hours—depending on the island—and the return ferry leaves around 2:30 pm. By speedboat and hydrofoil, the same trip takes one hour. Inquire at Putri Pulau Seribu Paradise office in Djakarta Theatre building.

DIVE CHARTERS

It is far less complicated to book your entire trip with one of the above listed dive outfits. Dive weekends average $110–$150, including round trip transportation, 4 boat dives, and one night in basic, air-conditioned, accommodations.

West Java

Travel to Krakatau or Ujung Kulon is more of an effort than Pulau Seribu. It requires an overland journey to Anyer or Labuhan, and then a fairly long boat ride. Again, it is much better to organize such a trip with a reliable Jakarta dive outfit.

Krakatau

Boats can be chartered from Labuhan or Carita beach, just 8 kilometers north of Labuhan. A forestry official in either town can help arrange boats for up to 20 people—about $100—or local fisherman can be contacted to charter a smaller vessel, about $50. It is impossible to determine the seaworthiness of these boats, or just how reliable are their motors. Remember, this is a 4-hour crossing over rather unpredictable seas.

Ujung Kulon

The peninsula can be reached only by boat, or by a lengthy hike—good for seeing wildlife, but not practical for diving. You can arrange a boat at Labuhan, but again, it's best to organize the whole thing with a Jakarta dive agency. A government forestry boat at Labuhan will run about $100 for the 9-hr. trip to Peucang Island or Taman Jaya. To reach the actual dive sites, figure on some intense bargaining with local fishermen.

— *Janet Boileau, Debe Campbell,*
and Kal Muller

Sumatra PRACTICALITIES

Diving is still in its infancy on Sumatra. Spectacular sea life and unspoiled beaches await the adventurous. Much of the diving activity on the island is from either Singapore or Thailand.

Prices in US dollars. S = Single; D = Double; T = Triple; AC = Air-conditioning.

Bintan and Riau

Batuta Resort Mapor Island, Riau Indonesia. Agent in Singapore: Yacht Construction (SEA) Pte. Ltd., #50, Track 24, Punggol Road, Singapore 1954. ☎ (65) 3833036; fax: (65) 3833037. This outfit runs divers to Mapor island, north of Bintan. The trip begins and ends at the World Trade Centre dock in Singapore. Passengers are taken by ferry to Tanjung Pinang on Bintan Island, driven across Bintan, where they board the *Mapor I*. The trip to Mapor takes about an hour.

Round-trip to Mapor, $100; cottage accommodations,$40D, additional bed, $13 ; lunch or dinner, $8. Boat dives: single tank, $28; 2 tanks, $42. Rental equipment: regulator and BC, $18; mask, snorkel and fins, $12; skin suit, $4; whole kit, $26.

Marsden Bros Dive Centre 25 Faber Park, Singapore 129113. ☎ (65) 778-8287, fax: (65) 773-2265, E-mail: marsbros@pacific.net.sg. Operating out of Singapore, the *Reclaim II* is a 56' motor yacht beautifully equipped for cruising and diving. Sleeps eight passengers. One of the pioneers of the underwater world of the eastern Riau islands, it is the only company to frequent the waters on a regular basis. Liveaboard trips can be scheduled to the Riau archipelago can be scheduled between April and October. The crew are British zoologists and PADI master scuba diver trainers who specialize in marine research and scuba diving training.

North Sumatra

The oldest established outfit is on We island, off the northernmost tip of Sumatra (Sabang, the biggest town on the island, is better known than the island itself). This is as far east as you can get and still be in Indonesia. **Stingray Divers** (see Jakarta practicalities) have a small dive center there. Check with them for details.

Padang

Diving in Padang, in central Sumatra on the Andaman Sea side, is said to be good year-round, with the best season being April–September.

Merpati has direct 45-minute flights between Singapore and Padang. The city is well connected to the rest of the islands through Jakarta.

Padang Diving Wisata Jl. Batang Arau No. 88 B/6, Padang 25001, West Sumatra. ☎ (0751) 25876; fax: (0751) 28121. Shore-based diving. Efficient family run business, down by the river. Operates 2 x 9m boutboard boats for day dives near Padang. Has a very basic 20m wooden vessel for more extended lie-aboard trips. Day dives, including 2 full tanks, transport, diving guide, weights, and lunch, $98 (one diver)— $63 (4 divers). Equipment available for rent, but better to bring your own. PADI open water diving course, $375.

Live-aboard Charters, Inc. P.O. Box 22, Patong Beach, Phuket, Thailand. ☎ (6676) 340088; fax: (6676) 340309. Fantasea Divers of Phuket are planning to operate their live-aboard M.B. Fantasea in the Mentawai Islands, based out of Padang. Superb diving on the equator. 9-day/10-night cruise, $1,999.

Pusako Island Resort on Pulau Sikuai. Jl. Muara No. 38B, Padang, West Sumatra. ☎ 35311, fax: (0751) 22895. 21 cottages. Luxury beach resort on an otherwise uninhabited island, just south of Padang. Good and varied snorkelling. $90–$110S, $100–$120D. Boat transfer roundtrip, $15/person.

ACCOMMODATIONS

Dipo Hotel ☎ 34261; fax: 34265. Owner, Osman Iskander, is the local contact for Fantasea Diver Live-aboard. $20–$30.

Pengaran Beach Hotel Jl. Ir. H. Juanda 79, Padang. ☎ 51333; fax: 54613. North of town; full service beach resort. $64–$88 standard, $150–$375 suite.

—Charles Anderson

Bali PRACTICALITIES

INCLUDES LIVE-ABOARDS

Bali, a verdant, volcanic island with nearly three million people, is the tourist center of Indonesia. The Balinese are themselves not especially focused toward the sea, but the waters off Bali are very rich. The diving is not as immediately impressive as that in Eastern Indonesia, but it is very good, and gets more interesting the more you dive. Bali's combination of beautiful surroundings, convenient diving, plenty of tourist services, and colorful and interesting culture is hard to beat.

Prices in US dollars. S = Single; D = Double; T = Triple; AC = Air-conditioning.
City codes: South Bali 0361, North Bali 0362, East Bali 0363.

GETTING THERE

The best way to arrive in Bali is at the Ngurah Rai International Airport which, despite its often being referred to as "Denpasar" is actually on the isthmus connecting the Bukit Badung peninsula to Bali, much nearer to Kuta Beach than Bali's capital city. Daily Garuda flights from Jakarta, Yogyakarta, and many other Indonesian cities connect to Ngurah Rai, and a growing number of international flights—including those from Australia, Hong Kong, Japan, the Netherlands, Singapore and the United States—land here as well.

By Air

Flights from the Soekarno-Hatta International Airport in Jakarta are frequent, and if you land in Jakarta before 5 pm you can usually get a connection to Bali. (Although in peak season, these 90-min flights are almost always full. Book your flight all the way to Bali.) From the airport, hire a taxi to the place you intend to stay.

Domestic airline offices:
Garuda Jl. Melati 61, Denpasar, ☎ (0361) 235139.
Merpati Jl. Melati 51, Denpasar, ☎ (0361) 235358.

The following international airlines have offices in the Grand Bali Beach in Sanur, ☎ (0361) 288511. Direct phone lines are: Air France, ☎ 755523; Ansett Australia, ☎ 289636; Cathay Pacific, ☎ 753942; Continental-Micronesia, ☎ 287065/287774; Garuda, ☎ 288243; Japan Airlines and Japan Asia Airways, ☎ 287476/287577; Lufthansa, ☎ 286952; Malaysia Air Service, ☎ 288716 and 288511; Qantas, ☎ 288331; Singapore Airlines, ☎ 287940; Thai International, ☎ 285071 through –3.

Wisti Sabha Building at the Airport houses:

Air New Zealand, ☎ 756170 and 751011 ext. 1116; China Airlines, ☎ 754856 and 757298; EVA Air, ☎ 298935; KLM, ☎ 756127; Korean Air Lines, ☎ 754856 and 757298, fax: 757275; Royal Brunei, ☎ 757292.

By Train

One can also take a train from Jakarta (slow, and a nightmare with scuba gear) which connects to Surabaya (12 hrs on Bima, $43 Executive; 8 hrs. on the new Express, $44 Executive class), then a train to Bayuwangi (4 hrs, $7.50 Business class), then a bus to and across the Ketapang, Java–Gilimanuk, Bali ferry ($3) and on to Denpasar (4 hrs, $2).

By Bus

Taking a night bus the entire way is probably a better option (24 hrs, Jakarta–Denpasar, $30.) From Ubung Terminal outside Denpasar, where you are dropped off, a minibus to the tourist triangle of Kuta–Sanur–Nusa Dua runs $3–$5. All in all, best to arrive by plane.

LOCAL TRANSPORTATION

Airport taxis One-way fares from Ngurah Rai airport to the tourist centers are fixed. You pay a cashier inside, and receive a coupon which you surrender to your driver. (Of course, there will be plenty of touts and free-lancers offering you their services. These are never a better deal.) Fares range from $3 to nearby Kuta Beach to $17 to Ubud, far inland.
Minibuses All hotels have bemos for hire with a driver or with an English-speaking driver/guide. Rates run $3–$5/hr, with a 2-hr minimum. Day rates run $30–$40, more for an air-conditioned vehicle.
Bemos Public minibuses in Bali are called "bemos," a compression of becak (bicycle-

like pedicabs) and *mobil*. This is the way the Balinese travel and the cheapest way to get around the island. Fares are very inexpensive and you could probably get all the way across the island for less than $2, but you will need to know some Indonesian or be very good at charades to make sense of the routes and drop-off points. Public *bemos* can be rented for the day, usually for $20–$30. Still, it's probably better to get one through your hotel.

For a diving visitor to Bali, *bemos* are most useful for short day trips around the area or to hop locally around town. Get one of your diving guides or someone at the hotel to explain the ins and outs of the local routes.

Vehicle rental In almost all cases, it is best to leave the driving in Bali to someone who knows how to negotiate the roads and traffic. The roads are narrow, twisting, and full of hazards: unmarked construction sites, chickens, dogs, children, Vespas as wide as cars due to huge baskets of produce, and tough, unflinching truck drivers, to name just a few. You can rent a small (150cc) motorcycle for $5–$7/day if you have an international motorcycle driver's license, but you better know how to ride.

Renting a car—particularly since you will be carrying diving gear—is perhaps a more practical solution. These run $25–$35/day for little Suzuki jeeps; more for larger, more comfortable Toyota Kijangs. Rent through an agency (even Avis has outlets) or from numerous local rental companies. Ask your hotel or comb the streets where there's an agent on nearly every block. Be sure your rental includes insurance for loss and damage.

MEDICAL

Emergency Care

Call the Bali Hyatt for emergency evacuation services—☎ (0361) 288271 ext. 8160 (Bali Hyatt), 281127 (house clinic). The affiliated clinic is an SOS member of the international evacuation service and on 24-hr standby. The clinic is associated with Dr. Darmianti & Associates, which has clinics in the Nusa Dua Beach and Sanur Beach hotels. Set fees. Open 24 hours daily. (See page 259 for information on medical evacuation insurance.)

The two largest hospitals (*rumah sakit*) in Bali are in Denpasar. Both have emergency units with English-speaking doctors on duty 24 hrs:
Sanglah General Hospital RSUP Sanglah Denpasar, Diponegoro Street, Denpasar 80114. ☎ (0361) 227911–227915 (general), 223190 (ICCU), 232603 (VIP) and 224556 (director). Fax: (0361) 224206 (director), 226363 (emergency unit).
General Hospital Wangaya Jl. Kartini 109,

☎ (0361) 222141.

DCS Emergencies

There are two hyperbaric chambers in the area, one at Sanglah hospital in Denpasar, Bali, and the other in Surabaya, East Java.
Sanglah General Hospital RSUP Sanglah Denpasar, Diponegoro Street, Denpasar 80114. ☎ (0361) 227911–227915 ext. 232 for the hyperbaric medicine department. The chief doctor for the chamber is Dr. Antonius Natasamudra (home: 0361/420842), and Dr. Etty Herawati (home: 0361/223570) works the chamber as well. Both speak English and are very competent. The chamber is used regularly for beauty treatments, so it is kept in good service and the doctors and nurses are familiar with its operation. They use the United States Navy tables for their treatment regime. The chamber was built by an American fabrication outfit in Houston, Texas and is a model PVHO-1. It has capacity for six patients, and a working pressue of up to 80 psi (5.4 atmospheres). It began operation in 1996.
LAKELSLA Direktorat Kesehatan TNI-AL, Lembaga Kesehatan, Keangakatan Lautan, Jl. Gadung No. 1, Surabaya, Java. ☎ (031) 45750 and 41731. This chamber, operated by the Indonesian Navy, is run by Dr. Suharsono, who was trained in Australia and speaks English very well. The chamber has a volume of 75 cubic meters, with a capacity for five patients at a maximum working pressure of 6 atmospheres. The unit was built in 1981 by Aqualogistics International, St. Helena, UK. Other instrumentation includes spirometry, audiometery, EKG, and chromatography.

General

Doctor Dr. Handris Prasetya hasa private practice on Jl. Sumatra No. 21 in Denpasar, open Mon–Sat 5–8 pm. He speaks English well and is accustomed to treating foreigners.
Dentist For dental treatment, Dr. Indra Guizot's private practice is on Jl. Pattimura 19, Tel: 222445, Mon–Fri 10 am–8 pm.

PHOTOGRAPHIC SUPPLIES

P.T. Modern Foto This outfit is the local Fuji agent, with a huge showroom in Kuta just opposite the gas station and Gelael supermarket. They have the best E-6 processing in Bali and the freshest film. For prints, there are many instant mini-labs in all the larger towns and tourist centers offering while-you-wait service. You cannot buy Kodachrome film in Bali.

The biggest range of photographic equipment and supplies can be found in Denpasar at **Tati Photo**, Jl. Sumatra 72, ☎ (0361) 226912, and **Prima Photo**, Jl. Gajah Mada 14, ☎ 222505.

DIVE OPERATORS

Diving tour operators in Bali are concentrated in the tourist triangle—Kuta, Nusa Dua and Sanur—and in two places close to good dive spots—Candidasa on the east coast and Lovina, between the Tulamben wreck and Menjangan Island, in the north. The bigger outfits maintain desks at the major hotels, or at least keep brochures at the desk.

Almost all the local dive guides speak some English (and/or Japanese) and dive very well. Where many fall short, however, is in dive planning—particularly tailoring a dive for your specific needs—and emergency assistance.

Most outfits, chiefly for financial reasons, offer "initial" introductory dive courses to non-divers (we highly discourage this). These courses vary widely in price, $65–$100. Operators also offer 4–5 day "resort courses" with CMAS (French), PADI, PAUI (Australian), or POSSI (Indonesian) certification. These courses range in price from $250 to $400. If the course is advertised for less than $350, find out if it includes manuals, dive tables and certification—sometimes a cheap initial price sucks in customers, but you may end up paying more in the long run by the time all the "extras" are factored in.

With scuba diving currently booming on Bali, new operators spring out of thin air almost daily. Horror stories abound: young local kid who barely knows how to dive himself buys two tanks, fills them God knows how, and sets himself up as dive operator. Cheap prices. Inexperienced client dies after surfacing too fast.

While more and more Indonesians are qualified dive instructors/guides, we suggest checking out the operator carefully. Indonesian certification, CMAS or POSSI, can be lax (as can PADI, in fact, or any of the others) and none of these is a guarantee of a good operator.

A resort course will give you some of the basics, but definitely does not make you at ease in currents, caves or at night. We suggest that after taking a resort course, you accumulate at least 20–30 dives before diving some of the more challenging sites. And stay above the 25-meter mark and plan your dives well.

Experienced divers should request, if at all possible, that their group does not include beginners. All outfits require a minimum of two passengers per trip, with a surcharge of 50 percent or more for single divers. Some offer the possibility of a third day dive or one at night. All offer snorkeling for non-divers. Serious divers should take time to plan a dive series with the operator, taking into consideration time, budget and weather.

Prices are fairly standard. The following ranges (based on 2 divers) reflect southern-based operators, and include two full tanks and weights, guides, transportation, and lunch:

Nusa Dua (one dive)	$30–$50
Sanur (one dive)	$30–$50
Padangbai	$50–$70
Tepekong or Mimpang	$60–$80
Amed	$60–$80
Tulamben	$60–$80
Lovina	$60–$80
Menjangan	$80–$120
Nusa Penida (near side)	$80–$110
Nusa Penida (far side)	$90–$130

Most operators offer 2-day to 5-day packages, which are more economical. Cost per dive in these runs maybe $30–$40.

All operators have equipment for rent for casual divers. Average rental rates, per day: BC and regulator, $10–$12; mask/snorkel/fins, $3–$5; wet suit $5–$7; flashlight $5.

At last count, there were over 30 dive operators in Bali, mostly around the Kuta/Sanur/Nusa Dua area. Five of these cater only to the Japanese market. Of those remaining, we can recommend those we have listed by area below. Prices are roughly similar, but the quality of the instruction, facilities and dive guides vary considerably, as does the English proficiency of the guides and instructors.

The area listings work their way counterclockwise around the island from the southern tourist triangle, which follows the diving. If you stay anywhere in Kuta and Legian, Sanur, Nusa Dua, or Tanjung Benoa there is no reason to pick an operator in that particular town, as they will all pick up clients in the southern area.

ACCOMMODATIONS

Bali has a very wide range of accommodations, from 5-star hotels to modest *losmen*. You can spend $1,200/night in a lavish suite at Nusa Dua or $3/night at a friendly little *losmen* in Candi Dasa. It's your choice.

Bali, the land of 10,000 temples, has more than that number of hotel rooms and it would be impossible for us to list all the available lodgings here. We keep the list short in popular areas, such as the Kuta–Sanur–Nusa Dua triangle, and concentrate on those places divers might have a special interest in staying, particularly Candi Dasa and Lovina. All the more up-market hotels charge 21% government tax and service on top of the listed prices.

Kuta and Legian City code: 0361

A town has grown up around the beach here that has become the tourist center of Bali. Robert and Louise Koke, surfers from southern California, first built their Kuta Beach Hotel here in 1936. Still, it wasn't until the late '60s and early '70s, when a generation of hippies and other western drop-outs "discovered" Bali, that Kuta exploded.

Today, the town, which now extends north up to Legian, bustles with activity, its streets and tiny *gangs* (alleyways) lined with shops, restaurants, discos, and *losmen*. It is even an international fashion center with a distinct, colorful style falling somewhere between neon sporting wear and a Grateful Dead T-shirt. Although it is currently fashionable to malign Kuta, the place does have an irrepressible, youthful charm.

DIVE OPERATORS

Bali International Diving Service Jl. Kuta Raya, Kuta 16M (in front of the Gelael Supermarket and gas station). ☎ (0361) 751342; Fax: (0361) 752956. Seven instructors, five dive masters, all CMAS-certified. Some 2–3 day dive packages available.

Baruna Water Sports Head office: Jl. Bypass Ngurah Rai 300B, Kuta (in back of gas station) Mailing address: P.O. Box 3419 Denpasar, Bali 80034. ☎ (0361) 753820, 753821; fax: (0361) 753809. Baruna, named after the Balinese water deity, is Bali's oldest and largest scuba diving operator. They operate two outriggered speedboats and a larger diesel-powered boat. Baruna organizes tours to all of Bali's dive sites, and many other sites in Indonesia. This includes obtaining airplane reservations and tickets, which can be quite difficult to do on your own for remote places. They also run special-interest diving tours, fixed program tours and can arrange yacht charters (with compressor) for groups of two to six.

Baruna owns a very attractive 50-room, bungalows-style hotel, the Puri Bagus Beach, beachside, at the extreme eastern end of Candi Dasa (see below). The architecture, grounds and pool are all in good taste and well maintained. Although you can make bookings from elsewhere, it is best to stay here if you are diving in the area, especially if you are on one of Baruna's package tours, as their dive operations for eastern Bali are run from here.

Pineapple Divers c/o Legian Beach Hotel, Jl. Melasti, P.O. Box 308, Kuta, Bali. ☎ (0361) 751313, Fax: (0361) 752651. A reputable outfit, specializing in Japanese clients.

ACCOMMODATIONS

Budget (under $20)

Blue Ocean south of Jl. Double Six. 29 rooms. A popular hangout for locals and surfers, right on Legian Beach. $9–$10.

Rita's House, Gang Poppies I, Kuta. ☎ (0361) 751760, 222390; fax: 236021. 13 rooms. Very

quiet, clean, well-kept, and friendly; right in the center of Kuta. Rooms with shower and toilet. $4.50–$7 fan, $11–$16 AC, incl. breakfast.

Sorga Beach Inn Gang Menuh, between Jl. Melasti and Jl. Padma, Legian. ☎ 751609. 10 rooms. Fan only. Walk to the beach. $8–$10.

Yulia Beach Inn Jl. Pantai Kuta 43. ☎ 751893; fax: 751055. 48 rooms. One of the original Kuta places near the beach, where you have an ample choice of rooms. $3 w/o private bath, up to $30 for AC.

Intermediate ($25–$75)

Asana Santhi Willy Jl. Tegalwangi 18, Kuta. ☎ 751281, 752641. 10 rooms. In the heart of Kuta. Pleasant, newly renovated with antique furnishings and semi-open bathrooms, swimming pool. Willy II (14 rooms) next door has large rooms, but no character. $30–$35.

Bali Niksoma Beach Cottages Jl. Padma, Legian. ☎ 751946; fax: 753587. 52 rooms. A quiet beachfront place in Legian. Rooms with fan $21–$25, AC $45–$55,deluxe $65–$80, suites $95.

Bruna Beach Inn Jl. Pantai Kuta. ☎ 751565. 36 rooms. Across the road from Kuta beach. Attached or bungalow style, AC and non-AC. $12, $30–$35. Family room for $65 sleeps 5.

Garden View Cottages Jl. Padma Utara 4, Legian. ☎ 751559; fax: 753265. 56 rms. Secluded, on a Legian backlane. Short walk to beach. $38–$45.

Kuta Beach Club Jl. Bakung Sari, Kuta. ☎ 751261; fax: 752896. 100 rooms. A tranquil setting with garden and bungalows, right in the center of Kuta. $38–$40.

Poppies Cottages I Gang Poppies I, Jl. Legian, Kuta (behind Jl. Pantai Kuta). ☎ 751059; fax: 752364. 20 rooms. Well-designed cottages in a beautiful garden. Refrigerator in every room. 300 metres from the beach and always filled to capacity; reservations a must. $65–$70.

Poppies Cottages II Poppies Lane II, Kuta. ☎ 751059; fax: 52364. 4 rooms with fans, showers and fridges. $23–$28, $5 extra for a private kitchen.

Sandi Phala Jl. Kartika Plaza, Kuta. ☎ 753042; fax: 754889. 12 rooms. Two-story bungalows overlooking the beach in a big compound with pool and beachfront restaurant. $30–$45.

First Class ($75 and up)

Bali Oberoi Jl. Kayu Aya, Petitenget. ☎ 730361; fax: 730791. 75 rms. Tucked between ricefields and the sea at the northern end of the beach; bungalows of coral rock scattered tastefully about landscaped grounds. Beds are hand-carved 4-posters and the baths have open-air gardens. $225–$850 for a beachside villa with private pool.

Bali Intan Cottages Jl. Melasti 1, Legian.

☎ 751770; fax: 751891. 150 rms. Across the road from Legian beach. Standard $80–$90, superior $90–$100, cottage $100–$110, suite $180.

Bali Mandira Jl. Padma, Legian. ☎ 751381; fax: 752377. 120 rooms. Rows of cottages clustered around tidy courtyards. Tennis and squash. $80–$100, suites $135–170.

Jayakarta Bali Jl. Pura Bagus Teruna, Legian. ☎ 751433; fax: 752074. 281 rooms. Right on the beach; rooms are in large, two-story blocks. Standard $95–$100, up to $250 for a suite.

Kuta Beach Hotel Jl. Pantai Kuta. PO Box 3393. ☎ 751361; fax: 751362. 137 rooms right on Kuta Beach. $80–$90, bungalow $90–$100, suite $135–$300.

Patra Jasa Bali Jl. Kuta Beach, Tuban. ☎ 751161, 752810; fax: 752030. 206 rooms. Just five minutes from the airport, on the beach at the southern end of Kuta. Tennis courts, golf course, badminton and watersports. $130, up to $800 for a suite.

Sanur City code: 0361

Sanur was Bali's first resort town and is, in a sense, the grey eminence of the tourist triangle. Compared to Kuta, it is quiet and dignified (or just dull, depending on your point of view and, inescapably, your age) and compares to Nusa Dua as old wealth does to new. The town is very quiet at night and the beach here, protected by the reef flat, is very calm. People who intend to spend a long time on Bali often stay in Sanur.

DIVE OPERATORS

Ambisi Dive Center Jl. Tukad Pakerisan 98, Sanur. Mailing address: P.O. Box 3734, Denpasar 80228. ☎ (0361) 241428; fax: (0361) 241421. Formerly Oceana. Has changed management along with the name and location. Osanu Okuno is manager-instructor and caters to Japanese-speaking divers.

Bali Marine Sports Jl. Bypass Ngurah Rai, Belanjong, Sanur. ☎ (0361) 289308, fax: (0361) 287872. Good organization, equipment and guides. Basic and advanced dive courses. A PADI International Dive Center, run by very professional westerners. They own three 12-person dive boats with radio communications to the dive center. All divers insured. Cross-certification and specialty courses offered. Various all-inclusive dive tours of Bali. Highly recommended if the same people stay on staff.

Dive & Dive's Jl. Bypass Ngurah Rai 198, Sanur, Denpasar, Bali. ☎ (0361) 288052, fax: (0361) 289309. One of the best outfits in Bali at the time of this writing. Highly recommended. Dive shop with gear for sale and rent, small cafe, nice diver ambiance. They can arrange multi-day dive tour packages and trips around Bali or anywhere else in Indonesia.

ENA Dive Centre and Water Sports Jl. Tirta Ening 1, P.O. Box 3798, Sanur, Denpasar, Bali 80227. ☎ (0361) 288829, 287945, and 281751, Fax: (0361) 287945.
E-mail: enadive@denpasar.wasantara.net.id
Web: www.indo.com/diving/ena/
On a back street in Sanur, not easy to find, but like the other operators, they'll pick you up at your hotel. ENA owns the Saya Resort in Tulamben (see below). Various all-inclusive dive and accommodation packages are offered. PADI courses in English or Japanese. Also offers jetski, parasailing and other water sports.

Pro Dive Bali Jl. Sekar Waru No. 25, Sanur, Bali 80238. ☎ (0361) 286336, ☎ /fax: (0361) 288756.
E-mail: prodivebali@bali-paradise.com
Web: www.prodive.com.au
Australian-operated company offering PADI open water dive courses for $350 and continuing education programs in advanced open water diving, rescue diving, divemaster and specialty courses. Their 10-meter custom dive boat, *Pro Diver,* speeds you to the sites so you can spend more time in the water instead of on the water. The outfit's two- and five-day packages are popular.

ACCOMMODATIONS

Budget (under $25)

Sanur Plaza Jl. Bypass Ngurah Rai. ☎ 288808. 40 rooms. Spacious bungalows with thatched roof and hot water. A pool is available. They also have a family room. $12–$20.

Taman Agung Beach Inn Jl. Danau Tamblingan 146, Batujimbar. ☎ 289161, 288549; fax: 289161. 24 rooms. One of the best *losmen* in Sanur. Pleasant atmosphere. Five minutes from the beach. $25 fan, $50 suite.

Intermediate ($25–$75)

Baruna Beach Inn Jl. Sindhu 17, Sindhu. ☎ 288546; fax: 289629. 8 rooms. Pleasant old bungalows on the beach with lots of character, furnished with antiques and opening onto a courtyard by the sea. Cozy, very popular. $35–$40 with fridge. $65 suite. Breakfast, tax and service included. Credit cards not accepted. There is a house nearby for long stays.

Bali Sanur Besakih Beach Bungalows Jl. Danau Tamblingan 45, Batujimbar. ☎ 288424; fax: 286059. 50 rooms. Set in a garden leading to the sea. $65–$75.

Palm Garden Jl. Kesumasari No. 3, Semawang. ☎ 287041; fax: 289571. 23 rooms, all with

living room. $100 standard, $200–$300 suite.
Sindhu Beach Hotel at the beach end of Jl. Sindhu. Mailing address: Jl. Danau Tondano 14, Batujimbar. ☎ 288351; fax: 289268. 104 rooms in beachside bungalows. Owned by Natour chain. $40–$100.

First Class ($75 and up)

Bali Hyatt Jl. Danau Tamblingan, Semawang. ☎ 288271; fax: 287693. 390 rooms. With thatched-roof and terra-cotta-tiled lobby, open, relaxed reel, and magnificently landscaped garden, this is not your typical luxury chain hotel. For years, this has been *the* place to stay in Bali. Renovations completed in 1994 returned it to its classical Balinese roots. Several indoor and outdoor restaurants. Complete sports facilities. One pool has a replica of the famous Goa Gajah—plus waterfall, Jacuzzi and cold dip. $140–$185 superior/deluxe, $165–$185 executive/king, $180–$215 Regency Club, $400–$685 suite.
La Taverna Bali Jl. Tanjung Sari. ☎ 288387, 288497; fax: 287126. 34 rooms. Noted for its unique blend of Mediterranean and Balinese architecture combining thatched roofs and stucco. Tasteful antique-furnished rooms set in a tropical garden. Excellent beachside restaurant serves a variety of Italian and Indonesian specialities. $120–$160 standard, $195–$260 suite.
Sanur Beach Hotel Jl. Mertasari, Semawang; P.O. Box 279, Sanur. ☎ 288011; fax: 287566. 425 rooms. This four-story block is one of the older beachfront hotels in Sanur. Known for its friendly service. $125–$135 standard, $145–$170 deluxe, $200–$425 Studio, $350–$900 suite. Super-deluxe bungalow with marbled bathroom and private swimming pool $850. Group rates: $85–$95/person. Garuda office on 2nd floor.
Sativa Sanur Cottages off Jl. Mertasari, Semawang, ☎ /fax: 287881. 50 rooms. Shaded by coconut trees, this well-managed hotel is one of the coziest places to stay in Sanur, but it is away from the beach. The restaurant is excellent. $74–$184.
Segara Village Hotel Jl. Segara Ayu, Sindhu. ☎ 288407, fax: 287242. 120 rooms. Mini-villages of private bungalows by the sea, "rustic Balinese" (some look like *lumbung*, traditional rice granaries). Efficient, friendly staff. Balinese dance classes, a children's recreation room, gym, sauna. $65–$135, suite $210.
Tandjung Sari Hotel Jl. Tanjung Sari ☎ 288441; fax: 287930. 26 rooms. Built in 1962, this remains the top choice for many visitors. Charming decor, tranquil, elegant. The bungalows are reminiscent of those found in the pleasure gardens of the Balinese *rajas*. Caters to a celebrity clientele. The restaurant is highly recommended. $200–$1,250 standard,

$300–$380 suites.
The Grand Bali Beach (formerly Hotel Bali Beach) Jl. Hang Tuah. ☎ 288511; fax: 287917. The first large luxury hotel in Bali. Offers the most complete hotel facilities in Bali. One of its restaurants is a rooftop supper club with panoramic views. The golf course may be the reason why lots of Japanese groups stay here. Bowling alleys, tennis courts, local banks, American Express TRS office, and airline offices. $165–185.

Nusa Dua and Tanjung Benoa

City code: 0361

Nusa Dua offers luxury, and isolation from touts, peddlers, stray dogs, cold-water showers and other indignities. It's also quite antiseptic. Preferred by the international jet set. There are no cheap lodgings here.

Tanjung Benoa is a recently established resort just north of Nusa Dua. The beach hotels here are small and cozy, although there are some newly opened larger hotels. The nice, white-sand beach here is popular for water sports: parasailing, windsurfing, waterskiing and, of course, snorkeling and diving. All the accommodations are intermediate or budget, and provide a nice complement to nearby Nusa Dua's deluxe digs.

DIVE OPERATORS

Bali Hai Diving Adventures Contact Michael Cortenbach at PO Box 3548, Denpasar, Bali 80001. Tel: (0361) 720331, and Fax: (0361) 720334. Runs diving around Lembongan Island, and specializes in diving for *Mola mola* at a site dubbed "Blue Corner." Mike offers several packages, and we recommend the ten-dive package ($425) which includes the ride to Lembongan and back. While on the island, accommodation choices are two: the lovely Waka Nusa ($100/night) or the Mushroom Losmen, around $20, but much more basic. Mike will make the arrangements. The best time to see *Mola mola* is at the autumnal equinox.
Barrakuda Bali Dive At the Bali Tropic Palace Hotel, Jl. Pratama 34A, Nusa Dua. ☎ 772130, ext. 731; fax 772131. Located at the hotel. One instructor and two guides, all CMAS-certified. Also has counters in Candi Dasa and Lovina.
Wally's Special Tours Perumahan Wisma, Nusa Permai, Blok C. 35, Nusa Dua, Kampial, Bali. (0361) 772784. Cell: (087) 812-7243. Wally can also be contacted through YOS Diving in Tanjung Benoa (see below).
E-mail: walldive@denpasar.wasantara.net.id
Dive guide Wally Siagian (see profile, page

102) is really in a category of his own. Wally caters to small groups whose special interests include marine life and photography. He offers custom tours to any of Bali's dive spots and can arrange yacht charters for diving further afield. He is particularly familiar with Komodo diving, which he pioneered several years back. Wally (who holds an advanced instructor ranking from SSI) can also certify divers and offer advanced courses.

His strength is his knowledge of the sites, which he has been diving longer than anyone else on the island, and particularly of the unique biology of each. He has guided, worked with, and spotted animals for Gerald R. Allen, Gary Bell, David Doubilet, Rudie Kuiter, Jack Randall, and Roger Steene, among other notables. If you are a serious about your photography, you should work with Wally, especially if you want to photograph rare animals.

He gives a briefing before every dive, and nights are spent going over the day's dives and talking about the client's special interests over cold beer. We cannot recommend these tours highly enough—but give yourself plenty of time. Optionals include shopping (Wally doesn't take commissions), sightseeing, lunch at the special "super chicken" Taliwang stall, *tuak*-drinking, whatever. It's up to you—Wally's schedule is flexible and his knowlege of the island is encyclopedic. He owns his own Bauer compressor and equipment, and his rates are no higher than the other operators.

YOS Diving Centre and Marine Sports Jalan Pratama, Tanjung Benoa, Nusa Dua, Bali, Indonesia. ☎ (0361) 773774, 752005; fax 752985. This is a very well-run operation managed by Yos W.K. Amerta. They run fast boats from the main Tanjung Benoa center to Nusa Penida, and take divers by land to any of the other sites. YOS maintains counters at the Nusa Dua hotels, and full dive centers at Lovina and at the Pondok Sari Bungalows in Pemuteran. Good compressors and new, high-quality rental gear. A professional outfit that can take divers to any site in Bali. Also fishing, parasailing, jetskiing, and other marine sports.

ACCOMMODATIONS

Bualu Village P.O. Box 6, Denpasar. ☎ 771310; fax: 771313. 50 rms. Sports activities are free and the hotel has a PADI-certified diving instructor. The beach is five minutes away by foot or horsecart. $69–$112.
Club Méditerranée Nusa Dua P.O. Box 7, Denpasar. ☎ 771521, 771523; fax: 771831. 350 rooms. Looks more like a traditional luxury hotel than other Club Meds around the world. A fun place; attractive international staff. No room service, TVs or telephones. Packages including airfare, meals and entertainment

through your travel agent.
Melia Bali Sol P.O. Box 1048, Tuban. ☎ 771410, 771510; fax: 771362, 771360. 496 rooms. Recently renovated; managed by the Spanish Sol Melia chain, the Bali Sol reflects a certain Spanish ambience, including a replica of the Alhambra fountain at the entrance. Popular with Japanese tourists. Indoor pool and spa, outdoor pool with sunken bar. $176–198 superior, up to $1,100 for the deluxe suite.
Nusa Dua Beach Hotel P.O. Box 1028, Denpasar. ☎ 771210; fax: 771229. 380 rooms. Recently renovated with luxury Nusa Dua Spa added. The spectacular Balinese *candi bentar* gate at the entrance is a Nusa Dua landmark. Elaborately decorated with stone carvings in the manner of a Klungkung palace. Where then-U.S. President and Mrs. Ronald Reagan stayed. Gym and squash courts. $165 superior, $3,200 for a suite with private pool and entrance.
Putri Bali P.O. Box 1, Denpasar. ☎ 771020; fax: 771139. 384 rooms. Managed by the Hotel Indonesia chain. Book the cottages for more privacy. $120–$155 superior, $155–175 cottages, $210–$600 suites.

Tanjung Benoa

Matahari Terbit Bungalows ☎ 771018; fax: 772027. 8 rooms. Overlooking pool, restaurant in center. $60.
Puri Joma Bungalows ☎/fax: 771526. 10 rooms. For people who like staying in a small hotel away from the crowds. Very relaxing beachfront pool. $55–$60.

Candi Dasa City code: 0363

This town is quiet and relatively uncrowded compared to Kuta and Sanur to the south. There are at least 50 hotels, *losmen,* and homestays, and plenty of restaurants. The availability of services and its location—halfway between Nusa Penida and Tulamben—make it a reasonable place for a diver to settle.

DIVE OPERATORS

Spice Dive Balina Beach Resort. Buitan Manggis, Karangasem. ☎ (0363) 41720, Fax: (0363) 41001.
E-mail: spicedive@denpasar.wasantara.net.id
Well-known for their Lovina operation, Spice Dive now runs the concession at Balina.
Baruna Water Sports (see above under Kuta).
Sea Lion Diving Club (Stingray Dive Service) Bali Samudra Indah Hotel. ☎ (0363) 41062, 41181. Inclusive, two-dive tours: Nusa Penida ($70), Padangbai Blue Lagoon ($50), Gili Tepekong ($55), Tulamben ($55), Menjangan, min-

imum 4 persons ($70). Night dive at Tulamben ($40), Padangbai ($35). Two dives at any location, with accommodation ($90). Five-day course, with CMAS certification ($250). Introductory dive ($85).

ACCOMMODATIONS

There is a wide range of accommodations in Candi Dasa, from small, practically windowless cement block cells to large suites overlooking the ocean. Prices vary accordingly.

Bayu Paneeda Beach Inn ☎ (0363) 41104. 14 rooms. West of town. Medium-sized twin huts set in a huge tract of land. A large, grassy lawn makes this a favorite spot for families with kids. Blankets, reading lights and towels are supplied. Some hot water units with fans and screens. $9–$16.

Candi Beach Cottage Desa Sengkidu, kecamatan Manggis. ☎ (0363) 41234; fax: (0363) 41111. 64 rooms. Hotel and cotage rooms with satellite TV, mini-bar, verandah. Also has a pool, spa, open water diving school, fitness center, and tennis court. $75–$100.

Candi Dasa Beach Bungalows II ☎ (0363) 41536; fax: (0363) 41537. 69 spacious rooms overlooking the sea. A large two-story block of rooms. Swimming pool and open-air bar. Some rooms have refrigerators and TVs. $60–$85, bungalow $100, suite $150.

Homestay Pelangi 9 rooms. West of town in a quiet oceanside setting. Private garden. Decent-sized bamboo rooms, bathrooms with open-air garden. The owner, Pak Gelgel, is very friendly. Often a pair of bamboo gamelans with flute lull one to sleep. $7–$9, breakfast included. You can join organized treks to Tenganan via Kestala for as little as $5/person.

Ida Homestay Jl. Raya Candi Dasa. ☎ (0363) 41096. 6 rooms. East of town on the beach. Private thatched bamboo bungalows in a large, grassy coconut grove. Two-story houses provide upstairs bedrooms with wide ocean views. Beautiful open-air bathrooms. Carved furniture in some units. No hot water. $9–$23.

Losman Geringsing 15 rms. The best bargain in town. This friendly place offers small bamboo and brick bungalows in a banana grove on the beach. One of the few places to have any beach left, though only at low tide. $9–$14, includes breakfast, but not tax and service.

Puri Bagus Beach Hotel Jl. Raya Candi Dasa. P.O. Box 129, Amlapura. ☎ (0363) 41291/2; fax: (0363) 41290. 50 rms. Clean, spacious bungalows with semi-open bathroom and mini-bar. Pool and restaurant overlooking the ocean. $65–$125. Ocean view/front room surcharge $10–$15.

Puri Pundak ☎ (0363) 33978. 17 rooms. In the banana groves east of town, near the homes of local fishermen. Large bamboo rooms,

Western bathrooms, some with bathtubs. Overlooks the bay. $7–$23.

Rama Ocean View Bungalows Balina. ☎ (0363) 33974; fax: (0363) 233975. 74 rms. West of Candi Dasa, away from the noise and bustle. A beachside enclave with a pool, restaurant, mini bar, and satellite TV. Fitness center, sauna, tennis court, and games rooms. $75–$90, suite $250–$350.

Serai Desa Buitan, Manggis. P.O. Box 13, Karangasem 80871. ☎ (0363) 41011/2; fax: (0363) 41015. 58 rooms. Just west of Candi Dasa. Secluded beachfront hotel with swimming pool, restaurant. $90 superior, deluxe $105, $175 suite.

The Water Garden ☎ (0363) 41540; fax: (0363) 41164. 12 rooms. This hotel venture of TJ's Restaurant in Kuta has been designed with their usual attention to detail and quality. Gorgeous bungalows set in a network of cascading streams, pools and elegant gardens. Mountain bikes, hiking maps and information about local events and places of interest available. Swimming pool. $60–$65.

DINING

There are lots of restaurants in Candi Dasa. The typical menu will contain salads, Indonesian and Chinese standards and a few basic western dishes. Prices are very reasonable, averaging $4–$5/person, with drinks. Seafood, though delicious, can be considerably more expensive. Most restaurants close up by 10 pm.

Arie Bar and Restaurant 8 tables. Down-to-earth, family-run establishment with a good selection of Balinese, Chinese and Western dishes. Good quality and cheap prices.

Kubu Bali ☎ (0363) 41532. 36 tables. Serves a bit of everything, but excels in seafood—grilled, steamed or fried. Their open kitchen is fun to watch. Finish up with peach melba, chilled fruit or a cognac.

Lotus Sea View Larger and more formal than the neighboring Toke Cafe, but it has great seafood and its location near the water gives it a Venetian flavor.

Pandan Restaurant ☎ (0363) 41541. 30 tables. By the beach. Well-known for its Balinese buffet of *babi guling* (roast pork), chicken, fish, vegetables, noodles and salads. Experience this feast or sample one of the many other delicious local or Chinese dishes.

Rama Bungalow and Restaurant Has added Swiss dishes, such as *Roschti*, *Kartoffel* and *Puffer Mitgemuse* to an already good menu.

TJ's Cafe ☎ (0363) 41540. 22 tables. The best grilled fish, stuffed baked potatoes and salads around. Elegant open pavilions overlook a carp pond. Popular western music and the delicious desserts.

Toke Cafe Near the bend in the road, beachside. Wonderful combination of Balinese ambience and Western intimacy. Great welcoming drink and good pasta, all of this just for a couple of dollars.

Warung Ibu Rasmini The best *nasi campur* (mixed vegetables, *tempe*, and chicken over rice) in town for under $1, plus a range of other simple Indonesian dishes.

Tulamben

City code: 0362, but no phones yet.

Most divers travel to Tulamben (or nearby Cemeluk) on a package tour from Kuta, Sanur, Nusa Dua, or Candi Dasa, but independent-minded divers can make their way by rented car or, if not carrying gear, motorcycle. It's about 4 hrs from Kuta or Nusa Dua, 30 min. less from Sanur. The traffic through Candi Dasa will likely be heavy, but the last hour of the trip—from Candi Dasa onward—is very scenic. From Tulamben to Menjangan takes another 3 hrs.

Operators in Tulamben offer tanks, weights, and equipment rental, along with guides for independent divers who arrive on their own, and we highly recommend staying in Tulamben if you want to dive here or in Cemeluk. The wreck, in particular, is far less crowded in the morning before the hordes arrive from the South.

DIVE OPERATORS

Bali Dive has a branch office at the turnoff to the parking area near the entry point for the wreck. Tanks, regulators and BCs for rent.

Dive Paradise Tulamben Attached to the Paradise Palm Beach Hotel, P.O. Box 111, Amlapura 80811, Bali. No phone yet, but they can be contacted through the Friendship Shop in Candi Dasa, ☎/Fax: (0363) 41052. This outfit, run by Emiko Shibuya, is the most experienced operator in the Tulamben area. Emiko, who has been in Bali for 11 years, keeps her compressor, tanks and equipment in fine order. There is no telephone yet (the village has unapologetically voted PDI for years) but you can get fresh Fuji Velvia at the counter. Dive Paradise's guide, Nengah Putu, holds an advanced diver rating. One wreck dive with instructor-guide ($30), two dives ($50). The dive shop also organizes dives at other spots around Bali. Prices include transportation from Tulamben, dive guide, two dives, and all equipment, are reasonable, as are the room rates. For snorkelers at Tulamben, the Paradise has fins, masks and snorkels, $1.50/day.

Tulamben Dive Center P.O. Box 31, Amlapura 80811. ☎ (0363) 41032. Next to the Paradise on the main road. Has a compressor, tanks and rental gear. Same prices as the Paradise. Associated with the *losmen* Tulamben Beach Pondok Wisata, 4 rooms $5–$10.

ACCOMMODATIONS

Ganda Mayu ("Fragrant Flower") 7 rooms. Simple beachfront accommodations. Near dive entry point to wreck site. Bali Coral Dive Center in front of bungalows. $7–$14.

Mimpi Resort Sales office: Kawasan Bukit Permai, Jimaran, Denpasar 80361. ☎ (0361) 701070; fax: (0361) 701074. 16 new bungalows. Swimming pool, restaurant, and Bukit Kencana Dive Center on beachfront grounds. Fan and AC. $75–$125. Minibuses of daydivers park next to this *losmen*.

Paradise Palm Beach P.O. Box 31, Amlapura 80811. ☎ (0363) 41032. 22 nice, thatched bungalows, each with two beds, fan and toilet. Pleasant, simple accommodations, geared toward divers. Beach restaurant, souvenir shop and Dive Center attached. Reserve in high season. Meals at the beachside restaurant are inexpensive, but not wonderful, but the beer is cold and the waitresses are charming and good-humored. On busy afternoons this restaurant is the unofficial nerve center of Bali's diving community. From the Paradise, it's about 300 m to the entry point for the wreck. Porters carry your gear for about $1.50 for two dives ($1.75 at night.) Rooms (w/breakfast) $11–$16. Rooms with AC and hot water, $35.

Saya Resort 5 AC rooms, mini-bar, hot water, private balconies. Attached restaurant. Snorkeling and dive excursions with hotel's Ena Dive Center. Rooms $35–$50, w/breakfast.

Dining

Sunrise Next to the Paradise, away from the wreck, on the beach. Chicken or fish ($2), also —less expensive—vegetables, *gado-gado,* and sandwiches. Soft drinks and beer.

Cemeluk and Sambirenteng

City code: 0362

There is no compressor or rental gear in the immediate vicinity of this dive site. Bring your own from Tulamben, Candi Dasa or wherever, or join a group from Kuta/Sanur/Nusa Dua for a day trip. Past Cemeluk, on the way to Karangasem, there are a few *losmen*, on the bad, but paved and spectacular road that follows the coast around Bali's easternmost peninsula. There's a small sunken wooden boat in shallow (snorkelable) depth at Banyuning/ Waru, close to the beach, between the Vienna and

Bali 3

the Good Karma (see below).

ACCOMMODATIONS

Coral View. New resort with 19 thatched bungalows, swimming pol, bar, and restaurant. Motorboat available for dolphin cruises. All rooms with hot water. $29 economy with fan, $40 standard with fan, $52 AC, $104 suite.

Good Karma Dusun Selang, Amed. 10 bamboo bungalows on the beach. Small, friendly, quiet place favored by young Europeans. $9–$11.

Hidden Paradise Cottages Lipah, Bunutan, Abang, Amed. ☎ (0361) 431273; fax: (0363) 21044, (0361) 423820. 16 rooms. Hot water, fan and AC. Complete facilities: swimming pool, bicycles and watersports. Snorkeling equipment, boat available. $35–$87, including American breakfast.

Kusuma Jaya Beach Inn Jemuluk village, 12 km from Amlapura. ☎ (0363) 21250. 12 rooms. On a steep hill above the pool with wonderful vistas. Beautiful sunrises and sunsets. Take the steep steps on the left past the bridge. Snorkeling gear available for guests. $13–$16, including breakfast.

Vienna Cottage P.O. Box 112, Lipah, Amed. 12 bungalows. Watersports facilities: diving, snorkeling, fishing, sailing. $11–$21, including breakfast.

Sambirenteng

Alam Anda Sambirenteng. Contact Astawa Enterprises, c/o Nyumpene, Jl. Legian Tengah 436N, Legian. ☎ /fax: (0361) 752296. 9 bungalows, 4-room house. Unique, new seaside resort devoted to relaxation. Organizes trips through unspoilt landscapes, as well as sailing, snorkeling, and dive trips to Amed, Tulamben, Menjangan, and Nusa Penida. They have an experienced dive master in residence and diving equipment in top condition for rent. $24–$29 rooms, $39–$44 bungalows, including breakfast.

Lovina City code: 0362

Lovina is the generic name for a cluster of villages spread along Bali's north coast. They are, from east to west: Tukad Munggah, Anturan, Kalibukbuk (Lovina), and Temukus. The beach is shiny black sand and the surf is calm. If you want to dive at Menjangan and if you don't stay in Pemuteran, then Lovina, about an hour's drive away, is the next closest place to stay. Operators can arrange diving (in Lovina and Menjangan) as well as local snorkeling ($3–$4), trip to the dolphins ($5) and fishing ($5).

Lovina is a good spot for beginning divers,

with shallow depths and often excellent visibility (15–30 meters). The reef has a good variety of hard corals, sponges, crinoids and anemones, and abundant small reef fish.

DIVE OPERATORS

Spice Dive On the south side of the main coastal road. P.O. Box 157, Singaraja, Bali. ☎ (0362) 41305, Fax: (0362) 41171. E-mail: spicedive@denpasar.wasantara.net.id A small, well-run operation. Introductory dives available. Now a PADI operation. Two dives, all-inclusive, including all gear: Tulamben ($65), Lovina ($45), Menjangan ($65). Knock off 10% if you bring your own gear. Menjangan package requires a minimum of two clients. You can also arrange dives at Nusa Penida, Padangbai and Gili Tepekong (however, because of distance, just one dive per day).

Barrakuda At Bali Lovina Beach Cottages in Singaraja. ☎ /fax: (0362) 41385, 21836. In Sanur, ☎ /fax: (0361) 233386 and 287694. This dive operator's head office is in Sanur. Prices similar to those at Spice Dive.

ACCOMMODATIONS

Most lodgings here are budget *losmen* or intermediate lodgings. Prices are a bargain compared to the tourist towns in the south.

Aditya Jl. Seririt. P.O. Box 35, Lovina. ☎ 41059; fax: 41342. 75 rooms. Some spacious new suites with AC, hot water, tub, and phone are available. $20–$25 fan, $35–$45 AC, including Continental breakfast.

Agung Homestay, Bar & Restaurant P.O. Box 124, Anturan. 5 rooms. One of the first hotels in Lovina, the building uses bamboo throughout. Very friendly atmosphere. No private baths. $3–$4.50. Reservations are needed.

Angsoka Kalibukbuk. ☎ 41841. 26 rooms. Comfortable two-story bungalows, some with hot water. $4–$7.50 fan, $20–$25 AC.

Angsoka Seaside Cottages Jl. Lovina. ☎41841; fax: 41023. 26 rooms. Special facilities for bungalows include split AC, bathtub and hot water. $7–$18 fan, $12 open Bali-style baths.

Astina Kalibukbuk. 8 km west of Singaraja, PO Box 141, Singaraja 81151. ☎ 41803 (c/o Ayodya). 12 rooms, 5 cottages. On the beach. Bamboo-walled rooms around a nice garden. $5.50–$7 with common bath, $8–$9 with private bath $11–$12.50 cottages with fan, mosquito net, private bath.

Awangga Tukad Munggah, Banjar Banyualik, Desa Kalibukbuk. ☎ 41561. 8 clean and spacious rooms, close to the beach. $7, including American breakfast.

Ayodya Kalibukbuk. ☎ 41803. 5 bamboo-walled rooms in a well-kept old house. Despite its location on the main road, pleasantly calm. No private bathrooms. $3–$4.

Bali Lovina Beach Cottage Jl. Seririt, Singaraja, Lovina. PO Box 186. ☎/fax: 41285; fax: 41478. 34 bungalow-style rooms. $30–$35 fan, $40–$45 AC, $50–$60 superior, including a generous breakfast, with bacon eggs and toast. $30S, $35D, $35S, $40D w/AC.

Bali Taman Beach Hotel Jl. Raya Seririt, Desa Tukad Mungga, PO Box 99. ☎ 41126; fax: 41478. 18 bungalow-stlye rooms. Tennis court, fridge and TV available. $22.50–$27.50 fan, $45–$55 AC and hot water.

Banyualit Beach Inn Jl. Singaraja, P.O. Box 116, Kalibukbuk. ☎ 41789; fax: 41563. 20 rooms. Simple to newly renovated AC with hot water. Some of the verandahs are literally on the water's edge. Friendly and helpful staff. Ask for a room close to the beach. $12–$15 fan, $16–$23 AC.

Baruna Beach Cottages Desa Temaron. P.O. Box 149, Lovina. ☎ 41746; fax: 41252. 42 rooms. Several cottages overlooking the beach. All rooms with private bath. $17 budget w/fan, $24–$32 cottages w/fan, $40–$52 AC. Excluding tax, service and breakfast.

Janur's Dive Inn Kalibukbuk, Tukad Mungga. P.O. Box 100, Singaraja. ☎ 41056. 5 rooms with fans. Friendly family place run by Janur and Rose and Gede, who live in the same compound. Very simple accommodations, but special and cozy. Ask Janur to guide you around. $4.50.

Jati Reef Bungalows P.O. Box 52, Tukad Mungga. ☎ 41052. 16 rooms in four separate bungalows, with a short walk through the ricefields to get to your room. $7 fan.

Kalibukbuk Beach Inn Jl. Lafiana, Desa Kalibukbuk. ☎ 41701. 25 rooms. At the end of Banyualit lane, just a few steps from the beach. $9 budget, $11–$14 fan, $16–$20 AC.

Nirwana Desa Kalibukbuk, Lovina. ☎ 41288; fax: 41090. 32 rooms. Spacious, clean, right on the beach. The largest room can sleep four. Two-story bungalows with bamboo trim spread set in a lush garden. $14–$18, family suite $23.

Palma Hotel Jl. Raya Lovina-Singaraja. P.O. Box 131. ☎ 41775, 41658; fax: 41659. 45 rooms, standard and cottages, AC, hot showers. Other facilities include meeting room tennis court and recreation facilities, including boat sailing, push bikes. $72–$81 standard, $94–$102 cottages, $192–$210 suites, including American breakfast.

Perama Jl. Lovina, Anturan. ☎ 41161. 10 rooms very close to one another and right on the main road, so it can be rather noisy. $4.50 for rooms with private shower, $3.60 without.

Puri Tasik Madu/Tama ☎ 41376. 12 rooms. This was one of the first hotels in the area. Rooms are newly-renovated. Pleasant staff and a very friendly atmosphere. $8.50–$17.

Rini Kalibukbuk. ☎ 41386. 20 rooms. Clean,all rooms with private bath. No breakfast.

$15–$30.

Samudra Beach Cottage Jl. Seririt, Desa Temukus. P.O. Box 142, Temukus. ☎ 41751. 24 rooms. At the western end of the beach. Very quiet. $7–$11 fan, $9–$16 AC, including Continental breakfast.

Simon's Seaside Cottage Jl. Semit, Desa Anturan. P.O. Box 151, Tukad Mungga. ☎ 41183. 16 rooms in four two-story bungalows. Clean and roomy. Great upper rooms with verandahs front and back overlooking the beach and ricefields $11–$14.

Sri Homestay Jl. Singaraja, Seririt, Desa Anturan. ☎ 41135. 12 bamboo rooms by the beach. Bathrooms are not the cleanest, but it is pleasant to look at ricefields while taking a shower. Has a narrow veranda in front. The owner, Sri, is helpful and friendly. $11–$15.

DINING

Nearly all hotels in the area have restaurants. **Janur's Dive Inn** has one that is great value for money. Very pleasant atmosphere, serving standard favorites like *cap cay* (mixed vegetables) for $1. The most famous restaurant is **Khi Khi**. Grilled fish and fried prawns are the favorites here. Another popular restaurant is the **Kakatua**, near Lovina beach. Try their fried fish for $2. Or you can go to **Srikandi** for fried rice, which you eat sitting on a mat. For those who want live music, go to **Wina** or **Malibu**. The latter turns into a disco on Fridays.

Pemuteran Menjangan Area

City code: 0362

Park visitor's permit and the boat from Labuhan Lalang to Menjangan Island comes to about $15 (this fee is included in package tours).

DIVE OPERATORS

P.T. Arkipelago Selam Associated with the Taman Sari Bungalows Resort, Desa Pemuteran, Gerokgak, Singaraja 81155, Bali. ☎ (0362) 92623, Fax: (0362) 93264. Also keeps a shop at the Sol Elite Paradiso Hotel, Jl. Kartika Plaza, Kuta 80361 Bali. ☎ (0361) 761414 ext. 7153, Fax: (0361) 756944. E-mail: tamanri@indosat.net.id Web: baliwww.com/arkipelago/ A new outfit, which offers a Bali-wide program.

Reef Seen Aquatics Dive Centre Desa Pemuteran, Gerokgak, Singaraja, 81155, Bali. ☎/fax: (0362) 92339. Contact: Chris Brown. E-mail: reefseen@denpasar.wasantara.net.id Chris Brown pioneered the Pemuteran sites, and is always continuing his explorations, including unusual dives such as at a nearby pearl farm. He can book divers at any of the local hotels. The dive boats are traditional wooden craft, customized for diving. Oxygen and a good first aid kit are kept on board. Film and 110V or 220V charging facilities, multi-system video playback, separate freshwater rinse tanks for photo and video gear. Snorkeling, temple visits and nature walks in Bali Barat National Park are options. Two dives at the Pemuteran sites, just offshore, from boat, $55. Shore dives $10, with guide, $20; shore night dives $15, with guide, $25. Trips to Menjangan, including 2 dives and lunch, $75/person, minimum two divers ($65/person with three or more). Equipment rental: $10/dive.

YOS Diving Centre and Marine Sports Associated with the Pondok Sari Bungalows (see below). A branch of the well-run Tanjung Benoa–based operator. Permuteran Village, ☎/fax: (0361) 92337 (for contacts, see also above under Nusa Dua).

ACCOMMODATIONS

Matahari Beach Resort Pemuteran, Singaraja. ☎ 92312; fax: 92313. 32 rooms. New, exclusive 5-star resort. Built in Balinese style with German management, spacious bungalows, each with two rooms with marble terraces, living room, AC, and outdoor baths. Full facilities include tennis, watersports, mountain biking, and a dive center, David's Sport Center. Airport transfer for $30 is a luxury with dive gear. $140–$160 garden view, $170–$190 sea view, $220–$240 deluxe, $330–$350 super deluxe. All prices plus 20% tax and service.

Pondok Sari Beach Bungalows Desa Pemuteran, Gerokgak, Singaraja. ☎/fax: 92337. 20 rooms in 10 bungalows. The original resort in the area. The bungalows are clean and comfortable, and the setting is very peaceful. The tasteful room furnishings and the open-air bathrooms with Japanese touches—smooth river pebbles, dripping bamboo—are very nice. The restaurant offers good western and Indonesian cuisine, plus cold beer. $18 fan, $29 AC, plus 15% tax and service.

Pulau Menjangan Inn 3 km from the boat landing. 8 rooms, strictly basic accommodation. Simple meals ($1.25–$2). $5.

Taman Sari Beach Bungalows Desa Pemuteran, Gerokgak, Singaraja. ☎ (0362) 92623, (0361) 289031, (0361) 288096 c/o Putu Tini; fax: (0361) 289285. The successor to the Pondok Sari (built by the same partners) with similar features. More upscale, but still very tasteful. $35 fan, $50–$65 AC, $80 suite, plus 15% tax and service.

Live-aboards

Sea Contacts Dive Voyages Jl. Mertasari no. 64A, Sidakarya Batan Kendal, Suwung, Denpasar, Bali. ☎ (0361) 725430, Fax: (0361) 725431. Cruise director: Larry Smith. E-mail: smithdiv@dps.mega.net.id
This is a brand new operation, which wouldn't mean a lot except for the name of the cruise director. Larry Smith is the most experienced live-aboard director working in Indonesia today, and any dive operation he runs is certain to be exceptional. The planned 1999 schedule:

Season	Area	Length of runs
Feb.–March	Banda Sea	10–14 days
April	Sangihe-Talaud	8–9 days
May–July	Sangalaki	7–12 days
July–Sept.	Sangihe-Talaud	8–12 days
Oct.–Dec.	Komodo area	8–15 days

The runs are in the *Sea Contacts 1,* a very well-equipped 35-meter ship with capacity for 12 divers. This 360 hp vessel has Bauer K-14 and Mariner compressors, individual AC in each of six cabins (w/attached bathrooms), full GPS and other instrumentation, and two U.S. divemasters. Prices were unavailable as we went to press, but contact them.

Grand Komodo Tours & Travel (Komodo Alor Safari) Main office: Jl. Hang Tua No. 27, Sanur, Denpasar 80034, Bali. ☎ (0361) 287166, Fax: (0361) 287165. In Bima: Jl. Sukarno Hatta 45, Bima, Sumbawa, NTB, ☎ (0374) 42018, Fax: (0374) 42812. In Labuahanbajo: Jl. P.W. Papu, Labuahanbajo, Flores, NTT, ☎ (0385) 41377, Fax: (0385) 41378.
    E-mail: gkomodot@indosat.net.id
    Also: gkomodo@dps.mega.net.id
This Komodo and Alor specialist offers charters to many sites in the area. See "Komodo," page 291, for more details.

Pro Dive Bali Jl. Sekar Waru No. 25, Sanur, Bali 80238. ☎ (0361) 286336, ☎/fax: (0361) 288756. Contact: Richard Johnstone.
    E-mail: prodivebali@bali-paradise.com
    Web: www.prodive.com.au
This Australian-operated company runs the *Bali Sea Dancer,* a large ship that offers diving on its three- and four-day runs to Komodo. A newer operation, called "Oceanic Odyssey" offers luxury three- and four-day cruises and charters east of Bali.

Rasa Yacht Charters ☎ (0361) 71571. 2 fine yachts, the 14-meter steel-hulled ketches *Rasa III* and *Rasa V,* which have state-of-the-art electronics and twin 100 hp engines.

Tourdevco Bali Benoa Port, ☎ (0361) 31591; fax: 31592. Jakarta office is at Jl. Johar Menteng 2A, Menteng, Jakarta 10340, ☎ (021) 380-5011, Fax: (021) 720-0756.

    —*updated by Debe Campbell, David Pickell, and Andy Udayana*

⁴ Nusa Tenggara PRACTICALITIES

Most of Nusa Tenggara is not yet part of the standard Indonesian tourist circuit, although the infrastructure is developing rapidly. If you schedule ahead of time, most dive operators will meet you at the airport. The islands here are rugged and—in the northernmost part of the chain—volcanic. This is one of the best parts of Indonesia for traditional cloth, and in some areas, particularly Sumba and Flores, old animist religions are still followed.

Prices in US dollars. S = Single; D = Double; T = Triple; AC = Air-conditioning.

Gili Islands City code: 0364

These three small islands, because they are so close to Bali, have become a very popular destination. The simplest way to get here is to take the ferry from Padangbai, Bali (3.5 hrs). There are ferries daily every two hours, beginning at 6 am. Fare: $2.50 economy, $4 VIP. The ferry reaches Lombok at Labuhan Lembar. From Lembar, minibuses head to any of a number of destinations, including Mataram (the island's capital and largest city) and Senggigi Beach.

A more luxurious alternative is the Mabua Intan Express, a 40 m catamaran that speeds at 60 kn/h between Benoa and Lambar in just 2 hours. Reclining seats, overhead lockers, a bar, and even videos make this a luxury. In rough weather the cat literally jumps over the waves, causing a lot of upset stomachs. Departures from Benoa are at 8 am and 2:30 pm, from Lembar at 11:30 am and 5:30 pm. Economy class $12.50, middle class $17.50 and first class $25, including snack and beverage. ☎ (0361) 772521 on Bali or (0364) 37224 on Lombok.

You can also fly from Bali to Lombok's Selaparang airport. Merpati Nusantara and Sempati Air have several flights daily ($27, 25 min). The jump off point for the Gili Islands is Bangsal, north of Senggigi. You can take a public minibus to Pemenang ($1.50), and then hire a *cidomo,* a horse-drawn cart, for the short remaining trip to Bangsal harbor (35¢). Or you can just charter a minibus to take you directly to Bangsal (maybe $8–$15).

At the harbor, book your passage at the official ticket booth on one of the regular 20-seat boats to Gili Air (50¢), Gili Meno (60¢), or Gili Trawangan (75¢). These leave regularly in the early morning and late afternoon, and at other times when they fill up. You can also buy a one-way charter to Gilis Air (20 min, $6); Meno (30 min, $7); or Trawangan (45 min, $9).

DIVE OPERATORS

While there are several dive operators on Gili Trawangan and a couple on Gili Meno, they are not particularly reliable. We suggest taking a good look at their compressors and filters before diving with any of these outfits. It's not worth it to pay less and get bad or questionable air, along with unreliable rental gear. We also strongly discourage taking a dive course from any of the operators on the islands: we have encountered instructors with fake certifications who were unqualified.

It's much better to book with one of the operators from Senggigi, even if it's more expensive and requires a fairly long boat ride (an hour or so).

Albatross Jl. Raya Senggigi, near the Lina Hotel. PO Box 1066, Mataram 83010, Lombok. ☎ (0364) 93399; fax: (0364) 93388. This is currently the best dive operator on Lombok, under the direction of owner-manager Andy Chan. He has found several new dive locations just north of the Gilis, so ask about those.

Plan your dive itinerary with Andy, who will come up with spots for your level of experience. All-inclusive two-dive trips to the Gilis, $55 (min 2 people, price includes BC and regulator, if needed), night dive $35.

Baronang Divers Pak Sjahrul Nasution, P.O. Box 24, Mataram, Lombok. ☎ (0364) 27793. He keeps his dive boat at Teluk Nara, just off the main road from Senggigi going north along the coast and shortly before Bangsal. The man might be hard to find, but he gives good service at very reasonable prices.

Baruna A branch of this large, Bali-based diving operator is located at the Senggigi Beach Hotel. ☎ (0364) 93333, Fax: (0364) 93140. Two dives in the Senggigi area, $50, two dives off the Gilis, $65. To both prices add $10 for BC and regulator, plus $5 for a wet suit, the latter usually not necessary.

Rinjani Divers At Senggigi's Lombok Intan Laguna Hotel. ☎ (0364) 93090; Fax: (0364) 93185. Two-dive day trips to Gili Air, Trawangan, Tanjung Bonita $65 (2 people minimum); further away, to Gili Petangan or Pantai Karibu, $75.

Pulau Moyo

Moyo Island, 250 km from Bali, lies off the north coast of Sumbawa. Since 1976, approximately half of this island has been registered as a nature preserve. The vegetation varies from savannas to jungle, with majestic banyan, teak, tamarind and fig trees sheltering wild boar, rusa deer, macaque monkeys, banteng, and wild buffaloes along with abundant bird life: white-breasted sea eagles, brahminy kites, and megapodes. Eight small villages ring the island's periphery. The dry season on Moyo runs from April to November.

A concession covering some 50 hectares of this island (5 below water, 45 above) has been awarded to the Amanwana luxury resort, with its unique "tents"—actually canvas-topped bungalows, with full AC and conveniences. The Amanwana assists the monitoring of the game reserve, providing personnel and logistical support where needed.

The diving here is very good, and the Amanwana offers full facilities. For divers who cannot afford this luxury, ENA Dive Centre also offers diving off Moyo, from their base on Bali.

Amanwana Resort Pulau Moyo, Sumbawa. ☎ (0371) 22233, Fax: (0371) 22288. Contact: manager Michael DiLonardo. As resorts go, this one is something like a Range Rover—with plush leather seats and six-speaker sound. Guests fly from Bali to Sumbawa Besar, where the luxury begins. Resort personnel meet you and you are taken to the port for a one-and-one-half hour ride to the island, enjoying treats of champagne and salmon along the way. If you are in a big hurry, Amanwana will arrange a helicopter from Bali ($3,000 each way).

There are 20 tent/bungalows, and a staff of 130 to pamper the guests, usually about 25 at any given time. It is actually a good value for families (up to two children under 12 stay free), at least well-heeled families, and there's always something interesting for the kids to do. Prices: $625 for seaside tents and $525 for tents set back a short ways from the beach. All meals included. Add 21% government and service tax.

Ian White (formerly of H2O Divers in Phuket, Thailand) runs the diving at the Amanwana. He has also trained Indonesian divers up to the dive master level. His guests have occasionally seen manta rays and whale sharks, but these are by no means a common occurrence. Dive prices range from $35 to $150, depending on location and the number of divers. Various PADI courses are available, e.g. open water ($500).

Jimmy, a good-natured Australian and something of a legend among the Amanwana's guests, runs the resort's many boats and its game fishing operation. The fishing grounds are just 30 minutes from the resort, and very rich. Game fishing charters run from $225 for half day for a small but powerful boat to $1,200 for a full day in the queen of the fleet.

ENA Dive Centre and Water Sports Jl. Tirta Ening 1, P.O. Box 3798, Sanur, Denpasar, Bali 80227. ☎ (0361) 288829, 287945, and 281751, Fax: (0361) 287945.
E-mail: enadive@denpasar.wasantara.net.id
Web: www.indo.com/diving/ena/

This operator offers three packages to dive Moyo. Divers are met at their hotels in Bali, flown to Sumbawa, and put up at the Kencana Beach Cottage during the course of the diving. All prices are based on two divers. 4 days/3 nights (4 dives) $297; 5 days/4 nights (7 dives) $468; 6 days/5 nights (9 dives) $594. A non-diver joining a diver is about half-price.

Komodo

There are two ways of diving this relatively unexplored region; either by live-aboard vessels based outside of the immediate Komodo area, or by shore-based diving through one of the two dive operators in Labuanbajo. Live-aboard trips are best arranged in Bali, with the best known operation being Grand Komodo Tours & Travel.

GETTING THERE

Theoretically, you can fly from Bali to Labuanbajo, via Bima (eastern Sumbawa), every day at 9:20am ($98). In practice, however, the Bima-Labuanbajo air connection is very unreliable, and you would be better off debarking in Bima ($70 one way), taking a minibus to Sape (2 hrs, $1 public bus, $18 charter), and then boarding the ferry to Komodo and Labuanbajo (9–11 hours to Labuanbajo, departs daily from Sape at 8am, $6). To make this early morning connection, one can either overnight in Sape ($5 for very basic room at one of the local *losmens*) or spend the night in Bima and catch the 5am minibus to Sape.

A much more comfortable, quicker, and less expensive alternative is to board one of the Pelni oceanliners which service Labuanbajo from Bali, Ujung Pandang or Kupang/Waingapu. 1st and 2nd class cabins on the brand-new *Tilongkabila* are as comfortable as any hotel room, the meals excellent, and divers carrying heavy gear needn't worry about overweight baggage.

The *Tilongkbila* makes the 14 hour voyage to Labuanbajo from Ujung Pandang every other Sunday ($48 first class, $30 second) and from Denpasar to Labuanbajo every other Wednesday (24 hours, $78 first class, $60 second). The Pelni ships *Kelimutu* (from Denpasar, every other Tuesday and from Kupang every other Friday) and *Tatamailau* (from Denpasar, every third Tuesday) also service Labuanbajo. Check with any Pelni office for schedules and tickets.

DIVE OPERATORS

Bajo Beach Diving Club Hotel Bajo, Jl. Yos Sudarso, Labuanbajo, Flores, NTT. ☎ (0385) 41008; fax: 41009. Owner Pak Hendrik Chandra offers dive packages (minimum 2 divers) including gear, 2 tanks, guide, and lunch, to Bidadari, Sabolan/Sebayur, and Komodo/Rinca for $50–$75/diver. This is based on local diesel boat transport, although for a slight price increase he can arrange a speed boat. The club has 2 compressors, 30 tanks and 10 full sets of dive gear. Groups of 10 persons or more receive complimentary meals and lodging at the Hotel Bajo, otherwise, AC rooms $36D.

Should you want to take a break from diving, Pak Hendrik offers land-based tour packages. One includes a cave (*Batu Cermin*), a whip fight and an area where there is petrified wood. $50–$125/person depending on group size.

Grand Komodo Tours & Travel (Komodo Alor Safari) Main office: Jl. Hang Tua No. 27, Denpasar 80034, Bali. ☎ (0361) 287166, Fax: (0361) 287165. In Bima: Jl. Sukarno Hatta 45, Bima, Sumbawa, NTB, ☎ (0374) 42018, Fax: (0374) 42812. In Labuahanbajo: Jl. P.W. Papu, Labuanbajo, Flores, NTT, ☎ (0385) 41377, Fax: (0385) 41378.

E-mail: gkomodot@indosat.net.id
Also: gkomodo@dps.mega.net.id

This experienced outfit, run by the husband and wife team of Nyoman and Reno Kirtya, takes divers to Komodo, Alor and Selayar on two newly-built live-aboards, the *Komodo Plus I* and *II*, both 20-meter hardwood boats built in the Bugis style. Accomodations on the ship are simple, but comfortable. The *Komodo Plus I* sleeps up to 18 people in a large central cabin (non-private bunks), while the *KP II* has private cabins for 12 divers. Groups fly directly from Bali to Bima, Sumbawa, where they are met by Grand Komodo and driven overland to Sape, where the boats are docked. The southern—and best—sites were all pioneered by Grand Komodo, and this live-aboard is still the best way to dive them.

The outfit has a number of departures for Komodo, Alor and their newest site, Selayar Island south of Sulawesi. Basically, the packages offer a week of diving at each site. Some prices:

Komodo (1 week)	$750
Alor (1 week)	$750
Komodo and Alor (2 weeks)	$1,350
Selayar (1 week)	$750

These prices cover everything except airfare to Bima and drinks. Any of Grand Komodo's four Sape-based boats can also be chartered, and will meet your party in any of the diving areas:

Komodo Plus I or *II*	$800/day
Getting the boat in position	$350/day
Kembang Laut (4 divers)	$600/day
Getting the boat in position	$250/day
Kartika (capacity for 3 divers)	$400/day
Getting the boat in position	$175/day

An excellent combination for a small group is to charter one of the boats and hire Bali-based dive guide Wally Siagan—who did much of the initial pioneering for Grand Komodo, and who currently is familiar with almost 50 sites in the Komodo area—to come along as a guide. Contact Grand Komodo and Wally for details.

Grand Komodo also now offers a land-based dive operation from Labuahanbajo, which is convenient for some of the northern sites.

Grand Komodo runs live-aboard tours to Komodo for dragon-viewing: 3-day tour: $290/person (from Bima), 4 day tour: $330/person.

Komodo Kalypso Dive Center (Varanus Tours and Travel). Main office: Jl. Yos Sudarso 10, P.O. Box 3, Labuanbajo 86554 Flores NTT. ☎ (0385) 41007, fax: 41202. In Jakarta: Varanus Tours and Travel, Jl. Pulonangka Timur III C/3 Jakarta 13260. ☎ /Fax: (021) 4716360.

Owner/guide Pak Linus has been running dive tours in the Komodo area since 1992, and is very knowledgeable about diving in the area. This is a small, but safe and friendly operation, with 2 compressors, 26 tanks, 7 sets of rental gear and a twin-engined fiberglass speedboat. Day trips, including full gear, 2 dives, guide and lunch box run from $75/person for the closer reefs (Sabolan, Bididari, etc) up to $100/person for diving around Komodo and Rinca (using local wooden boats instead attracts a discount of $10/person). Expect a discount for multiple-day diving as well. Pak Linus is very flexible with his packages, and can also arrange night dives and land-based tours to Komodo/Rinca or Western Flores.

Pro Dive Komodo Batu Gosok, Labuanbajo, ☎ (0361) 286336. Bali office: Jl. Sekar Waru No. 25, Sanur, Bali 80238. ☎ (0361) 286336, ☎ /fax: (0361) 288756.

E-mail: prodivebali@bali-paradise.com
Web: www.prodive.com.au

This Australian-operated company maintains a diving resort—Puribagus Komodo—on Batu Gosok Island, near Labuanbajo. They have three dive boats, and the manager is a PADI assistant instructor. Pro Dive also runs three- and four-day cruises, including diving, to Komodo on its large ship the *Bali Sea Dancer*.

Maumere   City code: 0382

Maumere is the visitor's center of Flores, offering the best accommodations and infrastructure for tourists. With the recent closing of the most famous of the Maumere dive resorts, there is currently only one land-based operation here.

Merpati schedules daily flights between Maumere and Bali ($97); Bima, Sumbawa ($52); and Kupang ($33). Flights to Ujung Pandang, Sulawesi ($60) run three days/week. Connections to Surabaya and Jakarta through Bali.
Merpati Jl. Don Thomas 18, ☎ (0382) 21342.

DIVE OPERATORS

Seaworld Club (Waiara Cottages) P.O. Box 3, Maumere, Flores, NTT, ☎ (0382) 21570. 38 rooms and bungalows. Lunch ($4), dinner ($5) available. $10–$25S, $15–$30D including breakfast. Daily dive rates, with accommodations, $70–$80 S, $75–$85 D; diving only, $60 for two-tank day with boat. 6 day/6 night dive packages, $420–$480S, $390–$450 D. BC/regulator rental, $15/day. Various land tours available, including Kelimutu (minimum, 4 persons) $15 per head.

Sumba

Currently, the only diving available on Sumba is through a luxury resort on the southwest coast, south of the West Sumba capital of Waikabubak.
Sumba Reef Lodge P.T. Indonesia Adventure Sport, P.O. Box 1018, Tuban, Bali. ☎ /fax: (0361) 731172. A luxury resort with 23 villas, 7 of them with private swimming pools. The average room rate is $250/night. Diving: two boat dives, unlimited tanks for beach diving, accommodation and food runs $250/person per day. Game fishing is the same. For trips south to the camp at Rua Nature Reserve, including two dives, accommodation and food, $150/person per day.

Kupang   Includes Roti and Alor

Kupang city code: 0380

Kupang is a large town, the capital of the Nusa Tenggara Timur province, and has four one-star hotels and a good range of more moderately priced accommodations. English is spoken at most places.

Kupang's El Tari airport is 15 km east of downtown Kupang. A taxi from the airport costs $4. Try to get one to yourself or you could end up running all over town while others are dropped off.

Kupang receives daily Merpati flights from Jakarta ($200), Bali ($103), Ujung Pandang ($85), and Maumere ($40) among other cities in the region. Also, international flights from Darwin, Australia, land here.
Merpati Jl. Kosasih No. 2. ☎ (0380) 833833, 822884, 823111, 831949, and 832662.

DIVE OPERATORS

Dive Trek East A division of P.T. Asmara Duyung Mas watersports company. Jl. El Tari No. 19, P.O. Box 1120, Kupang, Timor, NTT. ☎ (0380) 821154, Fax: (0380) 824833.
E-mail: divealor@kupang.wasantara.net.id

This outfit is run by the Australian father and son team, divemaster Graeme Whitford and PADI dive instructor Donovan Whitford, that began diving this area while managing Pitoby Watersports. Theirs is an efficient agency, and the biggest in this part of Indonesia. They offer packages for diving Kupang, Roti, and Alor.

The Whitford's offer all-inclusive packages, beginning with a pick-up at Kupang airport, ranging from 4 days/3 nights to 11 days/10 nights. Here's a sample:
Kupang Bay 4 days/3 nights (5 dives), $245; 6 days/5 nights (9 dives) $345; 8 days/7 nights (11 dives) $595.
Roti 5 days/4 nights (3 dives) $375; 7 days/6 nights (7 dives) $575.
Kupang and Roti 8 days/7 nights (10 dives) $645; 11 days/10 nights (15 dives), $895.
Alor 6 days/5 nights (8 dives) $750 and 8 days/7 nights (12 dives) $1,150. Prices are twin share, and include everything—accommodation, boats, etc.—except airfare from Kupang to Kalabahi, Alor (Merpatai, $80 RT). Accommodation is in new AC rooms with attached bath at a *losmen* style hotel. Non-divers 50% of divers price; single supplement, $25 day. Gear rental 15% of package price.

Walk-in rates are $100/day (2 dives) including gear rental, transfers and lunch, but are subject to space available. Booking ahead is highly recommended. The Whitfords offer a full range of PADI diving courses as well, and can organize charters to other sites in Eastern Indonesia.
Grand Komodo Tours & Travel (Komodo Alor Safari (see above under Komodo). This outfit offers packages and charters to Alor in its liveaboards *Komodo Plus I* and *II*. See above under "Komodo" (pg. 291) for contact details.

Sulawesi PRACTICALITIES

5

Sulawesi is a rugged, forested volcanic island in north-central Indonesia. The island sends one of its strange, flailing peninsulas reaching northeast, and this is where the developed dive sites are: the Bunaken group near Manado, the capital of North Sulawesi, the Lembeh Strait on the east coast of the peninsula, north of the port town of Bitung, and the Sangihe and Talaud island groups, stretching to the north. Still unexplored sites off Selayar and the Tukang Besi archipelago, and the Togian Islands in south and central Sulawesi remain to be explored.

Prices in US dollars. S = Single; D = Double; T = Triple; AC = Air-conditioning.

Manado City code: 0431

Manado—the entry point to diving North Sulawesi—is a large city and is well-connected by air to the rest of Indonesia. The Dr. Sam Ratulangi airport Airport is 7 km outside of town, and taxi coupons to just about anywhere in town cost $3–$4. If you reserve ahead with one of the dive operators, they will meet you at the airport. Airport information, ☎ (0431) 852117 or 860865.

GETTING THERE

Because of the Garuda/Merpati monopoly on flights, in the past it was a long and expensive proposition to get to Manado. No international flights were allowed to land, except for a short-lived and mysteriously ended series of flights from Guam. This has now changed.

There is a direct, twice a week, 3.5-hour run from/to Singapore by SilkAir, the daughter airline of Singapore Airlines. There are also rumors of flights from Taiwan, Japan, and Korea. If these come to pass, the attractions of North Sulawesi will be appreciated by many more visitors.
Garuda Jl. Diponegoro 15, ☎ (0431) 864535, 852154, Fax: (0431) 862242. Open 8am to 4pm weekdays, Sat. 7:30am–12:30pm, Sun. 8am–12 noon. Airbus flights daily to Ujung Pandang ($153), Denpasar ($254) and Jakarta ($345).
Merpati Jl. Sudirman 132, ☎ (0431) 864027, 864028, 881512. Same hours as Garuda. Ambon, 4 weekly flights ($167); Bali, daily ($254) continuing to Jakarta ($414); also daily to Gorontalo, ($70) and Ternate ($73); four flights weekly to Naha, near Tahuna, Sagihe Besar ($79); twice weekly to Sorong ($158); twice weekly to Mangole ($90); twice weekly to Melanguane on Karakelong Island in the Talaud

group ($107); once weekly to Palu ($108); and once weekly to Poso ($120).
SilkAir Jl. Sarapung No. 5. ☎ (0431) 863744 and 863844, Fax: (0431) 853841. The direct singapore lfight route is welcome particularly by divers, as it is more convenient, less time-consuming and less exhausting than transferring through Jakarta. Punctual flight schedule, reliable reservations and bookings, and proficient service. Twice weekly to Singapore ($445 one-way, $742 RT).

LOCAL TRANSPORTATION

Any of the dive resorts will be able to arrange some kind of transport for you if you want to sightsee or travel anywhere. There are also several forms of public transportation around Manado.
Oplet. Travel around the city is by *oplet*, tiny minivans one enters by the rear. They run regular routes, and the destination is displayed on a sign in the front. The driver will stop for you anywhere along the route, just flag them down as you would a taxi. When you get to your stop, pull the cord inside (or bang on the window behind the driver if the cord is broken, as it often is) and the vehicle will stop sharply. The fare is Rp250. Larger minibuses (*mikrolet*) also run regular routes. These cost the same, but carry more people and one enters on the side.

The problem with this form of transportation (in addition to the fact that they are cramped) is making sure you get in the right one. If you are confident you have gotten past this hurdle, don't be overly alarmed if the little truck veers off the main road and starts heading down a tiny back alley somewhere. Passengers often make special requests to be dropped off at their doorsteps.
Taxis. Two types of *taksi* operate in Manado. One is unmarked with no meter, and you must

Sulawesi 5

negotiate a price to your particular destination. The other type are metered white sedans with signs on their roofs. The four taxi companies are: **Indra Kelana Taxi Company,** ☎ 852033, **Dian Taksi,** ☎ 851010, **Merit** ☎ 861195, 861465, and **Cender** ☎ 864422.The Merit fare for the first km is Rp900 and Rp450 for subsequent kms; Dian taxis run Rp 700 for the first km and Rp400 for each additional km. Indra and Cender fares vary considerably, depending on who's driving and what adjustments have been made on the meters—if there is one in the taxi. Your best bet is to negotiate the fare before you get into the car. Some drivers will try to take advantage of visitors, especially on night tours of the town, so be on your guard!

Charters. One can charter any of the above forms of transport. Empty *oplets* can be chartered for around $1.60/hr (no minimum), and *mikrolets* for a bit more. Taxis can be hired by the hour, around $2.75/hr (3-hr minimum around town, 5-hr minimum out of town).

Bunaken Island Small local passenger boats motor to Bunaken, usually in the early morning or late afternoon, with passage costing about $1.50. These boats leave from Kuala Jenkey, between the bridge and the mouth of the Tondano River and occasionally from the harbor area near the fish-auction market.

TOURIST SERVICES

Communications

Post office (*Kantor Pos*) Jl. Sam Ratulangi 23, 5 minutes walk south of Kawanua City Hotel: 8am–8pm, Mon.–Fri.; to 6 pm, Sat. and Sun. **Telephone office** (*Perumtel*) Jl. Sam Ratulangi between the Kawanua City Hotel and the post office (opposite side of the street). Open 24 hrs.

Photo Processing

There are many shops in Manado and the dive outfits can take your film in for you. If you are taking care of this yourself, we recommend these three services:

Angkasa Color Photo Service Jl. Yos Sudarso 20, ☎ 862467. One-day slide service.

Fuji Star Plaza Jl. Sam Ratulangi 203. ☎ 863469. Probably the most proficient in photo procesing in Manado. Good color reproduction and a professional choice of camera equipment.

Modern Photo Film Co Fuji Image Plaza, Jl. Wenang Permai, Bl. J/4, between Jumbo Supermarket and the central square. ☎ 868226.

Bookstores

Borobudur has a resonable choice of English, and German dictionaries, English language Indonesia travel books, and a good selection of postcards. **Jumbo Supermarket**, Jl. Letjen. Suprapto 1 (☎ 863236) gets regular supplies of *Asian Diver* magazine and has a good stock of Rudie Kuiter's *Tropical Reef-Fishes of the Western Pacific—Indonesia And Adjacent Waters*, Periplus postcards, and the English-language daily, *Jakarta Post*. **President**, located in the center of town (in the theater complex) has a selection of regional maps. The **Kawanua City Hotel** receives Time magazine, although a bit late.

PT Serimpi–Divex, located in the Wenang district, about 50m from the Plaza complex are the regional distributors for *Asian Diver* magazine and stocks Periplus postcards. Free magazine delivery within Manado. The first *Manado Diver's Log* is now available. The log book is designed for usage with PADI dive tables, good for 100 dives, $10. Contact Deby, ☎ 851123, 852123, Fax: 867667.

Tours and Guides

These can be arranged through the dive clubs, or at a travel agency or some of the hotels. Tours available include the popular day trip through the Minahasa area ($30), Tomohon and the crater lake of the Mahawu volcano ($25), and the much less frequent jaunt, with 4-wheel-drive vehicle, through a section of the Tangkoko–Batuangus–Dua Saudara Nature Reserve ($45). Prices based on a minimum of two clients.

North Sulawesi Tourism Office Easy to find, just beyond the Garuda Indonesia office on Jl. Diponegoro. ☎ 851723, 851835, Fax: 852730. Open 7am–2pm, Mon-Fri. Drs. Gromang and his staff will be happy to attend to any traveller or visitor seeking assistance, information or advice concerning tourism in Sulawesi. Maps and brochures of the North Sulawesi region are available upon request.

DIVE OPERATORS

There are a growing number of dive operators taking divers to the Bunaken group. Accommodations have also been built on Bunaken Island itself, and at least two operators offer diving from there. Since the island is part of a nature reserve, many have questioned the wisdom of allowing building there at all.

For serious diving, we suggest booking a package—including accommodations and board—with one of the more established dive centers on the mainland. At least three of the operators listed below have more than a decade of experience in the area.

Barracuda Molas Beach, Dusun II, Manado, Sulawesi, 9242. About 10 kms north of Manado. ☎ (0431) 854279, 854288, Fax: (0431) 864848. For reservations contact: Alfred R. Lefrandt. Barracuda, established in 1989, offers chalet-type accommodations on a small hill, the only one of the three resorts that has a view.

Like Murex, it has a quiet charm. They also have a glass-bottom boat, on-boat dive profiles; the larger craft are equipped with radio. They also carry oxygen onboard during their longer trips or for the shipwreck dives. Their boats are new, and in good shape: 3 large dive boats, and 6 dive boats, each with 80 hp engines. They also have a glass-bottom sight-seeing and dive boat—which carries up to 28—with two 80 hp engines. PADI courses available include (training and certification): open water ($395), advanced ($145), rescue ($300), divemaster ($450).

Day rate (2 dives, tanks, weights, boat, lunch)—$65, min. 2 persons. Sightseeing, $30; snorkeling, $40. Package rate, including full room and board and two dives, $80–$95/day. Night dive, $20 extra. 6 dive masters, 10 dive guides, 2 instructors. 100 tanks, 30 BCs, 25 regulators, and 8 UW lights.

Barracuda offers dives off Bangka Island, at no extra charge. They take you there by catamaran (2.5 hrs) and bring you back overland from Likupang (1.5 hrs).

Accommodations: 21 double rooms $25–$35 bungalow with fan, $35–$42 bungalow with AC. Good seafood restaurant.

Indo-Pacific Divers At the Boulevard Sea-View Hotel, P.O. Box 1014, Manado 95010. ☎ (0431) 859379, Fax: (0431) 859368.
E-mail: kudalaut@manado.wasantara.net.id
Web: www.wp.com/kudalaut
A new PADI-affiliated outfit, run by expat Europeans, specializing in PADI instruction. Two of the four dive managers are marine biologists. Their operation is 40 minutes from Bunaken. Two dives, $70. At least 15 different courses offered. Open water, $420.

Manado Diving Center (MDC) Jl. Bethesda 75. P.O. Box 11, Manado 95115. ☎ (0431) 862880, 866622, 865001, Fax: (0431) 863857. MDC has been around for several years and offers dive tours, hotel accommodations, as well as national and international package tours. They have bungalow accommodation on Bunaken Island at reasonable rates. 3 PADI divemasters, 5 dive guides and 1 instructor for an open-water dive course. Accommodations: 15 rooms. $17.50–$21 standard, $47.50 suite.

Dive packages (2 dives, tanks, weights, boat, dive guide, full board)—$86S, $75D standard; $120S, $100D suite. All rooms with AC, TV and phone. Additional third dive or night dive, $20. Snorkeling tour for min. 3 people, $35. Tour of

Bunaken island for min. 4 people, $25; Minahasa land tour, $50.

Murex (Manado Underwater Explorations). About 10 km south of Manado. Jl. Sudirman 28. P.O. Box 236, Manado 95123. ☎ (0431) 866280, ☎ /Fax: 852116. European representative: DIVEX Indonesia, P.O. Box 5352, 30053 Hannover, Germany. ☎ (49 511) 647-6129, Fax: (49 511) 647-6120.

Murex, which has been in operation since 1987, is the smallest, quietest and most "intimate" of the three pioneering resorts (NDC, Murex, Barracuda), with very nice landscaping featuring lotus pools. It has the best boats, and its guides all use computers and safe second stages. It is also located furthest from the dive sites. Murex is run by Dr. Hanny Batuna, a medical doctor and dive instructor, who divides his time between several occupations. Dr. Batuna has been diving in the area since the '70s. He started Murex in 1987.

Quite good, wide diving boats. The ride from here to Bunaken is a bit longer than that from the Molas-based clubs, and the boats cut through more open water (thus waves and spray). Good use of space on boats for tank and equipment storage and suiting up. Murex also runs two live-aboard dive boats, the Serenade and the Arlena. (See below under live-aboards.)

Accommodations: 19 rooms in both old-fashioned and modern cottages $25–$30 fan, $30–$35 standard AC, $35–$40 superior AC.

Day rate (2 dives, tanks, weights, boat, lunch), $70/person, minimum 3 in group. Package rate (double occupancy room, meals, 2 dives) $100/person. Dives to the Lembeh Strait or Bangka Island, $20 extra, as it's a lot further from this site. 60 tanks, 6 BCs, 12 regulators. Medical doctor and NAUI instructor Hanny Batuna offers a 40-hour dive course leading to NAUI certification ($250). 8 dive guides, 5 divemasters, and 2 instructors.

Nusantara Diving Centre (NDC) Molas Beach, P.O. Box 1015, Manado 95242, Sulawesi. ☎ (0431) 860638 and 863988, Fax: (0431) 860368 and 854668.

E-mail: ndc@mdo.mega.net.id
Web: mdo.mega.net.id/ndc

This is the oldest, largest, and liveliest resort in the area. The center was started by Loky Herlambang almost 25 years ago, and some of his devoted staff have been working for NDC for 15 years. Located close to the sea, but the beach is mangrove and mud. The operation has a fun, local feel, and at night the guitars often come out. NDC has 11 boats with double 40 hp outboards, 45 guides, 350 tanks, 50 sets of rental gear, and 4 dive instructors.

Day rate (2 dives, tanks, weights, boat, lunch), min. two persons, $60. Night dive (after two day dives) $20 extra. Package rates (2 dives, room, meals) run $70 to $100, depending on the room. Rooms (43 available)

w/o diving run $7.50–$10 economy, $15–$20 standard fan, $35–$40 AC. Full set of rental gear, $20/day, $15 if you have your own mask, snorkel and fins. Snorkeling or sightseeing available. Open water dive course (PADI or SSI) $500 including private instructor. No pool, all beginning underwater instruction takes place on a shallow reef. Reservations recommended, especially for July, August, and December. Mastercard, Visa and American Express accepted.

Novotel Manado Jl. Sam Ratulangi No. 22. ☎ (0431) 851245 and 851174, Fax: (0431) 863545. All marine activities operate under the supervision of two Australian dive professionals with PADI Instructor ratings. Novotel will operate 8 high-powered fiberglass dive boats, each with a capacity of 20 divers, plus two large passenger vessels (one for 100 passengers, the other for 200 passengers) for sightseeing cruises around the marine park. The largest vessel is ideal for special functions, banquets, and parties. A semi-submersible viewer boat, Aqua Scoop, with a capacity of 40, affords tours around the marine park. 5 divemasters, 30 dive guides, 2 instructors. Open water, advance, rescue, divemaster, and specialty courses offered.

Accommodations: Four-star hotel with all the amenities, including a swimming pool with a magnificent view of Bunaken Island, fitness center and cauna, and seafood restaurant. Jet-ski and windsurfing rentals, daily trips on semi-submersible viewer, fishing trips, and land excursions and sightseeing tours available. $105 standard, $120 superior.

Dive packages: 4 nights in four-star hotel, 4 days buffet breakfast, 3 days diving (2 dives/day), 1 night dive optional—$379, tanks, weights, boat, dive guide, airport transfer. Other dive package arrangements are available upon request. Additional third dive/night dive, $40. Glassbottom boat tour, $38.

Likupang

Paradise Beach Hotel & Resort Desa Maen, Likupang. ☎ (0431) 868200, 868868, 868222, 868880; Fax: (0431) 862200, 864888. 32 km from Sam Ratulangi International Airport at the northern tip of North Sulawesi. Opened in March 1996, Paradise Beach Hotel offers 5-star comfort combined with 450 hectares of unspoiled tropical jungle, 2.5 kms of white sand beaches, clear seas and good reefs.

The hotel runs joint ventures with Eurodivers, a PADI-affiliated dive operator. Two new compressors and 40 tanks, 30 regulators, 20 BCs, and several Aladdin computers for rent. Likupang is at the tip of Sulawesi's northern peninsula, and this outfit has pioneered some new sites in Lembeh and around Bangka island.

An impressive, well-organized outfit. Several dive courses available, open water $425.

Accommodations: 320 rooms and luxury suites. 3 restaurants, business center, tennis courts, watersports, diving center and golf course. $130–$150 standard, $250 deluxe, $350–$550 suite.

Day rate (includes tanks, weights, dive guide for lagoon and house reef dives): Single dive, $45; 5 dives, $210; 10 dives, $400; 15 dives, $550; six day no limit (including night dive), $420. Group rate for a minimum of 6 divers available, but must register 30 days before arrival. Fishing tour, $400.

Bunaken Island

Bastiaano's Island Cottages Bunaken Island Jl. Kol. Sugiono 31, Manado. ☎ (0431) 863417, 867648, 853566; fax: 863629. Any diver taking a lunch break on the Liang Beach of Bunaken Island will surely "discover" these cottages. Located in the heart of the marine park, all cottages are sited at the beachfront with an exceptional view of the lagoon and Manado Tua volcano on the horizon. Conveniently equipped, carefully landscaped. Sightseeing tours, open sea tuna fishing, and boat charter can be arranged. Diving rates are $65–$80/person, including 2 dives, tanks, weights, boat, and guide, minimum 2 divers. $20 for room, full board, coffee and tea. For guests wishing to stay more than 4 nights, free boat transportation from Manado to Bunaken can be arranged.

Tirta Satwa Diving Center P.O. Box 1082, Manado. ☎ (0431) 856954 and 856314, Fax: (0431) 865164. Offers CMAS courses. Scuba dive tour for minimum 2 divers, 2 dives plus boat, tanks, weights, and guide, $50. Additional third dive or night dive, $30. Economy bungalows on Bunaken, $25S, $30D. Bungalows on Siladen Island, $10S, $20D.

LIVE-ABOARDS

Liburan Adventure Diving Tours P.O. Box 1449, Manado 95001. ☎ /Fax: (0431) 869849. European reservations through DIVEX Indonesia, P.O. Box 5352, 30053 Hanover, Germany, ☎ /Fax: (49) 5043-3459.

This live-aboard boat started operations in June 1995 and offers dive tour cruises throughout the North Sulawesi and Maluku areas. This 16m boat has a cruising speed of 13 knots and offers accommodations for 10 divers. The boat is equipped with marine radio, sonar GPS, Bauer compressor, a new range of equipment, and 12 liter aluminium dive tanks. There are two toilets andshowers, a small conveniently equipped kitchen and a spacious upper deck. The food on board is excellent and there's always plenty of it. Cold beer and other beverages are available at moderate prices.

All diving activities are under the supervision of Henry Maulany, a master scuba diver who can tailor your diver excursions in these areas.

Package rates per person per day (all including tanks, weights, divemaster, and hotel/airport transfer): Bunaken Marine Park—3 dives, lunch, $85 (min. 2 divers); extra dive $20. Bunaken Marine Park with accommodation on the Liburan—no limit diving, all meals, $110 (min. 4 divers); Sangihe–Talaud Islands, Biaro, Siau, Togian Islands, or Maluku (Halmahera, Ternate, Ambon, Banda Naira, Saparua)—7 days, accommodation and all meals on board, no limit, additional land/island excursions, $145 (min. 6 divers).

Serenade See above under Murex for information and reservations. The *Serenade* is fully air-conditioned and has 7 twin sharing rooms. She has a depth sounder and radar, carries 35–40 tanks, and has two Bauer compressors on board. She is good for 8–10 knots. Tours the North Sulawesi district, including Bunaken Marine Park, Bangka, Biaro, Taliwei, and features spectacular dive sites around the remote Sangihe-Talaud islands. The package rates per person per day $165, includes accommodations in a twin-shared cabin, full board meals, no limit diving, airport pick-up, tanks, weights, and guides.

Also in Dr. Batuna's program is a smaller craft called the *Arlena,* which accommodates 4 divers, and has a cabin shower and an outdoor shower. Tour operations are similar to those of the *Serenade,* and rates are somewhat cheaper, about $125/person per day. Chartering the *Arlena* is more of a bargain for a smaller group.

ACCOMMODATIONS

Manado Beach Hotel Tasik Ria. ☎ 67001; fax: 67007. This four-star hotel lies 20 km south of Manado, just beyond Mokupa. An Australian-managed dive center and marina have just set up shop next door and will run joint diving operations with the hotel beginning in June. $110–$650.

Mokupa Palace Cottages Jl. Trans-Sulawesi, Mokupa, Kec. Tombariri, Minahasa, Manado. ☎ 54277, 54272, fax: 54277. Reservations in Europe: DIVEX Indonesia, see Murex above. 14 rooms. Small resort located 20 km south of Manado with an overwhelming view of the Minahasa mountains in the back and a small beach cove sheltered by mangroves and palm trees in the front. Several small lotus ponds, scenic beach front with view over Manado Bay. Fully AC, spacious bathrooms, plus separate tiled room for storing and rinsing dive equipment. The house reef is excellent for beginning divers and snorkeling, and there are still several unexplored reefs in the vicinity. Swimming pool, tennis court. sightseeing and snorkeling tours available; diving operations commence during the course of the high season. $40–$50 standard, $55–$65 superior.

Ranopaso Cottages, Restaurant & Hot Springs Koya Tondano, Minahasa 95618. ☎ (0436) 21585, 21600; fax: (0436) 21585. For a refreshing change from dive touring adventures. Ranopaso is located approximately 3 km from the Minahasan town of Tondano, in the midst of traditional rice fields. Because of the altitude, the climate is quite cool, so it may be advisable to bring along some extra T-shirts and long sleeves for the evenings. The hot water springs are renown for their healing effect of skin diseases, rheumatism and similar illnesses. For the healthy diver, it revitalizes the circulatory system. However, it is not recommended to take a hot bath after diving, and divers shold consider going to Ranopaso the day after diving because of the altitude. A hot bath costs $1.50/person/hour.

The resort location is an ideal starting point for Minahasa excursions. Lake Tondano is just a walk around the corner and offers a spectacular view of the former volcanic lake, traditional fishing villages, and a neverending plateau of rice fields. $15–$40, not including tax and service.

Tagaroa Seaside Cottages c/o Mrs. Gerry Lolong, P.O. Box 1068, Manado. ☎ /fax: 61100, fax: 67667. 6 rooms. This resort is probably one of the smallest of its kind in the Manado area, however, it is amongst the top ranking for landscaping, innovative bungalow design and resort location. Tucked away behind the Tanawangko hills, approximately 28 km south of Manado, the resort offers an intimate atmosphere and one of the most captivating scenic views of the surrounding rain forests and the Bunaken National Marine Park. Located virtually on top of the Arakan Wawontulap Marine Park, divers and snorkelers can encounter a vivacious underwater environment and a good variety of hard and soft corals.

Diving tours range between $75–$100, depending on location and distance, and include 2 dives, tanks, weights, divemaster, and boat, minimum 4 divers. Land tours can be arranged for 3 participants to Minahasa, $30/person, and Tangkoko, $40. Good food and service is standard. $50S, $60D, includes room, full board, airport transfers.

Lembeh Bitung city code: 0438

Lembeh Strait is on the other side of the peninsula from Manado, just north of the town of Bitung, North Sulawesi's busiest port. The long, narrow island of Lembeh blocks the weather, protecting the port year-round. Kungkungan Bay Resort is the only dive operator on the east coast of North Sulawesi, and the pioneer of most of the Lembeh Strait sites. The resorts on the other side will take you to Lembeh upon special request, but it is far easier at Kungkungan. There are a few *losmen* in Bitung, but Kungkungan is a self-contained resort, not set up for walk-on dive customers. If you want to dive here, you need to book with Kungkungan.

Kungkungan Bay Resort On a bay of the same name in the village of Tanduk Rusa, about 5 kilometers north of Bitung. Mailing address: P.O. Box 16, Bitung, Sulawesi Utara, Indonesia. ☎ (0438) 30300; Fax: (0438) 31400. Make reservations through the U.S. office: Jeremy H. Burns, P.O. Box 5577, Concord, CA 94521. ☎ (510) 825-1939, Fax: (510) 825-0105.

This quiet, beautifully designed resort sits on the site of an old coconut plantation, facing a small bay north of Bitung, in the protected waters of the Lembeh Strait. The suites are spacious, all face the water, and have comfortable porches. A large lobby/restaurant, built out over the water, is the center of activities. The operation has one dive boat, several dozen tanks and a new Bauer compressor.

Accommodations only: $156S, $182D, plus tax and service charge. Day rate for 2 dives, lunch, boat, tanks, weights, and guide, $80. Additional third dive/night dive, $45.

Packages: 7 nights/8 days ($2,035S, $1,503D/person; 3 nights/4 days ($820S, $592D/person); additional days ($307S, $231D/person). Prices include beach-front suite, 2 boat dives a day, all meals, taxes, service charges and transfers. Beach dives are included, at the discretion of the divemaster.

Ujung Pandang

City code: 0411

Caraka Travel Indo Jl. Samalona 12, Ujung Pandang 90174 Sulawesi. ☎ 318877; fax: 318889. Dutch general manager Jan Wezendonk and his assistant Andrea can arrange a wide variety of quality, unique tours throughout Indonesia, including snorkelling/island hopping trips within the Spermonde. They specialize in Sulawesi and can arrange trips anywhere within this little-explored island.

Hiu Martil 152 G. Latimojong, Ujung Pandang. ☎ 322717; fax: 314170.

E-mail: hiumart@indosat.net.id

Maintains cottages on Kapopsang island, 1.5 hrs from Ujung Pandang. Variety of dive sites. Equipment rental. CMAS and PADI instruction.

Makassar Diving Center Jl. Ujung Pandang 3, opposite Fort Rotterdam, ☎ 326056; fax: (c/o Shogun Restaurant) ☎ 319842. The manager of MDC, Pak Jeffrey, is also an excellent dive guide and runs a very professional operation.

One day dive trips to sites in the Spermonde archipelago $50–$75/person, depending on distance (minimum 2 divers). The 2 day/1 night trip to Kapoposang (4 dives) $150/person (3 person minimum, all meals included); 3 day/2 night trips (6 dives) costing $200/person. Accomodation on this beautiful coconut-fringed island is in a spacious traditional cottage.

Discount of 10%–20% is given for larger groups. MDC's well-maintained gear includes, per day, mask, snorkel, fins ($5), BC ($7), regulator ($7). Pak Jeffrey speaks good English. **Makassar Gate Beach Hotel** Jl. Pasar Ikan 10, Ujung Pandang. ☎ 325791; fax: 316303. The general manager of this hotel, Australian Robert Hotson, is knowledgeable on the reefs of the area and can arrange boat trips to any of the local islands. He also has jet skiis for hire.

Selayar

The Bali-based Komodo and Alor specialist Grand Komodo has recently added trips to Selayar on its live-aboard itinerary.
Grand Komodo Tours & Travel (Komodo Alor Safari) Main office: Jl. Hang Tua No. 27, Denpasar 80034, Bali. ☎ (0361) 287166, Fax: (0361) 287165. In Bima: Jl. Sukarno Hatta 45, Bima, Sumbawa, NTB, ☎ (0374) 42018, Fax: (0374) 42812. In Labuhanbajo: Jl. P.W. Papu, Labuhanbajo, Flores, NTT, ☎ (0385) 41377, Fax: (0385) 41378.

E-mail: gkomodot@indosat.net.id
Also: gkomodo@dps.mega.net.id
This experienced outfit, run by the husband and wife team of Nyoman and Reno Kirtya, takes divers to Komodo, Alor, and Selayar on two newly-built live-aboards, the *Komodo Plus I* and *II*, both 20-meter hardwood boats built in the Bugis style. Accomodations on the ship are simple, but comfortable. The *Komodo Plus I* sleeps up to 18 people in a large central cabin (non-private bunks), while the *KP II* has private cabins for 12 divers. Groups fly directly from Bali to Bima, Sumbawa, where they are met by Grand Komodo and driven overland to Sape, where the boats are docked.

The outfit has recently added departures to Selayar Island south of Sulawesi:

Selayar (1 week)	$750

This price covers everything except airfare to Bima and drinks, and a week of diving in Komodo can be added on. Any of Grand Komodo's four Sape-based boats can also be chartered:

Komodo Plus I or *II*	$800/day
Getting the boat in position	$350/day
Kembang Laut (4 divers)	$600/day
Getting the boat in position	$250/day
Kartika (capacity for 3 divers)	$400/day
Getting the boat in position	$175/day

OTHER OPTIONS

For those who are independent-mined, another option is to rent gear and several tanks from the **Makassar Diving Center** in Ujung Pandang, take the 4 hour minibus ride to Bira ($4 public bus, $35 charter), and then charter a wooden boat at Bira ($20-$50/day, depending on size of boat and distance of journey). There are a number of charming little homestays in Bira, and David at **Anda Bungalows** is especially helpful in setting up boat charters (including week-long sailboat voyages around Selayar). On your way back to Ujung Pandang, be sure to stop at Tana Beru (25 km from Bira) to observe the amazing craftsmanship displayed in traditional Pinisi boatbuilding.

Tukang Besi

Tukang Besi is the name of a small archipelago extending off from Buton Island, in southeast Sulawesi. This is a remote, and rarely visited area, and offers probably some of the finest diving in Indonesia and, in fact, the world.

A new resort, Wakatobi Divers, has been operating here for the past two years, and the diving has received rave reviews, including in *Undercurrent*. The resort is on the small island of Tolandono, just beside Tomea Island, towards the south of the chain. Another option is joining an Operation Wallacea expedition.
Wakatobi Divers Booking office: 10 Anson Road, 33-17 International Plaza, Singapore 079903. Tel: (65) 235-5060 and 737-0001, Fax: (65) 738-4548 and 732-7077.

E-mail: wakatobi@singnet.com.sg
The resort is run by two expatriate Swiss, Lorenz Mäder and Erwin Wober. It has six guest rooms, in a modest, traditionally designed thatched building. Getting to the area is difficult, but the operators will pick up guests in Kendari, the capital of Southeast Sulawesi, a daily plane ride ($50) from Ujung Pandang. Package rates vary, but a 12-day, unlimited diving package runs $1,650. Contact the Singapore office for more details.
Operation Wallacea Contact: Marine director, Operation Wallacea, 6A Robin Drive, Lew Mansions, Singapore 258264. ☎ (65) 7347693 fax: (65) 7389945. Operation Wallacea offers 2 and 4 week expeditions for divers with a minimum of 20 hours diving experience. No scientific experience necessary. 2 week expeditions cost $1550/person, including boat transfer from Kendari, accommodation,food, and all diving (group discounts available). 4 week expeditions, $2800/person.

Sulawesi **5**

Togian Islands

Getting to the Togians is no small task. One possibility is to hire a minivan with driver from Caraka Travel Indo in Ujung Pandang ($40/day, see Ujung Pandang Practicalities) and make the 20 hour drive to Ampana (the jump-off point for Togian trips), perhaps stopping in Tana Toraja or the Bada Valley in the Sulawesi highlands for sleep and/or cultural sightseeing. From Ampana, catch one of the medium-sized ferries which cross Tomini Bay between Poso and Gorontalo, stopping in the Togians ($5, 4-6 hrs). If coming from Manado, fly ($60, 1 hr) or bus ($10, 12 hrs) to Gorontalo and catch these same ferries to the Togians on their return journey. You can also fly from Ujung Pandang to Palu ($66 one way, daily flights at 9:30 am), and then catch a bus to Ampana ($10, 10 hrs).

The Tomini Bay ferries have several ports of call in the Togians; Wakai is perhaps the best for diving. Local businessman Edi Yusuf and his charming wife Huntje run the Togian Islands Hotel there, and they arrange flexible snorkelling/diving trips throughout the Togians for very reasonable rates. Pak Edi can suggest good dive sites (and warn you of the areas that are damaged from blast fishing) or simply consult the detailed bathymetric chart they have at the hotel and explore your own best hunches—its hard to go wrong.

You can also debark at Ketupat, rumoured to have a small dive operation as well, or try the island of Melenge-the Indonesian nature NGO YABSHI has a station there and may be willing to rent their dive gear.

DIVE OPERATORS

Togian Islands Hotel Wakai, Kabupaten Poso, Sulawesi Tengah. Owner Pak Edi has 4 sets of dive gear, 7 tanks, a compressor and a twin-engined speedboat. He has a standard 1 day diving package that includes gear, 2 tanks, lunchbox and transport by local wooden boat ($32/person, minimum 2 people), but a far better option is to rent the speedboat for the day ($120, driver, fuel and lunch included) , rent gear if necessary, and explore. Rooms in this charming wooden hotel over the water are $8–$22D, breakfast included. Ibu Huntje can give you suggestions for day walks through the island's forests, home of the elusive *babirusa* (pig-deer).

Donggala

There is a little-known piece of tropical paradise, at Donggala near Palu, in Central Sulawesi— Prince John Dive Resort. The setting is idyllic:

well-built wood-and-thatch cottages, excellent meals, no electricity or TV, white sand beach, and year-round water sports, including scuba diving. Expert divers can explore the wrecks just off Donggala Harbor. The best one, recently discovered and completely unmolested since it sank, lies on her side at 32–50 meters. The boatman at the Prince John can find it.

Prince John Dive Resort Tanjung Karang, Donggala, Sulawesi Tengah. ☎ (0457) 71710. Booking office: P.T. Kathulistiwa Sulawesi, Jl. Mt. Haryono 5, Palu, Sulawesi Tengah, ☎ /Fax: (0451) 23027. Contact: Maureen and Peter Meroniak.

Several bungalows plus 10 rooms. Owner Peter Meroniak is almost always there on weekends. Diver director Irmi Schmidbauer offers PADI courses up to divemaster level.

Accommodations: $8 to $12.50S, $15 to $17.50D, meals included.

Diving: Two-dive package (minimum four divers) $62; with all equipment, $82. 6% discount for six dives, 10% discount for ten dives, 20% discount for 20 dives. Snorkeling tour $20. PADI open water certification, $380.

Sangalaki

At the time of this writing, Borneo Divers, the pioneers of Sangalaki, had ended their operations there. They may try to restart, however, so if you interested in diving Sangalaki or Kakaban you might try to contact them via their office in Malaysia.

Borneo Divers and Sea Sports Head office: 9th Floor, Menara Jubili 88000, Kota Kinabalu, Sabah, Malaysia. ☎ 60 (88) 222226 (8 lines), Fax: (88) 221550.
E-mail: bdivers@po.jaring.my
Web: www.jaring.my/bdivers/

Derawan Island

Currently, the only way to dive Sangalaki and Kakaban is with Derawan Resort on Derawan Island.
Derawan Resort Derawan Island. Bookings through: Benakutai Hotel OSA 202, Jl. A. Yani, Balikpapan, East Kalimantan 76113, ☎ (0542) 20258, 35997, 31896, Fax: (0542) 20293.

This is a well-run operation that has been in business for three years. Two PADI-certified dive masters, both from Bali.

Diving: Around Derawan, $75 for two dives. To either Sangalaki or Kakaban, $120 for two dives plus $40 for the boat, to be split among the divers. Night dive, $35. Regulator and BC rental, $15/day.

Accommodations: 11 AC cottages with attached toilet. $30S, $50D, meals $7.50.

6

Maluku PRACTICALITIES

Maluku consists of three island-strewn provinces, the most spread-out and lightly populated part of Indonesia. Maluku, with thousands of islands, seems a natural for diving. The fish and invertebrate life here is rich, and little disturbed, but in all but a few areas access is difficult. In some of the areas where diving has been developed for a while, such as the Bandas, the airplanes are small, have limited weight allowance, and and are still rather irregular. It is certainly worth any effort to dive here, however.

Prices in US dollars. S = Single; D = Double; T = Triple; AC = Air-conditioning.

Ambon

City code 0911

Pattimura Airport is on Ambon Island's Hitu Peninsula across the bay from Ambon City—37 kilometers and 45 minutes by road. A vehicle and passenger ferry runs every few minutes between Poka and Galala, where the bay narrows, which cuts the traveling distance in half. Sometimes a long queue of vehicles waits at the ferry, so it might be faster to take the long way around. In either case, the airport taxis charge either $9 or $10 (air-conditioned cars) for the trip.
Merpati Jl. A. Yani. ☎ (0911) 42480; fax: 52572.

GETTING THERE

Merpati flies daily to Ujung Pandang and Jakarta; four times weekly to Denpasar; four times weekly to Tual (Kei Islands); three times weekly to Banda; six times weekly to Ternate and once a week to Manado.

From Ambon to/from Ujung Pandang, $138; Jakarta $282; Surabaya $246; Denpasar (Bali) $204; Manado $200; Ternate $96; Tual $180 and Banda $60.

LOCAL TRANSPORTATION

Taxis and public minibuses (and *becaks*, three-wheeled bicycle carts) provide transportation in and around Ambon town. Taxis run about $3/hr, sometimes with a two-hour minimum. The main transportation center is in the Mardika market.

Private taxis out of town run about $3/hr ($5/hr w/AC). For a round-trip to Hila, including waiting time, a non-AC taxis would cost $20–$30. For a run to Liang, stopping at Natsepa and Waai

(to see the eels) on the way, figure about $30–$35 w/AC, $18 w/o AC.

Crowded minibuses go everywhere around the island, more often in the early morning and late afternoon. Fares run from 15¢ to nearby Galala (6 km) to $ 1.25 to Asilulu (70 km). You can charter one of these for about $5–$7.50/hr.

DIVE OPERATORS

P.T. Daya Patal Tour and Travel Jl. Said Perintah 53, Ambon 97126. ☎ (0911) 53344, 52498, 41136, 41821; fax: 54127. Contact: Tony Tomasoa.

P.T. Daya Patal is at present one of two dive operators (and one new club) in Ambon. They specialize in diving around Saparua and nearby islands. (See below for their resort on Saparua.) They can arrange boats, tanks, guides, food, and, if needed, a compressor. While there are no certified dive guides yet, staff members can show you where the good spots are located. We had superb diving with this outfit, with all arrangements running as planned. See below, under Saparua, for prices, including pickup at the Ambon airport and transfer direct to Saparua.
Ambon Dive Centre Jl. Pantai Namalatu, Latuhalat, Ambon 97118 Maluku. ☎ (0911) 62101; fax: 62104. Contacts: Sonny and Carol.

Two dives with lunch, tanks, weights, guide, and boat, $70. Gear for rent : mask/snorkel/fins, $5; regulators, $5; BC, $5; wetsuit, $5; or full set for $15. Video playback, all systems, at the operator's base. Planned E6 slide processing. NAUI courses available, as well as Easy Scuba Experience for non divers, $50.
Amboina Diving Club Jl. A.J. Patty 50. ☎ (0911) 52528; fax: 41364. Also: Jl. Skip SK27/4. ☎ (0911) 42275. Ask for Wempy Sietolus or Robert Chandra.

Two-dive day trips with tanks and weight belts, cost from $45–$100, depending on distance. The Pintu Kota/Seri locations, at $50, are a good value-for-money. Equipment for rent: mask, snorkel, fins $5/day; BC $10/day; regulator with gauges $13. Nikonos V, with macro and wide angle adapters, plus SB102 flash, $95/day. Sony F340 video in housing with one light, $125/day. Nikon 801s in housing with SB 103 flash, $110/day. Both of their dive boats, one 8 meters, the other 10 meters, are powered by twin 40hp Yamaha outboards.

Maulana Ambon Hotel At the roadside, a short way before reaching Tulehu from Ambon City. For inquiries and reservations, contact their Jakarta office: Maulana Hotels, Jl. Bangka Raya 85, Pela Mampang, Jakarta 12720. ☎ (021) 7994885.

Due to open shortly after this writing. A new hotel offering diving in the area. With large swimming pool, bar and restaurant. Room prices $35–$65. Dive packages (min. 2 persons), first dive, $55, then $35 per additional dives. (4 to 6 persons, 20% discount). Additional charges for "intermediary zone" $10/diver plus $40 boat charge; for the "outer zone," $10/person, plus $80 boat charge. PADI dive instruction available.

LAND TOURS

The **Daya Patal** agency also runs non-diving tours to Banda, Ternate, Tanimbar and elsewhere in the Moluccas. Contact Hans Rijoly or Karole, they both speak excellent English. Other operators offering tours:

Sumber Budi Tour and Travel Jl. Mutiara 2/16, ☎ (0911) 51744; fax: 53205

Pedoman Pratama Tours Jl. Dr. Soetono SK 3/2 #65, ☎ (0911) 51703, 53905; fax: 54761.

Lorihua Tropis Jl. Pattimura 12. ☎ (0911) 53075; fax: 72324.

Novita Sari Jl. Mutiara 79. ☎ (0911) 41866; fax: 51444.

ACCOMMODATIONS

We recommend the following hotels and *losmen* in Ambon:

Amboina Jl. Kapitan Ulupaha. ☎ (0911) 41725. 38 rooms. Restaurant, bar, shops, conference room, and TV room. $21S, $32D. New rooms will be 20%–30% more expensive.

Ambon Manise Jl. Pantai Mardika 53A, Ambon 97123. ☎ (0911) 53888, 54888, 55888; fax: 54492, 54493. 99 rooms. A large, new hotel, hosting tourist groups and businessmen, with restaurant, bar, and conference facilities. $40 economy, $50 standard, $60 deluxe, $70 executive, $80–$125 suite. All prices for single occupancy. Add $5 for double; $10 for extra bed.

Beta Jl. Wim Reawaru, ☎ (0911) 53463. 26 rooms. One of the best of the cheaper hotels. $5–8S, $8–$10D.

Cenderawasih Jl. Tulukabessy. ☎ (0911) 52487. 18 rooms with TV. Restaurant. $41S, $45D.

Game Jl. A. Yani. 14 rooms. One of the best of the cheaper hotels. $12.

Manise Jl. W.R. Spratman. ☎ (0911) 42905. 56 rooms. A businessman's hotel. $25–$40S, $30–$45D. Add 20% service charge.

Mutiara Jl. Raya Pattimura, ☎ (0911) 53075, 53076. 31 rooms, all with TV and AC. Pleasant staff, nice atmosphere; many interesting people stay here. Restaurant and bar. English language *Jakarta Post* newspaper available in the lobby for guests. Discount possible if staying more than a couple of days. $29S, $49D.

Santai Beach Resort Contact: Ambon Dive Centre, Pantai Namalatu. ☎ (0911) 62101, fax: 62104. Relaxing, friendly, overlooking the beach.10 minutes walk from Ambon Dive Centre. $26 standard, $42 deluxe.

DINING

The traditional cuisine of Ambon is not one of the archipelago's most exciting. The staples—such as sago cakes—are generally bland. The fruit, however, is excellent, and lobsters ($6–$10 each, best at the Hotel Manise) can often be obtained. We recommend the following:

Amboina Jl. A. Y. Pattimura 63. Best bakery in town, locally-made ice cream. A nice place for a quick meal. Makes a good *roti saucise,* a hot dog in a bun.

Kakatoa Jl. Said Perintah 20. European cooking, run by Belgian couple, the only place in town for a real change from Asian cooking. Very pleasant atmosphere, well run. Count an about $4–$10 per person per meal.

Pondok Asri Next to the Hotel Manise. Features Chinese and Indonesian dishes, as well as Japanese meals ($12–$14), imported US beef ($11–$12) and lots of seafood. Nice decor and quiet setting.

TOURIST SERVICES

Banks and Money-changing

There are plenty of banks around Ambon for money-changing, and credit cards are becoming more popular—the best are Visa and the card issued by Bank Central Asia.

Medical

Kantor Kesehatan Wilayah (District Health Office). ☎ (0911) 52861, 52392. Three doctors—Dr. Krishna (clinic telephone: 52715), Dr. Polanunu and Dr. Ristianto (home phone: 53411, 51526)—speak English.

Rumah Sakit Umum (Public Hospital). ☎ (0911) 53438 ext. 118 or 348.

Pelita Farma pharmacy Jl. Setia Budi. Open 24-hours.

PERIPLUS TRAVEL MAPS
Detailed maps of the Asia Pacific region

This map program was launched in 1993 with the goal of producing accurate and up-to-date maps of every major city and country in the Asia Pacific region. About 12 new titles are published each year, along with numerous revised editions. Titles in **BOLDFACE** are already available. Titles in *ITALICS* are scheduled for publication in 1999/2000.

Yogyakarta	ISBN 0-945971-42-7

JAPAN REGIONAL MAPS
Kyoto	ISBN 962-593-143-0
Osaka	ISBN 962-593-110-4
Tokyo	ISBN 962-593-109-0

KOREA REGIONAL MAPS
Pusan	ISBN 962-593-128-7
Seoul	ISBN 962-593-127-9

MALAYSIA REGIONAL MAPS
Johor Bahru	ISBN 0-945971-98-2
Kuala Lumpur	ISBN 0-945971-75-3
Malacca	ISBN 0-945971-77-X
Penang	ISBN 0-945971-76-1
West Malaysia	ISBN 962-593-129-5
Sabah	ISBN 0-945971-78-8
Sarawak	ISBN 0-945971-79-6

NEPAL REGIONAL MAP
Kathmandu	ISBN 962-593-063-9

NEW ZEALAND REGIONAL MAPS
Auckland	ISBN 962-593-130-9
Wellington	ISBN 962-593-131-7

THE PHILIPPINES REGIONAL MAPS
Cebu	ISBN 962-593-126-0
Manila	ISBN 962-593-124-4

TAIWAN REGIONAL MAPS
Kaohsiung	ISBN 962-593-133-3
Taipei	ISBN 962-593-132-5

THAILAND REGIONAL MAPS
Bangkok	ISBN 0-945971-81-8
Chiang Mai	ISBN 0-945971-88-5
Phuket	ISBN 0-945971-82-6
Ko Samui	ISBN 962-593-036-1

INDIVIDUAL COUNTRY TITLES
Australia	ISBN 962-593-150-3
Cambodia	ISBN 0-945971-87-7
China	ISBN 962-593-107-4
India	ISBN 962-593-047-7
Indonesia	ISBN 962-593-042-6
Japan	ISBN 962-593-108-2
Korea	ISBN 962-593-111-2
Laos	ISBN 962-593-069-8
Malaysia	ISBN 962-593-043-4
Myanmar	ISBN 962-593-070-1
Nepal	ISBN 962-593-062-0
New Zealand	ISBN 962-593-092-2
Philippines	ISBN 962-593-113-9
Singapore	ISBN 0-945971-41-9
Taiwan	ISBN 962-593-090-6
Thailand	ISBN 962-593-044-2
Vietnam	ISBN 0-945971-72-9

AUSTRALIA REGIONAL MAPS
Brisbane	ISBN 962-593-049-3
Cairns	ISBN 962-593-048-5
Darwin	ISBN 962-593-089-2
Melbourne	ISBN 962-593-050-7
Perth	ISBN 962-593-088-4
Sydney	ISBN 962-593-087-6

CHINA REGIONAL MAPS
Beijing	ISBN 962-593-031-0
Shanghai	ISBN 962-593-032-9
Hong Kong	ISBN 0-945971-74-5

INDIA REGIONAL MAPS
Bombay	ISBN 962-593-051-5
Delhi	ISBN 962-593-053-1

INDONESIA REGIONAL MAPS
Bali	ISBN 0-945971-49-4
Bandung	ISBN 0-945971-43-5
Batam	ISBN 962-593-144-9
Bintan	ISBN 962-593-139-2
Jakarta	ISBN 0-945971-62-1
Java	ISBN 962-593-040-X
Lake Toba	ISBN 0-945971-71-0
Lombok	ISBN 0-945971-46-X
Medan	ISBN 0-945971-70-2
Sulawesi	ISBN 962-593-162-7
Sumatra	ISBN 0-945971-67-2
Surabaya	ISBN 0-945971-48-6
Tana Toraja	ISBN 0-945971-44-3
Ujung Pandang	ISBN 962-593-138-4

Periplus Travel Maps are available at bookshops around the world. If you cannot find them where you live, please write to us for the name of a distributor closest to you:

Berkeley Books Pte Ltd
5 Little Road, #08-01, Singapore 536983.   Tel: (65) 280 1330   Fax: (65) 280 6290

Communications

Telephone Office Jl. Raya Pattimura. In general, phone connections are good, both nationally and internationally. Fax and telex machines are available as well as telephones.

Like everywhere else in the world, hotels in Ambon take a cut on long distance telephone calls and can charge a bundle for fax and telex services. Ask before making a call. Much cheaper to go to one of the several *wartel* mini-offices around town for international phone calls (via satellite) where you pay just about the same as a direct-dialed. Not much English spoken but easy enough to make yourself understood.

Photography

Union Photo Jl. A.Y. Pattimura No. 3, Ambon. ☎ (0911) 53569. In-store print processing, $1 for negatives, 15¢ for each print. Kodacolor and Fujicolor negative films; Ektachrome 100 slide film, but no slide processing. No Fuji Velvia or other specialized films.

AMBON UNDERWATER FESTIVAL

A yearly underwater festival in Ambon began in 1993. The week-long event, usually held in late October, features 4 days of diving with 10 plunges, including two night dives.

The highlight is an underwater photo competition, with $10,000 prize money split among three categories—wide angle, macro and animal behavior. Fuji from Jakarta provides film and processing. There is lots of local entertainment, including traditional song and dance.

The festival package is almost incredibly cheap: $750/person, which includes all diving, six days room and full board plus round-trip ticket from Bali. Information, reservations and registration through the Ambon Dive Centre (see above).

DIVE SEASON

As a general rule, the best diving in the Ambon and Lease area is between September and December. During this period, all areas are available for diving, and visibility is at its greatest. From April through August, diving is limited to the north coast of Ambon and the Lease Islands, and the nearby south coast of Seram. From January through March, diving is best along the south, with occasional journeys to the north, if weather permits.

Saparua

GETTING THERE

Regular boats leave from Tulehu on Ambon Island's east coat to the bigger villages on Haruku and Saparua. The regular boat from Tulehu to Pelau, on the north coast of Haruku and the island's largest village, costs $1.50. A regular ferry leaves for Saparua at 9am and 2pm, Mon–Sat and at 11 on Sun, and stops at Tuhaha ($5) on the east coast of Tuhaha Bay in the north. Another boat goes to Saparua Town ($2) and then continues on to Amahai on Seram Island to the north (another $2 and 2.5 hours).

Regular boats from Saparua Town head to Nusa Laut only on Wednesdays and Saturdays, when they have lots of business ferrying people back and forth to Saparua's market. If you want to go to the little island on another day, you will have to charter a boat.

Chartering speedboats. You can also charter a speedboat—able to carry 3–6 passengers—from Ambon to various villages on Haruku and Saparua. Prices vary, depending on distance, traffic and your bargaining ability, approx. $80.

LAND TRANSPORTATION

On the two big islands, buses wait for passengers in the morning at the ferry terminals. Fares range from 15¢ to 75¢ from the ferry terminal on either Haruku or Saparua to anywhere else on the islands. Charters run $5–$7.50/hour.

DIVE OPERATORS

Tony Tomasoa (of P.T. Daya Patal in Ambon, see above) operates a resort on Saparua, near Mahu Village. Two compressors and dive gear are kept on the premises. Although you can dive with Daya Patal from a base in one of the hotels in Ambon City, it is much more pleasant and convenient on Saparua, as you don't have to take the long boat ride in the morning and returning in the afternoon to Ambon.

Mahu Diving Lodge Desa Mahu, Saparua. All bookings through Daya Patal Tours, Jl. Said Perintah SK II / 27A, Ambon. ☎ (0911) 53344, 41136; fax: 54127, 53287.

The resort consists of attractive bungalows facing mangrove trees at the sea's edge in a coconut plantation. The resort is locally called "Kelapa Indah" ("Beautiful Coconut"). Dugongs have been occasionally seen feeding in the shallow beds of sea grass not far from the resort. The cottages are spacious, airy, thatch-roofed structures with showers and flush toilets. Electricity (220/240 volts) available.

The diving just in front of the resort is not good, but the coral on the other side of the bay is fine for snorkeling, in 2–3 m depths. The resort has "self-paddle" outrigger canoes to make the short cross-bay run. Light tackle available for fishing trips with boat and pilot/guide. In August and September, black marlin and also tuna in the 50–100 kg range hit regularly.

Two dives to Nusa Laut or Maulana Island, $55; Moloth, Itawaka or Kulor, $45; two divers minimum. Package (room, meals, 2 dives, boat, guide, tanks and weights) $85–$100, depending on distance, two diver minimum. Regulator rental $10/day, BC $10/day. Extra (third) dive $15, night dive $20.

Accommodations at the Mahu Resort Lodge only: $45S, $55D, includes full board. Airport pickup $20 per person to Tulehu. Speedboat charter, round trip to Mahu, $80 for up to 6 people. Normal ferry boat to Saparua (two departures daily) $5. Payment possible by Visa or Mastercard or travelers' cheques; 3% surcharge if credit card payment.

OTHER ACCOMMODATIONS

Losmen Siri Sore In Siri Sore Saram, on the east shore of Saparua Bay. 12 clean rooms, breakfast included. Land and sea excursions can be organized. $12–$14S; $13–$18D.

On Haruku and Nusa Laut, travelers must negotiate for a place to stay with a family.

Pindito

The live-aboard *Pindito* is based in Ambon. Trips—around the Banda Sea and the Islands off Western Irian Jaya, depending on the season—are usually of 12 days, with all but one day for diving. Rate: $220/day, all-inclusive (even beer, liquor, equipment rental). Note: we still recommend divers bring their own, recently checked dive gear. The ship can also be chartered, for $3,000/day, with a capacity of up to 16 divers. As the *Pindito* is a busy ship, we advise bookings well ahead of time (6 months or even a year) for confirmed space. However, one or two beds are often available on short notice, but, of course, not guaranteed. So far, marketing has been aimed at Germany and Switzerland. The *Pindito's* main office can also arrange flights, hotel bookings, and extensions to other parts of Indonesia. **Pindito** Main office: Pindito Travel Ltd., Fallackerstrasse 48, P.O. Box CH-8105 Watt, Regensdorf, Switzerland. ☎ (41-1) 870-0207, Fax: (41-1) 870-0215. In Ambon: Pondok Permai RT 18/RW 03, Hative Kecil, Ambon, Maluku, Indonesia. ☎/fax: (0911) 51569. Contact:

Ambon-based manager, Edi Frommenwiler. E-mail: pindito@eyekon.ch Web: www.eyekon.ch/pindito

Banda

City code: 0910

Merpati flies one of its 18-passenger Twin Otters to Bandaneira from Ambon on Mondays, Wednesdays and Saturdays (1 hr, $50). The possibility of cancellations (weather or technical problems) is very real and should always be taken into account.

A local passenger ship makes the Banda–Ambon run on a semi-regular basis or when too many flights have been canceled or there are too many air passengers. Inter-island mixed freighters or large Pelni passenger liners also make the trip about every three weeks (see Travel Advisory, page 266.) You can easily walk from the airstrip to the Bandaneira hotels, but not with dive gear. Hop into one of the mini-buses that will be waiting.

DIVE OPERATORS

Diving is available to guests at the Maulana Inn or the Laguna Inn. For reservations, contact: Hotel Maulana, P.O. Box 3193, Jakarta. ☎ (021) 360372; fax: 360308. In Banda: ☎ (0910) 21022 or 21023; fax: 21024. **Laguna Inn** 12 rooms. Three meals $22. $25–$60S; $29–$70D. Some bungalows at $15 on twin-share basis. All plus 10% tax. **Maulana Inn** 50 rooms. The best rooms in Bandaneira. The hotel offers a nice view of Gunung Api across the lagoon. Three meals $22/person + 10%. Cold beer, small can $2. Bottle of *arak* $3. Meals are okay, but boring. The *sushi*, however, is great when available (order one day ahead; $4.50 for a big plate of *sashimi* tuna). $60–$87S; $70–$140D, plus 10% tax.

Diving for people staying at either of these hotels (min of 4 people): To Ai, Hatta and Run, $60 (with your own gear); $75 (regulator and BC provided), $80 (all gear provided). The ride to the dive sites takes 60–70 minutes by speedboat. For other, nearby locations, the rates are: $50, $65, $70, with a two-person minimum. 5–30 minutes by speedboat. Night dives, $30.

For snorkeling off Bandaneira, the near coast of Lontar, and Gunung Api, a boat can drop you off and pick you up at predetermined time for $6/person (6 persons or more). The same arrangement for Sjahrir Island and the far side of the Lontar, $10/person.

For a special trip to Manukang (Suangi) Island or Manuk Island (lots of birds), contact the manager of the Maulana Hotel. It is, essentially, the cost of the boat charter—to Manukang, 4 hours each way by diesel, 1.5 to 2 hours by speedboat; to Manuk, about 11 hours each way (diesel only).

Other watersports Windsurfing, mid June to September, January to March, $2/hr; water-skiing $30/hr; fishing is included in price of boat rental. May to September, the yellowtail tuna, sailfish, swordfish, and Spanish mackerel run; from October to June, it's barracuda. Jacks are caught all year round.

OTHER ACCOMMODATIONS

Aside from the above places owned by Des Alwi, there are some simple *losmen*: the **Delfika** with 8 rooms, all enclosed facilities, $9.50/person including tax and three meals; the **Selecta** with 7 rooms, also offering full board, $10 with attached toilet facilities, $8.50 for rooms with shared facilities.

These *losmen* are all quite close to the main mosque and its blaring loudspeakers. All accommodations on Banda tend to fill during the last two weeks of December as well as most of October. Make sure to reserve ahead during these times.

DINING

Best at the Maulana and the Laguna, where you usually are served two kinds of fish and a vegetable. There are many little restaurants in Bandaneira town where the simple meals of rice or noodles with chicken cost about 75¢. We found the **Selecta II** the most pleasant of these—there is cold beer available here (sometimes) for a $1.40 per can.

TOURIST SERVICES

Excursions

Sunset cruise Two-hour cruise around Gunung Api by boat, and a stop at Sambayang to visit a cinnamon plantation and to snorkel in the sea and in hot water springs. $6 (6 person minimum).
Climbing Gunung Api It takes one to three hours to climb the 656-meter-high volcano. One day's notice is required. Guide $5.50 per person (whether he carries anything or not) and round-trip boat $5. Upon returning, you obtain a certificate declaring you an honorary citizen of Banda. This document requires a $2 donation to the museum.
Lontar Village This is a trip to Lontar island to see a nutmeg plantation, sacred wells and Fort Hollandia, this last reached by climbing 360 steps. The tour starts at 4 pm, and takes about two hours. $6/person, minimum of two; if guide needed, extra $5.

Cultural Events

In April and October, 37-man *kora-kora* (war canoe) races are held. The rest of the year, you can commission a demonstration: $150 for one *kora-kora* and crew. A *cakalele* war dance costs $350 and requires 10-day's notice.

Banks and Money-changing

There are no banks on Banda, so bring all the rupiah you will need from Ambon.

DIVING SEASON

The best diving is March through June, and October through November. From July/August to mid-September, diving is usually restricted to locations close to Bandaneira, due to heavy seas. December to February is supposed to be Banda's driest period, but in 1993 and 1994 there were heavy rains at this time.

7   Irian Jaya PRACTICALITIES

Irian Jaya, the Indonesian province that covers the western half of the large island of New Guinea, is one of the world's last unknown expanses, especially underwater. Diving is excellent—diverse coral, stunning fish life, turtles, dugongs, sharks, rays, whales are common sights, not to mention an abundance of ship and aircraft wrecks just now being discovered.

Prices in US dollars. S = Single; D = Double; T = Triple; AC = Air-conditioning. City code for Sorong 0951.

Currently, aside from the *Pindito's* seasonal trips to the Raja Ampat islands, the only way to dive Irian is with Irian Diving, which operates out of Sorong on the Bird's Head peninsula. Divers will be met by this outfit in either Sorong to dive in the Raja Ampat Islands, or Manokwari, departure point for dives in Dore and Cenderawasih Bays.

GETTING THERE

Merpati flights connect Sorong (departure point for the Raja Ampat Islands) with other diving centers throughout the country:

Ambon	Daily	$ 67
Denpasar	Daily (via Ambon, U.P.)	$236
Jakarta	Daily (via Ambon, U.P.)	$296
Manado	Th,Su	$110
Ujung Pandang	Daily (via Ambon)	$176
Jayapura	M,W,Th,Su (via Biak)	$152
Manokwari	W,F,Sa	$ 79

For diving in Cenderawasih Bay, head for Manokwari on the north coast:

Ambon	M,T,W,Th,Su (via Biak)	$172
Manado	Sa	$175
Ujung Pandang	F (3 stops)	$265
Jayapura	Tu,Th,F,Su	$120

Both cities are stopovers for Pelni Lines' two passenger boats, the *Dobonsolo* and the *Ciremai* every two weeks on their way from Jakarta to Jayapura and the *Tatamailau* (Denpasar–Jayapura) calls monthly.

DIVE OPERATOR

Irian Diving Jl. Gn. Gamalama No. 3, Kampung Baru, Sorong, Irian Jaya, P.O. Box 187 98414. ☎/Fax: (0951) 25274 and 27371. Mailing address: P.O. Box 187, Sorong. Contact in the Netherlands: Irian Diving. ☎/Fax: (31-38) 4478293, (31-183) 443430. Contact: Max Ammer.

The usual three-week dive programs begin on Sunday and end on Friday. This includes a week at each of the Wai and Kri Island base camps. Fax Max Ammer for the schedule and possible space during the next year. Most of the clients during the past three years of operation have been from Germany (80%) with the rest coming from Holland (15%) and the odd American or Singaporean.

The base price is $2,000 for three weeks. It is possible to cut the first or last week of these three-week periods. At the Wai base camp, 220 V. electricity is available for recharging batteries. Some scuba rental equipment is available. As Max is a Seventh Day Adventist, he prefers not working on Saturdays if at all possible. On request, he will be buy and provide at cost beer and keep it nice and cold in an ice chest.

Equipment includes 1 wooden boat, 2 fiberglass dive boats, 1 long boat, GPS navigation used to locate wreck and dive sites, a generator to charge batteries, 3 Bauer compressors, 60 tanks, and 8 complete sets of diving equipment. Occasionally rides can be rough but this should get better with a new, bigger fiberglass boat which should be operating by the time you read this, powered by two 85 Hp outboards.

All trips are guided by Max Ammer, who, with more than 6 years diving experience in Irian Jaya, has located more than 60 ship and 30 aircraft wrecks. Small groups (6–12 divers) only, accompanied by 3 or 4 Irianese staff and one diving instructor/guide. All his staff are certified divers.

Contact them as early as possible, as they work on with small groups and are often booked far in advance. Additional information in English, Dutch, German, or Indonesian available upon request. Airport transfers can be arranged.

Underwater Hazards

We have all heard far too many shark attack stories. There is a remote possibility of a shark attack of course, but the odds are against it. You are far safer diving in Indonesian waters than riding around Bali on a motorcycle.

Above: *The colubrine sea snake,* Laticauda colubrina.

The biggest hazards are currents and cold water, and cuts and scrapes on coral. Still, there are a number of dangerous animals on Indonesia's reefs, and they should not be toyed with. In 1991, a diver died from trying to ride a large reef stingray. He must have thought it was a manta, and climbed on its back.

In almost 300 dives in Indonesia, my problems have been few. I brushed stinging hydroids with my exposed wrists, and small jellyfish stung the area around my throat. And I was once attacked by a Titan triggerfish (*Balistoides viridescens*), although all he got were a few clumps of hair.

My biggest problem in the beginning was cold. I had a 1mm suit, but this left me shivering in some of the cold water off Bali. Later, I added a 3mm shorty on top when we encountered cold water. A few times, I wished I had a hood as well.

ANIMALS THAT BITE

Sharks

Of the hundreds of species of sharks, only 12 have been known to attack humans, and another 28 are considered capable of such an act. The great white shark (*Carcharodon carcharias*), reaching 6.5 meters, is probably the most fearsome of these. This animal prefers cool waters, and sticks to Australia and the west coast of the United States. We only know of one great white sighting, off Bali. The diver held still, stuck to the coral wall and prayed (he's an atheist) as he watched the monster cruise by. Jacques Cousteau considers the oceanic whitetip (*Carcharhinus longimanus*)—a chiefly pelagic species almost never seen by divers in Indonesia—to be the most unpredictable and dangerous species.

The only really dangerous species one is likely to see diving off Indonesia's reefs is the tiger shark (*Galeocerdo cuvier*), a large deepwater fish that sometimes comes up onto the reefs to feed, particularly in the late afternoon and at night. It is probably not worth tempting fate with this animal, which is occasionally sighted by divers.

The common reef sharks you will see in Indonesia are not considered dangerous, and one never hears of attacks. (In fact, your big problem will be that they're so shy it's hard to get good photos.) But still, don't harass them, and spearfishing always dramatically increases the risk of attack.

Sharks are very highly developed predators, with a very keen sense of smell, and a lateral line sensitive to the vibrations given off by a wounded or distressed fish. Since there is easier prey around—smaller, more familiar and less menacing—sharks very seldom attack humans. When they do, it is more likely to be a territorial defense than an attempt at getting a meal.

Prior to a territory related attack, sharks will warn divers with a "dance" display: the circling animals shake their heads back and forth, arch their backs, and point their pectoral fins downward. It is very distinctive (much like a big dog defending his territory) and even without this description you would probably get the message.

The classic shark feeding behavior consists of circling the prey, gradually increasing in speed and moving in closer. Sharks are more cautious than you might think they need to be, and the animals often test their potential prey's defenses by brushing against it with their abrasive skin.

Should either of these behaviors develop while you are underwater, it is best to get out of there as soon as possible. Stay calm, stick to your buddy, and back up against the reef wall. Work your way steadily up and get back to the beach or the dive boat. If one or more of the animals comes too close, try banging it on its sensitive nose with your camera, a dive light, or your fist—whichever is most handy.

Barracuda

Barracuda are far less dangerous than sharks, but have sharp teeth and the great barracuda (*Sphyraena barracuda*) grows to 2 meters. These fish are sometimes drawn to flashy jewelry (and speared fish). Dive lights occasionally attract them at night, and if temporarily blinded, they could become disoriented and dangerous. For some reason, Atlantic Ocean barracuda are much more likely to attack than their Pacific Ocean brethren.

Sea snakes

Sea snakes carry some of the most deadly poison known (they are the most poisonous of snakes). The species seen in Indonesia, however, are not aggressive. Sea snakes are sometimes inquisitive, and don't panic if one should explore your face underwater. Remember: they have very short teeth, very rarely bite, and even if they do bite, often they do not inject their venom. It seems that it takes the snakes a day or more to regenerate their venom supply, and they are loath to use it unless faced with a real emergency. Do not make them feel they are facing an emergency.

If bitten (with poison), restrict circulation from the affected limb, and get the victim to a doctor. There is little pain at first, but paralysis and death can follow hours later.

Others

Sea turtles, and even small reef fish, particularly triggers and puffers, have powerful jaws and strong teeth that can do damage. It may seem silly to run from a foot-long fish, but better that than a painful wound.

STINGING FISH

Stingrays

These common animals use their tail stinger when stepped on or startled. They frequent sandy areas, and are sometimes practically invisible. A good habit if walking in the shallows is to shuffle your feet giving them time to get out of your way. When diving, don't try to sneak up on a stingray. Approach slowly, from in front. The sting from a ray is rarely fatal to an adult, although it is extremely painful. (Note: in the example cited above, the stinger literally pierced the victim's heart.)

Scorpionfish

All scorpionfish carry poison in their dorsal, anal and pelvic fins. The pain from most can be excruciating, but only the stonefish (*Synanceia*

Above: *(Top to bottom) Grey reef shark,* Carcharhinus amblyrhynchos; *reef whitetip shark,* Triaenodon obesus; *tiger shark,* Galeocerdo cuvier; *oceanic whitetip shark,* Carcharhinus longimanus.

verrucosa) has been responsible for human fatalities. The stonefish is the world's most venomous fish, and being stung by one is a real disaster—at best you can expect local tissue death and perhaps the loss of your toes; at worst, a painful death. Be careful! Many scorpionfish are masters of camouflage, making it easy to step on or brush one.

Lionfish (*Pterois* spp.) are more conspicuous. They sometimes travel in packs, however, and particularly at night, when they are attracted to the small fish stunned by your lights, you could accidentally bump one.

A sting from a ray or scorpionfish causes excruciating pain, which can bring on unconsciousness. Get the victim topside immediately. Remove any spine still stuck in the skin, and wash and slightly bleed the puncture area. As quickly as possible, immerse the wound in hot water, up to 50°C (use tea if you have some on the boat), or use hot compresses. If attended to quickly enough, good results are likely from this method. Treat for shock, and take the victim to a doctor.

PRICKS AND CUTS

Sea urchins

The long, black spines of the *Diadema* spp. sea urchins are not something one would voluntarily bump against. But it happens. These animals are found more often in harbors, lagoons and rather eutrophic back-reef areas than on the forereef where divers spend their time. Be careful walking out, particularly through cloudy water! Other urchins are not as dramatic, but can still be a real irritation, and some are venomous.

Try to remove the spines with a tweezers, but if this is impossible, try crushing them: use a shoe or a weight from your belt. This will relieve the pain somewhat, and the spines will eventually be absorbed.

Coral scrapes

Infected coral cuts are the divers' most frequent problems in Indonesia. Do not neglect any broken skin in the tropics. A festering, pus-filled sore will develop, possibly swelling your lymph glands and starting real trouble.

Don't let things get this far. Clean and disinfect the wound as soon as you are finished diving. Keep a loose open bandage on it and change it frequently.

ANIMALS THAT 'BURN'

The hazard presented by these animals can usually be prevented by even a thin suit. Often it is the areas around the face or the wrist where you can get stung.

Jellyfish

The most dangerous jellyfish is the sea wasp (*Chironex fleckeri*). It is a problem in Australia, and swimming is prohibited in the Darwin area when the mature animals are about. Children and adults with cardio-respiratory problems are the most at risk from this transparent, 20-centimeter creature. A coma and death can result. Remove the victim from the water, and gently remove any still-adhering tentacles. Vinegar may reduce further discharge of nematocysts, or use local anaesthetic sprays or ointments. Resuscitation may be required. Other jellyfish are more unpleasant than dangerous, but vinegar or creams may help with them as well.

Stinging hydroids

The stinging hydroid *Aglaophenia* is common in Indonesia, looking like a beige or pinkish fern. Fire coral (*Millepora*) grows as smooth, wrinkled sheets (brownish or greenish) or as encrusting forms. Gloves and even Lycra suits offer protection, but a brush against it with bare skin will burn, and leave an itchy, bumpy rash. This is irritating, but not enough to make you abort a dive.

Indonesian Reef Fishes

WITH ENGLISH, LATIN, INDONESIAN AND LOCAL LANGUAGES

Family name (Latin family name) English common name (*Genus species*); standard length (does not include tail)	Indonesian; Bajo (Ba); Bugis (Bu); Manado dialect (M); Ambon dialect (A) —In Indonesian, almost all fish names begin with "ikan" (*fish*) which we omit below.
Sharks (Rhincodontidae, whale shark; Orectolobidae, nurse and zebra sharks; Hemigaleidae, reef whitetip; Sphyrnidae, hammerheads; Alopiidae, thresher sharks; Carcharhinidae, requiem shark)	Ikan hiu; cucut (*kiss, suck*); kareo (Ba); mengihang (Bu); gorango (M); kalayu (A); also bengiwang
Whale shark (*Rhincodon typus*); 12m, perhaps more	Hiu Abu-abu (*ashes*) Hiu gender (*gamelan instrument*), cucut lintang, ikan hiu bodoh (*stupid*)
Nurse shark (*Nebrius concolor*); 3.2m	Hiu buta (*blind*); kareo bisu (*deaf*) (Ba)
Leopard shark (*Stegastoma varium*); 2.3m	Hiu kembang (*a flower*), cucut tokek
Reef whitetip shark (*Triaenodon obesus*); 1.7m	Hiu sirip putih (*white fin*); kareo batu (Ba)
Silvertip shark (*Carcharhinus albimarginatus*); 2.8m	
Grey reef shark (*C. amblyrhynchos*); 2.3m	
Oceanic whitetip shark (*C. longimanus*); 2.7m	Hiu samudera (*ocean*), berujung (*top*), putih Hiu sirip putih laut dalam (*deep sea white fin*); kareo pansa (Ba)
Reef blacktip shark (*C. melanopterus*); 1.8m	Hiu sirip hitam (*black fin*); kareo mengali (Ba), hiu karang berujung hitam
Tiger shark (*Galeocerdo cuvier*); 5.5m, perhaps more	Hiu macan (*tiger*)
Hammerhead shark (*Sphyrna sp.*); perhaps 5m	Hiu ronggeng (*Javanese dancer/bar girl*), cucut rongceng, ikan hiu martil (*ham- mer*); kareo bingkoh (Ba); gorango martelu (M)
Thresher shark (*Alopias pelagicus*); 3.3m	Hiu penebah
Rays in general (Rajidae)	Ikan pari; pari luncur
Guitarfishes (Rhinobatidae) White-spotted guitarfish (*Rhynchobatus djiddensis*); 3m	Cucut biola (*violin*), cucut panrong
Stingrays (Dasyatididae)	Pari sengat (*sting*)
Leopard ray (*Himantura uarnak*); 1.8m width	Pari, Pareh; Pai (Ba); Pari, Nyoa (*bird*) (Bu)
Blue-spotted stingray (*Taenura lymma*); 1m width	Pari macan (*tiger*), pari kembang Pari pasir bintik biru (*blue spotted sand ray*); pai kiam (Ba); nunang, nyoa pasir (*sand*) (Bu)
Black-spotted stingray (*T. melanospilos*); 1.7m width	Pari pasir; pai kikir (Ba)
Eagle rays (Myliobatidae) Spotted eagle ray (*Aetobatis narinari*); 2.3m width	Pari burung (*bird*), pari ayam (*chicken, for the taste*); pai mano (Ba); pari mano, nyoa burung (Bu)
Manta rays (Mobulidae) Manta ray (*Manta alfredi*); 6.7m width; usually to 3m	Pari hantu (*ghost*), pari manta Pari jurig, pari satan (Sundanese); pai saranga (Ba); pari pangka (Bu); bele-

lang, bou, moku (*Lamalera dialect*)

Moray eels (Muraenidae)
Snowflake moray (*Echidna nebulosa*); 75cm
Fimbriated moray (*Gymnothorax fimbriatus*); 80cm
Yellow-margined moray (*G. flavimarginatus*); 1.2m
Giant moray (*G. javanicus*); 2.4m, maybe 3m
Spotted moray (*G. meelagris*); 1.2m
Black-spotted moray (*G. melanospilos*); 1m
Zonipectis moray (*G. zonipectis*); 46cm
Blue ribbon eel (*Rhinomuraena quaesita*); 1.2m

Sidat morena/Sidat moa
Ladu (*lava*), morea, kerundung (*veil*); ndoh
(Ba); lado (M). [Note: belut for "eel" in
Indonesian; belut (usually means fresh-
water species) of the Synbranchi-
formes order]

Garden eels (Congridae; subfamily Heterocongridae)
Spotted garden eel (*Heteroconger hassi*); 35cm

Sidat conger
Sidat kebun (*garden*)

Snake eels (Ophichthidae)
Banded snake eel (*Myrichthys colubrinus*); 88cm
Spotted snake eel (*M. maculosus*); 1m

Milkfishes (Chanidae)
Milkfish (*Chanos chanos*); 50cm, rarely to 1.8m

Ikan bandeng
Gelondongan (*adult*), nener (*fry*) [Note:
these are farmed in fishponds]

Eel catfishes (Plotosidae)
Striped eel catfish (*Plotosus lineatus*); 30cm

Sembilang karang (*coral catfish*); titinagan
(Ba)

Anchovies (Engraulididae)
Anchovies (*Stolephorus* spp.); 5–10cm

Teri; puri (A); ikan bilis (Malay)

Herrings (Clupeidae)
Sprats (*Dussumieria* spp. and *Spratelloides* spp.); 10cm
Herrings (*Herklotsichthys* spp.); 15cm

Ikan haring
Japuh [also terubuk (*Clupes toli*), tembang
and lemuru (*Sardinella* sp.)]

Lizardfishes (Synodontidae)
Graceful lizardfish (*Saurida gracilis*); 31cm
Nebulous lizardfish (*S. nebulosa*); 17cm
Twin-spot lizardfish (*Synodus binotatus*); 13cm
Reef lizardfish (*S. englemani*)
Black-blotch lizardfish (*S. jaculum*); 14cm
Variegated lizardfish (*S. variegatus*); 20cm

Ikan kadal
Beloso, gabus, ikan kepala busok (*fish
with depraved expression*); taropatau
(Ba); gosi cina (M)

Frogfishes (Antennariidae)
Painted frogfish (*Antennarius pictus*); 16cm
Sargassumfish (*Histrio histrio*); 14cm

Needlefishes (Belonidae)
Keeled needlefish (*Platybelone argalus platyura*); 37cm
Reef needlefish (*Strongylura incisa*); 1m
Crocodile needlefish (*Tylosaurus crocodilis*); 1.3m

Cendro, ikan julung-julung (*unlucky*);
timbaloah (Ba); sori (Bu); sako (M)

Halfbeaks (Hemirhamphidae)
Island halfbeack (*Hemiramphus archipelagicus*); 25cm
Spotted halfbeak (*H. far*); 40cm

Ikan kacang-kachang (*beans*), ikan julung-
julung (*unlucky*); pipilangan (Ba); cado-
cado (Bu); sako (M)

Flashlightfishes (Anomalopidae)
Flashlightfish (*Anomalops katoptron*); 9cm
Flashlightfish (*Photoblepheron palpebratus*); 9cm

Ikan leweri air, ikan leweri bau; oho (Ba)

Soldierfishes and Squirrelfishes (Holocentridae)
Bronze soldierfish (*Myripristis adusta*); 25cm
Bigscale soldierfish (*M. berndti*); 24cm

Ikan tupai (*squirrel*)
Karoo, kabakok, ikan mata bulan (*moon-
eyed*), ikan mata besar (*big-eyed*);

Red soldierfish (*M. murdjan*); 22cm Fine-lined squirrelfish (*Sargocentron microstoma*); 16cm Soldierfishes (in general) (*Myrptis sp*)	karango (Ba); susunu, gora (Bu) Serdadu (*soldier*)

Trumpetfishes (Aulostomidae) Trumpetfish (*Aulostomus chinensis*); 62cm	Mulut (*mouth*), pipa (*pipe*) Manok, ikan terompet; tarigonoh (Ba)

Cornetfishes (Fistulariidae) Flutemouth cornetfish (*Fistularia commersonii*); 1m	Seruling, tangkur, moncong (*snout, muzzle*); ikan terompet; teligonoh (Ba); malo (Bu)

Shrimpfishes (Centriscidae) Shrimpfish (*Aeoliscus strigatus*); 15cm	Ikan udang, piso-piso; Ikan pisau-pisau (*knife*); barbadisamo (Ba)

Ghost pipefishes (Solenostomus) Ghost pipefish (*Solenostomus cyanopterus*); 16cm Ornate ghost pipefish (*S. paradoxus*)	Ikan hantu (*ghost*)

Pipefishes and Seahorses (Syngnathidae)
Thorny seahorse (*Hippocampus histrix*); 15cm
Common seahorse (*H. kuda*); 30cm
Crowned seahorse (*H. planifrons*); 15cm
Network pipefish (*Corythoichthys flavofasciatus*); 11cm
Scribbled pipefish (*C. intestinalis*); 16cm
Double-headed pipefish (*Trachyramphus bicoarctata*);
   39cm
	Tangkur kuda (*javanese*)
	Tangkur, tangkur buaya (*crocodile*), ikan
	   kuda (*horse*); pipilando (Ba)
	Pipilando samo (Ba)
	Tangkur kuda; pipilando jarang (Ba)

Dragonfishes (Pegasidae) Sea moth (*Pegasus sp*)	Ikan ngengat (*moth*) laut

Flatheads (Platycephalidae) Crocodilefish (*Cymbacephalus beauforti*); 50cm Longsnout flathead (*Platycephalus chiltonae*); 20cm	Ikan kepala (*head*), pipih (*flat, thin*) Papangao (Ba)

Scorpionfishes (Scorpaenidae)
 	
Devil scorpionfish (*Scorpaenopsis diabolus*); 19cm
Tassled scorpionfish (*S. oxycephala*); 19cm
Weedy scorpionfish (*Rhinopias frondosa*); 19cm
Stonefish (*Synanceia verrucosa*); 35cm
 	
Devilfish (*Inimicus didactylus*); 15cm
Twinspot lionfish (*Dendrochirus biocellatus*); 8cm
Shortfin lionfish (*D. brachypterus*); 15cm
Zebra lionfish (*D. zebra*); 25cm
Spotfin lionfish (*Pterois antennata*); 19cm
Tailbar lionfish (*P. radiata*); 20cm
Lionfish (*P. volitans*); 30cm
	Ikan pipi-perisai (*cheek-shield*)
	Ikan kalajengking
	Lepu (*fish with toxic spines*), ikan anjing
	   (*dog fish*), pangaten, ikan suanggi
	   (*witch doctor*); kelopo (Ba)
	Ikan tembaga (*copper*); laroh (Ba)
	Lepu batu
	
	Lepu ayam (*chicken*)—all lionfishes
	
	Lepu
	
	Lepu ayam (*chicken*)

Perciformes: Bangsa Kerapu (Grouper clan)

Fairy Basslets and Groupers (Serranidae)
Magenta slender basslet (*Luzonichthys waitei*); 5cm
Peach fairy basslet (*Pseudanthias dispar*); 8cm
Red-cheeked anthias (*P. huchtii*); 8cm
Lyretail coralfish (*P. squammipinnis*); 10cm
Purple queen (*P. pascalus*); 12cm
Pink-square anthias (*P. pleurotaenia*); 10cm
Purple queen (*P. tuka*); 8cm
White-lined grouper (*Anyperodon leucogrammicus*); 41cm
Peacock grouper (*Cephalopholis argus*); 42cm
Leopard grouper (*C. leopardus*); 20cm
	All fairy basslets: Nona manis (*sweet girl*),
	   ikan pisang-pisang (*bananas*); daya-
	   suboh (Ba)
	All groupers: kerapu, garupa; kiapu (Ba);
	   suno (Bu)
	
	Argus bintik (*spot, stain*), biru (*blue*)
	Kiapu tongko, kiapu geang (Ba)

Coral grouper (*C. miniata*); 30cm
Flagtail grouper (*C. urodeta*); 19cm
Polkadot grouper, pantherfish (*Cromileptes altivelis*); 70cm
Black-tipped grouper (*Ephinephelus fasciatus*); 29cm
Blotchy grouper (*E. fuscogattatus*); 89cm
Honeycomb grouper (*E. merra*); 23cm
Giant grouper (*E. lanceolatus*); 3m total length, 400 kg
Saddleback grouper (*Plectropomus laevis*); 1m
Lyretail grouper (*Variola louti*); 56cm

Kiapu mirah (Ba)
Kiapu pedi betah (Ba); loong (Bu)
Kerapu bebek (*duck*), Geris Keli (*Grace Kelly!*)

Kerapu macan (*tiger*)

Kerapu lumpur; kiapu lohong (Ba)
Suno Bendera (Bu)
Suno enro (Bu)

Soapfishes (Grammistidae)
Lined soapfish (*Grammistes sexlineatus*); 27cm

Cantik jelita (*lovely, usually to girls*)

Prettyfins (Plesiopidae)
Comet (*Calloplesiops altivelis*); 11cm
Argus comet (*C. argus*); 11cm

Dottybacks (Pseudochromidae)
Paccagnalle's dottyback (*Pseudochromis paccagnallae*); 6cm
Magenta dottyback (*P. porphyreus*); 5cm

Ikan jentung

Hawkfishes (Cirrhitidae)
Falco hawkfish (*Cirrhitichthys falco*); 5cm
Pixy hawkfish (*C. oxycephalus*); 7cm
Longnose hawkfish (*Oxycirrhites typus*); 8cm
Arc-eye hawkfish (*Paracirrhites arcatus*); 11cm
Forster's hawkfish (*P. forsteri*); 17cm

Cardinalfishes (Apogonidae)
Cardinalfishes (*Apogon* spp.); av. 5–8cm
Pajama cardinalfish (*Sphaeramia nematoptera*); 6cm

Serinding, ikan sang karang; bebeseh (Ba)

Bigeyes (Priacanthidae)
Glasseye (*Heteropriacanthus cruentatus*); 23cm
Goggle-eye (*Priacanthus hamrur*); 26cm

Gora suanggi (*witch doctor*), serinding tembako (*tobacco cardinalfish*)

Remoras (Echeneididae)
Striped sharksucker (*Echeneis naucrates*); 90cm
Remora (*Remora remora*); 40cm

Kutu (*louse*); keluyu
Gemih
Gemih besar (*big*)

Jacks and Trevallies (Carangidae)

Kuwe or kuweh, bubara (*jacks*), selar (*Selar* sp. *scads*), ikan layang (*scads*), tetengkek (*hardtail scads*); pipili (Ba) (*jacks*)

Slender scad (*Decapterus macrosoma*); 35cm
Bigeye scad (*Selar crumenophthalmus*); 30cm
Threadfin pompano (*Alectis ciliaris*); 65cm
Indian threadfish (*A. indicus*); 1.5m
Golden trevally (*Gnathanodon speciosus*); 1.1m
Giant trevally (*Caranx ignobilis*); 1.7m
Black jack (*C. lugubris*); 91cm
Bluefin trevally (*C. melampygus*); 80cm
Bigeye jack (*C. sexfasciatus*); 85cm
Leatherback (*Scomberoides lysan*); 70cm

Ikan layang
Selar bentong
Kuwe rambut (*hair*)
Kuwe rambut (*hair*)
Kuwe macan (*tiger*)

Dayah nyumbah (Ba)

Lasi (*forbidden eating*), lima jari (*five fingers*); manok (Ba)

Rainbow runner (*Elagatis bipinnulatus*); 1.2m
Greater amberjack (*Seriola dumerili*); 1.9m
Silver pompano (*Trachinotus blochii*); 1.1m

Sunglir; uroh-uroh (Ba); suru (Bu)
Bangaya (Ba)

Mojarras (Gerreidae)
Common mojarra (*Gerres argyreus*); 19cm

Ikan kapas-kapas (*cotton*)

Snappers (Lutjanidae)
Blue-lined sea bream (*Symphorichthys spilurus*); 50cm
Black-and-white snapper (*Macolor macularis*); 50cm
Black snapper (*M. niger*); 60cm
River snapper (*Lutjanus argentimaculatus*); 70cm
Red snapper (*L. bohar*); 80cm

Bambangan, gerot-gerot; sulasaya (Ba)
Dayah sangai (Ba)
Kakap
Ikan tanda-tanda (*signs, markers*)

Ikan merah (*red fish*), jenaha, kakap;
ahrang (Ba)

Blackspot snapper (*L. ehrenbergi*); 26cm
Flametail snapper (*L. fulvus*); 35cm
Humpback snapper (*L. gibbus*); 42cm
Bluelined snapper (*L. kasmira*); 26cm
Onespot snapper (*L. monostigmus*); 45cm

Dapa

Fusiliers (Caesionidae)
Yellowtail fusilier (*Caesio cuning*); 23cm
Lunar fusilier (*C. lunaris*); 26cm
Yellowback fusilier (*C. teres*); 27cm
Bluestreak fusilier (*Pterocaesio tile*); 22cm
Three-striped fusilier (*P. trilineata*); 13cm

Pisang-pisang, lalosi
Ekor kuning (*yellowtail*); bulek kuneh (Ba)

Sweetlips and Grunts (Haemulidae)

Slatey sweetlips (*Diagramma pictum*); 78cm
Sulawesi sweetlips (*Plectorhinchus celebecus*); 41cm
Clown sweetlips (*P. chaetodonoides*); 60cm
Goldman's sweetlips (*P. goldmanni*); 60cm
Oriental sweetlips (*P. orientalis*); 72cm
Spotted sweetlips (*P. picus*); 70cm
Yellow-ribbon sweetlips (*P. polytaenia*); 70cm

Ikan gerot-gerot, raja bau (*smell*), raja caci,
pepondok.
Kerong-kerong (Ba); kokoreh (Bu)

Laundung (Ba)
Balekeh (Ba)
Balekeh (Ba)
Lepeh (Ba)
Gaiji

Threadfin breams (Nemipteridae)
Black-and-white spinecheeks (*Scolopsis lineatus*); 20cm
Redfin mid-water bream (*Pentapodus macrurus*); 30cm

Suelala (Ba)

Emperors (Lethrinidae)
Yellowspot emperor (*Gnathodentex aurolineatus*); 21cm
Bigeye emperor (*Monotaxis grandoculus*); 45cm
Ambon emperor (*Lethrinus amboinensis*); 57cm
Blackspot emperor (*L. harak*); 50cm
Longnose emperor (*L. olivaceus*); 84cm

Lencam, ketambak, asunan
Lalanga (Ba)

Sikuda; lausa (Ba); anduping (Bu)

Goatfishes (Mullidae)
Yellowstripe goatfish (*Mulloides flavolineatus*); 36cm
Yellowfin goatfish (*M. vanicolensis*); 31cm
Dash-dot goatfish (*Parupeneus barberinus*); 50cm
Multibarred goatfish (*P. multifasciatus*); 24cm

Biji nangka (*jackfruit seed*), jangut kuniran
(*yellow beard*), ikan kambing (*goat
fish*); jajango (Ba); salmoneti,
matadung (Bu)

Sweepers (Pempherididae)
Pigmy sweep (*Parapriacanthus ransonneti*); 6cm

Chubs (Kyphosidae)
Snubnose chub (*Kyphosus cinerascens*); 37cm

Batfishes (Ephippidae)
Orbiculate batfish (*Platax orbicularis*); 47cm
Pinnate batfish (*P. pinnatus*); 37cm
Round-faced batfish (*P. tiera*); 41cm

Kalong (*fruit-eating bat/flying fox*)
Gebel, ikan bawal, ikan bendera (*flag*)
Gebel bunder
Gebel asli (*native*)
Gebel biasa (*ordinary*)

Butterflyfishes (Chaetodontidae)
Threadfin butterflyfish (*Chaetodon auriga*); 15cm
Baroness butterflyfish (*C. barronessa*); 11cm
Bennett's butterflyfish (*C. bennetti*); 15cm
Saddleback butterflyfish (*C. ephippium*); 17cm
Klein's butterflyfish (*C. kleinii*); 11cm
Lined butterflyfish (*C. lineolatus*); 24cm
Raccoon butterflyfish (*C. lunula*); 16cm
Meyer's butterflyfish (*C. meyeri*); 14cm
Ornate butterflyfish (*C. ornatissimus*); 15cm
Spotnape butterflyfish (*C. oxycephalus*); 17cm
Raffles' butterflyfish (*C. rafflesii*); 11cm
Red-finned butterflyfish (*C. trifasciatus*); 12cm
Vagabond butterflyfish (*C. vagabundus*); 16cm
Copperband butterflyfish (*Chelmon rostratus*); 18cm
Longnose butterflyfish (*Forcipiger flavissimus*); 18cm
Big longnose butterflyfish (*F. longirostris*); 18cm
Pyramid butterflyfish (*Hemitaurichthys polylepis*); 13cm
Bannerfish (*Heniochus acuminatus*); 20cm
Bannerfish (*H. diphreutes*); 19cm
Pennant bannerfish (*H. chrysostomus*); 13cm
Masked bannerfish (*H. monoceros*); 18cm
Singular bannerfish (*H. singularis*); 24cm
Humphead bannerfish (*H. varius*); 15cm

Kepe-kepe, ikan kupu-kupu (*butterfly*),
   ikan daun-daun (*leaves*), kiper laut
[Note: Colorful reef fishes in general, butterflyfish, angelfish, damselfish: ikan
   karang (*coral*), ikan prong or ikan hias
   (*ornamental*), ikan cincin (*ring*)]

Kepe-kepe monyung asli (*native, true*)
Kepe-kepe monyung palsu (*false*)

Angelfishes (Pomacanthidae)
Three-spot angelfish (*Apolemichthys trimaculatus*); 26cm
Bicolor angelfish (*Centropyge bicolor*); 14cm
Dusky angelfish (*C. bispinosus*); 10cm
Lemonpeel angelfish (*C. flavissimus*); 8cm
Keyhole angelfish (*C. tibicen*); 15cm
Pearlscale angelfish (*C. vrolikii*); 8cm
Blackspot angelfish (*Genicanthus melanospilos*); 15cm
Regal angelfish (*Pygoplites diacanthus*); 21cm
Blue-ring angelfish (*Pomacanthus annularis*); 30cm
Emperor angelfish (*P. imperator*); 30cm

Blue-girdled angelfish (*P. navarchus*); 20cm
Semicircle angelfish (*P. semicirculatus*); 29cm
Six-banded angelfish (*P. sextriatus*); 38cm
Blue-faced angelfish (*P. xanthometopon*); 32cm

Injel (*"angel"*), ikan kupu-kupu (*butterfly*);
   edo (Ba)
Injel biru-kuning (*blue and yellow*)

Injel hitam (*black*)

Injel lurik (*type of striped cloth*)

Kambing (*goat*), raja (*king*)
Kaiser, beluston, betman (*"batman"*)
Injel piyama (*yes, "pyjamas"*)
kambing (*goat*), koran (*Muslim holy book*)

Beluston, beluboran

Damselfishes (Pomacentridae)
Sergeant-major (*Abudefduf vaigiensis*); 17cm
Golden damsel (*Amblygliphidodon aureus*); 10cm
Staghorn damsel (*A. curacao*); 9cm
Skunk anemonefish (*Amphiprion akallopisos*); 9cm
Orange-fin anemonefish (*A. chrysopterus*); 13cm
Clark's anemonefish (*A. clarkii*); 10cm
Red saddleback anemonefish (*A. ephippium*); 11cm
Tomato anemonefish (*A. frenatus*); 11cm
Dusky anemonefish (*A. melanopus*); 9cm
Clown anemonefish (*A. ocellaris*); 8cm
Pink anemonefish (*A. perideraion*); 8cm
Saddleback anemonefish (*A. polymnus*); 10cm
Orange anemonefish (*A. sandaracinos*); 11cm
Reef chromis (*Chromis agilis*); 8cm
Yellow-speckled chromis (*C. alpha*); 9cm
Ambon chromis (*C. amboinensis*); 6cm
Yellow chromis (*C analis*); 14cm
Black-axil chromis (*C. atripectoralis*); 9cm

Asan, giru
Bonang-bonang, sersan major

For all anemonefishes: Klon (*"clown"*),
   klon asan, giru prong, gemutu, ikan
   jamur (*mushroom*); kinsang (Ba)

For all *Chromis* spp.: Gucia, betok laut,
   kapas-kapas (*cotton fleece*)

Bicolor chromis (*C. margaritifer*); 6cm
Blue-green chromis (*C. viridis*); 7cm
Blue devil (*Chrysiptera cyanea*); 6cm
Blue-spot damsel (*C. oxycephala*); 7cm
Three-striped dascyllus (*Dascyllus aruanus*); 7cm
Black-tailed dascyllus (*D. melanurus*); 7cm
Reticulated dascyllus (*D. reticulatus*); 6cm
Three-spot dascyllus (*D. trimaculatus*); 11cm
Black damsel (*Neoglyphidodon melas*); 13cm
Java damsel (*N. oxyodon*); 12cm
Behn's damsel (*N. nigroris*); 9cm
Neon damsel (*Pomacentrus coelestis*); 7cm
Lemon damsel (*P. moluccensis*); 6cm
Peacock damsel (*P. pavo*); 9cm
Spine-cheek anemonefish (*Premnas biaculeatus*); 17cm
Farmerfish (*Stegastes lividus*); 13cm
Dusky farmerfish (*S. nigricans*); 12cm

Dakocan (*black puppet*), giru bolong (*pierced*), giru gete-gete

Wrasses (Labridae)
Lyretail hogfish (*Bodianus anthoides*); 24cm
Axilspot hogfish (*B. axillaris*); 16cm

Red-breasted wrasse (*Cheilinus fasciatus*); 28cm
Napoleon wrasse; humphead wrasse (*C. undulatus*);
    1.8m; total length to 2.3m
Ringtail wrasse (*C. unifasciatus*); 38cm
Slingjaw wrasse (*Epibulus insidiator*); 30cm
Clown coris (*Coris aygula*); 1m
Yellowtail coris (*C. gaimard*); 35cm
Bird wrasse (*Gomphosus varius*); 18cm
Two-tone wrasse (*Thalassoma amblycephalum*); 12cm
Lunar wrasse (*T. lunare*); 18cm
Bicolor cleaner wrasse (*Labroides bicolor*); 10cm
Bluestreak cleaner wrasse (*L. dimidiatus*); 9cm

Keling (*small wrasses*). Babi (*pig*) or Nuri-nuri (*a type of parrot*) (*large wrasses*). Gigi anjing (*dog's tooth*) (*tuskfishes*). Lamboso; lampah (Ba) (*hogfishes*).
Besiparai (Ba)
Napoleon; langkoeh, angkeh (Ba)

Keling merah putih (*red-white*)

Ikan doktor (*doctor fish*)
Ikan doktor (*doctor fish*)

Parrotfishes (Scaridae)
Bumphead parrotfish (*Bolbometopon muricatum*); 1m
Bicolor parrotfish (*Cetoscarus bicolor*); 60cm
Filament-finned parrotfish (*Scarus altipinnis*); 41cm
Blue-chin parrotfish (*S. atropectoralis*); 42cm
Bleeker's parrotfish (*S. bleekeri*); 39cm
Festive parrotfish (*S. festivus*); 34cm
Yellowfin parrotfish (*S. flavipectoralis*); 21cm
Blue-barred parrotfish (*S. ghobban*); 57cm
Java parrotfish (*S. hypselopterus*); 26cm
Pale-nose parrotfish (*S. psittacus*); 27cm
Rivulated parrotfish (*S. rivulatus*); 34cm
Redlip parrotfish (*S. rubroviolaceus*); 48cm
Bullethead parrotfish (*S. sordidus*); 26cm

Ikan kakatua (*cockatoo*); pelo, mogoh (Ba)
Ankeh (Ba); Loong (Bu)
Mogoh (Ba)

Mullets (Mugilidae)
Fringelip mullet (*Crenimugil crenilabis*); 50cm
Engel's mullet (*Valamugil engeli*); 15cm
Mullet (*V. speigleri*)

Mul abu-abu (*ashes*)
Belanak, tikus-tikus (*mice*), kuro, sumbal
Ikan janggut (*beard*); depoh (Ba)
Bunteh (Ba)

Barracudas (Sphyraenidae)
Great barracuda (*Sphyraena barracuda*); 1.7m
Blackfin barracuda (*S. genie*); 1.5m
Arrow barracuda (*S. novaehollandiae*); 50cm

Senuk, alu-alu, barakuda
Pangaluang (Ba), barakuda besar

Sandperches (Pinguipedidae)

Sandperches (*Parapercis* spp.); approx. 14cm

Blennies (Blenniidae) — Ikan tembakul
Bicolor blenny (*Ecsenius bicolor*); 8cm
Red-spotted blenny (*Istiblennius chrysospilos*); 11cm
Cleaner mimic blenny (*Aspidontus taeniatus*); 10cm
Scale-eating blenny (*Plagiotremus tapienosoma*); 12cm

Dragonets (Callionymidae)
Mandarinfish (*Synchiropus splendidus*); 5cm

Dartfishes (Microdesmidae)
Zebra dartfish (*Ptereleotris zebra*); 10cm
Decorated dartfish (*Nemateleotris decora*); 7cm
Firefish (*N. magnifica*); 5cm

Gobies (Gobiidae) — Beladok cina; belosoh
Prawn gobies (various); ave. 7cm
Gorgonian goby (*Bryaninops amplus*); 5cm — Belosoh karang (*coral*)
Coral gobies (*Gobiodon* and *Paragobiodon* spp.); ave. 4cm
Mudskipper (*Periophthalmus kalolo*); 10cm — Beladok, glodok

Surgeonfishes (Acanthuridae) — Surgeonfishes—Gron, Botana; kadodoh (Ba). Unicornfishes—Gutana; kumai (Ba).
Ringtail surgeonfish (*Acanthurus blochii*); 32cm
Clown surgeonfish (*A. lineatus*); 24cm
Whitecheek surgeonfish (*A. nigricans*); 16cm — Botana kasur (*mattress*)
Powder-blue surgeonfish (*A. leucosternun*); 20cm
Orangeband surgeonfish (*A. olivaceus*); 25cm — Kecamata (*eyeglasses*)
Mimic tang (*A. pyroferus*); 19cm
Thompson's surgeonfish (*A. thompsoni*); 19cm
Convict tang (*A. triostegus*); 21cm — Gron Lorek (*stripe*), Lima (*five*)
Yellowfin surgeonfish (*A. xanthopterus*); 43cm
Striped bristletooth tang (*Ctenochaetus striatus*); 20cm
Goldring surgeonfish (*C. strigosus*); 14cm
Tomini surgeonfish (*C. tominiensis*); 10cm
Hepatus tang (*Paracanthurus hepatus*); 20cm — Angka enam (*the numeral 6*)
Brown tang (*Zebrasomas scopas*); 15cm — Tetpai tambako (*makes you "drunk"*) (Ba)
Sailfin tang (*Z. veliferum*); 30cm
Whitemargin unicornfish (*Naso annulatus*); 1m
Humpback unicornfish (*N. brachycentron*); 90cm
Spotted unicornfish (*N. brevirostris*); 60cm — Kumai tandoh (Ba)
Sleek unicornfish (*N. hexacanthus*); 75cm
Orangespine unicornfish (*N. literatus*); 31cm
Humpnosed unicornfish (*N. tuberosus*); 60cm
Bluespine unicornfish (*N. unicornis*); 70cm
Bignose unicornfish (*N. vlamingii*); 50cm

Moorish Idol (Zanclidae) — Ikan bendera (*flag*), gayam, moris idol
Moorish Idol (*Zanclus cornutus*); 14cm

Rabbitfishes (Siganidae) — Baronang, bihang, masadar; uhi, bulawis (Ba); belawis (Bu); bete-bete (M)

Foxface (*Siganus [Lo] volpinus*); 18cm — Berah (Ba)
Seagrass rabbitfish (*S. canaliculatus*); 23cm — Lingkis, bulawis samo
Coral rabbitfish (*S. corallinus*); 23cm
Pencil-streaked rabbitfish (*S. doliatus*); 20cm — Kea-kea
Golden rabbitfish (*S. guttatus*); 33cm — Baronang lada; berah (Ba)
Lined rabbitfish (*S. lineatus*); 34cm
Scribbled rabbitfish (*S. spinus*); 23cm — Bulawis jantang (Ba)
Double-barred rabbitfish (*S. virgatus*); 20cm

Tunas and mackerels (Scombridae) — Tuna (*tunas and billfish*), tongkol (*little tunas, makerels*), tenggiri (*makerels*)

Frigate mackerel (*Auxis thazard*) — Tongkol, makelel fregat
Double-lined mackerel (*Grammatorcynos bilineatus*); 60cm — Andeh-andeh (Ba)

Dogtooth tuna (*Gymnosarda unicolor*); 2m — Bambuloh (Ba); pakukul (Bu)
Striped mackerel (*Rastrelliger kanagurta*); 35cm — Kembung lelaki
Narrow-barred king mackerel (*Scomberomorus commersoni*); 2.2m — Tenggiri

Skipjack tuna (*Katsuwonus pelamis*) — Cakalang
Albacore (*Thunnus alalunga*) — Albakor
Yellowfin tuna (*T. albacares*) — Madidihang, pane, tuna sirip (*fin*) kuning (*yellow*)

Southern bluefin tuna (*T. maccoyii*) — Tuna sirip biru (*blue-fin*)
Bigeye tuna (*T. obesus*) — Tuna mata besar (*big-eye*)
Longtail tuna (*T. tonggol*) — Abu-abu (*ashes*), tuna ekor panjang (*longtail*)

Flounders (Pleuronectiformes) — Ikan sebelah (*one-half*)

Flatfishes (Bothidae) — Kalankan, ikan lidah (*tongue*)
Peacock flounder (*Bothus mancus*); 40cm
Black-spotted sole (*Aseraggodes melanostictus*); 5cm

Triggerfishes (Balistidae) — Triger, ikan tato, ikan tatul (*wound*); ampala (Ba); pogo (Bu); sunga (M)

Orange-striped triggerfish (*Balistapus undulatus*); 23cm — Kauk; popogo batu (Ba); kau (Bu)
Clown triggerfish (*Balistoides conspicillum*); 25cm — Triger kembang (*flower*), triger ceplok (*polkadot*); ampala bulunti (Ba)

Titan triggerfish (*B. viridescens*); 63cm — Triger sisir (*comb*); ampala gila (*crazy*) (Ba)
Grey triggerfish (*Melichthys niger*); 28cm
Black triggerfish, red-tooth triggerfish (*Odonus niger*); 29cm — Triger abu-abu (*ashes*)
Yellow-margined triggerfish (*Pseudobalistes flavomarginatus*); 53cm
Undulate triggerfish (*P. fuscus*); 41cm — Triger liris (*batik pattern*)
Picasso triggerfish (*Rhinecanthus aculeatus*); 20cm — Triger matahari (*sun*)
Rectangular triggerfish (*R. rectangulus*); 18cm — Triger segi tiga (*triangle*)
Blackbelly Picasso triggerfish (*R. verrucosa*); 19cm

Filefishes (Monacanthidae) — Bulusan babi (*pig*), hayam
Scribbled filefish (*Aluterus scriptus*); 71cm
Barred filefish (*Cantherhines dumerili*); 25cm
Wire-net filefish (*C. pardalis*); 20cm
Longnose filefish (*Oxymonacanthus longirostris*); 10cm
Blackbar filefish (*Pervagor janthinosoma*); 11cm

Trunkfishes (Ostraciidae) — Ikan buntel kotak (*swelled box*); pogo, lumis, kepe (Ba)

Longhorn cowfish (*Lactoria cornuta*); 30cm — Ikan buntel tanduk (*horn*); cocoring (Ba); kabila, tatumbu (Bu)

Cubefish (*Ostracion cubicus*); 31cm
Spotted trunkfish (*O. meleagris*); 15cm
Reticulate boxfish (*O. solorensis*); 10cm

Puffers (Tetradontidae) — Ikan buntal (*swollen, bloated*)
Whitespotted puffer (*Arothron hispidus*); 45cm
Map puffer (*A. mappa*); 54cm — Gurisang (Ba)
Guineafowl puffer (*A. melagris*); 40cm
Dog-faced puffer, black-spotted puffer (*A. nigropunctatus*); 27cm

Star puffer (*A. stellatus*); 90cm
Ambon sharpnose puffer (*Canthigaster amboinensis*);
   10cm
Crowned sharpnose puffer (*C. cornata*); 10cm
Spotted sharpnose puffer (*C. solandri*); 9cm
Valentini's sharpnose puffer (*C. valentini*); 8cm

Porcupinefishes (Diodontidae)	Ikan duren (*spiky, delicious fruit*); konkeh
Porcupinefish (*Diodon hystrix*); 80cm	(Ba); landah (Bu), landak (*porcupine*)

Boxfishes (Ostraciidae)	
Cowfish (*Lactoria cornuta*)	Buntal lembu (*ox, cow, bull*)
Boxfish (*Ostrocion sp.*)	Buntal kotak (*box*)
	Buntal tanduk (*horns*)

Other animals	Ular laut

Sea snakes (famlly Hydrophiidae)	
Colubrine sea snake (*Laticauda colubrina*)	
Yellow-bellied sea snake (*Pelamis platurus*)	

Sea turtles (order Chelonia)	Penyu (*any kind of turtle*)
Loggerhead (*Caretta caretta*)	Penyu tempayan (*large water jar*)
Green turtle (*Chelonia mydas*)	Penyu hijau (*green*), penyu daging (*meat*)
Leatherback turtle (*Dermochelys coriacea*)	Penyu belimbing (*like a starfruit*)
Hawksbill turtle (*Eremochelys imbricata*)	Penyu sisik (*tortoiseshell*), penyu kembang
Flatback turtle (*Natator depressus*)	Penyu pipih
Olive ridley turtle (*Lepidochelys olivacea*)	Penyu lekang

Dugong (order Sirenia)	Dugung
Dugong (*Dugong dugon*)	

Whales (order Cetacea)	Ikan paus (*pope fish*)
Shortfin pilot whale (*Globicephala macrorhynchus*)	Temu bela (*Lamalera*)
Great killer whale (*Orcinus orca*)	Seguni
Pygmy killer whale (*Feresa attenuata*)	
Striped dolphin (*Stenella coeruleoalba*)	Lumba-lumba (*all dolphins*)
Spinner dolphin (*S. longirostris*)	Timu kira (*Lamalera language*)
Common dolphin (*Delphinus delphis*)	
Bottlenose dolphin (*Tursiops truncatus*)	Lumba-lumba berhidung botol (*bottlenose*)
Pygmy sperm whale (*Kogis* spp.)	
Sperm whale (*Physeter catodon*)	Lodan, kotal lema
Minke whale (*Balaenoptera acutorostrata*)	Kararu
Sei whale (*B. borealis*)	Kararu
Bryde's whale (*B. edeni*)	Kararu
Blue whale (*B. musculus*)	Ikan paus biru (*blue*)
Fin whale (*B. physalus*)	Kararu
Humpback whale (*Megaptera novaeangliae*)	

Indonesian Dive Terms
WITH ENGLISH, GERMAN AND FRENCH

ENGLISH	INDONESIAN	GERMAN	FRENCH
Dive	Selam	Tauchgang	Plonger
Flipper/fin	Sepatu bebek ("duck shoe")	Flosse	Palmes
Regulator	Regulator	Lungenautomat	Détendeur
Mask	Masker or Kacamata Selam	Maske or Taucherbrille	Masque or Combinaison
Snorkel	Snorkel	Schnorchel	Tuba
BC	Pelampung	Tarierweste	Bouée
Weight	Timbah or pemberat	Gewicht	Plomb
Weight belt	Ikat pinggang	Bleigurt	Ceinture
Tank	Tenki or tabung	Pressluftflasche	Bouteille
O-ring	Oli sel or karet	Dichtung/O Ring	Joint thorique
Flashlight	Senter	Taschenlampe	Pile
Compressor	Kompresor	Kompressor	Compresseur
Air	Angin	Luft	Air
Follow	Ikut	Befolgen	Suivre
Bubble	Gelembung udara	Luftblase	Bulle
The air is no good (oily)	Angin kurang baik (rasa oli)	Die Luft ist nicht gut (ölig)	Mauvais air (huile)
Current	Arus	Strömung	Courant
Strong current	Arus kuat	Starke Strömung	Courant fort
Fast	Cepat	Schnell	Vite
Slow	Palan-palan	Langsam	Lentement
Danger	Berbahaya	Gefahr	Dangereux
Look out!	Awas!	Pass auf!	Attention!
Careful	Hati-hati	Vorsichtig	Attention
Water	Air	Wasser	Eau
High tide	Air pasang	Flut	Marée haute
Low tide	Air surut	Ebbe	Marée basse
Wave	Ombak	Welle	Vague
Big wave	Ombak besar	Grosse Welle	Grosse vague
Little wave	Ombak kecil	Kleine Welle	Petite vague
East	Timur	Osten	Est
West	Barat	Westen	Ouest
North	Utara	Norden	Nord
South	Selatan	Süden	Sud
Full moon	Purnama	Vollmond	Pleine lune
Deep	Dalam	Tief	Profond
How deep?	Berapa dalam?	Wie tief?	Quelle profondeur?
Shallow	Dankal	Seicht	Peu profond
Sand	Pasir	Sand	Sable
Coral	Karang	Koralle	Corail
Sea urchin	Bulu babi (*pig bristle*)	Seeigel	Oursin
Boat	Kapal	Boot	bateau
Canoe	Prahu	Kanu	Pirogue
Outrigger	Tangah (also *ladder*)	Ausleger	Echelle
Outboard	Jonson (Johnson)	Aussenborder	Horsbord
Horsepower	P.K.	Pferdestärken, PS	Chevaux
How much horse-power?	Berapa P.K.	Wieviel PS?	Quelle puissance?
How long?	Berapa panjang?	Wie lang?	Quelle longueur?
Rent, charter	Carter, sewa	Mieten, chartern	Louer
How much?	Berapa?	Wieviel?	Combien?
	Per jam, per hari	Pro Stunde, pro Tag	Par heure, par jour

Further Reading

In addition to a good guide, a diver is probably most interested in a fish identification book, to help make some order out of the more than 2,500 species swimming around the reefs of Indonesia. Two excellent resources recently became available.

TROPICAL REEF-FISHES

Tropical Reef-Fishes Of The Western Pacific— Indonesia And Adjacent Waters, by Rudie H. Kuiter is the first extensive guide to the reef fishes of Indonesia.

This compact, handsome book is a manageable 300 pages long, and includes 1,300 excellent color photographs, illustrating 1,027 species including males, females and juveniles, where color or morphological differences exist. *Tropical Reef-Fishes* covers more than 50 families of reef fishes, just about every species you are likely to see around Indonesia's reefs down to about 30 meters.

Each family receives a brief description, headed by a large photo and followed by several smaller ones, usually six to the page. The common names are Australian usage (Kuiter lives in Australia). Kuiter is one of the world's leading authorities on Pacific reef fishes, being the principal author of the description of a half-dozen new species and associate author for a dozen more. Some of these new species are included in this book. Because of space constraints, however, not all families are listed. In particular, there is nothing on sharks, rays and some of the roving lagoon species, and pelagic species are skipped over lightly. Some of these, of course, are of great interest to the diver. Still, it is an indispensable work.

MICRONESIAN REEF FISHES

Micronesian Reef Fishes: A Practical Guide to the Identification of the Inshore Marine Fishes of the Tropical Central and Western Pacific, 2d ed., by Robert F. Myers, also belongs in the library of every diver in Indonesia. While Myers has not sought to write a book about Indonesian species, there is a great deal of overlap in the faunas of the two regions, and well over 90 percent of the species discussed can be found in Indonesia.

Myers' book is a model of accuracy and detail, with clear color photos of more than 1,000 species, complete meristics, and a dense 50–100 word description of the habitat and behavior of each species. A large number of black-and-white photos of preserved specimens and line drawings are particularly useful, showing such details as the location of cirri and mouth shapes where it is important in identification.

Myers covers the sharks and rays, and a number of other families Kuiter leaves out. Still, Kuiter's book describes 15–20 more butterflyfish, and 30 more damsels. The best solution is to get both.

OTHER WORKS OF INTEREST

The grandfather of all Indonesian fish guides is of course Bleeker's Atlas Ichthyologique. It is still very accurate, although not even close to being portable, or even available. Another very valuable book that became available as we were in production is Gerald R. Allen's *Damselfishes of the World.* This fine book describes and illustrates some 321 damselfish, all that are currently known, including 16 new species. Full meristics, and range and habitat descriptions of all the species are included.

The most available series of books on Indo-Pacific reef life in the United States are those put out by Tropical Fish Hobbyist publications in New Jersey. Unfortunately, however, these books are almost universally awful. They are really badly edited, with misidentified photos and poor organization.

Unfortunately, we were unable to find any books on the rich invertebrate life of Indonesian reefs as thorough and compact as the above-mentioned fish books. We have listed some below, however, that may prove helpful.

FISHES

Allen, Gerald R. *Butterfly And Angelfishes Of The World.* New York: Wiley Interscience, 1979.

——*Damselfishes of the World.* Hong Kong: Mergus, 1991. (Distributed in the United States by Aquarium Systems, 8141 Tyler Blvd., Mentor OH 44060.)

Allen, Gerald R. and Roger C. Steene. *Reef Fishes Of The Indian Ocean* (Pacific Marine

Fishes, Book 10). Neptune, N.J.: T.F.H. Publications, 1988.

Bleeker, Pieter. *Atlas Ichthyologique des Indes Orientales Neerlandaises* (9 volumes). Amsterdam, 1877. (Dr. Bleeker's classic "Atlas." Out of print and very valuable. Look for it at a good library.)

Burgess, Warren E. *Atlas Of Marine Aquarium Fishes.* Neptune, N.J.: T.F.H. Publications, 1988. (Full of inaccuracies and misidentified photos; no scientific value.)

Burgess, Warren E. and Herbert R. Axelrod. *Fishes of the Great Barrier Reef* (Pacific Marine Fishes, Book 7). Neptune, N.J.: T.F.H. Publications. 1975.

——*Fishes of Melanesia* (Pacific Marine Fishes Book 7). Neptune, N.J.: T.F.H. Publications, 1975.

Carcasson, R. H. *A Guide To Coral Reef Fishes Of The Indian And West Pacific Regions.* London: Collins, 1977. (Out of date, hard to recognize fishes from the drawings.)

Kuiter, Rudie H. *Tropical Reef-Fishes Of The Western Pacific—Indonesia And Adjacent Waters.* Jakarta: Gramedia, 1992. (Excellent, see above.)

Myers, Robert F. *Micronesian Reef Fishes: A Practical Guide to the Identification of the Inshore Marine Fishes of the Tropical Central and Western Pacific, 2d ed.* Guam: Coral Graphics, 1991. (Excellent, see text above. Order through Coral Graphics, P.O. Box 21153, Guam Main Facility, Barrigada, Territory of Guam 96921.)

Nelson, J.S. *Fishes Of The World.* New York: John Wiley and Sons, 1984.

Piesch, Ted and D.B. Grobecker. *Frogfishes Of The World.* Stanford, CA: Stanford University Press, 1987.

Randall, John E., Gerald R. Allen and Roger Steene. *Fishes of the Great Barrier Reef and the Coral Sea.* Bathhurst, Australia: Crawford House Press, University of Hawaii Press, 1990.

Sawada, T. *Fishes in Indonesia.* Japan International Cooperation Agency, 1980.

Schuster W.H. and R.R. Djajadiredja. *Local Common Names For Indonesia Fishes.* Bandung, Java: N.V. Penerbit W. Van Hoeve, 1952.

Weber, M. and de Beaufort, L.F. *The Fishes Of The Indo- Australian Archipelago* (11 volumes, 404–607 pages each). Leiden, E.J. Brill. 1913–1962.

INVERTEBRATES

Debelius, Helmut. *Armoured Nights of the Sea.* Kernan Verlag, 1984.

Ditlev, Hans A. *A Field-Guide to the Reef-Building Corals of the Indo-Pacific.* Klampenborg: Scandinavian Science Press, 1980. (Good, compact volume.)

Randall, Richard H. and Robert F. Myers. *Guide to the Coastal Resources of Guam, vol. 2: the Corals.* Guam: University of Guam Press, 1983.

Usher, G.F. "Coral Reef Invertebrates In Indonesia." IUNC/WWF Report, 1984.

Walls, Jerry G., ed. *Encyclopedia of Marine Invertebrates.* Neptune, N.J.:T.F.H. Publications, 1982. (The text of this 700-page book is often good. There are the usual mistakes with photos, however, and many of the names have not kept up with recent changes. A preponderance of the illustrations are Caribbean.)

Wells, Sue, *et al,* eds. *The IUNC Invertebrate Red Data Book.* Gland, Switzerland: International Union for Conservation of Nature and Natural Resources, 1983.

Wood, Elizabeth M. *Corals of the World.* Neptune, N.J.: T.F.H. Publications, 1983.

REEF ECOLOGY

Darwin, Charles. *The Structure and Distribution of Coral Reefs.* Tucson, AZ: University of Arizona Press, 1984.

——*The Voyage of the Beagle.* New York: Mentor (Penguin), 1988.

George, G. *Marine Life.* Sydney: Rigby Ltd, 1976 (also: New York: John Wiley & Sons).

Goreau, Thomas F., Nora I. Goreau and Thomas J. Goreau. "Corals and Coral Reefs," *Scientific American* vol. 241, 1979.

Henry, L.E. *Coral Reefs of Malaysia.* Kuala Lumpur: Longman, 1980.

Randall, Richard H. and L.G. Eldredge. "A Marine Survey Of The Shoalwater Habitats Of Ambon, Pulau Pombo, Pulau Kasa and Pulau Babi." Guam: University of Guam Marine Laboratory, 1983.

Salm, R.V. and M. Halim. *Marine Conservation Data Atlas.* IUNV/WWF Project 3108, 1984.

Soegiarto, A. and N. Polunin. "The Marine Environment Of Indonesia." A Report Prepared for the Government of the Republic of Indonesia, under the sponsorship of the IUNC and WWF, 1982.

Umbgrove, J.H.F. "Coral Reefs of the East Indies," *Bulletin Of The Geological Society of America,* vol. 58, 1947.

Wallace, Alfred Russel. *The Malay Archipelago.* Singapore: Oxford University Press, 1986.

Wells, Sue, *et al. Coral Reefs Of The World* (3 volumes). Gland, Switzerland: United Nations Environmental Program, 1988.

Whitten, Anthony J., Muslimin Mustafa and Gregory S. Henderson. *The Ecology of Sulawesi.* Yogyakarta, Java: Gadjah Mada University Press, 1987. (Though not exclusively or even particularly marine in focus, a very interesting work.)

Wyrtri, K. "Physical Oceanography of the Southeast Asian Waters, Naga Report Vol. 2." La Jolla, CA: University of California, Scripps Institute of Oceanography, 1961.

Index

Map Index